ISBN 978-1-4400-7519-3
PIBN 10036980

1 MONTH OF
FREE
READING

at

www.ForgottenBooks.com

By purchasing this book you are eligible for one month membership to ForgottenBooks.com, giving you unlimited access to our entire collection of over 700,000 titles via our web site and mobile apps.

To claim your free month visit:

www.forgottenbooks.com/free36980

English
Français
Deutsche
Italiano
Español
Português

www.forgottenbooks.com

Mythology Photography **Fiction**
Fishing Christianity **Art** Cooking
Essays Buddhism Freemasonry
Medicine **Biology** Music **Ancient
Egypt** Evolution Carpentry Physics
Dance Geology **Mathematics** Fitness
Shakespeare **Folklore** Yoga Marketing
Confidence Immortality Biographies
Poetry **Psychology** Witchcraft
Electronics Chemistry History **Law**
Accounting **Philosophy** Anthropology
Alchemy Drama Quantum Mechanics
Atheism Sexual Health **Ancient History**
Entrepreneurship Languages Sport
Paleontology Needlework Islam
Metaphysics Investment Archaeology
Parenting Statistics Criminology
Motivational

EPISTEMOLOGY

OR THE

THEORY OF KNOWLEDGE

4e

EPISTEMOLOGY

OR THE

THEORY OF KNOWLEDGE

AN INTRODUCTION TO GENERAL METAPHYSICS

BY

P. COFFEY, Ph.D. (Louvain)

PROFESSOR OF LOGIC AND METAPHYSICS, MAYNOOTH COLLEGE, IRELAND

IN TWO VOLUMES

VOL. I

LONGMANS, GREEN AND CO.

39 PATERNOSTER ROW, LONDON

FOURTH AVENUE & 30TH STREET, NEW YORK

BOMBAY, CALCUTTA, AND MADRAS

1917

TO

HIS EMINENCE, CARDINAL MERCIER

ARCHBISHOP OF MECHLIN

FOUNDER AND FIRST DIRECTOR

OF THE *INSTITUT SUPÉRIEUR DE PHILOSOPHIE*

AT THE

CATHOLIC UNIVERSITY OF LOUVAIN—

ENLIGHTENED EXPONENT

OF THE CHRISTIAN PHILOSOPHY OF LIFE

AND FEARLESS ADVOCATE

OF ITS RIGHTFUL SUPREMACY IN TROUBLED TIMES

AS A SMALL TOKEN

OF GRATITUDE AND VENERATION

FROM A FORMER PUPIL

THIS WORK

IS RESPECTFULLY DEDICATED

BY

THE AUTHOR

PREFACE.

THE present work, which was commenced on the publication of the author's *Ontology*, is written from the same general standpoint as the *Ontology* and his earlier treatise on *The Science of Logic*. It aims at applying the principles of Scholasticism to the solution of the problems raised by a critical inquiry into the validity of knowledge and the grounds of certitude. It does not purport to be in any sense a history of theories of knowledge, or to supply anything like an adequate bibliography of works on the subject. It is primarily a text-book for the use of university students in philosophy, though it is hoped that a perusal of it may be found helpful to all who desire a closer acquaintance with the attitude of modern scholastic writers towards the critical problems which almost monopolize the attention of philosophers nowadays. It is needless to emphasize the growing importance of such problems in this age of restless inquiry and scepticism. Nor will a text-book in English from the standpoint of Scholasticism be deemed superfluous.

Kant's theory of knowledge is the only non-scholastic theory examined in any considerable detail : because most of the modern theories draw their inspiration directly or indirectly from principles propounded in the *Critiques*, so that the student who can appraise these principles on their merits will be in a position to deal with those theories in whatever guise they may confront him. In his exposition and criticism of Kant's speculative philosophy the author has made free use of H. A. PRICHARD'S valuable work on *Kant's Theory of Knowledge*,[1] and begs gratefully to acknowledge his deep indebtedness.   He owes much, likewise, to CARDINAL MERCIER's well-known treatise on *Criteriology*,[2]—the first serious attempt to vindicate the superiority of the Scholastic theory of knowledge as compared with the Kantian and other non-scholastic theories. Finally, his acknowledgments are due to the Rev. PÈRE JEANNIÈRE, S.J., whose recently published Latin text-book,[3] breathing the spirit and developing the teaching of the Louvain neo-scholasticism, is in every way excellent, and has been consulted with profit.   Clear, comprehensive, compendious, and extensively documented, it deserves a wide welcome in Catholic colleges and seminaries.

For the rest, the doctrines and views propounded in the present work are of course drawn from, and based on, the rational principles embodied in the teaching of St. Thomas Aquinas and the other great masters of the traditional Aristotelian Scholasticism : which, it may perhaps be necessary to observe, does *not* mean what non-scholastic philosophers might be tempted to interpret it as meaning, that those doctrines are presented for acceptance on the ground of authority.   They are put forward on their intrinsic merits, and by these alone they must be judged.

. . . .

As a rule the more advanced portions and detailed discussions are printed in smaller type, so that these, as well as certain sections or even whole chapters, may be omitted or postponed for a second reading at the discretion of the teacher when the book is being used for class

[1] *Kant's Theory of Knowledge*, by H. A. PRICHARD, Fellow of Trinity College, Oxford.   Oxford : at the Clarendon Press, 1909.

[2] CRITÉRIOLOGIE GÉNÉRALE, *ou Théorie Générale de la Certitude*, par D. MERCIER, Professeur de philosophie et directeur de l'institut supérieur de philosophie, à l'université catholique de Louvain.   6me édit., 1906.

[3] CRITERIOLOGIA, vel Critica Cognitionis Certae.   Auctore RENATO JEANNIÈRE, S.J., in Collegio Jersiensi Professore.   Paris ; Beauchesne, 1912.   Pp. 616, 8vo,

work.   Moreover, since the same general problems recur
repeatedly in different contexts, and are discussed and
illustrated from a variety of standpoints, it is only by
collating these that the student will gain an adequate
understanding and appreciation of the solutions arrived
at in the course of the inquiry.   He will be enabled to
bring together in this way all that is said on any particular
topic, not only by making use of the indexes at the end
of each volume, but by consulting the cross-references to
the various sections, as given in parentheses, in the text
itself.

CONTENTS OF VOLUME I.

CHAPTER III.

THE METHOD OF THE INQUIRY.

CHAPTER IV.

UNJUSTIFIABLE ISSUE OF THE INQUIRY: SCEPTICISM.

PART II.

INTELLECTUAL KNOWLEDGE: JUDGMENT.

CHAPTER V.

NECESSARY JUDGMENTS: ENGLISH SUBJECTIVISM.

CHAPTER VI.

NECESSARY JUDGMENTS: KANT'S THEORY EXPOUNDED.

CHAPTER VII.

NECESSARY JUDGMENTS: KANT'S THEORY EXAMINED.

CHAPTER VIII.

NECESSARY JUDGMENTS: SCHOLASTIC THEORY.

PART III.

INTELLECTUAL KNOWLEDGE: CONCEPTION.

CHAPTER IX.

ORIGIN AND VALIDITY OF CONCEPTS: MODERATE REALISM.

CHAPTER X.

VALIDITY OF CONCEPTS: EXTREME REALISM.

CHAPTER XI.

VALIDITY OF CONCEPTS: NOMINALISM.

CHAPTER XII.

VALIDITY OF CONCEPTS: CONCEPTUALISM; KANT'S DOCTRINE.

INTRODUCTION.

1. EPISTEMOLOGY : ITS PLACE IN PHILOSOPHY.—While the special or positive sciences explore each a limited portion of human experience, philosophy explores the whole domain. While they raise immediate questions and offer partial and proximate explanations, it raises ultimate problems and offers the fullest explanations which the mind of man can discover. What is the nature of man and the universe? What is their origin? What is their destiny? What is the meaning of life? How should man live? What can man know of these things? Of how much can he be certain? What is knowledge itself? Is any knowledge reliable? And if so, what are its limits and conditions? These are some of the problems investigated in the various departments of philosophy—Cosmology, Psychology Logic, Ethics, etc.

Assuming a division of Speculative Philosophy, or Metaphysics, into General and Special—the former embracing Ontology and · Epistemology, the latter embracing Cosmology, Psychology, and Natural Theology—a division which has been set forth elsewhere [1]—we assign to *Epistemology* or the *Theory of Knowledge* (ἐπιστήμη, λόγος, *doctrina scientiae seu cognitionis*) the philosophical investigation of human knowledge itself, from the standpoint of the certitude, validity, or truth-value of this knowledge.

Epistemology and Logic.—The relation of Epistemology to *Logic* is thus apparent. Logic as a practical science brings to light from an analysis of our thought processes certain normative principles which guide these processes towards the discovery of truth. In doing so it makes a number of assumptions, as, for instance, that by thinking correctly, *i.e.* by judging and reasoning according to logical canons, the attainment of truth and certitude is possible. All such assumptions it devolves on Epistemo-

---

[1] *Ontology, or The Theory of Being.* P. COFFEY, Ph.D. (Longmans, 1914), Introd., pp. 14-23.

logy to justify.[1]   But in fact the line of division between these
two branches of study has not been clearly recognized either in
theory or in practice : for all the problems claimed by Epistemology arise naturally out of the reflective analysis to which Logic
subjects our thought processes.   Down to comparatively recent
times the practice among scholastic exponents of philosophy has
been to treat this group of questions under the title of *Logica
Critica*, or Critical Logic, in immediate connexion with *Logica
Dialectica*, the Logic of Inference and Scientific Method.[2]

Towards the end of the eighteenth century the influence of
Kant's Critical Philosophy gave an extraordinary impetus to the
study of problems concerning the scope and limitations of human
certitude.   This influence was felt among the exponents of the
traditional " Philosophy of the Schools ".   It resulted in the
grouping of such problems into a definite department for fuller
exposition and treatment, and called forth special scholastic
treatises, of which MERCIER'S *Critériologie Générale*,[3] and more
recently JEANNIÈRE'S *Criteriologia*,[4] may be taken as typical.
The title *Criteriology* (Κριτήριον, λόγος,—the science of the
criteria or tests, *i.e.* of true and certain knowledge) emphasizes
the special aim of the investigation as being an analysis of the
tests by the application of which to our knowledge and beliefs we
may be able to discern and sift out the true from the false ; while
the title *Epistemology* ("Theory of Knowledge," *Erkenntnis-
theorie, Erkenntnislehre*) reminds us that the subject-matter of the
investigation is human knowledge.[5]   While, then, the aim of the
various human sciences, and of the other departments of philosophy, is to *extend* our knowledge of the data of human experience,
the aim of this particular investigation is not exactly to extend

---

[1] *Cf. Science of Logic.*   P. COFFEY, Ph.D. (Longmans, 1912), i., § 17, pp. 28-9.

[2] *Cf.* HICKEY, *Summula Philosophiae Scholasticae* (Dublin, Gill, 1912), vol. i. ;
REINSTADLER, *Elementa Philosophiae Scholasticae* (Herder, 1901), vol. i.

[3] Mercier's treatise, one of the many works from the pen of the illustrious
Belgian Cardinal when he was Director of the Philosophical Institute at the Catholic
University of Louvain, was published in 1899, and forms the fourth volume of the
Louvain *Cours de Philosophie*.   Mainly on account of its searching analysis of
Kantism it gained a wide publicity, reaching its sixth edition in 1911.

[4] *Criteriologia, vel Critica Cognitionis Certae.*   Auctore R. JEANNIÈRE, S.J.
Paris, Beauchesne, 1912.

[5] Not angelic or divine knowledge, or the knowledge of an imaginary abstract
pure intelligence, but such knowledge as may be attained by the minds of concrete
individual human beings.   About the former kinds of knowledge we can know only
what we can infer by analogy from the knowledge of which we have direct experience, *i.e.* human knowledge.   *Cf.* F. S. TURNER, *Knowledge, Belief, and Certitude*
(London, 1900), p. 59.

our knowledge but rather to *perfect* our acquired knowledge by teaching us WHAT IT IS TO KNOW.

Our method, therefore, as in psychology, will be mainly introspection, supplemented of course by external observation of the cognitive experiences of the human race, and by rational inference from the internal and external data so observed.

Epistemology and Psychology.—If we understand by *Psychology*, as a department of philosophy, the philosophical investigation of the whole domain of living things, the highest branch of its subject-matter will be the phenomena of the human mind, and among these latter cognitive phenomena hold a prominent place. On account of the naturally close connexion of problems concerning the origin and development of knowledge with problems concerning its scope, validity, and significance, epistemology is closely allied with psychology.[1] They have, however, definitely distinct standpoints. The cognitive activities of the mind, considered as facts, as mental events, belong to psychology ; considered as apprehending truth they belong to epistemology. For while as mental events they arise and develop according to laws of mental association and conjunction which it is the duty of psychology to elucidate, they have another and distinct aspect in that they claim to apprehend truth. It is precisely this claim which epistemology has to investigate.

Reflecting on our conscious life we easily distinguish between two orders of movement and combination among our conscious states. We find things occurring together in our mental life without any inner connexion, and recurring together for no other reason than that they have occurred together. The connexion of language with thought is a good example of this association of mental states. . The spoken or written word suggests a certain idea not because it has any internal connexion with the latter, but because they have always occurred together in our experience. Memory depends on this sort of grouping and reproduction of mental states. The states so connected might conceivably not have been so connected. It is a *de facto* grouping according to mental tendencies which psychology has to examine and analyse. But there is another connexion of a different kind, not a *de facto* conjunction but a connexion which is seen by our reason to be *necessary and immutable.*

---

[1] Hence, apart from special treatises on the Theory of Knowledge, such as Father Rickaby's volume in the *Stonyhurst Philosophical Series* (*The First Principles of Knowledge*, by JOHN RICKABY, S.J., 2nd edit., Longmans, 1901), much epistemological matter is to be found in such treatises as Father Maher's work on *Psychology* (*Psychology, Empirical and Rational*, by MICHAEL MAHER, S.J. Longmans, 1890, 6th edit., 1910) in the same series. MERCIER (*op. cit.*, 5th edit., § 3) regards the Theory of Knowledge as a specially important tributary or dependency of the domain of Psychology.

Such, for instance, is the connexion between our concepts of the various properties of a triangle, or our concepts of whole and part, or our concepts of ground and consequent, premisses and conclusion. Here the elements not merely occur together *de facto*, they "belong together" so to speak ; they are internally, *i.e.* rationally, logically connected. Now among the *de facto* groupings and movements the mind is constantly seeking for those rational groupings and movements whereby we interpret our cognitive processes and discover their significance as embodying truth or knowledge of reality. It is with connexions of this latter kind that epistemology is concerned.

Or, again, we might illustrate the distinction in this way. Psychology deals with all conscious experiences as mental events. Some of these experiences are nothing more than individual mental events in an individual mind, as, for example, an impulse, an emotion, a feeling of pleasure or pain. That is, they simply are what they are, and they report nothing beyond themselves. But there are other conscious experiences which do report an object beyond and independent of the individual mental event itself, which claim to represent a something beyond themselves and common to all minds, a something which they do not make but only discover as portion of the total system or order which reveals itself more or less to all of us and which we call *reality*. This is true of those conscious experiences which we describe as *thought* or *thinking*, *cognition* or *knowledge*, *knowing*, in the stricter sense of these terms, *i.e.* interpreting, judging, affirming or denying. Now it is with such conscious experiences, as representative of reality, that epistemology deals. Indeed, this very question,—how a judgment which is an individual event of an individual mind can validly apprehend something beyond itself as real and true for all minds,—is not the least of the mysteries which epistemology has to examine. *How* thought can have this objective reference it may be difficult to understand ; but to deny the fact—as some philosophers have attempted—is equivalently to distort and destroy the function of thought altogether.

Epistemology and Ontology.—We have referred to the division of General Metaphysics into the Theory of Knowing (Epistemology) and the Theory of Being (Ontology). The aim of all metaphysics is to arrive at a rational and systematic comprehension of reality. From the nature of the case, this of course is an ideal to which the finite mind of man can only approximate. Again, while the understanding of reality, of real being, is the ultimate aim of metaphysics, it is clear that this understanding cannot be satisfactory without an investigation into the nature of "knowing" itself. Thus the Theory of Being has for its counterpart and condition the Theory of Knowing.

And since all knowing involves a knowing subject and a known object the two lines of investigation deal with two aspects of the same domain, this domain being the sum-total of human experience, or reality as revealed in and through this experience. Historically some systems of speculative philosophy might be roughly described as theories of knowing and others as theories of being, according as the one or the other of these two lines of investigation is found to predominate. Thus, while the systems of Aristotle, the mediæval Schoolmen, Spinoza, and Leibniz are fundamentally theories of being, those of Plato, Descartes, Locke, Hume, and Kant are pre-eminently theories of knowing. The distinction, however, is not to be taken as absolute, for neither line of investigation can be pursued without reference to the other, though the two groups of problems are sufficiently distinct to admit of separate treatment.

2. BEARING OF EPISTEMOLOGY ON SPONTANEOUS CONVICTIONS, ON THE SCIENCES, AND ON RELIGIOUS BELIEF.—It is primarily for the guidance of the beginner that the present treatise is intended. It may be well, therefore, to set down here a few practical considerations which will at once arouse his interest and help to adjust his initial outlook.

In the first place what is true of the study of philosophy generally—that it demands the effort of personal thought and reflection from the individual learner, and is not to be achieved by any mere passive and unreflecting assimilation of the teaching of text-books or professors—is particularly true of the study of Epistemology. At the same time many of its problems are such that the youthful student finds it very difficult to regard them as serious or to approach them seriously. When he sees what appear to him to be self-evident truths or dictates of plain common sense called into question by people whom he hears dignified by the title of great philosophers, he is apt to lose patience unless he be modest enough to accept the assurance that there is really *something* to be said for such apparently extravagant positions, and sincere enough to endeavour to enter sympathetically into standpoints so novel and so completely at variance with his own outlook. But while such an attitude is necessary not merely for the understanding of these novel theories, but even for an intelligent appreciation of the common-sense standpoint and its difficulties, he must remember that it is quite compatible with a robust faith in the soundness of this latter, nor has he any need to be unduly alarmed about the competence of the mind for truth by the spectacle of so many able minds missing truth from the very outset.

Moreover, the really just and fully satisfactory solution of some of the problems, when once they are raised, demands a

ripeness of thought and experience, a breadth and depth of outlook on men and things, which the youthful student can scarcely
be expected to bring to bear upon them.   However, an average
acquaintance with logic and scientific method, a general knowledge of psychology, a moderate familiarity with the main conclusions and theories of the physical and natural sciences, with
history, literature, and the arts, and with the great world-facts
of morality and religion—all these ordinary acquisitions will enable him to appreciate the importance of epistemological problems, and, what is better still, to weigh the evidences from all
sources perhaps more justly and impartially than many of those
more mature inquirers who happen to have lost the sense of due
proportion by long years devoted to some specialized study which
has made them experts in a particular domain.   The specialist
is always exposed to the danger of overrating evidence from his
own department, of interpreting all reality in terms of its particular laws, of ignoring facts that do not fit in with these.   The
history of philosophy is strewn with the wreckage of false philosophical theories propounded by scientific or other specialists.
The mechanical, evolutionary, and agnostic philosophies based on
the physical sciences about the middle of the last century by
such men as Huxley, Spencer, Büchner, and Haeckel are cases in
point.   The youthful student, approaching the study of Epistemology for the first time, will be free from such prejudices ; but
he must learn to think out the problems for himself, to seek the
truth sincerely and for its own sake, to recognize that the human
mind has its limits, that there are many questions which it may
raise indeed but cannot adequately answer, while at the same
time it can discover and hold firmly to all the truths that are
requisite for the realization of the supreme purpose of man's
existence in the universe.

   In the next place the student will appreciate the importance
of epistemological problems when he learns that upon their right
solution depends the value or the worthlessness of scientific truth.
We all spontaneously believe in the trustworthiness of our cognitive faculties : that our senses reveal to us a real, material universe distinct from our minds ; that by the use of our reason in
the physical, natural, human, and social sciences we can and do
discover a certain amount of "truth," of genuine "knowledge"
about the real existence and the real nature of the persons, things,
and happenings which constitute this universe ; that what we

call the necessary and universal truths brought to light in these sciences are not mere subjective constructions of our own mental processes, signifying nothing beyond themselves, but that on the contrary they really do give us an insight into the nature of that which they purport to reveal to us, namely, the real world; that the concepts assumed not merely by ordinary thought but by the thought of the scientist to be concepts representative of the real world are indeed really such, — concepts of "number," "quantity," "space," "time," "cause," "effect," "action," "quality," "substance," "matter," "spirit," "good," "evil," "freedom," "purpose," "duty," "happiness," etc., etc. ;—that what are assumed by the plain man to be self-evident truths underlying all knowledge, and what are assumed by the scientist as principles or starting-points from which, and with the aid of which, he proceeds to discover and establish "scientific truths," are really themselves "truths," *i.e.* valid information or items of knowledge about the real world. Now all these spontaneous beliefs of the plain man, of the scientist, and indeed of the philosopher in other departments, must be examined and tested in Epistemology. Every single department of human science and investigation makes, in regard to the possibility and fact of certain knowledge, many assumptions which it is not only legitimate but even necessary to criticize. For when we come to reflect on it we find that human cognition is a very complex process ; that we distinguish truth from error and have often fallen into the latter ; that if we have been deceived once and again we may perhaps be victims of a wider and deeper deception than we dream of in respect to much, or possibly all, of what we think we know.

Again, the student will take a deeper interest in epistemological problems when he learns that nowadays it is in this domain rather than in the positive sciences, or in supernatural theology, or in any other department of philosophy, he will encounter questions by the right or wrong solution of which all faith in Christianity, or indeed in supernatural religion as such, must stand or fall. The foundations of faith in the truth of Christianity cannot be laid in the quicksands of a mind that is swept by the withering winds of philosophical scepticism. The Theism implied by Christianity can find no home in the mind that is a prey to Agnosticism. Nor is belief in a Supreme Being, distinct from the world, compatible with the acceptance of any form of Monism. It is of the first importance for the catholic

student to realize that among all peoples who have inherited
Christian culture and civilization the choice of ever-increasing
multitudes of those whom we may describe as the leaders of
thought—and consequently also of the masses influenced by them
—is now no longer so much as formerly between Catholicism and
some other form of Christianity, but rather between Catholicism
and the rejection of supernatural religion altogether.   Nowadays
the religious question in the main resolves itself into Catholicism
versus Unbelief, Agnosticism, Monism, Naturalism.   The intellectual difficulties which impede the acceptance of catholic truth
by the modern mind are not concerned with individual dogmas ;
they lie deeper down ; they refer to the possibility of Divine
Revelation, to the existence of a Supreme Being, to the binding
force of morality, to the very capacity of the human mind for
attaining to any certain knowledge about the origin, nature, and
destiny of man and the universe.   These difficulties, arising out
of false theories of knowledge, enhance both the interest and the
importance of Epistemology for the catholic student.

At the same time our investigation, if it is to attain its object,
must be wholly impartial and disinterested.   A treatise on the
Theory of Knowledge cannot possibly be apologetic or polemical
in the religious sense.   It must be purely philosophical ; it must
appeal to reason, not to authority; it must be grounded on
universal human experience ; it must assume nothing except on
grounds of reason ; in this sense it must be " presuppositionless "
But only in this sense ; for it will bring to light many presuppositions without which no rational investigation and no intelligent
thought would be possible.   The believer in the Christian religion may legitimately indeed entertain not only the expectation, but even the unwavering confidence throughout, that a
purely rational investigation of the sources, scope, and limits of
human certitude, will, if rightly conducted, inevitably justify the
foundations of his faith and make of this a *rationabile obsequium*,
a reasonable service ;[1] but were he to attempt to construct a
theory of knowledge on the assumed truth of his religious beliefs,
the task attempted in thus " putting the cart before the horse "
would obviously be worse than useless.

3. CONSPECTUS OF PROBLEMS RAISED BY REFLECTIVE
THOUGHT.—All men have spontaneous and firm convictions
about many things.   Prompted by nature itself they believe

[1] Rom. xii. 1.

that there is a distinction between truth and error; that they can and do discover some truths. It is likewise the general experience of men to discover occasionally that they have been deceived, that some of their firm convictions were not true but false, were not "knowledge" but error,—for by the term "knowledge," used simply and without qualification, we understand true knowledge and not merely seeming, spurious knowledge. Nor is the ordinary man disconcerted by the discovery that time and again he has been deceived, for he knows that man is not infallible in the pursuit of truth. With wider experience he may learn to exercise greater caution in regard to what he will accept as certainly true, and he may be more easily disposed to admit that even some of what he still holds for certain knowledge may turn out after all to have been false; but none the less he will continue to follow the inclination of his rational nature to hold on firmly to each and every one of his spontaneous convictions as long as he sees no reason for abandoning them. Thus, as he passes through life he may retain his early "religious" convictions—about God, the soul, a future life of rewards and punishments, moral responsibility, etc.—if he ever had such; or it may happen that he may modify them. If he be comparatively uneducated, or prevented by material preoccupations from pursuing the cultivation of his mind, it is not likely that he will ever systematically examine and revise his beliefs, even those that most intimately concern his own nature and destiny. And this is the case with the masses of mankind.

But with those who have leisure to cultivate their minds by the study of the arts and sciences, of literature and history, of philosophy and religion, of human civilization in any of its varied and manifold modes of expression; with those, too, on whom the duty devolves of instructing, educating, enlightening their fellow-men, the duty of promoting the intellectual, moral, and religious progress of humanity,—the case is different. When we reflect on the profoundly divergent and conflicting views that have at all times divided humanity in regard to the very questions that concern human destiny most intimately,—the existence and nature of a Supreme Being, the reality of a future life, the origin and binding force of moral principles, etc.,—we cannot help asking ourselves whether after all the human mind is capable of attaining to certitude about such matters. When we learn from the history of human thought as exercised in its fullest intensity by its ablest representatives and exponents on those and similar fundamental questions,—in other words, from the history of philosophy,—that many have questioned the power of the human mind to know even if there exist a suprasensible world, we must perforce examine the question : Can the human mind know for certain whether there is any reality other than the material things of time and space revealed in our sense experience? When from an acquaintance with the various positive sciences which deal with the material universe and with organic life we find no small disagreement prevailing as to what are " established conclusions " and what are merely " probable hypotheses " in these domains, we are led naturally to inquire whether, if truth be at all attainable, there are any satisfactory tests whereby we can recognize it. Moreover, we can see by a little reflection that not merely the ordinary convictions of the plain man, but even the sciences themselves,—even the abstract sciences, such as mathematics, no less than the concrete, positive sciences,—*assume* as true certain principles which they do not prove, and assume thereby that the notions embodied in these principles are validly applicable to reality and give us a genuine insight into reality. For by " science " we certainly understand a genuine knowledge *of reality*, and if those fundamental notions that enter into the sciences did not somehow reveal reality to us the sciences would be no better than a vast array of mental illusions. Not only so, but knowledge of whatsoever kind would be an illusion, inasmuch as all knowledge is embodied in judgments and all judgments involve notions and purport to interpret reality for us by analysis, synthesis, and comparison of notions.

We need not anticipate the illustrations that will be duly given in the course of our inquiry. What we have here to observe is this, that the principles and notions in question suggest an investigation of the rational grounds on which we accept them as giving us genuine knowledge. In other words, the general problem presents itself of re-examining critically our spontaneous convictions and beliefs with a view to determining whether, or within what limits and under what conditions, we can have well grounded and certain knowledge about anything. And no sooner do we attempt to enter on our task than we come to realize how exceedingly complex is the simplest act of knowledge,—in its sources, in its objects, in its processes, in its grounds and motives.

We find ourselves endowed with external sense faculties whereby we think that we apprehend a real, material universe existing in space and time, distinct from and independent of, our own minds, and with which we think we are brought into conscious or cognitive relation by means of our own living human bodies. But does the individual human mind, or can it, really apprehend anything beyond or distinct from itself? and if so, how? We have the power of reflecting on whatever we become aware of, and on the mental acts or processes involved in this awareness. Does this reflection bear out our spontaneous conviction that our knowledge can and does reach beyond the cognitive process, the mental state itself, and apprehend a reality distinct from the latter? We have the power of interpreting the data, the contents, of our acts and processes of sense cognition; we have the power of rational or intellectual cognition, of judging these data and reasoning from them. When we interpret them as giving us some insight into the existence and nature of a real material universe, is our interpretation well-grounded? When we infer from these data of sense experience the reality and existence of an order of beings beyond the scope of sense knowledge and knowable only by intellect or reason, the existence of a suprasensible order of realities, intelligent, immaterial or spiritual, free and immortal, and the existence of a Supreme Personal Spirit, will the validity of such inferences stand the test of the deliberate critical reflection to which reason can and must subject them? The validity of all such inferences depends on the validity of the fundamental rational principles and notions on which they rest, and of which they are applications: are these principles and notions themselves valid? In other words, do they give the individual mind an insight into any reality beyond itself? Or will a critical analysis of them perhaps disclose them to be, for aught we know, mere products of the cognitive activity of the individual mind,—products which spontaneously and of their very nature refer us, no doubt, to a supposed world of reality which they purport to represent, but whose genuine representative character we can never rely on, or satisfactorily vindicate and justify?

Are any, therefore, of our spontaneous convictions rationally justifiable? Are any of the objects attained by our knowledge real? Or, in other words, is any of our knowledge true? Does knowledge attain to reality as it is, or is reality so transformed in and through the very process of cognition itself that reality can never be known by the mind as it really is in itself and apart from the mind? Is knowledge a purely passive mirroring of reality? and if so how is error possible? Or is the mind active in cognition? and if so can we distinguish what it does, or contributes, to the total "known object," from what is really there to be known antecedently to the actual cognition of it?

Truth is commonly understood to be the conformity of knowledge, or of the mind knowing, with the reality known; and error to be the opposite relation. And it is commonly assumed that we have the power of testing our knowledge, and of discerning between genuine knowledge and misleading or erroneous knowledge. But this seems to imply that we can grasp not merely the mental or subjective term but also the extramental or objective or real term of the knowledge-relation, in order to judge whether this relation is one of conformity or not. But how can we grasp the extramental term otherwise than by knowing it and thereby making it mental? What then is truth at all?

All our knowledge,—nay, all our consciousness,—involves a duality, a

distinction between the subjective factor, the subject and act or process of
consciousness or cognition on the one hand, and the object, of which the
subject is made aware by this act or process, on the other hand.   When we
reflect even upon the mere awareness which characterizes the most rudimentary conscious feeling or sensation, we see that by describing it as conscious, as a conscious act or conscious state, we mean that there is an object
presented, however dimly, to a subject that becomes aware of it, however
vaguely.   And such a sensation is not yet knowledge ; for we have not
knowledge proper until we interpret or judge,—at least implicitly, as we
generally if not invariably do in sense perception,—until we interpret, until
we say, mentally, "this" or "that" "is" or "is not," or "is" or "is not"
"so-and-so".   In external sense perception this duality of subject and object
is more clearly marked, as also in all judgments referring to the data of external sense experience.   It is likewise present in our consciousness of our
own bodies, in our feelings of bodily pleasure or pain, etc., though here we
spontaneously believe in some sort of a unity or continuity of the object with
the subject : for here *we* are the knowing subjects and the bodies which are
the known objects are *our* bodies.   Nay even when we make our minds, our
cognitive activities themselves, the objects of our contemplation, as we can
and do by introspective reflection, there is still the duality, the distinction between the mind as knowing subject and the mind as known object.   What
bearing has this duality on the possibility of our discovering the nature of our
own selves and cognitive processes on the one hand, or of realities (other than
our own selves) as known objects on the other hand ?

It is manifest that an examination of all those and many other similar
questions will involve an inquiry into the main sources of our knowledge, the
nature and modes of our cognitive processes, the characteristics of objectivity
and universality in the concepts and judgments formed by our individual
minds, and the ultimate grounds of our spontaneous belief that we can and
do attain to some certain knowledge concerning our own real nature and the
real nature of the universe in which we have our being.

4. RISE AND DEVELOPMENT OF THEORIES OF KNOWLEDGE :
HISTORICAL OUTLINES.—An analogy is sometimes drawn between the mental development of the individual and that of the
race.   As the child is at first wholly preoccupied with external
objects, and only as its mental powers develop does it begin to
reflect, to look inward, and finally in adult years to puzzle over
the meaning, the reliability and the limits of its acquired knowledge and beliefs,—so the philosophical speculation of the race has
been at first concerned mainly with the external world (*Cosmology*), then with the nature of the knowing self or subject (*Psychology*), and finally with the meaning, scope, and value of knowledge
itself (*Epistemology*).   In the main the analogy is true of certain
great epochs of philosophical inquiry : for instance, after the
earliest of the ancient Grecian thinkers had busied themselves

with speculations on the nature of the *cosmos*, attention was directed by Socrates, and by his contemporaries and successors, to problems concerning the soul and the possibility of certain knowledge. But the analogy is not true of the progress of philosophical thought as a whole. The erroneous impression is sometimes conveyed by modern writers that the age of philosophical criticism, first prepared by Descartes (1596-1650), only dawned with Kant (1724-1804); that previously philosophers in the main had naïvely and unreflectingly taken for granted as unquestionable a multitude of epistemological assumptions which post-Kantian criticism has at all events fearlessly analysed. As a matter of fact the critical analysis of knowledge is as old as philosophy itself. In the fifth century before the Christian era the Kantian Criticism had its forerunner in the *Homo mensura omnium* of the Grecian sophist, Protagoras ; and modern subjectivism had its prototype in the scepticism of the Platonic academies. The scholasticism of the Middle Ages,—which it has been so customary among modern advocates of untrammelled criticism to regard as a system truly typical of naïve dogmatism,—devoted its highest efforts of thought for centuries to distinctively epistemological problems in its controversies on universal ideas, on individuation and distinctions, and on the respective domains of reason and faith. It is probably because, in contrast with much of modern thought, those mediæval investigations did not issue in widespread scepticism and intellectual chaos, that their real value to philosophy has been so commonly underrated. The conclusions they reached were in harmony with the revealed truths of the Christian Religion ; and this was enough to render them suspect to the non-catholic mind, which, since the religious revolt of the sixteenth century, has preferred to philosophize on purely individualistic lines, and without respect to the great world-fact of Christianity in the religious experience of humanity. None the less, the fruits of so many centuries of critical reflection on the scope and limits of human knowledge and certitude cannot be lightly ignored by the modern student of epistemology.

It is, however, undeniable that the philosophical criticism of the last two centuries has prosecuted a very searching analysis of the cognitive capacity of the human mind, that it has persistently explored the motives of human certitude, that it has sounded many depths and shoals in the ocean of human beliefs : a legitimate and even laudable enterprise, but grave and delicate, and

full of peril for the rash and incautious adventurer.   That it has
been prosecuted *wisely* in the main during these few centuries,
that fruitful results have rewarded its labours, the actual chaotic
conditions of the intellectual world will scarcely permit even the
most sanguine to maintain.   Indeed for Catholics its net result
seems to confirm their traditional teaching that it is morally
impossible for men generally, without the aid of Divine Revelation, to hold fast to such a knowledge of truth as will preserve
them from grave intellectual error and consequent moral decadence.   However this may be, at anyrate the problems raised, the
doubts suggested, the subjectivism fostered, by the divers and
often bewildering speculations of modern philosophers in regard
to the scope and limits of human certitude, impose on the present-
day Catholic student of philosophy the serious task of equipping
himself with a sound *Theory of Knowledge.*

Such questions as those indicated in the preceding section
(3) have been repeatedly raised and discussed since the first
beginnings of philosophical speculation ; and the various " theories
of knowledge " that have marked its development through the
centuries are characterized by the various forms in which those
questions have been raised, and the various solutions they have
received.   According to some of these theories the senses are the
only source of genuine knowledge, and the only knowable reality
is that which reveals itself through the senses, *i.e.* the material
universe.   The supposed suprasensible world, which intellect
with its reasoning processes purports to reveal to us, is chimerical, or its reality at best problematical.   Such theories of knowledge may be described as various forms of *Sensualism*, the
corresponding theories of reality being forms of *Materialism.*
According to others intellectual thought is the only source of
genuine knowledge : reality is only as thought conceives it and
not at all as the senses present it.   Such theories may be regarded as forms of *Intellectualism*, the corresponding theories
of reality being forms of *Idealism* or *Spiritualism.*   But it may
not be amiss to warn the student at the outset that all such
general descriptive titles of philosophical theories and systems
have been used, and are still used, in a variety of quite distinct
senses, so that he will always need to look to the context for
their exact meaning in each case.   Another class of theories
arose, perhaps as a logical and natural outcome of the opposition between the two just mentioned, namely, sceptical theories,

forms of *Scepticism*, *i.e.* of doubt about the existence of any reliable source of knowledge, about the possibility of attaining to any justifiable certitude whatsoever.

Other theories, again, have recognized both in the senses and in the intellect reliable sources of knowledge ; but differ in the parts which they ascribe to each source, in their modes of effecting a harmony between these sources, and of removing apparent contradictions between their respective verdicts concerning the ultimate nature of reality in so far as reality falls within human experience. Such theories are generally described as *dogmatic*, or as *critical*,—as *Dogmatism*, or as *Criticism*,—according as they tend to accept certain fundamental *principles* or postulates underlying thought and sensation as ultimate, unquestionable, and absolutely reliable, or endeavour to call even these into question and subject them to further and more searching critical analysis. Criticism pushed *too* far leads by excess to Scepticism.

Ancient Philosophy.—Some of these positions we find illustrated already in the philosophy of ancient Greece. Thus, about the fifth century B.C. the *Eleatic* philosophers (PARMENIDES and ZENO), failing to reconcile the manifoldness and changing character of reality as revealed through the senses with the unity of being as conceived by abstract thought, rejected the testimony of the senses as untrustworthy and held all reality to be *one* and *immutable*, while the later *Ionians* (represented by HERACLITUS) arrived at exactly the opposite conclusion that all reality consists essentially in *change*. The earlier Ionians had previously sought the fundamental and all-explaining factor of the universe in a material principle such as earth or water or air, while the *Pythagoreans*, impressed by the manifest order in the movements of the heavenly bodies, the succession of the seasons, etc., a harmony which makes the universe a *cosmos*, had sought to explain the latter by the aid of a more abstract concept, proclaiming the essences of all things to be numbers and numerical relations. The upshot of these conflicting theories was that earliest form of philosophical scepticism propounded by the *Sophists* (PROTAGORAS and GORGIAS). Against their destructive tendencies SOCRATES (469-399) vindicated the power of human reason to discover a solid groundwork of truth as a basis for a right system of ethics. PLATO (427-347) unduly extolled the function of abstract intellectual thought and underrated the testimony of the senses. ARISTOTLE (384-322), profiting by the precious fruits of the Socratic-Platonic teaching, successfully harmonized in his theory of knowledge the respective contributions of senses and intellect. The objects of intellectual thought, which were for Plato realities *transcending* the domain of sense experience, Aristotle proclaimed to be really *immanent* in the data of the latter, thus ascribing both to sensation and to thought their respective rôles as reliable sources of genuine knowledge. From this high-water mark in ancient Greek speculation the succeeding centuries witnessed a speedy relapse into sensualism with DEMOCRITUS, the *Stoics* and the *Epicureans*, and into scepticism with PYRRHO and the later Platonic academies.

As the waning culture of Greece migrated to Rome the great world-fact of the coming of Christ and the establishment of Christianity leavened all human thought with a rich wealth of new and profoundly significant experiences.   Graeco-Roman speculation was fused with the tradition of Hebrew culture and made to subserve the formation of a Christian world-view embracing such conceptions as that of the *Creation* of all finite reality by One Supreme, All-Perfect, Transcendent Spirit ; the *Redemption* of mankind by the Incarnation ; the full *Revelation* to man of his supernatural origin and destiny ; the reasonableness of *Faith* in truths which, revealed by God to man concerning his place and purpose in the universe, yet surpass the power of human reason to comprehend or fathom fully.   In the intellectual and moral ferment of the early Christian centuries, in the struggle between the conceptions embodied in the Christian religion and those that underlay the natural religions and beliefs of Paganism, the human mind was forced to reconsider the grounds of its deepest convictions concerning the great fundamental problems of philosophy and religion.   While the *Neo-Platonists* sought to oppose Christianity by a naturalistic system which largely substituted for the pure intellectualism of Plato an affective mysticism permeated with pantheism, the *Fathers of the Church* and after them the *Mediæval Schoolmen* gradually evolved a theory of knowledge and reality which, while harmonizing with the doctrines of the Christian religion, borrowed considerably from Plato, particularly through St. Augustine (354-430), but was moulded mainly by the philosophical teachings of Aristotle.

Mediæval Philosophy.—The two main problems of epistemology which occupied the Mediæval Schoolmen from the days of the Carlovingian revival of learning with ALCUIN (735-804), SCOTUS ERIUGENA (*c.* 815-80), and ST. ANSELM (1033-1109), to the golden age of Scholasticism in the thirteenth century with ST. BONAVENTURE (1221-74), ALBERTUS MAGNUS (1193-1280), DUNS SCOTUS (1266-1308), and St. THOMAS AQUINAS (1224-74)—were the harmonizing of the respective functions of senses and intellect in the genesis of natural knowledge, and the harmonizing of the latter in its entirety with supernatural faith in divinely revealed truth.   The former of these two problems was discussed in the copious mediæval *controversies concerning the validity and import of universal ideas,*—reaching in the thirteenth century what was for the time a definitive solution on the lines laid down by Aristotle. The latter was likewise settled by the doctrine so fully and clearly formulated by Aquinas concerning the power of the human mind to establish the existence of God and the fact of Revelation as *preambula fidei,* and the reasonableness of believing all revealed truths, including mysteries, on the authority of God revealing.

But just as an interval of decadence and retrogression succeeded the culmination of Greek philosophy in the fourth century B.C., so the culmination of Scholasticism in the thirteenth century of the Christian era was succeeded by the intellectual and religious chaos which marked the revolutions known as the Renaissance and the Reformation.   Down through the Middle Ages the contents of the Christian Revelation, authoritatively propounded to mankind by the Divine teaching prerogative claimed and exercised by the Catholic Church, had been universally accepted as in harmony with the dictates of human reason and the needs of human nature : whole nations now rejected the Church's claim to that prerogative, and claiming for themselves the privilege of individual private judgment went their own divergent ways, selecting divers fragments of Christianity and classical Paganism wherewith to form religious systems after their own hearts. Similarly in regard to natural knowledge few thinkers of any note during the Middle Ages had ever seriously questioned the trustworthiness either of senses or of intellect, or doubted the capacity of the human mind to reach certitude regarding the questions of deepest import to humanity : now, however, the abandonment of the Aristotelian-Scholastic teaching in regard to the co-operation of senses and intellect in the genesis of true and certain knowledge led to a manifold recrudescence of Sensualism and Scepticism.

Modern Philosophy.—This marks the transition to modern philosophy, whose first notable representative, DESCARTES (1596-1650), did much towards concentrating all subsequent philosophical speculation *explicitly* on the problem of the possibility and limits of human certitude. Not that this general problem had not been already discussed for centuries ; it had been repeatedly discussed, not however *ex professo*, but inasmuch as it inevitably entered into ontological problems concerning the nature of reality itself which was assumed to be the object of knowledge., But Descartes' method of starting in search of certitude by making a clean sweep of all philosophical tradition, trying to assume absolutely nothing, and laying down as the basis of all knowledge his own consciousness that he was doubting everything,—this method and its consequences pushed the problem of knowledge, the critical problem, to the forefront of philosophical speculation, and led to the development of epistemology as a distinct and substantive department of philosophy.

Starting from the fact of self-consciousness Descartes developed a form of intellectualism which, while depreciating unduly the rôle of the senses, issued in an irreconcilable dualism of spirit and matter. With his disciples, GEULINCX (1625-69) and MALEBRANCHE (1638-1715), this passed over into *Occasionalism*, with SPINOZA (1632-77) into *Pantheism*, and with LEIBNIZ (1646-1716) into a sort of pan-psychism known as *Monadism*. Malebranche's theory of knowledge turned on the contention that the human mind has its knowledge not from the senses but from an intuitive intellectual vision of truth in the Divine Mind ; Spinoza likewise regarded not the senses but only intellectual intuition and reasoning as the source of genuine knowledge ; while Leibniz taught that the perceptions of sense and the conceptions of reason are innate and derive their validity from a harmony pre-established between them and their objects by God.

Alongside this continental current of extreme intellectualism there developed in England a very strong and influential current of sensualism. The rapid development of the sciences of observation and experiment from the sixteenth century onward had shifted the interest of scholars from the apparently barren occupation of the intellect in deductive reasoning to the more promising occupation of the senses in observing and experimenting in the domain of external nature. LORD BACON (1561-1626) had already called attention to the importance of thus " interrogating " nature instead of " anticipating " nature by futile *a priori* speculations, and JOHN HOBBES (1588-1679) had already revived in substance the sensualism of the school of Democritus, when JOHN LOCKE (1632-1704) in his *Essay Concerning the Human Understanding* laid

the foundations of modern English sensualism by so analysing the sources
and processes of knowledge as to raise serious doubts about its scope and
validity.   Intellectual processes were misinterpreted and partly confounded
with those of the senses and imagination, and all knowledge was apparently
reduced to a knowledge of mental states.   The attempt to evolve a knowledge
of extramental reality from this subjective awareness was so unsuccessful that
with Locke's immediate disciples, BERKELEY (1685-1753) and HUME (1711-
1776), the supposed barrier against the power of the mind to transcend itself
in knowledge appeared only to become more and more insuperable.   The
former argued from Locke's principles that the universe perceived by our
senses and supposed to be a world of material substances can be only a system
of *perceived* objects, *i.e.* of immaterial *ideas* which have no existence other
than their mental existence,—their *esse* being *percipi*,—and which derive this
mental existence from God, the Supreme Spirit, who places them in the created
spirits which we call our minds.   The latter pushed Locke's principles so far
as to argue that not merely can we know nothing of material substances, but
that we cannot know anything even of spiritual substances : all knowledge is
reduced to a mere consciousness of a flow of transient states of the individual
mind.   This current of sensualism, which reached its *reductio ad absurdum*
in the nihilistic scepticism of Hume, is variously described as *Empiricism*
owing to its exaggeration of the function of sense experience in knowledge and
its attempted reduction of all thought to sense processes ; as *Idealism* or
Phenomenism owing to its reduction of all knowledge to knowledge of mental
states, impressions, ideas, or appearances ; and as *Subjectivism* on account of
its implied or expressed denial of any power in the knowing subject to transcend itself in the process of cognition and so attain to any knowledge of extramental reality.   The logical issue of subjectivism is the absurd conclusion
known as *Solipsism*, *i.e.* the fancy that the individual conscious mind is the
sole existing reality, the whole universe being a sort of self-evolved panorama
passing within it.   An alternative to this absurd conclusion is, however, the
metaphysical theory of Idealistic Monism according to which individual finite
minds are but transient centres of partial self-consciousness in the eternal
evolution of the one sole reality which is at once Subject and Object, or Mind
and Nature.   Notwithstanding the suicidal destructiveness of Hume's philosophy, phenomenism was still widely prevalent among English philosophers
in the last century, finding typical exponents of its principles in such writers
as JOHN STUART MILL (1806-73), HUXLEY (1825-95), BAIN (1818-1903), and
SPENCER (1820-1903).   Under the title of *Positivism* (COMTE, 1798-1857) it
proclaimed the validity of the positive sciences as embodying knowledge of
the time and space relations of co-existence and sequence among the data
which constitute the domain of sense experience ; while on its negative side it
denied, under the title of *Agnosticism*, the validity of metaphysical knowledge,
i.e. knowledge of any domain of reality beyond that of sense experience.

   Towards the end of the eighteenth century the German philosopher,
IMMANUEL KANT (1724-1804),—aroused from the " dogmatic slumber" in
which he accepted the intellectualism of Leibniz and WOLFF (1679-1754),
by coming into contact with the thorough-going scepticism of Hume,—undertook the ambitious task of finding a *via media* between intellectualist dogmatism on the one side and sensualist scepticism on the other.   He sought this

via media by what he called the *Transcendental Criticism* of the mind's faculties of knowledge. In the spirit of Descartes he proclaimed the necessity of instituting a critical analysis of the mind, antecedently to all metaphysical investigation of man and the universe, with a view to discovering the scope and limitations of man's faculties of knowledge, and the conditions under which these faculties can attain to such knowledge as they are capable of reaching. The results of his life-long investigations were given to the world mainly in his three *Critiques,* the *Critique of Pure Reason,* the *Critique of Practical Reason,* and the *Critique of Judgment.* Praiseworthy in their purpose, but in their main drift misleading, they have exercised a profound, but on the whole an unhealthy and mischievous, influence on subsequent speculation. They reach the general conclusion that the human intellect, speculating reflectively on the data of sense experience, is confined to a knowledge of mental appearances or phenomena, and can attain to no knowledge of extra-subjective or extramental reality ; but that by a consideration of the practical or moral dictates of our conscience each of us can attain to subjective, personal certitude or conviction in regard to the principles of morals and religion,—the existence of God, the immortality of the soul, and the reality of human freedom and moral responsibility. Thus in effect he splits the human mind into two isolated compartments, and tries to reconcile speculative scepticism with moral dogmatism.

To his moral dogmatism may be traced the unfortunate anti-intellectualist tendency of modern thought to base all certitude concerning the principles which underlie religion and morality on the individual will and its aspirations, the individual feelings and emotions, the affective tendencies and activities of the individual mind. Thus, *Voluntarism* (RENAN, NIETZSCHE), *Sentimentalism* (JACOBI, 1743-1819), and in our own days *Pragmatism* (C. S. PIERCE, W. JAMES, G. SIMNEL, F. C. SCHILLER, etc.) have been propounded by those who while adhering to Kant's critical standpoint, and accepting his doctrine on the phenomenism of all speculative knowledge, display the same anxiety as he did to avoid the logical issue of a paralysing scepticism. At the same time the subjectivism reached by his defective analysis of speculative knowledge has sown in modern philosophy a deep distrust in the capacity of man to arrive by way of intellect at a valid knowledge of reality.

Hence we have multitudes of those modern writers who cultivate what we may call the philosophy of the sciences, proclaiming that even these elaborate systems, built up as they have been by intellectual interpretation of experience, give us no true insight into the nature of reality : their laws do not mirror or *represent* reality, but are only *regulative* principles whereby we systematize the contents of the subjective domain of our mental experience. This tendency is manifest in the writings of such men as HELMHOLTZ, HERTZ, MACH, POINCARÉ, LE ROY, etc.

Another manifestation of this sceptical attitude towards the power of the intellect may be recognized in the widely prevalent actual tendency to depreciate the value of a logical use of the intellect, to deny all validity or truth-value to the abstract intellectual concept and treat it as a mere symbol, to belittle the function of discursive reasoning by means of such concepts, to proclaim that not that way lies the road to real knowledge, but only by way of an alleged direct and immediate mental intuition which would bring the

conscious subject into living contact with the real.   Abstract thought presents
its object as one, inert, static, lifeless, etc.   But reality is manifold, dynamic,
vital, moving, etc. ; it is a process ; and only by direct conscious intuition can
it be grasped as such.   This attitude, already traceable in the writings of the
pragmatists (*cf.* DEWEY, SMITH, BREWSTER, WELLS, PAPINI, etc.) finds its
fullest development in the works of BERGSON,—who is *par excellence* the
philosopher most in fashion at the present time.   It is the old problem which
divided the Eleatics and the later Ionians, and in Bergson we rightly recognize the modern Heraclitus.

Reverting again for a moment to Kant's philosophy we observe that the
more notable of his *immediate* disciples, abandoning his critical standpoint,
developed what was for him a *theory of knowledge* into a *theory of reality*.
Thus FICHTE (1762-1814) and SCHELLING (1775-1854) constructed from
Kant's conclusions metaphysical systems of idealistic monism ; while HEGEL
(1770-1831), whose influence has rivalled that of Kant himself, constructed on
the lines of a purely intellectualist dialectic a monistic system in which he
identifies the logical with the ontological, subject with object, spirit or mind
with matter or nature, and represents the Sole Reality as a dialectically self-
evolving Thought or Idea.   While SCHOPENHAUER (1788-1860) opposed to
this Hegelian monism a voluntarist monism in which Reality is conceived as
Will, some of the immediate disciples of Hegel, such as FEUERBACH (1804-72)
and STRAUSS (1808-74), gave it an interpretation which issued in absolute
materialism.   Thus the most ambitious efforts of German speculation to
sound all the depths of Being with the plummet of the finite human mind, its
implied claim to clear up all mystery by comprehension of the Infinite, and
its equivalent deification of the creature, were speedily overtaken by the
nemesis of pride in a precipitous descent to the ignoble depths of the brute
philosophy.

Not all modern thought was, however, so deeply affected by subjectivism
as the various currents just indicated.   A truer appreciation of the relations
between senses and intellect, and between reason and faith, was retained by
many during the intellectual and religious revolutions which had ushered in
modern philosophy.   At the same time the enervating influence of the Cartesian and Kantian theories of knowledge weakened in some quarters that
healthy and robust confidence in the powers of the mind which had characterized the traditional Aristotelian philosophy as expounded in the Catholic
schools.   For this philosophy the certitude of knowledge is ultimately
grounded in the native capacity of the human intellect to reach a genuine
knowledge of reality by reasoning carefully from the data of sense experience
in the light of objective evidence.   Dissatisfied with this position some now
sought to claim for the human mind an immediate intuition of reality in the
Divine Mind as the only guarantee of the real validity of knowledge.   This
tendency found varied expressions in the *Theosophy* of OETINGER (1702-82)
and BAADER (1765-1841) in Germany, and in the *Ontologism* of ROSMINI
(1797-1855) and GIOBERTI (1801-52) in Italy.   Others sought to supplement
the supposed native incapacity of the mind by appealing to the necessity of
a Divine Revelation as the ultimate ground of human certitude, a theory
which found its formulation in the *Fideism* of HUET (1630-1721) and BAUTAIN
(1796-1867) in France, and in the *Traditionalism* of DE BONALD (1754-1840),

DE LAMENNAIS (1782-1854), BONNETTY (1798-1879), VENTURA (1792-1861), and UBAGHS (1800-75), in France, Italy, and Belgium.

In the main, however, the *traditional Aristotelian and scholastic theory* of knowledge found uninterrupted acceptance and support in Catholic centres of thought throughout the modern period. After the first shock of the sixteenth century revolutions it gained a remarkably brilliant series of advocates and exponents in the Catholic schools of Southern Europe, and especially of Spain. In this revival movement the most notable names are those of CAJETAN (1468-1534), SYLVESTER (1474-1528), SUAREZ (1548-1617), and JOHN OF ST. THOMAS (1589-1644).

Another and perhaps a more remarkable revival, or rather what is at once a revival, an adaptation, an amplification and development, of this traditional philosophy has taken place in our own days. The modern mind was prepared for it partly by the historical research of the last century,[1] which has dispelled so many prejudices concerning the Middle Ages, and partly by the intellectual unrest and discontent evoked by the modern chaos of ephemeral philosophical theories. It is characterized on the one hand by a more earnest study of mediæval scholasticism, especially as expounded in the works of St. Thomas Aquinas and the other great masters of the thirteenth century, and on the other hand by a thorough-going critical analysis of its principles both by comparison with other current theories of knowledge and reality, and by application to the achieved results of modern science and research in every department of human experience. It is in the spirit of this *present-day scholasticism* that problems are dealt with in this treatise.

The student will understand, of course, that the bald historical outlines in which we have just touched upon various theories of knowledge leave many theories unmentioned altogether, and have been set down merely with a view to acquainting the beginner with the general historical setting of the many questions to be investigated. About the modern scholastic movement just referred to it will suffice to say here that it had its origin in the seventies of the last century, during the pontificate of Leo XIII, and in no small measure owing to his enlightened and authoritative advocacy. While earnestly espoused in all Catholic schools, its two leading centres have been Rome and Louvain. Through the writings of the Louvain school, many of which have passed into English, German, Spanish, and Italian, its influence has been appreciably felt in not a few non-catholic and non-scholastic centres of thought.[2] Besides MERCIER'S *Criteriologie générale*, his *Logique*, *Ontologie*, and *Psychologie* (in the larger Louvain *Cours de philosophie*) may be consulted with profit, as also his *Origines de la psychologie contemporaine*. Among the leading exponents of the new scholasticism we may mention also : in Italy, LIBERATORE, SANSEVERINO, SIGNORIELLO, CORNOLDI, TONGIORGI, PAL-

---

[1] For historical research into mediæval philosophy, *cf.* the valuable collection consisting of some twelve volumes edited by BAEUMKER and VON HERTHING, *Beitraege zur Geschichte der Philosophie des Mittelalters;* the works of MANDONNET, EHRLÉ, and DENIFLÉ ; and the Louvain collection *Les Philosophes Belges*, edited by DE WULF and PELZER.

[2] For a fully documented account of the Neo-Scholastic Movement, *cf.* PERRIER, *The Revival of Scholastic Philosophy* (New York, 1909); also DE WULF, *Scholasticism Old and New* (2nd edit., Dublin, Gill, 1910).

MIERI, ZIGLIARA, LEPIDI,[1] SCHIFFINI and DE MARIA ;—in Spain, BALMES,
GONZALEZ, URRABURU ;—in Germany, KLEUTGEN,[2] STOECKL, VON HER-
THING, PESCH, BAEUMKER, WERNER, KAUFMANN, GRABMANN, GUTBERLET,
SCHMIDT ;[3]—in France, PEILLAUBE, SERTILLANGES, ROUSELLOT,[4] GARDEIL,
MANDONNET, PIAT, FARGES, DOMET DE VORGES, TONQUEDEC ;—in Eng-
land, HARPER, W. G. WARD, MAHER, RICKABY, and the other writers of the
Stonyhurst Philosophical Series ;—in Belgium, the Louvain school, including
MERCIER, NYS, THIERY, DEPLOIGE, DE WULF, NOEL, SENTROUL, VAN
WEDDINGEN, HALLEUX, FONTAINE, JANSSENS ; also DE SAN, DE MUN-
NYNCK, LAHOUSSE, etc., etc.

5. EPISTEMOLOGY NOT AN INTRODUCTION TO METAPHYSICS
BUT A DEPARTMENT OF METAPHYSICS.—The historical outlines
given above will have revealed the fact that since the time of
Descartes the notion has been widely entertained that a critical
investigation of the mind's capacity to reach certain knowledge
ought properly to *precede* any attempt to investigate any of the
fundamental problems of philosophy, that only when we have
first discovered the scope and limits of this capacity are we in a
position to carry on metaphysical research. Nay more, Kant is
said even to have urged that we must bring this critical analysis
to bear on the mind's cognitive *faculties* themselves without taking into account the *spontaneous working* of these faculties or
building in any way on the *experienced results* of our spontaneous
cognitive activities ; that looking at the mind itself,—irrespectively
of anything that it spontaneously thinks, judges, or believes,—the
general question we have to ask and try to answer is the question
whether, or how far, within what limits and under what conditions,
can such a mind have knowledge. Such is the sort of criticism
which Kant is said to have called " transcendental " and to have
himself undertaken. This standpoint is not easily intelligible ;
nor is it easy to see how the real, as distinct from the merely os-
tensible, adoption of such a standpoint could render a single step
of investigation possible,—in other words, how it would be possible
for us to investigate *knowledge*, which is at any rate an activity
of the mind (or its faculties) by attempting to examine the mind
(or its faculties) *apart from all activities of the latter.* For in what
other way can we hope to discover anything about knowledge,
about its scope and limits, about the conditions of its validity,
unless by examining the mind and its faculties *as revealed in its
cognitive activities ?*

---

[1] *Della conoscenza intellettuale.*
[2] Author of *Die Philosophie der Vorzeit ;* French tr., *La philosophie scolastique.*
[3] *Erkenntnislehre,* 2 vols., Freiburg im Br., 1890.
[4] *L'intellectualisme de Saint Thomas,* Paris, 1908.

Furthermore, it does not seem necessary to institute such an analysis *antecedently* to all other philosophical investigations. Just as a man's ·spontaneous reasonings can be correct without his having previously learned from the science of logic the canons to which they must have conformed, so can he by his spontaneous convictions have attained to true and certain knowledge without his having previously assured himself from the science of epistem ology that he was not misled by those convictions. As a matter of fact all men can and do acquire a more or less extensive stock of truth before ever adverting to the desirability or necessity of examining explicitly their capability to attain to any truth ; and most men never trouble themselves to raise such a question at all. Moreover, as we have seen already, it is only gradually and from a deeper study of scientific, philosophical, and religious questions, that the various problems arise with which epistemology has to deal. The aim of this sort of investigation, therefore, is not to prepare the way for metaphysical investigation, but rather to complete and consolidate this latter. Its problems are not problems which must be solved as an antecedent condition to the attainment of truth about any other matter. Hence epistem-ology is not a preparatory or introductory study which must pre cede metaphysics and make the latter possible ; it is a department of metaphysics, and not the first in order either.

Of course the reason for the post-Cartesian and post-Kantian view is not far to seek. In order that the mind discover truth with certitude *it must be capable of doing so.* Is anything else necessary ? Is it necessary also that the mind *be convinced of its own capability ?* Here we must distinguish. It does indeed seem necessary that the mind be *aware* of its own capability, that it have a *natural and spontaneous conviction* of its capability, not perhaps explicitly and as a result of reflection on the matter, but that an implicit, concomitant belief in its own capability must accompany all its cognitive activities : for no knowledge of truth, no conviction of knowledge certainly attained, would be compat-ible with a serious doubt on the part of the mind regarding its capacity to reach truth. This spontaneous belief in the general trustworthiness of his cognitive faculties is, however, a natural endowment of every man ; it is a condition which does not re-sult from, but precedes, all epistemological investigation.

But is it further necessary,—in order that the mind discover any truth with certitude,—not only that it be, and spontaneously believe itself to be, capable of so doing, but also that it should have by deliberate reflection and *ex professo* called this spontaneous belief into question, and examined critically whether or not the grounds for this spontaneous belief are really sufficient? No ; such an investigation is not a prerequisite condition for the certain possession of truth : provided that sufficient grounds for the spontaneous belief *are really there* we can reach truth without having *ex professo* examined into their sufficiency. Of course when we do deliberately institute a critical inquiry into the whole question of the sufficiency of the grounds for our spontaneous convictions,—an inquiry involving an analysis of the sources and processes of knowledge, etc.,—and when by such inquiry we satisfy ourselves that although we are not infallible and have sometimes fallen into error, and although our minds are not infinite and must therefore remain ignorant of many things, still we are really capable of reaching some truth and our spontaneous knowledge was in the main genuine,—when we have done all this we naturally thereby strengthen and confirm our spontaneous convictions. But this does not imply that they were not already convictions whereby we attained to true and genuine knowledge, or that the critical investigations undertaken in Epistemology must precede the acquisition of genuine certitude about anything. Nevertheless, the method of doubt employed by Descartes, and the method of transcendental criticism employed by Kant, seem to imply that a critical inquiry into the possibility of knowledge and certitude in general should precede the employment of our cognitive faculties to reach a reasoned solution of any fundamental or philosophical problem whatsoever. The one purports to start from an attempted universal doubt, the other to conduct the inquiry without any appeal to experience ; and both alike seem to imply that the mind can have no genuine certitude or real knowledge, at least about fundamental or philosophical problems, until it has first prosecuted to a successful issue the preliminary question as to whether it is at all capable of attaining to a certain solution of such problems. In connexion with these methods we shall see whether such a preliminary and presuppositionless theory of knowledge is at all possible. From what has been just said the student will be able to conclude that Epistemology is a department of metaphysics rather than an introduction to metaphysics, and this is the only point with which we are just now concerned.

PART I.

THE NATURE OF THE INQUIRY.

CHAPTER I.

THE TERMS AND DATA OF THE INQUIRY.

6. COGNITION. KNOWLEDGE. SCIENCE. BELIEF. FAITH.—
By *cognition* (L. *cognitio*) we mean simply the act or process of knowing. By *knowledge* we mean the result of this process, or sometimes—according to the context—the process of cognition itself. It is usually taken as a collective term : the collection of accumulated results of our cognitive activities. Sometimes, however, we find authors speaking of *a* knowledge, and *knowledges* in the plural,—meaning an individual cognition or its result, and a number of these, respectively. We may notice here that knowing, cognition, knowledge, is *sui generis*, that therefore it cannot properly speaking be defined, or explained in terms of anything other than itself.[1] It is of course a complex process which admits of analysis, examination, description, illustration ; but we must be always careful to remember that the terms of our descriptions and illustrations are only metaphors and analogies, and may therefore easily mislead instead of aiding us if we take them as conveying to us anything better known to us than knowledge itself. Nothing is more intimate to us than knowing. Hence there is no necessity for defining it even if we could ; but we cannot. No doubt, we may say that cognition is a process, an activity ; and so it is ; but this is not a definition, for if " activity " is the *genus*, what is the *differentia specifica ?* Cognition only bears

---

[1] " The very question, ' What does the process of knowing consist in ? ' at least suggests that knowing can be resolved into and stated in terms of something else · · · that it is possible to elucidate the nature of knowledge by means of something other than itself. Knowledge is *sui generis* and therefore a ' theory ' of it is impossible. Knowledge is simply knowledge, and any attempt to state it in terms of something else must end in describing something which is not knowledge." PRICHARD, *Kant's Theory of Knowledge*, pp. 23S-45.

an analogy to other forms of activity ; and no other form of activity is more intimate to us than that of knowing.   Moreover, we contrast "knowing" with "doing," and still more with "making". There is no more familiar distinction than that between "thought" and "action"; and thought[1] is a form of knowing.   No doubt the mind is active in knowing; all cognition is an immanent mental activity, and has as result a mental state or condition— which we call knowledge.   But all knowledge must be knowledge *of* something, and what we have here to observe is that knowledge as such does not *make* this "something".   At least the common-sense view of knowledge is that it is not a producing, creating, or making of something, but a revealing or discovery of something.   Just as volition or willing is an immanent mental activity which produces the mental state or condition of decision, determination, resolution, etc., so cognition or knowing produces the mental acquirement we call knowledge, but it does not produce the object of the knowledge, the thing known.   It is not a production but a discovery of this latter ;[2] but then, again, such terms as "discovery," "revelation," "manifestation," "representation," etc., employed in describing knowledge, are no whit simpler or more familiar to us than the term "knowledge," or "cognition" itself.

The term *science* conveys the notion of knowledge in some way perfected.   "*Scientific* knowledge" (L. *scientia, cognitio scientifica*) is contrasted with "*ordinary* knowledge" (L. *cognitio vulgaris*), as knowledge systematized, thought over, reduced to order, in contrast with the scrappy, unassorted, promiscuous knowledge possessed by the uneducated masses (the *vulgus*, or

---

[1] The terms "thought" and "thinking" signify properly the higher or intellectual processes of knowledge, such as conception of ideas, judgment, and reasoning, as distinguished from the operations of the senses and imagination.

[2] We are here concerned only with setting down the currently accepted meaning of terms.   We shall examine in due course attempts to show that knowledge is something like what this "construction" theory would make it.   It is in criticism of such an attempt, on the part of Kant, that PRICHARD (*op. cit.*, p. 118—*cf.* also *ibid.*, pp. 235-6) has the following : ' Knowledge unconditionally presupposes that the reality known exists independently of the knowledge of it, and that we know it as it exists in this independence.   It is simply *impossible* to think that any reality depends upon our knowledge of it, or upon any knowledge of it.   If there is to be knowledge, there must first *be* something to be known.   In other words, knowledge is essentially discovery, or the finding of what already is.   If a reality could only be or come to be in virtue of some activity or process on the part of the mind, th t activity or process would not be "knowing," but "making" or "creating," and to make and to know must in the end be admitted to be mutually exclusive.'

common folk).[1]   When knowledge is thus systematized it forms what are called " the *sciences* ".

On these distinctions we have to observe two things.   Firstly, scientific knowledge is in its processes and objects continuous with ordinary knowledge ; it is a development of the latter, attained by the same human minds using the same faculties on the same subject-matter as in ordinary knowledge.   To conceive science as something wholly apart and removed from ordinary knowledge would be a mistaken and unjustifiable view.   Secondly, when we think of " the sciences " as distinct bodies of truth or knowledge, the distinction is a mental one, due to the mind's power of abstracting ; and hence we must guard against conceiving the sciences as " existing " separately from one another or apart from human minds.   There is and can be no " science," just as there is and can be no " knowledge," except in individual human minds.   The sciences do not exist even in books : what exists in books is a system of visible symbols of oral language,— which latter is the expression of thought or knowledge.   But thought or knowledge exists only in the mind : and not in any common, general, or universal " mind " or " subject " whose sole function should be conceived as cognition,—for this too is only an abstraction,—but in the minds of individual men, each of whom not merely " knows," but also lives, feels, wills, believes, hopes, acts, and has all the manifold conscious states and activities which constitute human experience.

Belief is commonly distinguished from and sometimes contrasted with knowledge, but this is because the term has a variety of meanings.   *To believe* in its primary meaning is to accept something as true on the word or authority of another.   One of the main sources of our knowledge is the authority of our fellow-men.   People do not generally realize—because it needs a little reflection to realize—what a vast proportion of our knowledge comes to each of us individually through this source.   Through it each of us has *all* his knowledge of the facts of history, *most* of his knowledge of the facts of geography, *all* his knowledge of what is actually going on in the world outside the very limited corner that falls under his own personal notice.   People who decry " religious knowledge " because it is accepted

---

[1] For other and kindred implications of the term—" knowledge of a thing through its causes," " knowledge reached by demonstration," etc.—see below, § 13, p. 54 ; *Science of Logic*, ii., §§ 251-4.

on authority seem to forget that nine-tenths of the human race accept "scientific knowledge" only on authority, and that of the other tenth, the scientists themselves, each accepts nine-tenths of *his* scientific knowledge on the authority of his fellow-scientists and without exploring or verifying it for himself,—inasmuch as ten lifetimes, not to speak of one lifetime, would be too short to carry out such verification.   Now knowledge accepted on authority is belief.   In this sense of the term, therefore, belief is a department of knowledge.   When we believe a person's statement we believe the person himself.   This means that we know for certain his authority is reliable ; and when we know this we know that what he tells us is true.   Of course if we do not happen to know for certain that his authority for what he tells us is reliable we cannot know for certain that what he tells us is true.   We cannot give to it the certain assent which will make it for us knowledge in the strict sense, *i.e.* certain possession of the truth.

All knowledge proper is embodied in judgments.   To assent to a judgment is to accept it and commit ourselves to it as true. When we do so we accept implicitly the grounds for the truth of the judgment as sufficient.   When these grounds are in the judgment itself, or intrinsically connected with the judgment, and are in the nature of reasons appealing solely to our intellects, we are said commonly to "know" that the judgment is true. When they are in the nature of authority we are said to " believe" that the judgment is true, and to "believe" the truth embodied in it ; but here, provided the grounds are sufficient for a certain, *i.e.* a firm assent, and that we are not deceived, the belief will be knowledge.

When the grounds are not in the nature of authority, nor yet, on the other hand, purely intellectual and such as to compel our assent, to amount to "demonstration," or admit of being stated in purely intellectual terms, but are nevertheless such that from their appeal to our whole mental nature, needs, and constitution, —including intellect, will, and emotions,—we pronounce them to be reasonably sufficient grounds for assenting to the judgment,— in such cases also we are commonly said to " believe" the latter to be true.   Here, too, provided the grounds are sufficient, and we are not deceived, our belief will be knowledge : it will be firm adherence to a true judgment.   Nevertheless, when we give assents of this latter kind we are commonly said to " believe"

rather than to "know" what is asserted in the judgments concerned, just as in the case of assents given on authority. Thus
we are not only said to believe, *e.g.*, that Socrates was put to death
by the Athenians, but also, *e.g.*, that "our faculties are capable
of reaching truth," or that "truth and error are distinct and distinguishable," or that "Nature is uniform". The grounds for
such assents as these will be duly examined. Here we wish
merely to point out that it is a fairly common usage to group together assents based on authority, and assents based on grounds
not exclusively intellectual, but in part volitional, affective, emotional, instinctive, and under the title of "belief" or "faith" to
distinguish them from the purely intellectual assents which are
supposed to give us "knowledge" or "science".

Seeing that the grounds for the classes of assents described
as "belief" are not so clear or cogent or capable of exact formulation as the grounds for those described as "knowledge," it
should naturally be expected that the former term would gradually
come to be applied to assents that are not firm or certain, to
probable as distinct from certain knowledge, to opinion as distinct
from certitude. And such is the actual usage. Hence the common form of expression, "I do not *know* whether that is really
so, but I *believe* it is" (or "I *think* it is"), where the term "know"
connotes certain knowledge and the term "believe" (or "think")
connotes belief in the sense of opinion or probable knowledge.
In this usage "belief" is distinguished from "knowledge" as
"opinion" from "certitude".

Faith differs little in its meaning—or rather, in its meanings
—from "belief". As a mental act or attitude or habit it is
belief especially *in religious truths on Divine authority*. It is
used objectively to signify a whole body or system of dogmas
believed, just as the term "science" is used objectively to signify
a whole body or system of truths known. In this sense "faith"
is practically synonymous with "religion," and is distinguished
from "science," as belief is from knowledge. The distinction is
not one of opposition. The truths of faith and the truths of
science are both alike truths; and truth cannot contradict truth.
In so far as the assents of faith or religion are given to truths,
and on sufficient grounds, they embody knowledge, and the
systematization of such knowledge belongs to the science of
Theology—the Theology of Faith.

Of course there are multitudes who regard all religions

or faiths objectively as systems of beliefs or assents based on instinctive, emotional needs, about matters concerning which knowledge is considered impossible. But if the motives of such assents are pronounced sufficient to produce certitude, when submitted to the judgment of our reason reflecting on them, we cannot help thinking that they are beliefs which give us *knowledge*, or in other words put us into possession of *truth*. If, however, the motives are not reasonably sufficient to produce certitude, then in such case our " faith " or " religion " is only a system of more or less probable opinions. The view that the assents of faith are concerned with a domain of realities wholly distinct from the domain of objects of knowledge we shall find to be erroneous. It exaggerates and misinterprets the distinction which we do undoubtedly find between two great classes of our assents, namely, those given on clear and cogent intellectual grounds to the demonstrated conclusions of the speculative sciences, and those given from much more complex, personal, practical motives to judgments of more intimate concern to the general outlook and ordering of our lives.[1]

We have to bear in mind, then, that according to fairly common usage the terms "belief" and "faith" are not confined to assents given on authority, but embrace assents given to judgments which we accept indeed as true but to which we assent on grounds that are too complex to admit of being resolved into purely intellectual reasons amounting to the demonstration or the self-evidence deemed necessary for judgments constituting "knowledge" or "science".

When the judgments which we accept as true on authority have an intimate practical bearing on our own future, as they have in the case of supernatural religious beliefs, our assents are accompanied by the mental attitude of expectation, anticipation, hope, trust, confidence, reliance. The authority *in* whom we "believe" or "have faith" not merely vouches for a truth but makes a promise. Hence to " believe in " or to " have faith in " a person, commonly implies not merely accepting his authority for a truth but relying on his fidelity for the fulfilment of a promise. Faith in this sense of trust, or confidence, or reliance (L. *fiducia*), implies not merely assent of the intellect to a truth but a whole complex mental attitude,—involving the activity of will,

---

[1] *Cf.* NEWMAN's distinction between " notional " and " real " assents, *Grammar of Assent (passim)*.

affections, emotions, etc.,—towards some person or persons as related to ourselves and influencing our lives. In so far as faith means merely assent to or belief in a truth, it is an act of the intellect ; in so far as it includes confidence, reliance, trust, etc., it is a much more complex mental process involving activities other than cognitive activities. Cognition, knowledge, science are processes and states of the mind *as cognitive.* Belief and faith involve assent to, or acceptance of, the knowledge acquired by these processes.

Let us see next what introspection reveals regarding the various attitudes of our mind towards knowledge.

7. DOUBT. OPINION. CONVICTION. CERTITUDE.—It is a common conviction of mankind that truth is distinguishable from error. It is an equally common conviction that although men easily fall into error, and easily remain in error, nevertheless they can and do possess some true knowledge concerning themselves and the universe. The human mind is recognized to be fallible in that it can adhere to error, mistaking this for truth. It is also recognized to be limited in its capacity inasmuch as no one believes that *all reality* falls within the experience of any individual human being, and, therefore, there is much reality of which even the wisest human being must remain in ignorance. Finally, no human individual will claim that he *fully understands all* the reality which does fall within his experience : he will admit that there is much he is unable to interpret, unable to reach the truth or make up his mind about, so that he must *suspend his judgment* in reference to it and remain in *doubt ;* and that there is much, perhaps, too, in regard to which, while he has a more or less strong *opinion* that he has reached the truth, still he is not *certain,* not *sure,* not *convinced* that he has, and so recognizes the possibility that he may be mistaken. But with all that,—at least if he be an ordinary man and not a philosopher of a certain school, —he will unhesitatingly declare and maintain that there are some things, indeed many things, about which he is absolutely *certain* that he has true knowledge, and in regard to which he is not and could not have been deceived. Nor will the most sceptical philosopher deny that all men, himself included, naturally and spontaneously have such convictions. What he may question or deny is that any of these convictions are well grounded or will stand the test of critical analysis. With that, however, we are not here concerned, but merely with the fact that all men have spontaneous

convictions, *i.e.* are naturally certain that they possess some true knowledge.

Let us now look into our own minds a little and examine those mental attitudes of *doubt, surmise, opinion* (or "*belief*"), *conviction*, and *certitude* or *certainty*, in regard to our knowledge. We are concerned at this stage only with noting the undisputed facts which are the data of our inquiry, and the meaning of the terms in which its problems will be stated.

Doubt[1] is the attitude of our minds towards a judgment which we find ourselves unable either to affirm or to deny: a state of *hesitancy, suspense.* Either we know nothing or practically nothing about the subject in question and have no grounds for determining whether or not the suggested judgment about it is true,—in which case our doubt is said to be *negative*,—or the grounds for and against the judgment appear practically equal, in which case the doubt is described as *positive.* In this latter case we form judgments, of course, about the grounds, but in neither case do we enunciate a judgment about the main subject itself. We suspend our judgment.

Besides doubt, there is another state of *uncertainty*,[2] *viz. opinion* or "belief". This is the attitude of the mind towards a judgment to which it inclines, and which it accepts and assents to provisionally as more or less likely to be true, more or less *probable* or "provable". The mind does not know it to be true, is not certain of its truth, is conscious that it may possibly be false, and therefore does not assent to it firmly and definitively, but accepts it only provisionally. The strength of the mind's assent, of its ,hold on such a judgment, may vary (with the weight of the motives) from a mere *suspicion* or *surmise* of its truth to a very steady adhesion whereby the mind accepts it— as it prudently may accept it—for a safe principle or rule of

---

[1] The etymology of the term reveals the oscillation of the mind between *two* objects, between affirming and denying. It is from the same root (*dub-*) as *double* (*dubius, dubitare*). *Cf.* also the German *zweifel* (doubt) from *zwei* (two).

[2] Sometimes the term "doubt" is used as the contradictory of conviction or certitude, as connoting merely the absence of the latter state, in which case it covers both suspense of all assent (positive or negative doubt in the strict sense) and opinion or probable assent. In this usage it is equivalent to "uncertainty". Sometimes, too, it is used in the wider and improper sense of positive disbelief in the truth of a judgment, meaning a firm belief or conviction that the judgment is *false.* This, of course, is not really a state of doubt or uncertainty but a state of conviction. The student must, therefore, attend to the context for the meaning actually given to the term.

action.[1] But even then there is the consciousness that in accepting it there is a possibility—not a mere abstract possibility, but
a real and concrete possibility—of error. This concrete possibility
of error, when seen to persist, *omnibus pensatis*, begets in the
mind a *fear* of error, which the mind deems it *prudent* to entertain, so that the mind does not *repose* in a *definitive* assent to the
judgment as true.

Over against these two states of *uncertainty*, and sharply contrasted with uncertainty, is the mental attitude of *conviction, certitude, certainty*. Whereas the main affective characteristic of
uncertainty, and more especially of doubt, as a psychic state or
condition, is that of *indetermination, unrest, instability, irksome-
ness*, that of certitude[2] is rest, repose, stability. For certitude is
the fixed or firm assent of the mind to a judgment as true. In this
state the mind reposes, convinced that it has attained its object,
that it is in possession of truth; whereas, while the mind is
doubting, or merely inclining to a judgment as probably true,
while it is still uncertain, while it is not sure, not convinced that
the judgment is true, it is not at rest but conscious that it has
still to work, to search, to examine, before it attains its object,
which is repose in the possession of truth.

So long as we entertain a *prudent fear of error* we have not
conviction or certitude. The factor of prudence refers, of course,
to our examination of the grounds and motives of our assent.
When we are conscious to ourselves that the grounds of our assent are reasonably sufficient, in other words, when by a reasonable consideration of them they *show* the judgment to be true,
then and then only can we have conviction or certitude, then
alone can we say to ourselves, " I *know* that to be true ". An
"*imprudent* fear of error " is a fear that it would be unreasonable
to entertain. If a person doubts merely because of such a fear

---

[1] This very high degree of probability is commonly called "*practical* certitude,"
i.e. it is practically equivalent to certitude because men commonly act upon it in the
practical affairs of life. Hence the saying, *Probability is the guide of life.* When
we are not certain about the lawfulness of a given course of action, Moralists lay
down principles whereby we can overcome the speculative doubt and determine the
lawful line of conduct.

[2] The term certitude (*certum*, for *cretum*, from *cerno*, κρίνειν, κριτής) is from
a root meaning to judge, decide, decree, pass sentence, after sifting, " discerning" (*dis-, cerno*), examining, the evidence. It therefore implies decision, finality,
settlement. Sometimes a distinction is drawn between *certitude* as the state of
mind and *certainty* as the characteristic of the judgment, as when we say, " That is
a *certainty* ".

it is because he misjudges it to be a prudent fear : if he considers it an imprudent fear he will reject it and assent firmly, *i.e.* with conviction or certitude, to the judgment in question.   And while he is certain and remains certain he may advert to several such grounds of imprudent misgiving.   It is about such that Newman somewhere says " a hundred difficulties do not make one doubt ". Such vague and merely subjective misgivings as may arise from the consciousness that we are not infallible, or from the remembrance that we have at times fallen into error, are not necessarily incompatible with the fixed or firm assent which constitutes conviction.   Men can and do retain multitudes of their spontaneous convictions even after full advertence to, and consideration of, their own mental limitations ; and if some philosophers assert that the process of testing critically the grounds of certitude has ended for them in universal scepticism and destroyed their spontaneous convictions, this assertion only proves that like the rest of mankind they too had such convictions.[1]   Nor has any one ever seriously denied the existence of spontaneous or natural certitude as a mental state distinct from that of doubt.   The recognition of the distinction is in fact the starting-point of all critical inquiry into the validity of knowledge.

The distinction between opinion on the one hand and conviction or certitude on the other lies in the presence or absence of a prudent fear of error.   If such fear is present it arises from the apprehended *concrete possibility* of error and impedes a firm assent ; if it is absent the assent is firm and amounts to conviction or certitude.

It is a fact of common experience that according to the weight of the motives for or against assent the mind may alternate between the states of doubt, opinion, and conviction or certitude in regard to the same judgment.   The evidence for the truth of a probable judgment may increase up to the point at which all prudent fear of error is excluded, and at this point opinion passes into conviction or certitude.   It is of the essence of opinion or probable assent that it admits of varying grades of intensity.

Does conviction or certain assent also admit of varying

---

[1] Even after theoretically rejecting these convictions as speculatively unjustifiable, sceptics nevertheless retain them as practical certitudes : they could not continue to live otherwise, for almost every act of man's daily life is based on such convictions.

degrees of firmness? The common usage of language will not assist us materially in answering this question, for the terms in which people describe the character of their assents do not indicate any great accuracy or exactness of mental analysis. People often say lightly, " I am sure," " I am quite certain," " I have no doubt," etc., when a little reflection would convince them they were not really sure at all. Indeed when a person vehemently reasserts and reiterates that he is certain of a thing, this very fact is a pretty sure sign that he is not without some misgiving as to his position. Hence the assertion " I am more certain of this than I am of that,"—which, though perhaps unusual, is not unheard of,—does not settle the question whether some certitudes are really firmer than others.

It is obvious that on the *negative* side all certain assents must equally exclude prudent fear of error. But while all have this feature in common, may not some of them be *positively* firmer than others? Introspection reveals this much at all events, that there are some of my convictions which are never disturbed by any fear of error inasmuch as I cannot conceive the possibility of the judgments in question being erroneous, *e.g.*, " two and two are four"; and that there are other convictions of mine accompanied by the consciousness that they might possibly cease to be convictions, or perhaps by the memory that they were at one time only opinions or matters of doubt. Such for instance is my conviction that without the aid of Divine Revelation it would be morally impossible for the masses of mankind to reach and retain the religious knowledge necessary for the guidance of their lives in accordance with their nature and destiny. Such, too, are the convictions we shall describe later (11) as "free convictions," —to which class belong most moral and religious beliefs. Introspection, moreover, reveals that these latter alone are accompanied by a fluctuating mass of volitional and emotional consciousness arising from their intimate personal influence on our lives. While the necessary assents which we give to *speculative* judgments on cogent evidence are characterized by an absence of emotion, a calmness and tranquillity, arising partly from the consciousness that they are indubitable and partly from the consciousness that they have no immediate practical bearing on the regulation of our lives and conduct, the assents which we freely give to the *practical* judgments of the other class are indeed firm, not however with the immovable and unassailable fixity of assents on cogent evidence, but with a steadfastness begotten of mental effort; and while we hold these so firmly that we may be prepared even to die rather than relinquish them, still we are conscious that they are exposed in our minds to the possibility of being shaken by the intrusion of fears, by suggestions of reasons for doubting, etc.,—though we see the imprudence of yielding to such suggestions, of entertaining such fears, of fostering such temptations.

It is perhaps on this account that at first sight we are inclined to say that the former certitudes are "firmer" than the latter. Reflection, however, while revealing profound differences between the total mental state in each case, does not corroborate the view that our assent to such a judgment, as, for instance, "the human soul is immortal," is one whit less firm,—provided we are convinced, and as long as we are convinced, of its truth,—than is our assent to such a judgment as "the whole is greater than its part". Provided I am convinced of the truth of both, *i.e.* provided I know for certain, or think that I know for certain, that both are true, then I hold them equally for true. My mental grasp is *de facto* equally firm in both cases, though I am quite conscious that in the one case I am exposed to mental influences which might possibly have the effect of loosening my grasp while in the other case I am not aware that any such influences are even possible.

8. COGNITIVE AND NON-COGNITIVE STATES OF CONSCIOUSNESS. CONSCIOUSNESS, KNOWLEDGE, AND OBJECTIVITY.—Those states—of doubt, opinion, conviction, certitude—are, it need hardly be pointed out, *cognitive* states, states of the mind *as cognitive*, attitudes of the mind towards *knowledge*. The mind has other conscious states and activities which are not cognitive: wishes, desires, decisions, or choices, appetitive movements of various kinds, emotional and passional affections and feelings such as joy, anger, fear, pleasure, melancholy, etc. About all such states two things here claim our notice.

Firstly : they are all distinct from the states mentioned above. Although volitional and emotional factors can and often do enter into the motives which produce the states of doubt, opinion, conviction, or certitude, nevertheless these states are attitudes of the mind towards *knowledge* and *truth :* they are all concerned with assent to, or acceptance of, judgments as true, as embodying knowledge. They all refer the mind to an object made present to the mind by the state or process of cognition itself. The other states and processes do not of themselves refer the mind to anything beyond themselves. Considered in themselves, apart from the cognitions out of which they may have arisen and by which they are generally accompanied, they are merely mental facts, of which the mind as a conscious subject is aware.

Secondly : although, therefore, they are not *cognitive* states they are *conscious* states : they are states of consciousness, of appetitive, volitional, emotional consciousness, as distinct from cognitive consciousness. All states of consciousness, all conscious acts or processes, have this in common, that they make the conscious being somehow aware of himself in the concrete, of himself as living, doing, suffering, experiencing something : otherwise he would not be conscious. But this awareness, which is of the essence of all conscious activity, need not necessarily be of anything but the vaguest and most indefinite character. It does not necessarily imply the possession, by the conscious being, of any *idea* of " self " or " other," or even a conscious distinction, on the part of the conscious being, between himself and that of which he is conscious. Such an explicit awareness of the " self " as affected by conscious states, or as distinct from other beings, implies the exercise of introspection or reflex consciousness,[1] and of the faculty of comparing, distinguishing, judging, *i.e.* it involves interpretation and therefore cognition in the strict sense. The simple awareness which is essential to direct consciousness even in its most rudimentary stage, involves none of all this.

Although, therefore, direct consciousness may be called "cognition" or "knowledge" in a wide and loose sense, it is not knowledge properly speaking. It is of course an essential condition of the cognitive process, and may be regarded as an initial stage of this latter. But cognition or knowledge proper is the *interpretation* of something, the *mental assertion* of something about something.

The mere *presentation* of something to a conscious being, and

---

[1] Psychologists are wont to puzzle over the question, how the mind can act consciously and *at the same time* by a reflex process watch or attend to its direct conscious processes : come arguing that what really happens is that the direct process when just past is immediately *recalled* or *represented*, that " all introspection is retrospection " ; others arguing that " all retrospection is introspection," inasmuch as when the mind does remember or recall a past process it must, *while* reproducing it, at that instant *also* attend to it. However it happens, the possibility of introspection is proved by the fact of introspection : about the fact there can be no dispute.

its consequent presence *in* or *to* or *before*[1] the mind of such a being, are not yet knowledge. It is only when the mind *re*-views or *re*-presents to itself the already present or presented something, and makes some mental assertion which in some way interprets this " something," that the mind begins to have knowledge (or possibly error) about it. In this process of interpretation or judgment,—the exercise of which implies, as we shall see, some degree of mental development by which the mind through sense perception has acquired a stock of notions or concepts utilized in judging,—the mind *characterizes* in some way what has been presented to it, makes it to some extent *definite*, in some sense *classifies* it. Hence it has been said that " all cognition is recognition " : *i.e.* all cognition in the strict sense, in the sense in which it attains to truth or involves error.

Hence mere sense perception, whereby through the functioning of the sense faculties we become aware of something consciously affecting us in one or other of the modes with which sense experience has familiarized us, is not knowledge proper—of itself and apart from the interpretation that as a rule implicitly accompanies it. *As interpreted*, it is no longer mere perception but *apperception*, to use this term in one of its many meanings.[2] As apperception, it is knowledge proper and must be either true or false. But as perception merely, it rather is or gives the raw material of knowledge. Hence, too, mere mental imagery is not of itself cognition, nor can the images formed by the constructive or reproductive exercise of the imagination be regarded as knowledge ; though the interpretation of them is knowledge.

Hence, finally, mere intellectual conception, whereby we form the abstract and universal concepts, notions, or ideas expressed by abstract and general logical terms, is not cognition or knowledge, —apart from the interpretation or judgment which accompanies it. Neither of sense percepts, nor of imagination images, nor of intellectual concepts, nor of the logical terms which express in language those mental factors of knowledge, can it be properly said that they are either " true " or " false "

No doubt these products or results of conscious activity are factors of knowledge. All of them have that peculiar characteristic which marks off cognition from other forms of conscious

---

[1] These prepositions have of course in the above and similar contexts no *local* or *spatial* significance.

[2] *Cf.* MAHER, *Psychology*, 5th edit., pp. 359-60.

activity, *viz.* the objective reference of the mind as conscious subject to a something as distinct from the mental process whereby
this "something" is made present to the mind as conscious. External sense perception refers us to a perceived material universe
as distinct from our minds; the organic sense refers us to states
of an organism felt as our own, yet distinct from our process of
feeling; abstract concepts (and the logical terms which express
them) refer us to a domain not identical with, but objective to,
the thought-process of conception itself.[1] But while this objective reference is indeed there in all those cognitive states and
processes, it is not and cannot be interpreted and *asserted to be
a valid reference to reality* except in the mental act of judgment.
It is only the copula of the logical judgment that asserts the objects of this mental reference to be *reality*, and the relation between mind and reality involved in this reference to be true or
objectively valid knowledge. We may say, then, that *all* cognitive states or processes of consciousness have, in virtue of their
natural objective reference, an *interpretative* objectivity, but that
in judgment alone we have that *consciously asserted* objectivity
(of the mental state as representative of reality) whereby the
judgment is *true* or *false.*[2]

9. TRUTH. ERROR. IGNORANCE.—By knowledge simply we
mean *true* knowledge. The absence of knowledge in a subject
deemed capable of possessing knowledge we designate *ignorance.*
The absence of knowledge in a subject not deemed capable of
possessing knowledge, *e.g.* in a stick or a stone, we do not speak
of as ignorance; we may describe it as *nescience.* Knowledge
proper is embodied in the mental act of assertion or denial, in
the judgment. So long as we abstain from judging we cannot
err; but when we judge, our judgment must be *either* true *or*
false. We never consciously assent to a judgment, *i.e.* accept it
as true, as knowledge, if we know it to be false; indeed we cannot do so except through momentary inadvertence, and therefore
unconsciously. But we can and do accept as true judgments
which are really false,—thinking them, of course, to be true.
When we accept a false or erroneous judgment as true we are
in error. As we afterwards say when we discover our mistake:
we thought we knew but in reality we did not; we thought
we had knowledge but we really had not; we were farther re-

---

[1] *Cf. Science of Logic,* i. pp. 248-52.
[2] *Cf.* JEANNIÈRE, *Criteriologia,* pp. 78-9.

moved from the possession of truth or true knowledge than if we had been merely in ignorance or in doubt, for we were in error.

Now what is this TRUTH to which knowledge lays claim, and failing which it is not knowledge at all but error? Well, whatever truth and error respectively may prove to be in the sequel, this much at all events is certain, that men universally believe truth and error to be distinct, and therefore distinguishable, and to be mutually exclusive opposites. This common conviction is one of the data of our general inquiry. And its existence implies that the broad conception or meaning attached to each of those two terms is familiar to, and understood by, men generally. What, then, do men generally mean by truth? They mean the *conformity* of thought with thing, the *agreement* of their knowledge with reality, the *correspondence* or *concord* of their judgments with the real state of things, the *fidelity* of their knowledge to facts. And by error they mean the exact opposite of all this, the *discord* of their judgment with facts, the *disconformity* of their supposed knowledge with reality, the *disagreement* of what they think to be with what really is. These are undoubtedly the notions which convey what men generally mean by truth and error respectively; and we have purposely varied the expressions in italics in order to bring out the common notions themselves underlying the varied expressions. Whether truth and error are really what these notions represent them to be, will appear in the sequel. We hope later by gradual explanation of them to show that they are valid notions. But whether these traditional and what we may call spontaneous conceptions of truth and error are correct or not, there is no denying the fact that they are the conceptions universally entertained by mankind. Even the small minority consisting of those philosophers who think this common view of truth and error indefensible—even they entertained this very view before they became so sophisticated as to reject it as untenable. When reality is as we "think," *i.e.* judge, it to be, then and then only does our "thinking" or judging deserve to be called "knowing"; then and then only is it true: when reality is otherwise, then is our "thinking" or judging false, then it is no longer "knowing" but, so to speak, *mis*-knowing, *mis*-judging, falling into error. Such, then, is what men ordinarily understand by truth and error. And we have seen that all men have spontaneous convictions: they are certain that they know some truths, *i.e.* that some of their judgments are certainly in conformity with facts, with reality.

Every judgment to which we assent with certitude is accompanied, in the very act of mentally asserting it (" *in actu exercito* " as the technical language of the schools has it), by an implicit "I know". Every judgment asserted as true implicitly announces its own truth. If, over and above this, we reflect on the judgment and by a distinct mental act assert its truth, we are said to become explicitly aware of its truth and to know the latter "*in actu signato*".

Are we justified in regarding truth or true knowledge as a conformity of our judgments with reality, a conformity whereby we get a genuine insight into reality as it is? Are we justified in entertaining the spontaneous conviction or certitude that we have any such knowledge? These are the main problems that confront us. So far we have been merely observing the terms and the data of such problems. It is clear that their solution can be arrived at only by a searching analysis of our cognitive processes and states,—supplemented for each individual inquirer by his observing, and noticing the significance of, what others spontaneously believe in regard to their capacity for, and progress in, the discovery of truth. St. Thomas, in a remarkable passage in the *Quaestiones Disputatae*, insists on the need of this introspection for what we may call a reasoned and certain knowledge of truth, implying that this introspection will confirm our fundamental natural conviction that it is the very nature of the mind to know reality. "We have certain knowledge of the truth," he says, "inasmuch as (1) we attain to truth by an act of the intellect, and (2) we know that we do so. We attain to truth by an operation of the intellect inasmuch as the judgment of the intellect gives us an insight *into reality as it is*. And we know that it does so by reflecting on that operation and seeing not merely that the judgment is formed, but that it is *conformed to the reality*. But to see that the conformity is there we must understand the nature of the act of judgment; which in turn can be known only by knowing the nature of the principle whence it springs; and this principle is the intellect itself, *the nature of which is to conform itself to reality*. Hence the intellect knows that it possesses truth by reflecting on itself." [1]

---

[1] The following is the passage freely rendered in the text. We have italicized the phrases implying the conviction that the mind can know reality as it is:—

"Veritas est in intellectu . . . sicut consequens actum intellectus, et sicut cog-

In searching out the data of our inquiries it is lawful for each of us to supplement introspection by observing the common convictions and beliefs of his fellow-men,—provided these convictions and beliefs are simply noted as facts. Of course the assumption by each individual inquirer that they are facts for him seems to imply the validity of his own conviction that he has fellow-inquirers distinct from himself, and that there is distinct from his own mind a real world in which he and they exist in common. But this conviction of his does not really prejudge the nature of the relation between his own mind on the one hand and the reality of the world and his fellow-men on the other. In so far as this conviction is a belief that the world and his fellow-men have a real existence distinct from, and independent of, his knowledge of them, it is a *provisional* belief which he can hold himself prepared to review with critical impartiality. But that the world and his fellow-men are undeniable facts which enter into his mental experience—this is not an assumption but a fundamental datum which he can and must take as a starting-point. The contention, which seems to have been fostered by Descartes and Kant, that when an individual in mature life undertakes the critical investigation of the possibility and validity of human knowledge and certitude he must discard all previous experience and all presuppositions, set out with the conception of a pure thinking entity thus reduced to a *tabula rasa* or pure potentiality, and endeavour to discover how such an entity can gain any knowledge or experience whatever,—such a contention, *if strictly adhered to*, as of course it never has been in fact, would paralyse all effort to criticize knowledge *by leaving nothing to investigate.* Deferring this for further elucidation when we come to deal with doubt as a method, let us here pursue somewhat further the psychological

---

nita per intellectum; consequitur namque intellectus operationem secundum quod judicium intellectus est *de re secundum quod est;* cognoscitur autem ab intellectu secundum quod intellectus reflectitur super suum actum, non solum secundum quod cognoscit actum suum, sed secundum quod cognoscit *proportionem ejus ad rem:* quod quidem cognosci non potest, nisi cognoscatur natura ipsius actus, quae cognosci non potest nisi cognoscatur natura principii activi, quod est ipse intellectus, *in cujus natura est quod rebus conformetur:* unde secundum hoc cognoscit veritatem intellectus quod supra seipsum reflectitur."—*De Veritate,* i., 9. When he says that we cannot know the nature of the act of judgment unless through knowledge of the nature of the intellect, he refers of course to a synthetic knowledge by "causal" demonstration [*cf. Science of Logic,* ii., §§ 252-4]. Our knowledge of the nature of intellect, as of any faculty, can be reached only through observation of, and reasoning from, its operations.

investigation by which we have already noted some of the most elementary data concerning truth and the mind's spontaneous convictions in regard to the possession of truth.

10. FACULTIES AND SOURCES OF KNOWLEDGE. CLASSIFICA-TION OF SPONTANEOUS CONVICTIONS.—A general glance at the faculties by the exercise of which men acquire what they believe to be certain knowledge will enable us to reach at least a rough classification of those spontaneous convictions. By means of our external senses,—sight, hearing, taste, smell, touch,—we have revealed to us certain data which are, so to speak, the raw materials of our knowledge of an external material universe. Then we have the internal sense of organic touch whereby we are made aware of what we interpret to be states or conditions of our own bodies. Furthermore we have the faculties of memory and im-agination whereby we recall past experiences, compound and construct mental images, associate and co-ordinate mental states according to laws discovered and formulated by psychologists. Finally we have the faculty of *thinking*, in the stricter sense, *i.e.* of *forming* the *intellectual concepts* or *notions* expressed in language by abstract and general logical terms, of *interpreting* or *judging* all the data of conscious experience by means of those concepts, of *reasoning* from those interpretations and so making progress in knowledge. For the present we assume nothing and assert nothing as to the nature of those processes or the ultimate origin of the data with which they are concerned. We simply observe by introspection the fact that not merely have we sense percep-tions, imagination images, processes of memory and mental as-sociation, but also that we have a fund of intellectual concepts or notions ; that we take these notions as representing aspects of reality ; that by means of them we interpret the data of our sense perceptions which we likewise believe to be perceptions of reality ; that by the mental analysis and synthesis involved in judgment and reasoning we think we reach some true and certain know-ledge of reality.

Now while all the other cognitive processes lead up to know-ledge, it is in the mental act of judgment, of affirming or denying, that knowledge is formally contained. Can we reach any classi-fication of knowledge, *i.e.* of our judgments, on the basis of the sources whence their contents are immediately derived, or which comes to the same thing—of the processes which immediately sub-serve the formation of them ?

(1) In the first place we have immediate judgments of sense perception, judgments whereby we interpret individual facts of internal or external sense experience, as " I am writing," " it is raining," " this is a shilling," " that is the sound of the night mail passing ".   Such judgments are all singular and contingent ; they assert the real existence or happening of some individual contingent thing or event ; or characterize it in some way.   Hence we may also call them judgments of identification, designation, classification,—whereby we recognize certain attributes as characterizing individual things or events and designate these accordingly.   They are *synthetic* judgments, *i.e.* the information given by such judgments is derived not from any analysis of our concept of their respective subjects, but from experience. In fact the only concept we have of the subject, as such, is the concept of " this *being, thing*, or *event* " : " *hoc aliquid* " ; τοδὲ τί.

They give rise to the broad critical question of the trustworthiness, or the proper interpretation, of the data of sense experience ; and also to the question : What relation does the content of our universal concepts bear to the data of our sense experience ?

(2) Secondly, we have immediate judgments derived from analysis and comparison of abstract ideas, as " the whole is greater than its part," " two and two are four," " a judgment cannot be both true and false," " injustice is wrong," " virtue is praiseworthy " Like those of the previous class, such judgments also appear to be immediately evident, but unlike the former they seem to be *necessarily* and therefore also *universally* true : they are *analytic*, for the relation between predicate and subject is seen, by analysis of these latter, to arise necessarily from a comparison of them. They are called axioms or first principles.   The existence of such a class of judgment is undisputed, though there has been much controversy as to whether such or such a judgment,—*e.g.* " Whatever happens has a cause " ; " the course of Nature is uniform,"— belongs to this class.   Likewise their necessary character, their power of compelling our intellectual assent, is undisputed, though the nature and origin of this necessity are variously explained. Moreover, the *significance* of such judgments, or in other words the question : What insight, if any, do such abstract, necessary, and universal judgments give us into reality ?—will also have to be examined.

They reveal to the mind a system or domain of thought-objects, within which such necessary relations seem to hold sway. Is this domain *real?* If not, then no knowledge of reality seems possible : for all science and knowledge, all reasoning and judging, involve such principles.[1] If the domain of these abstract thought-objects and the relations between them be *real,* then how is it related to the data revealed in sense experience?—the question of "universals" under another form.

(3) Thirdly, we have mediate judgments derived by deductive reasoning from those of the preceding class. The conclusions of the pure mathematical sciences are the best example of such judgments: *e.g.* "the three interior angles of any plane triangle are equal to two right angles". The faculty of apprehending the principles belonging to the preceding class is called *intelligence* or *intellect;* the faculty of deriving from them the conclusions belonging to the present class is called *reason.* In both classes the mind is contemplating what we may call pure or abstract thought-objects or essences, and the relations between such, without any *immediate* or *direct* reference of them to what we may describe as the domain of concrete existences and happenings revealed in sense experience ; whereas in judgments of class (1) we are explicitly interpreting these concrete existences and happenings. If we designate these latter judgments as truths *of the real order,* and judgments about abstract thought-objects or essences as truths *of the ideal order,* we must not be understood as prejudging in any way the validity of either class of judgments as conveying to our minds a genuine knowledge of reality. Conclusions reached by deductive reasoning, in the pure or abstract sciences, from the principles referred to in class (2) imply of

[1] Even the elementary contingent judgment, such as "I am writing," yields intelligible knowledge only by its embodying in itself the principles of identity and contradiction, and these principles appear to be *necessarily* and *universally* true. Furthermore, an admitted characteristic of scientific knowledge is that it is knowledge of *necessary* and *universal* judgments, whether these be first principles or derived conclusions. Are such judgments interpretations *of reality?* Are they interpretations of the data of sense experience, and does this latter reveal *reality?* How can a human being who is himself a contingent individual, and whose existence appears to be limited in time and space, attain to judgments which appear to be true *necessarily* and *universally* for all time and space, or rather independently of all time and space, and which appear also to give him genuine knowledge of reality? Are time and space then real? Are the data of our sense experience, which are interpreted by us to be temporal and spatial,—are they *really* temporal and spatial? Or is that alone *real* which is revealed to us through necessary and universal judgments,—*i.e.* the domain of static, purely intellectual thought-objects with their eternal and immutable relations? These are some of the questions which a more mature reflection on our cognitive processes has repeatedly suggested for solution— as far as solution may be possible—to the inquiring mind.

course for their own validity not only the validity of the principles *from which* they are inferred but also that of the formal or logical principles of deductive reasoning *according to which* they are inferred.

(4) Fourthly, we have what we may call judgments of generalization or induction, whereby we transcend by thought the limits of our past and present sense experience and assert that what we have found to be true of all experienced instances of some thing or event is likewise true of the unexperienced instances, and of all possible instances, of that thing or event. The judgments of classes (2) and (3) we saw to be universal *because necessary :* "*All* wholes are greater than their parts because the whole *as such* is *necessarily* greater than its part". "*All* plane triangles have the sum of their interior angles equal to two right angles because this is *necessarily* true of the plane triangle *as such.*" Now we encounter another class of universal judgments which are reached not by analysis and comparison of abstract concepts, or deductive reasoning from the necessary principles revealed by such analysis and comparison, but by a process of generalizing from actually experienced facts—not, however, without the aid of *some* "necessary" principles. These universal judgments, thus reached by inductive generalization, refer to, and are concerned with, what we have called *the real order*, the domain of the concrete things and events revealed through sense experience. And it needs but little reflection to convince us what a very considerable proportion of our knowledge has been reached by each of us through this generalizing process. It is not merely the inductive scientist who employs it. He does so in the most careful manner according to the canons of inductive logic ; but every human individual employs it in a quasi-instinctive, rough and ready way from the time he reaches the use of reason. By means of it, for instance, Newton discovered the law of universal gravitation ; but no less by means of it have we all learned that fire burns, that unsupported bodies fall to the earth, that food nourishes, that living things are born and die, that where only oats are sown we cannot reap wheat, that children imitate the example of their elders, etc., etc. By means of it we acquire some knowledge of the characteristic properties of the classes of things and events revealed in sense experience, and thence of their natures and modes of behaviour, and of the causes and conditions of their existence and occur-

rence. Thus we are led[1] from acquaintance with directly perceptible realities to the intellectual apprehension or discovery of
realities that are not themselves perceptible by the senses,—from
effects to causes, from actions to agents, from conduct to nature,
from singular to universal.

Now the process of reaching such universal judgments from
particular sense experiences involves on our part the tacit acceptance or assumption of the validity of this general principle :
that Nature is uniform in its modes of existence and action ; that
the world of which we have experience is not chaotic, capricious,
unreliable, but orderly, regular, reliable ; that it is, so to speak,
"of a piece" within and without our experience, so that from the
former portion we can learn about the latter ; that the domain of
our experience, which we find to be in some measure intelligible,
to admit of rational interpretation and explanation up to the
limits of the cognitive powers of our finite minds, is *the real universe*, and is verily as our knowledge represents it to be, so far as
our knowledge of it goes.

Whether or in what sense this conviction of ours is based upon our actual
experience ; whether or in what sense it is a necessary presupposition for
having intelligible experience ; whether or how far it springs from an instinct
of our nature as intelligent or rational ; whether the conviction is validly applicable to the *real* universe, or only to the domain of appearances or phenomena within the individual mind ; what is the exact scope or extent of the
domain to which it does apply ; on what rational grounds is it ultimately
justifiable,—these are some of the critical questions to which reflection on this
conviction naturally gives rise.[2] And reflection will also suggest that this
conviction is perhaps inseparably bound up with our spontaneous belief that
on the one hand the real world is knowable or intelligible, and that on the
other hand our minds are capable of attaining to some true and certain
knowledge concerning it.

Judgments reached by inductive generalization from sense
experience present themselves to our minds as distinct from those
of class (1) in that the latter are singular while the former are
universal ; but both classes alike are synthetic judgments. Those
of the present class likewise differ from the judgments of classes
(2) and (3) inasmuch as they do not present themselves to the

---

[1] Or *think* we are led—from what we *think* to be realities—to what we *think* to
be other realities. The validity of this spontaneous thinking is at the present stage
an open question.

[2] For a detailed treatment of some of those questions, *cf. Science of Logic*, ii.,
Part IV., chap. iv. ; Part V., chap. i.

mind with the same characteristics of *absolute* necessity and uni-versality as the latter.   The necessity of two and two being four, or of the sum of the interior angles of a plane triangle being equal to two right angles, does not appear to characterize the judgment that " fire burns " or that " water expands on freezing,"—or any other inductively established law.   Yet these latter are in some true sense " necessary " judgments : we call them " laws," and we recognize the propriety of using the term of necessity, " must," in enunciating them.   If, however, we say that " fire *must* burn," we are conscious that the " must " is not as absolute as when we say " two and two *must* be four ".   The necessity of inductively established laws is, we feel, not absolute, not the purely intellect-ual necessity which characterizes the conceptual relations between abstract thought-objects, but is in some way contingent and de-pendent, a necessity referring to the concrete existing and hap-pening of things, and of which the ultimate ground must be sought in the nature of the universe itself.[1]

(5) Fifthly, we have judgments accepted on authority, judg-ments to which we assent not because we have the testimony of our senses for them, or the insight of our reason into the truth of them, but because we are convinced that we have in and through the testimony of our fellow-men unquestionably adequate au-thority for accepting them as certainly true.   We have already noted the important and significant fact that every human indi-vidual has a very large proportion of his spontaneous convictions from this particular source.   They imply a firm belief in the trustworthiness of human testimony under certain conditions. This belief itself rests on grounds which are very complex in character, and which, while excluding all prudent and reasonable fear of error, nevertheless do not amount to cogent logical evidence or admit of statement in purely intellectual terms.

Can we discover any convictions or certitudes which do not properly find a place in any of the five classes just enumerated ?   We do not think so.   It would be a useful exercise for the student to look into his own mental assents and see if the classification just given is exhaustive.   It will at all events be helpful towards a clearer grasp of the problems of epistemology thus to have taken stock of our spontaneous convictions and classified the immediate pro-cesses and sources whence they are derived.

[1] *Cf. Science of Logic*, ii. pp. 78, 100-12, where it is shown that an ultimate ex-planation of the grounds of this contingent or conditional necessity of the actual course of nature must be a function of some reasoned view of the universe as a whole, —Theism referring it ultimately to the *Fiat* of the Divine Will.

Before passing to the critical work proper of revising and testing them, we have next to fix our attention on a few other broad and significant facts concerning their character, their objects, and their general bearing on human life and conduct.

11. IRRESISTIBLE CERTITUDE AND FREELY FORMED CONVICTIONS.—It is an undeniable fact that some of our spontaneous convictions or certitudes are irresistible, that they are compelled, that we cannot help entertaining them, while others are formed and firmly entertained *dependently on our own free will.* Take on the one hand, for example, the immediate judgments of experience such as " I am writing " ; or the self-evident axioms of mathematics such as " the whole is greater than its part," and the conclusions derived by pure deductive reasoning from such axioms. I simply cannot help assenting to them when they present themselves to my mind.[1] Take on the other hand such judgments as " the human will is free," " the human soul is immortal," " miracles are possible," " Christ arose from the dead "; I am *convinced* of the truth of all these judgments, I assent to them firmly, I am certain of their truth. But they do not compel my assent. I know that there are some who do not believe them, and many others who hold them merely as opinions. Reflecting on all the grounds and motives on account of which I hold them as certain, I am conscious that those grounds and motives have effectively excluded from my mind all prudent fear of error, and so I adhere to them with that steady, firm, unwavering mental grasp which constitutes conviction or certitude. But I am also conscious that with those grounds and motives still before my mind I could loosen my mental grasp on the judgments and allow myself seriously to question them [2] : I feel that I should be acting rashly and unreasonably, and possibly also against the clear dictate of my conscience, in doing so, but nevertheless that I am free to do so, that though it would be

---

[1] Descartes indeed seems to .have thought that he could. Later on we shall see why. He also regarded assent and dissent as acts of the will, as willing or not willing, a synthesis of terms revealed by the intellect ; " Assurer, nier, douter, sont des façons differents de vouloir ".—*Médit.* iv. 9. But assent and dissent are themselves clearly acts of the intellect, though they may be commanded by an act of the will.

[2] Determinists of course would contend that all convictions, and all mental states, are *necessarily* what they are, that man's natural, spontaneous conviction that his will is free is an illusion. This contention does not affect the present context. The spontaneous conviction of freedom is there, and it is only with spontaneous convictions as such, as mental states, we are at present concerned.

unreasonable and reprehensible it is not impossible: while I advert that it would be not only unreasonable but impossible for me to question such judgments as " I exist," " other beings exist," " the whole is greater than its part," etc.   Of course, while the grounds and motives for such " free" convictions as those illustrated are actually before my mind I cannot doubt about their *credibility*, *i.e.* about the *reasonableness* of holding them firmly, or with conviction, as true; but this reasonable and prudent act of assenting firmly is performed by my intellect *freely*, *i.e.* under the command of a free act of my will.   And I am conscious that instead of performing this act at any time I can freely fix the attention of my intellect upon grounds, and allow myself to be influenced by motives, which would or might have the effect of gradually altering my mental attitude towards those judgments, my mental estimate of their credibility, and so possibly eventuate in my holding them as mere opinions, or even in holding their contradictories as convictions.   Of course it is of the very nature of a conviction that being a firm assent it cannot be changed or abandoned at pleasure.   If at any time we find ourselves able without further consideration to doubt or abandon a belief we have been holding, this very fact is clear evidence that the belief was not a conviction but only an opinion.   But it will not be denied that multitudes of our genuine spontaneous convictions have been reached by long processes of mental experience whereby our minds have been gradually disposed, and our whole mental outlook shaped, to receive these convictions ; and since these processes were in some degree controlled and guided by our own free application of mind to the consideration and weighing of evidence, we are quite conscious that the convictions are freely held, and that we could at any time freely so direct and apply our minds to their subject-matter that we might come to doubt or reject such convictions.

We might supplement this verdict of introspection by an appeal to the general experience of our fellow-men.   What are called religious beliefs are, no doubt, in the case of some religions mostly, if not exclusively, *opinions* rather than *convictions*.   But there are multitudes of such beliefs, especially in the case of the Catholic Religion, which are among the best examples we could quote of convictions that are at once entirely free and absolutely firm.   If a man, believing a judgment to be true, and believing himself morally bound to hold it for true, is prepared to die rather than doubt or deny it, we are at liberty to call his belief obstinacy or superstition or folly, or fortitude and heroism ; but we cannot well deny that it deserves to be called a really firm conviction. Yet not merely is the man free to *profess* to abandon it ; he is free furthermore so to act that he *may gradually bring himself really to abandon it.* And the occasional apostacy of Catholics from the faith which they once held for certain is an admitted fact. But no one can " apostatize " from a necessary conviction like " two and two are four ". Such religious convictions are therefore *free* convictions ; nay, it is because they are free that they are *meritorious* or otherwise, and that men are morally *responsible* for holding them. Moral responsibility extends not merely to a man's ways of willing and acting, it extends to his ways of thinking, judging, assenting, believing ; this is admitted by all who admit moral responsibility at all, if only for the simple reason that a man's conduct is determined largely by his beliefs, by his mental outlook on life. But it is plain that the assents, convictions, beliefs, for which man is responsible must be *free ;* otherwise there could be neither right nor wrong, neither merit nor demerit, in forming, holding, or professing them.

There can be no doubt, therefore, that men can and do hold convictions that are free. They are for the most part convictions based on authority, but they also include the more difficult and remote conclusions based on scientific and philosophical research.

12. INFLUENCE OF THE WILL ON FREE CONVICTIONS.— The influence exerted by free will on the formation of such convictions is many-sided and complex. To explore it fully would involve a prolonged and subtle psychological analysis, in which introspection could be richly supplemented by a careful study of the personal confessions of religious converts, unbelievers, sceptics, etc. The modern tendency to make certitude exclusively an affair of the will and the heart emphasizes the necessity for further research in this direction. Here we can merely call attention to a few of the most obvious lines of influence.

Intellect and will are, no doubt, distinct faculties ; but they are faculties of *the same* individual. We must, therefore, be careful not to " hypostasize " them or separate them unduly : it is less proper to say that the intellect thinks and the will chooses than it is to say that *the man* thinks by his intellect and chooses by his will. Bearing this in mind it is clear that the will exerts *at least* an *indirect and remote* influence on *all* our convictions by (1) applying the intellect to the consideration of the subject matter of the conviction; (2) by fixing the attention of the intellect on the grounds for assenting, to the exclusion of the difficulties, or grounds against assenting, when these are seen to be reasonably negligible; (3) by checking and keeping under the control of reason the passions, prejudices, and impulses that tend to prevent us from assenting to a judgment which though apparently true is realized to be unpleasant and distasteful. The will can exercise a real control,—not despotic but persuasive ("dominium *politicum*"),—over the operations of the intellect ("quoad *exercitium* actus"),—choosing, directing, altering the line of thought to be followed, etc.

Secondly, the will has sometimes also a *direct and immediate* influence on our convictions. It not only moves the intellect to act, but it determines the specific act of assent which the intellect is to elicit ("quoad *specificationem* actus"). This happens when there is question of judgments for which the evidence is not cogent. When the evidence is extrinsic to the judgment,—*i.e.* when we assent to the judgment not because we see[1] the intrinsic grounds of its truth, but because we accept it on authority,—the evidence is never absolutely cogent. This is likewise the case in regard to the more remote and important conclusions of the philosophical sciences, and more particularly those which have a serious practical and moral bearing on the personal conduct of life,—*e.g.* the existence of God, the immortality of the soul, the possibility and the fact of Divine revelation, miracles, supernatural religion, etc. In all such cases the object presented to the mind (*i.e.* the judgment, the connexion between subject and predicate) is not so clearly evident as to *compel* intellectual assent. Both the terms and the grounds of the judgment are complex. And hence although we may see that the grounds are such as to exclude all prudent fear of error, that the judgment is clearly[2] *credible*, that it would be unreasonable not to assent to it firmly, we may nevertheless continue to entertain (what is

[1] Or *think* that we see. We are here concerned only with the mental facts, not with the critical question of their validity.

[2] When we thus distinguish between assenting to the judgment itself as true, and assenting to its *credibility*, there are some who hold that the latter can be scientifically demonstrated, *i.e.* that we can have *cogent* evidence for the *credibility* of a judgment even though we may not have cogent evidence for its truth. *Cf.* JEANNIÈRE, *op. cit.*, p. 48.

really) an imprudent fear of error. So long as we do so the intellect remains undetermined, and an act of the will is required to determine and fix the mental assent as a conviction. Thus the influence of the will on the assent is direct and immediate, and the latter may be regarded in such cases as a complex mental operation in which intellect and will co-operate, rather than as a purely intellectual activity. In some cases, where the evidence is not cogent,—as it never is when there is question of assent on authority,—its appeal is nevertheless so strong that the act whereby the will determines the assent is not a free but an instinctively necessary movement, as, for instance, when I assent to the existence of America though I have never been there. Such assents are scarcely distinguishable from necessary assents on clear and cogent intrinsic evidence. Yet there is in them an element of will excluding imprudent fear of error: though not free they are voluntary (whereas in assenting to "two and two are four" the will has no *direct* influence on the act of assent at all). In most cases, however, the act whereby the will commands the assent is a free act, and in such cases the act of intellectual assent itself, because commanded by a free act, is itself denominated a "free" assent or a "free" conviction.

Since the objects of intellect and will are the true and the good respectively, it is clear that just as a *judgment* must appear *true* in order that the intellect assent to it, so also the *act of assenting* must appear *good* in order that the will command the eliciting of this act. Now when all prudent fear of error is excluded, the act of assenting to the judgment as true can certainly present itself to the mind as a good, inasmuch as (1) by means of this act we attain to truth or true knowledge, the possession of which appears to be a good; (2) what appears to be reasonable, to be in conformity with our nature as rational, appears as a good, and this act appears reasonable; and (3) the act may moreover present itself as morally praiseworthy and meritorious (as in the case of religious beliefs) and therefore as a good. But a little reflection will show that the individual man's appreciation of these various features of a free conviction or belief will depend not merely on the clearness of his purely intellectual insight, but also and in a very large degree on his moral training and character, —in regard to which the influence of his free will is obvious.

13. REASONABLENESS OF FREE CONVICTIONS. CERTITUDE OF SCIENCE AND CERTITUDE OF BELIEF OR FAITH.—From the

preceding section the student will have grasped the broad distinction between convictions based on grounds that *compel* intellectual assent and those based on grounds which, while not
compelling assent, are deemed *sufficient to exclude all prudent
fear of error.* He will also have realized that most of the convictions which men spontaneously entertain in regard to matters
of the most profound importance to human life belong to the
latter class.

The term "science," in its strictest sense, is usually applied
only to judgments reached by the cogent evidence of *demonstration* from axioms or principles for which the immediate evidence
is likewise cogent ; and the *necessary* conviction produced by such
cogent evidence is not uncommonly described as " the certitude
of science," as distinct from " the certitude of belief (or faith) ".
This usage is common to Aristotle, the mediæval Schoolmen, and
modern writers, all alike. Scientific knowledge is demonstrated
knowledge, and demonstration is a purely intellectual process
which by excluding even the possibility of error shuts off the
scientific judgment from all direct influence of the will.[1]

On the other hand, suppose that a man has convinced himself
of the existence of God, and of the fact that God has revealed to
the human race certain truths which, while of supreme import for
man's destiny, are nevertheless above the power of the human
mind to have discovered without revelation, or to understand
fully even with revelation,—such, for instance, as the Trinity, the
Original Fall, and the Redemption of mankind through Christ,
the elevation of man through Divine Grace to the Supernatural
Order, and through the Beatific Vision to a Supernatural End.
Such a man will see the reasonableness of assenting, on Divine
authority, to those " mysteries," *i.e.* truths, which he may believe
but cannot " comprehend," or fully understand. His assent will
be an assent of *Faith* in the strict sense, *i.e.* it will be assent to a
truth which cannot be an object of science, which cannot be demonstrated or " seen ". It is in this strict sense that Faith is
understood by those who say, with St. Thomas, that the same
truth cannot be both an object of faith and an object of science.

But lying between these mysteries or strictly indemonstrable
truths on the one hand, and the strictly demonstrable truths of

[1] " Assensus · · · scientiae non subjicitur libero arbitrio, quia *sciens cogitur*
ad assentiendum per efficaciam demonstrationis."—St. Thomas, *Summa Theol.*, II.[2],
Q. ii., a. 9, ad 2.

such an exact science as mathematics on the other, there is a wide domain of supremely important truths [1] which can indeed be proved, or reached with certitude, by man's unaided powers, and are, therefore, objects of science in a wider sense. Yet they cannot be reached without a certain influence of the will, inasmuch as the evidence for them is not clearly cogent but leaves room for the play of freedom and for the possibility of real, though perhaps imprudent, doubt. And hence our assent to them is commonly described as *belief*. If it be asked whether we can both *believe* and *prove* or demonstrate them, the answer will depend on the precise meaning we attach to our terms. Nobody is said to "believe" that the three interior angles of a triangle are equal to two right angles,—unless indeed without seeing the intrinsic reasons for it he takes it on the word of another. If he sees the intrinsic reasons for it his assent is not a free assent, a belief; it is compelled, it is an assent of science. Similarly, no one is said to see or demonstrate or prove scientifically the truth of a mystery, but to believe it. We may, however, say with propriety that we can both prove or demonstrate and also believe such a truth as the existence of God or the immortality of the soul. For, on the one hand, we can by the earnest and diligent exercise of our reason on the facts of experience convince ourselves of these truths. And this process may rightly be called proof or demonstration.[2] On the other hand, since the conduct of this process depends on our free-will, and since, moreover, the evidence it brings to light is not of a nature to *compel* our assent as it does in mathematics, the free assent we base upon it may be rightly described as belief; while, of course, if we assent to such truths solely on authority, and without examining for ourselves the intrinsic evidence available

---

[1] Or judgments : by calling them "truths" in the present context we do not wish to prejudge the question of their real truth.

[2] The Vatican Council defined that the existence of God can *be known for certain* from the facts of experience by the natural light of human reason : " Si quis dixerit Deum unum ac verum, Creatorem ac Dominum nostrum, per ea quae facta sunt naturali rationis humanae lumine certo cognosci non posse, anathema sit ".—The *Motu Proprio* of Pope Pius X. against the errors of Modernism ("*Lamentabili Sane*," 3 July, 1907), proclaimed that reason can *demonstrate* the existence of God. The doctrine propounded by this teaching is not that the available evidence for the existence of God is of such a nature as to *compel* the assent of the mind that considers it attentively, but that it is of such a nature as to exclude all reasonable, prudent, legitimate fear of error, all ground for justifiable doubt. It condemns the view that this evidence is of itself, and without such supernatural aid as that of revelation, insufficient to exclude reasonable doubt and so produce certain knowledge.

to prove them, our assent will not be in any sense an assent of science but simply a belief.

14. BEARING OF INTELLECTUAL AND MORAL DISCIPLINE ON FREE CONVICTIONS AND ON "FREE THOUGHT".—If, therefore, a person who has been brought up in the Catholic faith proclaims that he can no longer believe in the doctrines of Christianity, this must either be because (1) their falsity seems to him so evident that he is intellectually compelled to reject them, as he would the assertion that " 2 and 2 are 5 " ; or because (2) assent to them no longer appears to him as a good and desirable thing.   From the very nature of the questions involved the former hypothesis can never be verified at least in the case of a person of normally sane and healthy mind.   The latter hypothesis, however, can and does arise.   If it springs from intellectual difficulties or objections which seem to furnish grounds for a prudent doubt about the truth of any Christian doctrine, then, —seeing that issues of the gravest possible import are at stake, issues concerning the person's own nature and destiny, the conduct of his life, and his place and meaning in the universe,— prudence imperatively dictates that he should steadily and courageously examine these difficulties with the sole and single-minded purpose of discovering the truth and shaping his life accordingly.   Belief in the doctrines of Christianity may, how ever, appear to him no longer good or desirable, not from intel lectual reasons but because he finds that such belief impedes or restrains the gratification of pride, avarice, lust, or some other such passions, yearnings, or impulses.   Here, however, the dictate of conscience will warn him against such an appreciation of moral " values " ; and it is moral courage and determination to follow the voice of conscience that will in such cases save him from entering the path which might lead to unbelief.

And if we turn to the case of a person who, without ever having had any strong convictions or definite views regarding the great fundamental problems of religion and philosophy, has been brought by his experience of life to investigate them seriously, it will at least be agreed that in his investigation he will be wise if he allow himself to be guided by what appears to him to be reasonable, to be in harmony with the dictates of his nature as a rational and moral being.   The man of ordinary and moderate mental development will recognize a distinction between the right and the wrong, between the true and the false ; and whatever he may think truth to be he will recognize as right the impulse to seek truth and avoid error. Of course the measure of his success will depend largely on the nature of his youthful training, both intellectual and moral : more especially perhaps on his moral training, for on this will depend his fidelity to the dictate of conscience to seek the truth disinterestedly. At all events, if he be faithful to this dictate he cannot wholly fail. Sooner or later the supreme importance of seeking the true solution of certain problems will force itself insistently upon him : Is there a Supreme Being on whom he depends ? What is his own nature and destiny? Is his soul immortal ? What is the significance of the Moral Law for him? Has God revealed a religion to mankind ? In reference to such questions there is at least one course which cannot recommend itself to him as reasonable, and that is to put them aside lightly and thoughtlessly on the pretext that they are insoluble, or too irksome or difficult, and allow himself to drift through life regardless of life's meaning. Again, when he comes to recognize, as he will, sooner or later, that man's power of reaching truth is limited, that men have reached divergent solutions, and entertain conflicting beliefs, in regard to most of those fundamental problems, he cannot reasonably infer from this that he is at liberty to think just as he pleases in regard to them. Where they are concerned the pursuit of truth cannot present itself to him as a mere matter of taste or temperament, or a legitimate pastime occupation for the dilettante. On the contrary, he will feel that the more fundamental they are the more seriously should they be treated, and that the more important is their bearing on his outlook and conduct of life the more unfaithful he would be to the highest dictates of his nature were he to neglect to follow steadily whither the weight of evidence may beckon him. When he is told that " it is man's privilege to doubt," he may reply that it is even man's *duty* (to his rational nature) to doubt when it would be unreasonable to believe on the evidence, but he will also reply that it is equally man's privilege *to believe* when he has sufficient grounds for believing, and even his *duty* to believe when it would be unreasonable to doubt in the face of the evidence available. And he will emphatically reject as unreasonable the insistent claim of the unthinking and unreflecting modern mind to what is called " freedom of thought " in regard to all questions for the solution of which the evidence available cannot from the very nature of the case be intellectually

cogent evidence.   He will recognize that submission to the truth
is no slavery, but rather the highest perfection of the intellect,
and that therefore to claim the liberty of believing what one likes
as long as the evidence is not cogent is to claim an unreasonable
licence.

We may go one step further and say that when once our inquirer realizes
that for many centuries multitudes have firmly believed that God has revealed
to man for their greater enlightenment a system of moral and religious doctrines of the highest practical import to the right ordering of human life, and
has left on earth an infallible teaching authority to expound and apply those
doctrines,—when he has realized all this he will admit the reasonableness of
their claim that the accredited repositories of this teaching authority have both
the right and the duty to proclaim to the world that men must not misuse
their finite and fallible faculties by believing what they please, but must so
use these faculties that by following with reverent and humble docility the
" kindly light " of evidence they will freely submit their minds to truth and
shape their lives accordingly.   Whether or not he himself comes to believe
what the Catholic Church teaches, he will at all events see only a calumny
and a misrepresentation in the cry that the Catholic Church, by proclaiming
untrammelled " free thought " to be an unreasonable licence, is imposing unjust
or injurious shackles on human thought, or impeding the progressive dominion
of truth over the minds and hearts of men.
Another fact which he cannot fail to notice is this, that the problems
presented by human experience for solution fall into two broadly distinct
categories.   Some are purely speculative, in the sense that the true solution
of them does not seem to be imperative for the right ordering of his life.   If
he discover the truth about them, so much gained ; but if he cannot—well, it
does not matter : they are not of grave concern.   Such problems we might
instance by the extreme example of the problems of higher mathematics, or
by many of the disputed questions of history, or many of the speculations and
hypotheses of the physical sciences concerning the genesis and explanation of
natural phenomena.   On the one hand, ignorance or doubt about such matters
need not seriously disturb his peace of mind.   On the other hand, his investigation of them, and his fidelity in following the weight of evidence and accepting the truth about them according as he finds it, will not, as a rule, be
impeded by any strong passions or prejudices.
But there are other questions of an entirely different sort, questions the
solution of which he feels to be a matter of supreme practical concern to
his whole outlook on life.   And these are precisely the questions which are
commonly described as the fundamental problems of philosophy, ethics, and
religion.   We have already illustrated them abundantly, and we need not restate them here.   When a man is brought face to face with any such question,
as long as he is uncertain of its true solution he is troubled in mind and ill at
ease, for he feels that he cannot shape his life regardless of it, and that in its
solution the very meaning of his existence is involved.   No sane man can
deny that it must somehow ultimately make a serious difference to him
whether there is a God, whether his soul is immortal, whether he will be re-

warded or punished in a future life for his conduct in this life, whether the moral law implies a supreme Lawgiver, whether religion is a matter of taste or a matter of duty, whether God has made a revelation to help man to accomplish his purpose in life, whether it is his duty to seek the truth on these matters and be guided by the weight of evidence, whether he should consider it reasonable for him to seek the truth, or rather to brush aside such questions and, without troubling about them, live for the passing pleasure of the hour and be guided solely by the impulse of the moment. No doubt there are many who follow this latter course and would fain persuade themselves that they do so reasonably, who not only profess agnosticism but proclaim it as a reasonable philosophy of life, who not only determine their own particular religious beliefs or disbeliefs by their personal tastes and predilections, but hold indifferentism to be the reasonable attitude towards the various alternative forms of religion. But when we reflect that what we may call the affirmative solutions of those ultimate questions—*e.g.* God exists, the soul is immortal, virtue will be rewarded and vice punished, religion is a matter of duty, God has made a revelation to man, etc.—impose a restraint on the passions and run counter to the lower tendencies of human nature, we can understand why so many fail to exert that strong effort and endure that sustained discipline of the will, without which those positive convictions cannot be reached and fostered and made operative in the guidance of life.[1]

15. Universally Entertained Spontaneous Convictions: their Bearing on Human Life.—In considering men's spontaneous convictions and beliefs there is another sort of general survey the results of which may prove significant when

---

[1] It is easy to see, therefore, that for the free acceptance and fruitful fostering of convictions which develop the virtuous and restrain the vicious tendencies of our nature, it is very desirable to cultivate a certain goodwill, and form a sympathetic attitude of mind, towards these convictions. A great deal can be done in this direction towards preparing the mind for the acceptance of the truths of the Christian Religion by showing that these truths,—supernatural though they are, and apart from the demonstrable credibility of the grounds on which they authoritatively impose themselves on the mind for acceptance,—harmonize completely with the highest aspirations, and satisfy most fully the noblest yearnings, of our nature. In Christian Apologetics, this method, which is known as the " Method of Immanence," helps and supplements the main method whereby the credibility and truth of the Christian Revelation are established by appeal to historical evidence. It is not to be confounded with the " Philosophy of Immanence," condemned in the Encyclical *Pascendi* of Pope Pius X. against the errors of Modernism (*apud* Denzinger, 2074): a philosophy which purports to show the impossibility, or at least the inutility, of all external revelation; which refuses to base Christianity on historical grounds; and which maintains that all religious truth is to be sought and found exclusively *within the individual,* being as it were the natural evolution or outgrowth or complement of his spiritual and moral impulses and aspirations. It is thus characterized in the Encyclical: " Explicatio autem, naturali theologia deleta, adituque ad revelationem ob rejecta credibilitatis argumenta intercluso, immo etiam revelatione qualibet externa penitus sublata, extra hominem inquiritur frustra. Est igitur, in ipso homine quaerenda, et . . . in vita omnino hominis reperienda est. In hoc immanentiae religiosae principium asseritur." *Cf.* Jeannière, *op. cit.*, p. 61 ; J. Wehrlé, *La Méthode d'Immanence* (Bloud, 1911).

we approach the main critical task of testing the grounds of human certitude. We have drawn a distinction between convictions that do not appear essential to human life and convictions that are of supreme concern to the right ordering of life. We may add to these latter, convictions that are absolutely indispensable to the individual for the very preservation and continuance of life itself. And if we look out upon the world of our experience we shall find that while there are many convictions which are only partial in extent and not entertained by all,—since men differ very much in the amount of certain knowledge which they think that they possess, some being better informed and more learned than others, —there are other convictions which are held spontaneously and universally by all men, which are found to prevail and to have prevailed among men throughout all time and space. And furthermore, we shall find that the convictions thus universally entertained are *generally* those that are *most necessary to enable men to preserve and develop their existence as physical, intellectual, moral, and religious beings.*

We are concerned here with convictions, *i.e.* fixed or firm assents, not with the multitudinous provisional assents which are more or less widespread among men, and which have given rise to the *dictum* that " probability is the guide of life ".

Moreover, the convictions in question are spontaneous convictions, inasmuch as they are possessed antecedently to all critical reflection. They are, therefore, not always held with a clear and distinct grasp of the grounds on which they rest ; but yet they are held with sufficient distinctness to be consciously operative in the guidance of life. They are called " truths of common sense " inasmuch as they naturally commend themselves as true to the intelligence of the ordinary man.

Furthermore, they are *practical* convictions or certitudes ; and some of them are so intensely practical that even the sceptic, who on reflection regards them as speculatively untenable, is forced to retain them as principles of action inasmuch as he could not preserve his life in practical disregard of them. Just as they are spontaneously formed by the mind, so they are naturally inseparable from the mind.

And it may be remarked in passing that this very fact should give serious pause to the sceptic. He might ask himself the question, Does not the very fact that he cannot live without assuming certain judgments to be true amount to strong presumptive evidence that they are really true ? Is he right in regarding that certitude alone as justifiable,—*i.e.* as attaining to *truth*,—which is begotten of purely intellectual and cogent evidence ?   We do not wish to raise here the question of the *criteria* or tests of truth, or to assert that the practical indispensability of certain convictions is such a test, but merely to suggest that this characteristic, which is shared in greater or less degree by many of our spontaneous convictions, is evidence which cannot reasonably be ignored when we come to ask ourselves whether such convictions are objectively valid. If life involves, as is generally admitted, a continuous process of adaptation of the living being to his surroundings, then those convictions or " knowledges " on which human life is dependent, and without which it could not be conserved, must, it would seem, put man into real contact with those surroundings, and inform him truly about them.   It is well to keep ourselves reminded that truth and knowledge are not speculative abstractions, or relations of an abstract intelligence to an abstract reality, but that they are a personal attainment and endowment of the individual human being in contact with his surroundings, and a means of contact and adjustment with these surroundings through the interpretation of his whole conscious experience.

Finally we may note that the very universality of the spontaneous convictions in question is itself a suggestive fact,—suggestive as a possible indication of the objective validity or truth of such convictions.   This, however, will be examined later. Here we are merely taking stock of spontaneous convictions as mental facts.

(1) First, then, as regards man's *physical* existence it is plain that in order to live at all he must possess quite a number of convictions regarding himself and his surroundings and his relations to his surroundings, and that he must live in accordance with these convictions.   He must know, for instance, that food nourishes, and fire burns, and water drowns, and unsupported bodies fall, etc., etc.   Such convictions are indispensable : he possesses such convictions, over and above the manifold probabilities which also help to guide his life ; and he acts according to these convictions.

(2) Secondly, in regard to his *intellectual* life, his progress in what is commonly assumed to be "knowledge," it is plain that,— apart altogether from the question of the truth of this knowledge, and even if it be a mere mental illusion instead of being what man spontaneously believes it to be, *viz.* insight into reality,—he can make no progress whatever in acquiring it without such fundamental convictions as that "the same judgment cannot be both true and false," "if two things are each equal to a third they are equal to each other," " whatever happens has a cause," "the world of experience is not chaotic but orderly," etc.   Such convictions are called principles of the speculative order.   Without them

thought as an intelligent process would be impossible. They are necessary for even the most elementary intellectual progress. They are possessed and utilized by men universally.

(3) Thirdly, man is a moral being, *i.e.* he is conscious of moral distinctions in his conduct. This is beyond question, for it is a mere statement of fact. Of course the nature, significance, and grounds of moral distinctions are not beyond dispute. But that men universally have such convictions as that "right is not wrong," "good is to be aimed at," "evil should be avoided," "lying, injustice, murder, and cruelty are wrong," "veracity, justice, fidelity, and beneficence are right and praiseworthy," is a fact beyond all dispute. Such convictions are called "principles of the moral order". Men are indeed often in ignorance, in doubt, or in error regarding the application of such principles to human conduct in detail; as, also, in regard to their source and significance and sanction. But some at least of the most elementary and fundamental ethical convictions are shared by all men. It is precisely because they are that human life has a moral or ethical aspect, that man is a moral being: without them this particular aspect of human life—which is an undeniable fact —would be simply unintelligible.

(4) Fourthly, man is not only a moral but a religious being: that is to say, there have been found to prevail at all times and in all places among men certain beliefs and convictions regarding what we may describe as "the unseen world". These beliefs are not found in the same form everywhere; but all their forms are expressions of belief in a future life or state of existence after death, and in the reality of a Supreme Being or Divinity. They are intimately connected with men's moral beliefs; for the conviction that there is a right and a wrong in human conduct, that right conduct deserves reward and wrong conduct punishment, naturally suggests belief in a future state of rightful retribution; and the conviction that morally right conduct is of obligation and imposes itself as a law similarly suggests belief in a Supreme Lawgiver. Moreover, we find as a fact that all races of men have at all times entertained in some form or other belief in immortality, and have by some form of worship or other recognized man's dependence on "higher powers".

Now it will not be denied that these two questions are of the gravest import to human life,—first, Is man's soul immortal, so that he does not wholly die but survives death and continues

to exist in another state?—and second, Is there a Supreme
Being by whom man exists, on whom he depends, and to whom
he owes worship? Indeed, it is not too much to say that it is
only by giving a certain answer to these questions that man can
have a certain knowledge of his own origin, nature, and destiny.
It is therefore a significant fact that *affirmative* answers to these
two questions are embodied in beliefs which are found to be,
morally speaking, universal among mankind. And if—in the
necessarily vague and rudimentary form in which they are thus
universal—it can be shown that these beliefs are also a *spontaneous* and *natural* product of the human mind in its contact with
the data of experience, this fact will be no less significant for us
when we come to consider their objective validity or truth value.
If they are spontaneous and natural, and therefore everywhere
and at all times prevalent among men, it will be obvious that the
philosophical *Materialism* which denies all survival of the individual soul, and the philosophical *Atheism* or *Agnosticism* which
denies or declares unknowable the existence of a Supreme Being,
run counter to the natural tendencies of the human mind and cannot be regarded as products of its normal functioning. This,
however, only creates a presumption against the soundness of
these philosophies of negation ; nor do we wish to pass judgment
on them here, for we are now considering man's beliefs in God
and immortality only as mental facts.

That at least some vague form of belief in a Supreme Being
is a spontaneous and natural attainment of human thought will
be apparent on a little reflection. For the existence of a Supreme
Being fits in with our sense of our own weakness and dependence,
with our yearning after a happiness beyond all that the visible
world can offer us (the affective and emotional needs of our
nature). It accounts for our consciousness of moral obligation
and satisfies the sense of justice involved in our spontaneous
conviction that moral conduct should have its adequate sanction
(the ethical or moral need in our nature). And finally it satisfies
our striving to find an explanation of the world of our experience,
a First, Supreme, and Adequate Cause of all finite reality (the
intellectual craving, or "*cupiditas sciendi*"). Similarly, some
vague form of belief in immortality arises spontaneously and
naturally from our instinctive clinging to life, our yearning for
happiness, our moral sense of justice, and our desire for a state
where a fuller knowledge may clear up the many questions which

man's experience on earth has permitted him to raise but has not enabled him to answer. These various conscious needs incite the mind to spontaneous thought; and the thought-process, thus naturally stimulated, brings the ordinary man,—not by any sustained and elaborate train of logical reasoning, but by an easy, direct, and half-unconscious movement,—to at least some vague form of belief in God and immortality. Of course it is only by a more mature, systematic, and critical analysis of experience that such beliefs, and the conceptions involved in them, are rendered clear and definite.

Having noted that the four classes of beliefs and convictions just enumerated are those that appear most necessary for human life, and that being spontaneous and natural they are possessed by men generally, we might inquire still further into the genesis of them as mental facts. This, however, will be done as far as necessary in connexion with our main inquiry into the objective validity of our knowledge generally. Here we may merely note the sense in which such convictions, and the concepts involved in them, are said to be *innate* or *inborn*, *instinctive*, etc.

They are not merely innate or inborn in the sense that we have from birth, as part of our very being, the various cognitive faculties, both sentient and intelligent, by the exercise or use of which we come gradually into conscious possession of those convictions, and of the notions involved in them: for in this wide sense *all* our knowledge might be said to be innate; whereas the convictions and beliefs in question seem to be acquired by all men more easily, promptly, indeliberately than any other convictions. Hence it is inferred by some that our cognitive faculties must have some sort of innate inclination, disposition, habit, or facility for forming the notions and acquiring the convictions with which we have just been dealing.

Thus, St. Thomas and scholastic philosophers generally attribute the prompt intuition of speculative axioms (of class 2, above) to a natural habit of the intellect which they call the *habitus primorum principiorum;* and that of the first principles of the moral order (class 3, above) to an analogous habit of intellect which they have entitled *synderesis.* Possibly in the former case the promptness and facility of acquisition might be sufficiently explained by the simplicity and clearness of the *objects* presented to the mind; but in the case of ethical notions and principles it does seem necessary to postulate a special natural inclination of the human intelligence to account for the uniform ease with which all men come into possession of them. At all events there would seem to be in our nature some kind of an inborn need which inclines and impels us to acquire those concepts and convictions rather than others that are in themselves equally attainable but not of such serious import to human life.

The same may be said with regard to the concepts of God and immortality, and belief in the validity of these concepts (class 4, above). Of course men generally come into possession of these concepts and beliefs in childhood and youth by way of authority,—by the teaching of their parents and elders. But it can hardly be denied that they seem to come natural to the human intelligence, that they are felt to satisfy not only a moral and religious, but also an intellectual need of our nature, that our reason promptly appreciates the grounds of those beliefs, and is inclined spontaneously and unquestioningly to accept those grounds as satisfactory and convincing.

Finally, with regard to those general judgments of the first class above, judgments so indispensable for the preservation of our physical life on earth, we have already noted the spontaneous inclination of the mind to generalize from sense experience. In the animal kingdom the great protecting and conserving factor of life is *instinct*, *i.e.* a natural tendency to pursue uniformly, but without consciousness of their ultimate purpose or their utility for this purpose, precisely those lines of conduct which are *de facto* useful for the preservation of life in the individual and in the species. In man instincts are largely overshadowed and supplanted by the use of reason, and come under the control of reason according as reason dawns in the individual. Why does reason so promptly and so universally derive from the data of sense experience just those judgments which are indispensable for the preservation of man's physical life? Why does it so operate in all men as to select just these for its earliest convictions? Because the natural needs of life fix the attention of the mind on them especially. May we not go farther and say: because *there is in our nature an inclination which prompts and impels our reason to reach out early towards those convictions*, so that we may be able to direct our life according to them?

The same indeed may be said of all four classes of the spontaneous beliefs and convictions we have been considering. When they are described as *instinctive*, as they often are, this is what is meant : that there is rooted in our nature an inclination, a tendency, an impulse to use our cognitive faculties and so attain to those convictions. Naturally, spontaneously, almost unconsciously, in virtue of this impulse we acquire by the use of our senses and reason those judgments which have such an essential bearing on our lives as physical, intellectual, moral, and religious beings. It is *not* meant that those judgments are themselves instinctive acts in the strict sense of being performed *blindly* or without conscious appreciation of their import and grounds, *i.e.* in the sense in which certain actions of animals are described as instinctive because performed without any conscious appreciation of their purpose. When we form these spontaneous judgments we do so because we *see*, or think we see, *sufficient grounds* for forming them ; otherwise we would not accept or assent to them. Before we assent to them we have, or think we have, either direct and cogent evidence for their truth, or else indirect evidence for their *truth* in the direct and cogent evidence which we have, or think we have, for their *credibility*, for the reasonableness of assenting to them with the firmness of conviction. They are therefore not instinctive *quoad specificationem actus :* it is not instinct but evidence that determines our mental assent to this or that specific judgment ; though they may be said to be instinctive *quoad exercitium actus*, inasmuch as it is an inclination of our nature that prompts us to exercise all the mental processes that lead up to, and terminate in, our assent to such judgments.

16. Spontaneous Conviction or Certitude not always True : Hence the Origin of Critical Investigation.— Our spontaneous convictions or certitudes are assents to judgments as true. This implies that these judgments are understood to be not merely *subjective* or mental facts, but to be mental facts which represent and refer us to a something which they render present to us as thinking subjects : which something we therefore think of as *objective*, and understand to be real. It implies furthermore that these judgments are taken not only to refer us to reality and represent reality to us, but that in so far as they do represent it they are taken to represent it *as it really is*. By the *objectivity* of the judgment we mean that *it has reality for its object*, that *it refers us to reality ;* by its *truth* we mean that *it represents reality to us faithfully*, or *as it really is*.

When, therefore, I assent firmly to a judgment, my conviction or certitude is not merely that I am judging, that I am carrying on a mental process, that I am comparing certain mental products which I call notions, concepts, ideas, but *that reality is as my judgment represents it to be.* In other words, I take my convictions or certitudes, of the judgments about which I am certain, to be *objective* and *true.* Thus when I judge with certitude that " the sun is shining " I mean not merely that I am making a mental comparison of two ideas, my idea of " sun " and my idea of " shining," but that there is a reality in which the objects of these two ideas are really found identified. If I meant *merely* the former, if men generally meant *merely* that in judging they were conscious of certain mental states and processes, if they did not mean further, and indeed principally, that they took these mental states and processes to represent accurately and faithfully *a reality objective* to these mental processes, and made present to them by means of these mental processes,—then the distinction between truth and error would be unintelligible. If truth or true knowledge means for me simply whatever goes on consciously in my mind, then *all* that I think is true, simply because I do think it ; and so for everyone else ; and there could be no such thing as error. But error is a fact; and it is a fact because men understand their judgments not only to refer to reality but to represent this reality accurately and faithfully to them, whereas sometimes their judgments, while referring them to reality, *do not represent this reality accurately and faithfully.*

Now it is almost superfluous to remark that men as a matter of course take their spontaneous convictions or certitudes to be objective and true ; or rather that it never occurs to them in their direct and spontaneous cognitions to distinguish between the subjective or mental aspect of these processes and the objective reality which they know, or think they know, in and through these processes. This spontaneous disposition of mind, whereby men recognize as real what their cognitive faculties reveal to them, involving as it does a reliance on those faculties so full and implicit as to be scarcely conscious, is known in philosophy as *naïf dogmatism* or *naïf realism*, to distinguish it from the more cautious and reasoned *critical dogmatism* or *critical realism* to which it may and ought to give place on mature philosophical reflection. It is a natural and spontaneous dictate of the human mind that its own cognitive states, processes, and products put it into con-

tact with something other than themselves, with that which really
exists ; and that when they themselves become by reflection the
objects of other reflex cognitive processes, they do so inasmuch
as they too are realities, parts of that which really is.

We have next to remark that whereas men *always* take their
spontaneous convictions or certitudes, or the judgments of which
they are convinced or certain, as objectively true, they are *sometimes* mistaken, they are sometimes in error, the judgments of
whose truth they are convinced or certain are in some cases not
true but false.   In other words, men can be, and sometimes are,
firmly convinced of the truth of judgments which are *de facto* false.
Whether an erroneous conviction of this kind should be called
certitude authors are not agreed.   Some authors so define certitude
as to confine it to convictions that are true, defining it as the firm
adherence of the mind *to a truth*, and holding it to be an abuse
of language to speak of a *false conviction* as a *certitude*.   It will
be noted that up to the present we have used the two terms " conviction " and " certitude " (" convinced " and " certain ") as synonymous.   It is of course only a matter of terminology.   But
however desirable it might be to retain the terms " certain " and
" certitude " for convictions that are objectively true, or at least
to describe false convictions as only *putative* certitudes, there is
no denying the fact that it is a common usage to apply the terms
without any such qualifying epithet to *all* firm assents, whether
they be true or false.   Whether the mind, if it acts prudently, is
ever obliged to give a *firm* assent to a judgment that is really false,
—in other words, whether to the mind that acts prudently *error* is
ever *inevitable*,—is another question, which may be solved in the
sequel.   But at present we are only looking at conviction or firm
assent under its psychological aspect ; and it is an undeniable
fact that men often do assent firmly to judgments that are false,
and that *while they do* they detect no difference between such an
assent and the assent they give to judgments that are really true.[1]
Indeed it is from this very fact, that men can be firmly persuaded
that they possess truth even when they are really in error, that
the critical problem arises : Is it possible, and if so how is it pos-

---

[1] *Afterwards*, when a person has discovered that he was in error, and in the light
of the new evidence looks back at his erroneous assent, he may be inclined to wonder
if it were really a firm assent, a conviction.   This arises from the prompting to read
the present evidence into the past state, and so to judge the latter as it might or
should have been rather than as it really was.

sible, for men so to distinguish between true and false judgments that they may attain to true knowledge and avoid error? If reflection on the grounds and motives of our spontaneous convictions can bring to light a test or tests whereby we can discern, between true and false convictions, differences which may have escaped the notice of our direct consciousness, and which will enable us to reject or avoid false convictions, then we shall have vindicated the possibility of objectively valid and reasoned certitude. But antecedently to critical reflection, and in the spontaneous assents themselves, there is no conscious difference between true and erroneous convictions.

There is hardly any need to illustrate either the fact that men sometimes firmly entertain erroneous convictions,—whether we call them certitudes or not does not matter: they think them certitudes, *i.e.* true or objectively valid convictions;—or the fact that it is from this very experience that critical inquiries into the possibility of objectively valid certitude in general have arisen. For instance, multitudes of men firmly believed for centuries that the sun really moved around the earth, that the heavens were solid, that the antipodes were uninhabitable, etc. Whether they ought to have been firmly convinced of these things is another question. Anyhow they were *de facto* convinced of them. Again, how many popular beliefs about historical matters, after having been firmly entertained and accepted for ages, have been afterwards shown to have been erroneous? Or look at the conflicting and contradictory beliefs that have been entertained and are still entertained by men regarding philosophical and religious questions. Even if these various beliefs are entertained merely as probabilities by many, are they not also entertained by many others with all the firmness and steadfastness that argues full persuasion and deep conviction? And yet some of them must be false, since they are mutually contradictory: There is a God distinct from the world—There is no God distinct from the world —The world is God; God is knowable—God is unknowable; Matter alone is real and Spirit is unreal—Spirit alone is real and Matter is unreal—Matter and Spirit are both real; The Soul of man is immortal—Man is wholly mortal; Man is Free—Freedom is an illusion; The world is ruled by an Intelligent Providence —Everything happens by blind chance; Miracles are possible— Miracles are impossible; etc., etc.

But if each one, appealing to his own experience, asks him-

self whether he remembers having believed something with all
the firmness of absolute conviction, without the faintest shadow
of a suspicion that he was in error, and afterwards finding to his
surprise, and perhaps with not a little bewilderment, that he
had been wholly in error, we venture to say that in all probability
he will remember such an experience ; at least there are few who
cannot.

Then as to the other fact, that it is such experiences that set
men inquiring into the grounds of human certitude, we have
already seen (3, 4) that this fact is borne out by the history of
philosophy. And if men find that they were really mistaken
when they were fully and firmly convinced that they had true
knowledge, is it not natural that this experience should lead them
in common prudence to meet the suspicion that they may perhaps be equally deceived in their other convictions, and to do so
by systematically examining the process of cognition, its grounds
and its faculties, in order to see if there be a reliable means of
discerning between true and false convictions ?

It may be admitted that the task of thus employing our
reason to probe into its own foundations by critically examining
the working of our cognitive faculties, their data, their presuppositions, their limitations, the validity of their processes, etc., is
a delicate task, not to be undertaken lightly or carried on in-
cautiously ; but at least nowadays, when no human belief is left
unquestioned, it is a task that imposes itself of necessity.

So far we have been merely taking a general view of the terms
and data of our inquiry from the purely psychological standpoint,
—reconnoitring our various cognitive processes and states, and
classifying our spontaneous convictions. We have now to inquire
into the nature and conditions of the general problem itself, the
attitude of mind in which to approach it, and the method of conducting the investigation.

CHAPTER II.

THE SCOPE AND INSTRUMENTS OF THE INQUIRY.

17. THE REAL PROBLEMS TO WHICH REFLECTION ON KNOWLEDGE GIVES RISE.—It is of the first importance for the student to realize what are the points, in relation to knowledge and certitude, which are open to serious inquiry, which are objects for legitimate investigation, which have been seriously doubted by sceptics; and what are the points on which there must be common agreement in order to make any discussion intelligible. Students are often bewildered and puzzled by misunderstanding the precise nature and objects of the doubts raised by sceptics—and by inquirers who are not sceptics—concerning knowledge and certitude.

Thus, no one can seriously doubt or deny that men have spontaneous convictions. The most thorough-going sceptic entertains them. He admits that there are some irresistible convictions which he cannot help entertaining. He admits that there are many judgments which he retains as subjective or mental facts whereby to shape his conduct and guide his life even after he has persuaded himself that they do not give him that insight into reality, which, before mature reflection, he spontaneously believed that they gave him. The question then is not whether men have spontaneous convictions which they believe to be objectively true. The sceptic has never denied that they have. He recognizes that men spontaneously believe that the judgments of which they are certain refer them to an objective world and faithfully represent (so far as they go) this objective world as it is, and that it is the real world. But, he may ask, is this objective world real in the sense of having a being or reality independent of the cognitive process which is supposed to reveal it? He may raise this doubt and cling to it, and so abandon the spontaneous conviction that human cognition reveals to the knower a world which has reality independently of the process of cognition: he will do so if he believes that because he cannot see clearly *how* his mind can transcend itself to know a reality distinct from itself, therefore the mind *cannot* and really does not do so.   But even if he does consider this attitude of subjective idealism to be the only reasonable issue of critical reflection on the matter, he still admits the irresistible tendency of his mind to believe in a world of realities distinct from its own states or processes; and while he doubts or denies that this tendency is speculatively justifiable he may continue to yield to it practically. He by no means ceases to believe that the world and his fellow-men are just as real as himself, but he persuades himself that for him their reality is either identical with, or in some sense dependent on, their presence in or to his mind in his process of knowing them.   Without pausing to cross-question him here as to what he can mean by true and false knowledge, or as to the other logical issues of his conception of knowledge, we can see that his attitude raises a very real and serious question as to whether knowledge in general by revealing objects to our minds —as it undoubtedly does, for we cannot know in any sense without being aware of something, which something we call the "objective world" or "objects"—thereby reveals to us a reality which is independent of, and not constituted by, the cognitive process itself.

Or again, supposing we take it as certain that our cognitive processes,—perception, conception, judgment, reasoning,—in presenting objects in or to our minds do not wholly construct those objects, but that these are in some way presented to us by a reality that is independent of those processes, the question still remains: Do we thereby get to know, in any degree or to any extent, this reality *as it really is?*   Perhaps in the very fact of getting itself presented to our minds in the form of objects of our various cognitive processes, in the very fact of becoming "objective" to these processes, the reality is so transformed, so metamorphosed, that the reality *as it is in itself,* is different from the reality *as it is in the various forms in which it appears as objects* in or to our minds?   If this were so, and if we could not discern what the mind or subject contributes, in knowing, to that which is known, from what the reality contributes to this latter, would it not follow that we could never know reality as it is in itself, and that the objectivity of knowledge would be after all illusory because intra-subjective or dependent on subjective factors, and not a genuine or real objectivity in the sense of being independent of such factors and presenting reality as it is? This misgiving may indeed be gratuitous and groundless and arbitrary. But that is not the point here. The point is that just such a doubt has been seriously raised and that some philosophers, and notably Kant, have been so influenced by it that it has led them, not willingly or consciously perhaps, but none the less effectively, into theories which really deny the validity of knowledge. This doubt or misgiving must therefore in its due place be candidly and impartially examined. We shall then also inquire what intelligible meaning the distinction between true and false knowledge can have in such theories.

But let us look at a conceivable alternative and observe its implications in regard to the possibility of truth and error. We instinctively repudiate,—as opposed to our natural, spontaneous, and deeply-rooted belief,—the notion that our knowledge is confined to wholly mental or subjective objects which would be the exclusive creation of our own mental processes, and also the notion that it is confined to objects which are still mental or subjective in the sense that though partly produced in our minds by a reality independent of our minds, still they give us no insight into this reality as it is. We spontaneously believe that our knowledge is knowledge of realities which are objective in the plain and obvious sense that, being real independently of our knowledge, they reveal themselves to us in and through our cognitive processes by becoming objects of those processes. But if they are realities independently of our cognition of them how do they become objects of cognition? How do they become objects in and for our minds? How do they reveal themselves, or become present to our minds? If we conceive our minds to be purely *passive*, so that these realities, in so far as they do reveal themselves, must always and necessarily reveal themselves just precisely as they are, is not all our knowledge necessarily true, and is not error impossible? This seems a necessary consequence of the assumption ; but it is false for it contradicts the fact that error is possible, and not only possible but also unfortunately very often actual ; therefore the assumption from which such a consequence necessarily follows must be likewise false.

Hence cognition is not a passive mirroring, in our minds, of reality as it is. Therefore cognition is—as, indeed, consciousness itself testifies—an *active* process whereby the mind has to interpret what it becomes aware of. That of which it becomes aware is objective to it, is given to it, is real, is independent of it, *i.e.* the mind spontaneously believes the matter of its awareness to be all this : a belief which reflection has to examine and if so be to justify.

But if what is thus given to the mind is reality, it is reality not *as known* but *as knowable*, not as interpreted but as calling for interpretation, not as revealed, discovered, or manifested, but as capable of being revealed, discovered, manifested by the process of mental interpretation or judgment. If, then, the reality supposed to be presented to our minds as an object for knowledge is sometimes misrepresented, misinterpreted, disfigured, distorted by the act of judgment, so that by this act we make it appear *otherwise than as it really is*, and thus think or judge it to be otherwise than as it really is, how can we be sure but this always happens? Have we any admittedly reliable means of correcting or avoiding error, of distinguishing between judgments which represent reality as it is, and those that misrepresent it, or represent it as it is not? and if so what are the means in question?

Thus we see that the main problems of knowledge are concerned with its *objectivity* and its *truth*. Are the objects of knowledge realities as they are in themselves? Have we any means of discerning between truth and error, between the knowledge which represents these realities as they are in themselves, and the knowledge which misrepresents them?

18. SUBJECT AND OBJECT OF KNOWLEDGE. THE KNOWING SUBJECT.—The distinctions between *subject* and *object*, *subjective* and *objective*, in knowledge, are of the first importance ; and as much confusion is caused by looseness of thought in regard to their meanings it is very necessary to understand the precise sense in which they are used in epistemology.

When we speak of " the subject ". or " the knowing subject " in epistemology,[1] we mean simply *the knower*, considered as

---

[1] (a) In the common and non-technical usage of language the term *subject* means what its etymology suggests, *viz.* whatever *lies under* or *below*, or *is inferior to*, something else. In politics, for instance, we speak of the people as *subjects* of their rulers, of *subject* races, etc. Whatever we think or speak of is the *subject* or subject-matter of our thought, etc., because we bring it *under* our consideration. In this usage *subject* is opposed, as inferior, to *superior*. (b) The *logical subject* of a judgment is so called partly because we subject or submit it to the process of predication, and partly because it usually comes under the higher and wider class-notion which is predicate, as the individual comes under the universal. In this sense *subject* is opposed to *predicate*. (c) In ontology we mean by *subject* that which under-

actually knowing, as actually having a cognitive experience, which experience always, of course, involves consciousness or awareness of something ; which something we call " the object," as distinguished from the knower and the cognitive process by which he knows it. Sometimes the term " consciousness," and sometimes again the term " mind," are used as synonymous with " subject " or "knowing subject ". But perhaps this usage is exposed to the charge of prejudging the nature of the latter. Really it is not my consciousness that becomes aware and knows ; it is *I* who become aware and know ; and consciousness is my state of being aware or knowing. When " consciousness " is thus hypostasized and used to designate the knower, we must not forget that in this transferred sense it means not the state of being aware but the knower, the " I myself" who am aware or conscious. Similarly, although I know by means of my mind, yet there is ambiguity in using the term " mind " as synonymous with " knower " or " knowing subject," for the simple reason that " mind " is usually thought of as distinct from, and correlative to " body," or in the sense of " spirit " as distinct from and correlative to " matter ". But when it is used as synonymous with " knowing subject " in epistemology it must not be taken as necessarily carrying these implications with it, but simply as designating the " knowing subject " without prejudging in any way the nature of the latter. Its denotation when used in this sense in epistemology must be clearly understood to be the individual human being or *Ego*, as knowing ; and its connotation must be understood to be indistinct, to be a matter for the metaphysics of psychology to determine. The " subject," then, or " knowing subject " in epistemology means the individual human *Ego*, as knowing ; for it is with *human* knowledge we are concerned. At least if we have occasion to refer to other than human " knowing subjects " the context will make it clear that we do so.

The term " subjective " accordingly signifies and designates whatever is understood to appertain to, or spring from, the knowing subject as such, in contradistinction from whatever is understood to characterize or belong to what he knows, what is object of his knowledge.

lies qualities or accidents, in other words, *substance :* while the qualities or accidents which determine, designate, and reveal or manifest the substance, we call *forms*. In this sense *subject* is opposed to *form*.

19. "OBJECT" IN THE SENSE OF (1) WHATEVER IS REAL, (2) WHATEVER WE ARE AWARE OF.—(1) In the ordinary usage of language the term *object* is synonymous with *thing, something, reality.* In this sense *object* is opposed to *nothingness :* whatever is real, or distinct from nothingness, is *objective* in this sense of the term.   Hence, since spontaneous convictions, whether true or false, and merely as states of the knowing subject, are real facts, real states, real occurrences, as distinct from nothingness, they are "objective," or "objects," in this sense.   It is not with such objectivity that epistemology is concerned.

(2) If we ask why whatever is real is thus called an object, or objective, we shall find it is because people spontaneously believe that whatever is real can be known, and that in the process of being known it is somehow thrown or placed before (*ob-jicere* to throw or cast before), or made present to, the knower. And according to the same spontaneous belief a reality can be thus made present to the knowing subject whether that reality be the knowing subject himself, or some conscious state, process, or activity of himself, *or whether it be a reality distinct from the knowing subject himself and his conscious states, processes, or activities.*

In the spontaneous order men do not trouble as to how a reality distinct from the knowing subject can become present to him so as to be an object of his cognition : they simply believe that it can and does happen.   Because they do not reflect they perceive no difficulty in it ; whereas to some men, when they reflect seriously on it, the difficulty—of the knowing subject "transcending" himself to know a reality distinct from himself —seems so insuperable that they pronounce such a feat an impossibility, and declare their belief that all knowable reality in order to be knowable must be in some sense really identical with the knowing subject.   They think that by this identification they surmount the "insuperable" difficulty.

It would appear, however, on further reflection that—apart altogether from the other insuperable difficulty into which such identification leads them, *viz.* the difficulty of successfully avoiding *solipsism*—the identification does not wholly surmount the original or "transcendence" difficulty.   And the reason why we think so is this.   Even when the knowing subject by an act of reflex cognition "knows" himself or his own conscious states, processes, or activities, or whatever it be that is thus consciously

identical with himself as knowing subject, has he not to make
himself, or such conscious phases or states of himself, an *object* of
his reflex cognition? For note that the direct, implicit concomitant awareness of self or subject, which we have seen (8) to
be essentially involved in all cognitive consciousness, is not itself
cognition or knowledge of the self as an object. If it were the
"identification" hypothesis might perhaps help to dispel or
lessen the mystery of all cognition. But the subject can
"know" himself in the proper sense of this term only by an act
of reflection whereby he makes himself *object* of himself as
reflecting subject. But is there no mystery or difficulty in the
possibility of this reflex cognition whereby the subject, by making
himself his own object, knows himself? It will not be denied
that there is ; and indeed to some serious students of knowledge
the question, "How can a subject know the reality which is himself?" presents a problem no less mysterious than the question,
"How can a subject know a reality which is other than himself?"[1] We are not raising these points here by way of discussion, but merely to help the student to think his way to clear
nominal definitions. We have seen that in the ordinary usage
of language the term "object" is synonymous with thing or
reality ; and we have suggested a reason why this is so. While
keeping clear of all contentious matter we can give another
intelligible meaning to the term *object* by the simple consideration that all cognition, indeed all consciousness in so far as it
involves the cognitive element of *awareness of something*, involves the presence of this "something" to the subject. In
other words, we cannot be conscious, or think, or know at all,
without being conscious or thinking of "something," without
knowing "something". Let us, following the etymology of the
word *object*, call this something an *object*,—without raising any
question whatsoever here about the nature, origin, or function of
this object, for it is just such questions that must be raised and
discussed in the sequel. And let us call it the *object of awareness*
to distinguish it from other senses of the term "object". Now
in this sense too, all knowledge whether true or false, valid or
invalid, genuine or illusory, has an object, and is admittedly
objective. It is not with such objectivity, any more than with
objectivity in the first sense above, that epistemology is concerned.

---

[1] *Cf.* PRICHARD, *op. cit.*, chap. vi., pp. 123-4.

20. "Mental Presence" or "Objectivity to Subject," and "Real Being" or "Real Objectivity".—(3) From the points raised above in (2) the student will be able to gather this much at least : that whether the reality known be the knowing subject himself (or whatever is partially identical with him, such as his conscious states, processes, etc.), or whether it be a reality distinct from himself, it must, in order to be known, have a presence as an object *to* or *in* or *before*[1] him as knowing subject (or to his "consciousness" or "mind" in the sense explained above). This unity or continuity of what is known with the knowing subject, this "rendering present" of the former to the latter, this "presentation" of the former to the latter, is something that happens in or to the subject, and is a necessary part of the cognitive process : because by it alone the subject gets an object and so becomes aware of something. This "mental *presence* or *presentation* or *existence*" (*ex-sistere*, to stand forth), by which *something* stands forth as object to the knowing subject, is essential to all cognition simply because cognition would be unintelligible without it. It is essential to every form of cognition : to sense perception whether internal or external, to simple intellectual apprehension or abstract conception, to the complex conception of relations in judgment and reasoning. It has been called *objectivity*,—objectivity whereby *something* stands before or is present or presented to the subject.

But mark well that it is a *subjective* or *intra-subjective* objectivity in the sense that this "becoming present of something as object" happens in or to the knowing subject, as an essential part of the cognitive process, and as a means whereby he becomes aware of the something through that process.

It has been called by scholastics "esse *ideale*," where *ideale* is taken in the wide sense of *mentale*, mental being or existence, the existence which the known has in or to the knower ; and also "esse *intentionale*," the subjective or mental being or happening whereby the mind stretches out, as it were, and apprehends, grasps, knows what it deems to be the reality as it is in itself (whether this reality be the subject itself or a reality distinct from the subject itself). They have also called it the *species sensibilis* in the case of sense cognition and the *species intelligibilis* or *verbum mentale* in the case of intellectual cognition ; and in both cases

---

[1] Note that these prepositions have here no spatial or local signification whatever.

they have described it as a *medium quo*, or *in quo*, or *per quod res cognoscitur*, a means *by* or *through* which, or a medium *in* which, the reality is known : at the same time observing that it is not *id quod cognoscitur*, or a *medium ex quo res cognoscitur*, *i.e.* that this *objective presence* of the reality *in the subject* is not the thing that is known, is not a something which is itself first and directly known and *from* which the reality would be indirectly known. From which it will be seen that the scholastics considered this mental being or existence, this mental presence or representation, of something *as an object in the mind or subject*, to be a means of making the cognition *indicative* or *representative* of a being or reality which this something is assumed to have independently of the subject and antecedently to the mental being or presence which it obtains in the subject by the process of cognition. Now it is this independent being or reality that is considered by them to be the *real object*, *i.e.* the *extra-subjective* or *extra-mental* object of knowledge ; and it is considered to be *extra-subjective* or *extra-mental* or *really objective*, not merely as opposed to the knowing subject himself, but also as distinct from the mental or subjective objectivity which it obtains in the actual process of cognition.[1]

21. ALTERNATE SOLUTIONS OF QUESTIONS RAISED BY MENTAL OBJECTIVITY.—Let us now revert to what was said above : that the mental presence of something in or to the mind or subject—which we have seen to be an admittedly essential condition of all knowledge—is an *intra-mental* or *intra-subjective* objectivity, in the sense that it is a happening of something in or to the subject and an essential part of the subjective cognitive process. A few extremely important questions have to be asked in reference to it : Is this "presence or presentation of something as object to the knowing subject" caused *exclusively* by the knowing subject

---

[1] When there is question of the subject knowing himself by an act of reflex cognition the reality known is of course really identical with the knowing subject, but logically distinct from the latter, inasmuch as the latter when regarded as a known object is considered under a different aspect from itself regarded as knowing subject. Furthermore, scholastics are not agreed as to whether in the case of reflex intellectual self-cognition, or in the case of the beatific vision, the known reality becomes present to the knower by an objective mental presence or being (or *verbum mentale*) distinct from the real being or essence of the known reality : some holding that in these cases the real self and the Divine Essence respectively are present as objects in or to the mind by their own real being or essence immediately, and without the intervention of any representative or "objectivating" factor such as the *verbum mentale;* others holding that even in these cases to make the self or God present as objects to the subject there is need of this representative, "objectivating" factor.

himself as such in the process of cognition, or is it caused *partly* by a reality distinct from him *as knowing subject ?*   And in the latter alternative does this reality, by partially contributing to the cognitive process, *present itself* to the subject, thus making him aware of it and offering itself for interpretation to him?   Let us mention four conceivable answers.

(1) First, it is caused exclusively by the knowing subject himself.   This is *Subjectivism* or *Subjective Idealism* in its extreme form. Observe what it seems to imply : that cognition is wholly a subjective process ; that the individual knowing subject wholly produces from his own subjectivity whatever he knows ; that the whole world, all reality, in so far as the world of reality is known to him or by him, is somehow an evolution, or emanation, or creation, of himself, of his own *Ego ;* that the "objective reference" of cognition, *i.e.* its suggestion of, or tendency to refer him to, realities beyond himself as knowing subject, and his spontaneous belief in the validity of this reference, are illusory ; that for.him reality has no other being than the being which it has by becoming an object or objects in or to himself or his own mind or consciousness ; and that this being is identical with, inasmuch as it is somehow a growth or efflorescence of, his own being : SOLIPSISM.   We may leave it at that for the present.

(2) Secondly, the subjective or mental objectivity or presence of something in knowledge is not exclusively a product of the knowing subject in the process of cognition ; but the *reality* by which it is also partly caused does not and cannot by so contributing to cognition be ever itself known : whether it be the reality of the knowing subject himself (the transcendental *Ego*) or a reality distinct from the latter (the transcendental *non-Ego*), it does not and cannot reveal itself as it is in itself to the knowing subject : its sole influence in the process of cognition is to produce in the subject, in combination with the latter's contribution, a set of intra-subjective or mental objects or appearances or phenomena, of which alone the subject can become aware : for the subject cannot transcend his own subjectivity but can become aware only of thóse mental objects as affected by cognitive factors belonging to his own subjectivity.   Thus it is the *esse mentale* or *mental being*, the subjective or mental objectivity, of reality that is known by the subject, and this alone is known by him ; the *esse reale*, the reality in its real or extra-subjective or extra-mental state or condition cannot be known by him : in a word,

real being as it is in itself is unknowable. This is the drift of Kant's theory of knowledge: *Phenomenism.*[1] It is really subjectivism, though not intentionally so, for there is in it an effort to show that knowledge is objective: an unsuccessful effort, however, inasmuch as the only objectivity that is really vindicated for knowledge is an objectivity that is limited and circumscribed by and shut up within the subject, and wholly determined by factors contributed to the cognitive process from the latter's own subjectivity.

(3) A third alternative: the presence or presentation of something as object to the knowing subject is not caused exclusively by the latter. In fact it is not caused by him at all. But this mental presentation of something in cognition is not a means by which the subject knows anything represented by this presence. What he knows is the presentations themselves, the objects in their mental presence, in the being they have in or to his mind; this mental presence or being he cannot transcend, *and he has no need to transcend*, for the objects present to him *have no other being:* their *esse* is *percipi:* their only reality consists in their being perceived, *i.e.* in their being present to a percipient mind. The knowing subject is mind or spirit and all realities are mental or spiritual, are simply ideas present to a mind. What we call the material universe, the world of sense perception, is a system of spiritual, mental, or ideal entities or objects, present to the perceiving mind: it is an illusion for the perceiving mind to think that they have or can have any being or reality beyond or independent of their presence in or to itself. But this ideal being that they have is not subjective in the sense of being produced by the percipient mind: it is objective in the sense that they are caused or produced or placed in or before the mind by another being distinct from the latter, *viz.* by the Divine Being.

In this theory, propounded by Berkeley, the necessity of transcendence seems to be avoided; the knowing subject (which is assumed to be mind in the sense of spirit) appears to be shut up or confined within itself in the sense that what it knows are ideas, *i.e.* entities which have no being or reality other than their presence in or to or for the mind, no extramental reality in the sense in which the material universe is supposed to have a being of its own distinct from its presence to the percipient mind in the

---

[1] *Cf.* PRICHARD, *op. cit.*, chap. vi.

act of perceptive cognition.   Hence the theory is *immaterialism*
in the sense of denying a substantive reality to matter ; it is
idealism in the sense that it claims all so-called material realities
to be a system of ideas present to a mind ; but it is not *subjectivism*
or *subjective* idealism, because it holds these ideas not to be products of the subjectivity of the knowing mind or subject, but to
be produced or placed in each individual human mind or subject
by the Supreme Being.   Hence it has been called *objective* idealism.   The objectivity in Kant's theory we have asserted to be
spurious, to be apparent rather than real, inasmuch as it is
wholly determined by factors belonging to the subjectivity of
the knowing subject, so that the latter cannot really know anything beyond his own individual subjectivity.   The objectivity
in Berkeley's theory is indeed an improvement on this, inasmuch
as the " ideas " which the mind knows are not products of its own
subjectivity ; but nevertheless it falls short of making knowledge
genuinely objective, because the only reality that objects of
knowledge are allowed in this theory is the presence they have
in each individual human mind while the latter is actually perceiving them : which reality is after all subjective at least in the
sense of being mind-dependent, *i.e.* limited to, and determined
by, and indeed identical with, the actual perceptions of individual
human minds.

(4) According to yet another alternative the mental presence
or presentation of something as an object to the knowing subject
in the process of cognition is not caused exclusively by the subject.   It happens of course in or to him and is necessarily subjective or mental in the sense that it is an essential feature of the
cognitive process, which is his process.   But it is a subjective or
mental event which happens through the influence of a *something
that has a reality which is extra-subjective*, *i.e.* a something whose
reality does not consist in, but is independent of, that mental
presentation or presence whereby it becomes an object in or to
the subject.   Moreover, it is by means of this presentation or
presence, this *esse ideale* or *esse intentionale*, that *this supposed real
something becomes known*.   And hence this mental being or existence or happening is *objective* not only in the sense that although
it happens in or to the subject it is not an exclusive product of
his subjectivity, but also and -especially because on this very
account, *i.e.* because it is partly due to something extra-subjective,
it is the means of bringing the subject into a cognitive union or rela-

tion of awareness with this latter, and of offering this latter to the subject for cognition in the full sense of what we have ventured to call (8) interpretation, apperception, recognition, etc.

When this extra-subjective reality is the subject himself, it is the subject as made present to himself by an act of reflex cognition : for the mere fact of identity does not involve cognition : a stick or a stone is really identical with itself and yet does not know itself. Reflection is necessary for self-knowledge, and though it involves a process perhaps scarcely less inexplicable than transcendence (*cf.* § 19 above), *viz.* the process whereby a real being opposes itself to itself as object to subject, as known to knower, still it is accepted by this theory as a fact. When on the other hand the extra-subjective reality is a reality distinct from the knowing subject, then the latter can and does, in and through the cognitive process (by means of the presentation, the objective mental happening), transcend not only his own subjectivity as in self-knowledge, but even his own reality : thus effecting that cognitive union or continuity of the knower with reality, without which knowledge, as genuinely objective knowledge of reality, would be impossible. Hence transcendence in the sense explained is also accepted by this theory as a fact.

Moreover, the supporters of this theory emphasize on the one hand their view that genuine knowledge does reach out to reality and grasp reality : *Objectum Intellectus est Ens :* knowledge is knowledge of reality. When the subject knows what he calls himself he knows not merely a product of his own subjectivity, or of factors belonging to his own subjectivity, a mental construction which he takes (or *mis*takes) for his real self, a subjective creation which certain philosophers have entitled "the empirical *Ego*" and held to be distinct from the real self, which they have called the "noumenal or transcendental *Ego*". No ; what he knows is his real self, and there is no other "self" for him to know. Similarly, when the knowing subject knows what he calls other things or other realities than himself, what he knows is not a system of subjectively evolved mental products ; or even a system of mental objects produced in or for his mind wholly by the Supreme Being, or partly by an extramental reality which must ever remain itself an unknowable *x*. What he knows is *a system of extramental realities.* And he knows them by means of their influence on him, an influence described in him as "mental presence," "objectivity," etc., and whereby he as knowing subject can attain to a genuine knowledge of these realities.

Hence, also, supporters of this theory emphasize on the other hand the view that when knowledge is of realities other than the knowing subject (as indeed, also, when it is of the knowing subject himself) the latter must effect, in and through the process of cognition, a union or continuity with the realities he knows; not however a *real* union or continuity or identity (even real identity does not of itself involve cognition, *cf.* § 19, above), but a cognitive union which is *sui generis* and which scholastics (whose theory we are describing) have called *intentionalis.* Here are a few of the profoundly significant phrases in which St. Thomas gives expression to this view (and they will repay serious reflection): "Sensibile in actu et sensus in actu *unum sunt*"; "Intelligibile in actu et intellectus in actu *unum sunt*"; "Mens cognoscendo *quodammodo fit omnia*".

22. EPISTEMOLOGICAL SENSE OF "OBJECT OF KNOWLEDGE" AND "OBJECTIVITY OF KNOWLEDGE". TRUTH OF KNOWLEDGE. —We are now in a position to give to the phrases "object of knowledge" and "objectivity of knowledge" the meaning we attach to them in epistemology. We give these meanings here as *nominal* definitions. It will be our concern in the sequel to endeavour to show that they are likewise real definitions, that knowledge and its objects are *really* what these definitions imply.

By the *object of knowledge* we mean the *reality* to which, according to the spontaneous belief of mankind, knowledge is supposed to attain, the *real* object *as it is in itself*, which is supposed to reveal itself to the subject in the cognitive process for interpretation, and to do so by means of the mental presentation or presence which gives to the subject an *object of awareness.* Whether this *object of awareness* is identical with the *real object of knowledge* will appear in the sequel. Anyhow, the real object of knowledge must in every case,—whether it be the reality of the subject himself or a reality distinct from him,—be rendered present to, or put into cognitive union or continuity with, the knowing subject: this is effected by means of the presentation or mental presence or existence, the *esse mentale* or *esse intentionale* which gives the subject an *object of awareness.* It is by means of this presentation that the subject obtains a *real object* for interpretation. This latter is always an interpretation of reality ; but it may be either true or false: for it is a process of comparing, analysing, and synthesizing those intra-subjective or mental objects which are the joint products, in the subject's process of cognition, of the subject's own cognitive activity and of the influence of the reality on the subject. If this process of interpretation is guided throughout by the presented *reality* (the *real object of knowledge*), so that the *re*presentation or *re*cognition, in which the process terminates, conforms the mind to this reality, then the knowledge is true ; if not, so that the mind judges that "what is" "is not," or that "what is not" "is," then the knowledge is erroneous.

By the *objectivity of knowledge* we mean, in epistemology (*a*), that *the object of knowledge* is *reality as it is in itself.* Such objectivity is denied to knowledge by Kant's theory, which is therefore a form of subjectivism. We mean, moreover, (*b*) that the subject can know not merely his *real* self by reflex cognition, but also *realities other than himself*—by ordinary or direct cognition as distinguished from introspective reflection. And we mean, of course, all that is involved in the cognition of realities other than himself. But this involves evidently that these realities become *cognitively* present to, or *cognitively* united or continuous with, the knowing subject. By this presentation they obtain in the process of cognition, an objectivity in or to the subject,—what we have called a mental or intra-subjective objectivity. Now (*c*) this mental objectivity is not an exclusive product of the subject's own cognitive factors or activities, a purely subjective construction, but is partly caused by the influence of extra-subjective realities : an objectivity which is denied by extreme subjectivism. Furthermore (*d*) it is not this " presence of something in or to the knowing subject" that is known by the latter, this presence is only the means by which the latter transcends his subjectivity to know extra-subjective realities : a position denied by all who hold that the only being or reality that can be known by the subject is the mental objectivity or presence of something in or to the subject,—whether this mental presence be exclusively a product of the subject, as extreme subjectivists hold, or whether it be produced in the subject by the Supreme Being, as Berkeley held. Reality is not "objectivity in or to the mind," as Berkeley held ("*Esse est percipi*") ; nor is "objectivity in or to the mind" that which is known, as he held in common with extreme subjectivists ; but it is by its "objectivity in or to the mind" that the extramental reality becomes for the knower an object for knowledge, for interpretation. Thus the subject can and does know extra-subjective and extramental reality as it is in itself: which is the main thesis of the *objectivity of knowledge.*

We can now see that the *truth* of knowledge is something more than its *objectivity,* that knowledge can be objective and yet false. For by the objectivity of knowledge we mean, as against subjectivist theories, that the knowing subject has presented to him in cognition *reality as it is in itself* for his interpretation. And, as we have seen, this process of interpretation, being a process or activity of the subject, under the influence of reality, may be so controlled by the reality as faithfully to represent this latter, *or it may not.*

The general theory which maintains the objectivity of knowledge, or that reality as it is in itself is attained by knowledge in the sense just explained, is described as *objectivism, realism, dogmatism,* as opposed to *subjectivism, phenomenism, scepticism.*

The thesis (*a*) that the *judgment* itself is not motived by purely subjective factors is described by Mercier[1] as the *objectivity of the judgment.* The thesis (*b*) that the *concepts* by which it interprets what is presented to the knowing subject in perception really represent this presented *datum* is described as the *reality* or *objective reality* of the judgment. And the thesis (*c*) that what is presented in *perception* is *reality, extramental reality,* is described as the *real validity of sense perception.*

23. ALTERNATIVE STATEMENTS OF THE GENERAL PROBLEM OF EPISTEMOLOGY.—In the preceding sections we have spoken as far as possible *in general terms, i.e.* about the problems to which *all* cognition gives rise, and without distinguishing the various cognitive processes or determining the forms taken by the general problem in regard to each kind of process,—sense perception, intellectual conception, intuition of axioms, judgment, reasoning, etc. But since knowledge attains to its fulness in the judgment, and since the possession of knowledge is fully attained by certain or firm assent, the general problem might be thus variously formulated with special reference to these :—

(*a*) Has the whole complex or intra-subjective object which is present to the mind in judging, or have any of the elements thereof, *e.g.* the subject and the predicate, corresponding to them

[1] *Critériologie Générale, passim.*

an extra-subjective or extramental reality to which they refer us,
—or is this reference an illusion?

(*b*) Is the synthesis of subject and predicate, to which the
mind assents in judging, effected or motived by the influence of
a reality distinct from the subjectivity of the mind judging,—or
is it wholly determined by the instinctive, sub-conscious operation or influence of factors or forms belonging to the mind's own
subjectivity?

(*c*) Is the subjective or mental state of conviction or certitude
produced wholly by the subject himself, by *subjective* factors, propensities, dispositions, instincts,—or is it produced in the subject
by the influence on him of an extra-subjective or extramental
reality?

(*d*) Does reflection reveal to us any *means* of solving the
questions *a*, *b* and *c*,—of determining whether the judgments we
spontaneously hold as true refer us to, and are formed under the
influence of, extra-subjective reality? And, furthermore, have
we any *means* or *tests* whereby we can discern when they are so
guided by this latter influence as to be *in conformity with this
reality as it is in itself*, and when, on the other hand, they are so
influenced by subjective or other factors that they do not represent
reality as it is? In other words, have we any satisfactory and
adequate test or tests of the truth of judgments,—of their *real
objective validity* in the full and complete sense?[1]

What, then, are the general conditions which make the investigation of these problems possible? What are their *data?*
And what is the proper method of approaching and conducting
the investigation? These three questions are intimately connected, and the consideration of the first two will lead to the
third.

24. GENERAL DATA AND CONDITIONS OF THE INVESTIGA-
TION.—Among the *data* are men's spontaneous convictions that
they have judgments which are not merely mental facts but are
also representative of reality, *i.e.* objectively valid and true. No
one denies or can deny that he has such spontaneous convictions,
and even some irresistible convictions. Their number differs from
one individual to another; but all have some, and they are the
very subject-matter of epistemological inquiry.

Secondly, the power of the human subject *to reflect* on his

---

[1] This latter statement of the problem, as an inquiry into *criteria* of truth, has
suggested the title *Criteriology.*

spontaneous assents, is an essential *condition* for raising and discussing the problems. It is by the exercise of reflection that he discovers he has sometimes erred in his spontaneous convictions, that he is led to raise doubt about his other convictions, to pass from the spontaneous, dogmatic attitude to the critical, questioning, doubting, sceptical attitude in regard to them. The brute beast, too, has spontaneously and irresistibly formed cognitive states. But because the brute beast has no faculty of reflection, he cannot control or criticize or question these states, but must continue to be irresistibly swayed and led and determined by them. Not so the human being. He has the power to summon them before the bar of his reflecting reason or intelligence and to consider whether he has adequate grounds for continuing to hold them for what he spontaneously took them to be. If he discovers a reliable test for them, then those that emerge successfully from the ordeal of its application to them will have become *reflex*, *scientific, philosophical* certitudes, and will now no longer be the merely direct, spontaneous convictions which they heretofore had been. If, unfortunately, he should fail to find a reliable test from which any of them could emerge successfully, then of course he would have no alternative to the despairing conclusion of the sceptic, that the human mind is a hopelessly botched apparatus,— "*que la machine humaine est mal faite*" [1]

What kind of reflection is required for the discussion of such problems? Evidently not the indirect, concomitant awareness of ourselves as subjects, the awareness that is essential to all cognition : this is not properly reflection at all, and is not sufficient for our present purpose. We need a formal, deliberate, introspective study of our spontaneous assents, and of these not merely as mental facts, but *as cognitive, as representative*, as characterized by the feature of *objective reference* which is peculiar to them. Reflection on them as mere mental facts belongs to psychology. It is reflection on their *objective* or *truth* claim that is called for in epistemology.

Furthermore, our reflection here must be methodic and systematic. It is not to be denied that men in their *spontaneous* assents reflect upon the grounds of these assents, make up their minds about the sufficiency of these grounds, and in doing so are conscious of their acts of judging and assenting as being reasoned and reasonable ; and in so far as they do their certitudes are

[1] MERCIER, *op. cit.*, p. 111.

implicitly scientific, reflex, philosophical ; nor is it claimed for a moment that men's convictions must be set down as unjustified and ill-considered until they have gone through a systematic study of epistemology. There is a certain moderate amount of reflection,—the reflection of the plain man, *reflectio vulgaris* as it is called,—permeating the plain man's spontaneous convictions and making them incipiently or moderately or implicitly philosophical ; nor is the systematic reflection required in epistemology different in kind, but only in degree and extent and intensity, from that of the plain man who is not an avowed philosopher or epistemologist.

Is a man's faculty of reflecting on his spontaneous judgments and assents essentially different, of a different kind or order, from his faculty of spontaneously forming and assenting to such judgments ? There is no ground for thinking so. It is the same general faculty, the same mind,—call it intellect, intelligence, reason, as you will,—which judges, assents, reasons, and reflects.

CHAPTER III.

THE METHOD OF THE INQUIRY.

25. INITIAL ATTITUDE OF THE SUBJECT TOWARDS HIS CAPACITY FOR DISCOVERING TRUTH WITH CERTITUDE.—We see, then, that in approaching the task of re-examining his spontaneous convictions the knowing subject must take his faculty of reflection for granted and make use of it for what it is worth,— exercising it with all the care and caution and circumspection he can command. We say he must take it "for what it is worth" He finds among his spontaneous convictions this particular one : that his mind is capable of discovering truth and that it has *de facto* discovered some truth. He finds himself believing spontaneously that his mind *is worth something* in this respect ; but he is quite conscious that he does not know just how much his mind may be able to discover with certitude. Moreover, he realizes that at this initial stage he has not yet deliberately tested by reflection his spontaneous belief that his mind can know at least something. And if he asks himself how is he to test the validity of this belief, the only answer he can give is : *by reflecting on it*, as on his other spontaneous beliefs, and seeing whether the grounds for it are adequate ; in other words, by exercising his mind and by studying its operations and observing its results, determining for himself whether his spontaneous belief in its capacity to discover truth is justified by those results.

No doubt, he is quite well aware that in doing so he is *using the faculty he is testing*, and that this is obviously inevitable. But provided his mind *is really* what he spontaneously believes it to be, *viz.* capable of discovering some truth with certitude, it will emerge successfully from the ordeal, provided the critical or testing process is judiciously conducted.

In order that his mind may actually discover truth all that is necessary is that it be really capable of discovering truth. And in order that he may actually come to know with reflex, philosophical certitude that it is thus really capable, he has simply to exercise it in the process of re-examining his spontaneous assents, to watch it while conducting that process, and while retaining provisionally .from the beginning his spontaneous belief in its validity, as a spontaneous belief, to see whether this belief will turn out to have been well grounded—in which case it will become a philosophical certitude,—or mayhap to have been groundless— in which case the result for the time at least would be scepticism.

It is therefore not *necessary* to presuppose at the outset of our inquiry *as philosophically certain*, the power of the mind to attain to the possession of truth. Nor is it *legitimate* to do so, for this very capacity of the mind is open to question, and has been questioned, and is one main point in regard to which we want to reach and establish philosophical or reflex certitude.

But it is both *legitimate* and *necessary* for us to *assume and retain provisionally our spontaneous conviction*, as a spontaneous conviction, that our minds are capable of discovering truth. It is legitimate, because the provisional retention of this spontaneous conviction does not in any way prejudge the critical question as to whether or not reflection will transform it into a reflex certi tude or show it to have been unjustifiable. And it is necessary, because *were we really to abandon* this spontaneous conviction by a *real and positive* doubt about our mental aptitude, all thought would be paralysed and all reflection rendered futile. For, sup- pose for a moment that we really lost this natural belief in our capacity to reach truth, suppose this conviction were really shat- tered by reasons that appeared to us sufficient to shatter them, suppose we were somehow landed in a state of genuine and serious misgiving about the capacity of our minds to attain to any certain knowledge whatsoever—what would happen? Well, either of two things might happen. (1) We might passively sub- mit in despair or indifference to the dominion of this doubt, in which case we should, under its withering influence, give up re- flection as hopeless and futile and live on as speculative sceptics. Nature might and probably would sooner or later revolt against this condition of mental paralysis ; but as long as it lasted re- flection would obviously be unmeaning because it would be con- sciously smitten with the blight of a *real and positive doubt* about its own efficacy. (2) We might, notwithstanding the considera- tions that appeared to us to strike at our spontaneous belief in our capacity to reach truth, determine to retain this spontaneous belief and continue to reflect, to examine, to explore, in the hope that we might find it on further reflection to have been well-grounded. But when this happens it shows that we have not *really* abandoned our spontaneous belief at all. And furthermore it reveals this other important corollary, that at least at the initial stage of our investigation no motives can occur to us really sufficient to shatter our spontaneous belief in the trustworthiness of our faculties. Let us consider the weight of the grounds for a few such possible initial misgivings.

26. DIFFICULTIES AGAINST THIS ATTITUDE.—(1) We have sometimes fallen into error in the past : our faculties deceived us, and of course we were not aware that we were being deceived : while in error we thought we were in possession of truth. Therefore perhaps *in all cases* we may be similarly deceived without knowing it.

This difficulty concerns the *individual acts* of assent elicited by us. Is it really sufficient to destroy our natural confidence in the capacity of our faculties to reach truth ? Manifestly it is not. Do not the premisses themselves imply that in some cases we believed ourselves to have discovered and corrected our errors, and that in doing so our faculties acted validly and were successful in discerning truth from error? The implied admission that we *know* truth to be distinct from error is a recognition that our faculties can discover some truth. So hard is it to *destroy effectively* our spontaneous trust in our faculties, that this difficulty certainly does not succeed in doing so.

The difficulty does not prove that we are always deceived. It merely suggests this as a possibility that should be seriously examined ; and it would be very imprudent and unreasonable to allow this possibility to destroy our spontaneous trust in our faculties, when it should rather stimulate us to further reflection. It proves merely that our faculties are fallible, and it should stimulate us to inquire whether this fallibility is *essential* ("*per se*") *and irremediable*, or *accidental* ("*per accidens*") *and remediable*. And on this point it will be enough to observe here that there are two possible alternatives. While we are deceived we of course do not know that we are deceived. But is the deception (*a*) always such that it *was* unavoidable, and *is* actually irremediable, *i.e.* such that while we are victims to it we have at our disposal no means of coming gradually to know that it was an error, and so of dispelling it ? or (*b*) always such that it *was not* really unavoidable, and that even while we are in error the deception *is not* actually irremediable, inasmuch as *by further reflection* we can discover the means of correcting the error? It is only reflection that can determine which of these alternatives is the right one. And since the former of the two does not at the outset of our inquiry impose itself irresistibly on us as the right one, it would be imprudent and unreasonable to allow such a misgiving to destroy our spontaneous belief in our capacity for truth and so, by paralysing thought, to render all investigation impossible.

(2) Whether from the fact that we have sometimes fallen into error, or from the fancy that for all we can know to the contrary we may be the sport of some Malignant Power [1] who gave us faculties that are radically and intrinsically and of their very nature deceptive, it may occur to us at the very outset to doubt whether this is not really the case. Therefore it would appear that we cannot reasonably retain our spontaneous belief in the trustworthiness of our faculties—even provisionally—throughout the course of our critical investigations.

This is the doubt which Descartes suggested to himself by his fancy that he might perhaps be the dupe of some "*malin génie*" [2]

Obviously no prudent person would allow such a possible contingency to " scare him out of his wits," so to speak. In the face of it he will very properly retain his spontaneous belief in the capacity of his mind to discover truth. And he will see, moreover, that the only possible way of settling the question raised by the fancy referred to is to examine by reflection, not the mind itself or its faculties apart from or antecedently to the mind's cognitive activities, but to examine it in and through these very activities. For it is clear that cognitive *faculties* cannot be tested or examined *in themselves* and abstracting from their *activities :* whatever we know or can know about the nature of the mind and its faculties we can know only through their activities : there is no other channel of information open to us.[3]

On this very point of method Kant is sometimes accused of having attempted to achieve the impossible task of determining, apart altogether from cognitive mental experience, and by a study of the mind exclusively in the state in which it must be antecedently to and apart from such experience,—

---

[1] " Peut-être quelque Dieu avait pû me donner une telle nature que je me trompasse même touchant les choses qui me semblent les plus manifestes."—DESCARTES, *Ire Méditation*, iii., nn. 34-6, *apud* MERCIER, *op. cit.*, p. 82. Cf. *Ire Méditation*, ix., 14, *ibid.*, p. 65.

[2] Cf. MERCIER, *op. cit.*, § 42, p. 86.

[3] Cf. *ibid.*, p. 87.

what the conditions are which the mind must fulfil in order that it may be capable of having cognitive experience at all (5). His way of formulating the general problem of knowledge may perhaps have laid him open to such a charge ; but it seems to us that he did not really attempt the impossible task of exploring a faculty apart from its activities. Rather what he attempted was, by studying and analysing the characteristics of human cognitive experience as he found it, *e.g.* the necessary and universal character of scientific judgments, etc., to work back to a knowledge of what the nature of the knowing subject must be, and what the subjective factors with which it must be conceived to be endowed, in order that it be capable of having the sort of cognitive experience which we find that it has *de facto*. If this be so the task is not an impossible one, whatever about Kant's success or failure in accomplishing it.

27. THE QUESTION OF METHOD IN CRITICAL INQUIRY. DOUBT AS A METHOD.—We have now seen that it is both unnecessary and unlawful for the knowing subject to assume, at the outset of his critical investigation, as already *philosophically certain* and as therefore itself *beyond the scope of such investigation*, his own capacity to discover truth : unnecessary, because the assumption of it *as a spontaneous conviction* is sufficient for his purpose ; unlawful, because the question whether or not this spontaneous conviction will stand the test of critical reflection and emerge therefrom as a philosophical certitude is a question that must not be prejudged but investigated.

We have seen secondly, however, that it is both lawful and necessary for him to retain provisionally throughout his investigation this spontaneous conviction *as a spontaneous conviction :* lawful, because its retention does not prejudge any critical problem ; necessary, because, this belief once *really lost*, thought is paralysed and investigation rendered impossible. And we have seen too that it is possible to start in possession of this spontaneous conviction because the difficulties that may occur at this initial stage are unavailing to deprive us of it by establishing in our minds a *real* and *serious* doubt in regard to this capacity.

What about all our other spontaneous beliefs and convictions ? Are we to retain them also as spontaneous beliefs and convictions ? Are we to continue to foster these convictions throughout our investigations, and to hold on to them as objectively valid and true as long as we fail to discover, by reflecting on them individually or by classes, good and valid reasons for doubting the truth of any individual conviction or class of convictions ? Our answer is that we certainly ought to do so ; and this is the only reasonable attitude of mind to adopt in regard to them.

How then, it may be asked, are we to investigate them? *Ex hypothesi* our task is to test them, to examine them critically by reflective thought, in order to find out whether they are really and objectively valid and true. But in order to do so must we not doubt them? How can we test them without holding them as questionable, as possibly groundless and illusory? And how is this questioning, interrogative attitude, this holding them as possibly false and as calling for justification,—compatible with our retaining the genuine spontaneous conviction we had hitherto entertained as to their objective validity and truth?

These are fair questions for consideration. They are also important questions of method. And it is imperative that the student should think his way clearly and candidly through them. Our spontaneous convictions are all convictions of the truth of individual judgments. We must see, therefore, whether we can entertain about the truth of a judgment any sort of doubt compatible with our spontaneous conviction that the judgment in question is true.

It is plain that while we are convinced that a judgment is true we cannot *really* doubt it, we cannot entertain a *real* doubt about it by judging *that it is really doubtful.* But perhaps we can freely determine, for some ulterior motive, to *regard it for the time as if it were doubtful,*—for the sake of re-examining the validity of the grounds on which we have assented to it, and the possible difficulties against it or grounds for doubting it? Such a doubt would be what is called a *methodic,* or a fictitious, simulated, supposititious, hypothetical doubt,—to distinguish it from a real or absolute doubt. Let us compare and illustrate those two sorts of doubt.

28. REAL DOUBT AND "METHODIC" DOUBT COMPARED. "METHODIC" DOUBT NEVER REAL. "NEGATIVE METHODIC" DOUBT.—Suppose I find the following statement made by a French astronomer:[1] "We can assert, without overstepping the conclusions warranted by the present condition of astronomical science, that although life has not yet been actually observed on the surface of any of the planets, nevertheless the most decisive reasons oblige us to hold that life does actually exist on many of them". I doubt *really* that the reasons referred to are decisive, and I doubt *really* that the planets are inhabited. Suppose I

---

[1] J. JANSSEN, *Les Époques dans l'histoire astronomique des planètes—apud* MERCIER, *op. cit.,* p. 67.

open a treatise on geometry and find in it this assertion : " If two angles of a triangle are equal, the sides opposite the equal angles are equal ".   I can freely determine to regard the statement for the moment as doubtful, not that I really doubt it, but because I want to recall or to discover the intrinsic reasons, which happen not to be here and now present to my mind, why the theorem in question is really true.   I look on it for the moment as if it were doubtful,—and for a purpose, as a method of investigating the grounds of its truth.   My doubt is *methodic.*

The first observable difference between those two doubts is that the former is not a matter of choice.   It imposes itself upon me necessarily.   However I may wish it were really true that the other planets were inhabited by organic and intelligent living beings so that the work of creation would be thus more sublime and grandiose, still my present knowledge forces me to remain in doubt on the point through lack of adequate reasons for conviction.   But in the second case my doubt is a matter of choice. I freely determine to regard the theorem for the moment as if it were doubtful, and I do so as a means to setting about proving it to myself.

Another observable difference between the two states is that the former is simpler psychologically than the latter.   In the former the whole state of mind consists in an attitude of doubt, an absence of conviction or firm adherence, in regard to the judgment " The other planets are inhabited ".   In the latter, however, the mental state is complex.   When, in order to prove a theorem of geometry, in order to reconsider the grounds for assenting to it, I decide to regard it for the time *as if it were* really doubtful, I have on the one hand *my habitual firm belief or conviction that it is true,*—whether because I remember having once proved it myself, or because of my habitual knowledge that the theorems of geometry are universally accepted as certain, and my implicit confidence in the authority of mathematicians.   But on the other hand I freely hold it for the moment as doubtful or questionable in order that by questioning it I may consider the grounds on account of which it must be held to be true ; and I do so *because for the moment these grounds are not here and now actually before me.*   It is to this complex attitude of mind, this combination of habitual, implicit certitude with actual, explicit doubt or questioning, that the title " *methodic* doubt " properly belongs.

Of course there arise out of our experience many questions and problems in regard to which we have not entertained spontaneous *convictions*, but only *opinions*, or even only an attitude of *ignorance* or of *negative doubt* (7), when we come to examine such questions critically ; and the *purely interrogative* attitude we assume for the purpose of exploring these might also be called, and has been called, *methodic doubt*, though it has no implicit conviction accompanying it.

The practice, however, of describing methodic doubt as a "negative doubt" may cause confusion. And the assertion that methodic doubt may be sometimes real, as distinct from simulated, is still more misleading.[1] Both Jeannière and Mercier speak of the initial doubt which it is legitimate to entertain regarding the aptitude of the mind to discover truth, as a "negative doubt". When there are positive reasons for doubting a given judgment our doubt will be either real or simulated according as we allow these reasons to prevent us from giving a firm assent to the judgment, or merely to induce us to examine these reasons while continuing to assent to the judgment. The important question is whether the doubt we ought to entertain about the aptitude of our mind to discover truth, at the outset of critical inquiry, and which these authors describe as a "negative doubt," does or does not, in their view, leave us in possession of our spontaneous conviction that the mind really has this aptitude. If it does,—and we believe this to be their view,—then it is not a real but a simulated doubt.

Here is Mercier's description of the doubt in question : "At the outset of the reflective work whereby the philosopher explores the nature of certain knowledge he has no right to *deny* or *declare doubtful*, any more than he has to *affirm*, the *aptitude of his faculties to reach a certain knowledge of truth*. Before it has reflected on its *acts*, and thus examined their nature, human reason does not and cannot know whether or not the exercise of its powers will lead it to truth. Hence the initial attitude of *reflecting reason* in regard to the *power* of our cognitive *faculties* is *deliberate ignorance, abstention* ('*ignorance voulue*,' '*abstention*').

[1] *Cf. e.g.* JEANNIÈRE, *op. cit.*, p. 112 : "Dubium *methodicum* (quod aliquando reale est, et aliquando fictum) est illud quod pendet ab aliqua hypothesi voluntarie inducta, et quod adhibetur tanquam medium aptum ad aliquam cognitionem obtinendam". But a *real* doubt, which the same author defines (p. 111) as "suspensio judicii . . . eo quod motiva determinationem mentis vere impediunt," cannot be assumed *ad libitum* or by the mere wish to adopt it. Such real doubt is, moreover, neither useful nor necessary as a means to reaching reflex certitude. A real doubt is real suspension of assent : because there are not *sufficient* reasons on either side of the contradictory to determine the assent to either side. Now if we *really* doubt this judgment, "*The mind is capable of discovering truth*," the withholding of our assent must be due to the presence of *positive* but insufficient reasons on both sides. This is a *positive* doubt, and in regard to this particular judgment JEANNIÈRE rightly says that such a doubt is almost impossible psychologically and wholly unjustifiable logically : "relate ad valorem facultatis in genere vix est psychologice possibilis nec potest logice justificari " (*ibid.*, p. 110).

" But this freely willed ignorance is not the universal methodic doubt which we have found to be self-contradictory in the case of Descartes.

" No; the ignorance we profess here is a *negative* doubt ; through lack of reasons for or against our cognitive *faculties* we systematically refuse to pronounce either for or against them.   Descartes on the contrary was far from suspending judgment on the aptitude of his senses and reason, for he called in arguments both of fact and of principle to proclaim the aptitude of human reason doubtful.

" Manifestly, between this wholly *negative* attitude of him who *refrains from prejudging* whether our faculties can lead us to truth and the attitude of him who *judges positively* that their trustworthiness *is doubtful*, there is an abyss of difference. . . .[1]

" We have no right to declare or to suppose by artifice in advance that human reason is *incapable* of leading us to truth.

" Neither have we the right to judge in advance that human reason is *capable* of leading us to truth.

" At the threshold of epistemology the inquirer must *abstain* from prejudging the *capacity* or the *incapacity* of our cognitive faculties ; on this point he should maintain a *deliberately willed ignorance* [*' ignorance voulue '*]. This state of mind is a universal *negative* doubt.   It is even more.   For a negative doubt implies powerlessness to judge, through lack of objective motives ; it is an attitude enforced on the subject.   But the state of freely willed ignorance which we demand for the inquirer in regard to the trustworthiness of our *faculties* does not spring from powerlessness ; it is a well-grounded law to which he must freely submit himself in order to escape acting from mere caprice." [2]

The general drift of these passages we take to be that the inquirer, at the outset of his investigations, should not allow any positive reasons or difficulties he may have encountered against the aptitude of his faculties to determine him to judge positively that their aptitude is doubtful and themselves not be trusted ; that while conscious that there are difficulties against their aptitude he should retain his spontaneous conviction that the aptitude is really there ; that while recognizing that this spontaneous conviction does not amount to reflex, reasoned knowledge or certitude, he should proceed open-mindedly to exercise his faculties with a view to testing them, of exploring and removing if he can all difficulties against their aptitude, and so reaching reflex certitude on the point.   But what are we to understand by calling this initial attitude a *negative* doubt ?

A negative doubt in the strict sense is the suspension of our assent to some judgment—say "A is B,"—or to its contradictory, "A is not B," *through a total or almost total lack of reasons on either side* (7).   Hence, it is regarded as practically equivalent to ignorance, or as barely removed from ignorance. But such a state of mind is *a real doubt*, a real suspension of assent.   The mind really refrains from judging that "A is B," or that "A is not B".   It does not form or assent to any judgment about "A " ; but neither would it in *positive* doubt.   The only difference between this state and positive doubt is that in the latter the mind withholds its assent *after* it has judged the grounds of assent to be insufficient, and *because* it has deemed them insufficient, whereas in the former it has no grounds to consider at all, or none worth considering, and hence it suspends its assent simply because it has nothing to influence it. It is equally true to say in both cases that the mind regards the judgment "A is B" as "doubtful" : for such predicates as "doubtful," "uncertain," "probable," "certain," applied in this way to a judgment, really refer not to the judgment in itself but to the attitude of the mind towards the judgment ; and in both cases, in positive and in negative doubt alike, the mind is really in doubt and really does not assent to the judgment. Both are *simple* states of mind ; and both alike are incompatible with a real conviction, even with a *spontaneous* conviction, that the judgment is true. This proposition, " The aptitude of my mind to discover truth is doubtful (or ' uncertain ')," can have for me no other meaning than this, that " I am doubtful, or uncertain, whether the judgment ' My mind is capable of discovering truth ' is a true judgment," whatever others may think of the aptitude of their minds. And if I *were* doubtful or uncertain of the truth of this latter judgment, whether because of insufficiency of positive reasons for it as compared with positive reasons against it (positive doubt), or because of my ignorance of any reasons or motives concerning it (negative doubt), it is plain that I could not at the same time have a spontaneous conviction of its truth.[1]

Now the "negative doubt" which Mercier adopts in regard to the aptitude of the mind to discover truth cannot be the negative doubt we have just described, for this latter is a *real* doubt, incompatible with even spontaneous conviction. We say this not because we think that such a *real and negative* doubt, or the mere absence of a spontaneous conviction that the mind is capable of discovering truth, would be fatal to critical investigation : it would not, for the mere exercise of the mind in the process of investigation, *e.g.* in examining assents to self-evident judgments, would very soon produce such conviction : it is only if we had convinced ourselves that our minds were *untrustworthy*, and thus found ourselves *disbelieving* in their aptitude, that we should have to put away this paralysing condition before we could reasonably proceed to exercise our faculties at all (*cf.* § 25). We say so rather because we think that such a *merely negative and real* doubt about *this particular matter* is psychologically impossible. We can have such a doubt only about a subject with which we are unfamiliar, a matter about which we know so little that we have practically no reasons worth considering for saying " yes " or " no " to any definite question about it.[2] Now if the subject is our

---

[1] Suppose a person were to attempt to set out by *assenting* himself, and claiming that all inquirers should assent with him, to this judgment as *true* : " The aptitude of the human mind in general to discover truth is uncertain," or to the same judgment in these terms, " The human mind is not to be trusted," his attitude would not be *positive doubt* about the aptitude of the mind, but *positive disbelief* in this aptitude : it would be that self-contradictory form of absolute scepticism which is not to be argued with. We refer to it only to dismiss it. *Cf. infra*, § 37.

[2] There are many subjects on which questions might be proposed which we should have no option of meeting otherwise than by a genuinely negative doubt—owing to our ignorance about such subjects. Now this negative doubt or mere ignorance would not be an obstacle to investigation. But that is the most that can be said of it. It would not be properly described as a " method " of investigation, or an attitude adopted for the sake of investigation. We pass from ignorance, and from the negative doubt involved therein, to knowledge : it is the necessary fore-

own mind, and if the question is its aptitude to discover truth, manifestly we have not here the conditions for a negative doubt. What is more familiar to us than our own mind? Have we not been exercising it from the dawn of reason, inquiring, believing, doubting, blundering and correcting blunders, falling into error and extricating ourselves, experiencing reasons both for trusting and for distrusting it? Clearly, at the threshold of critical investigation, recalling those reasons, we must find ourselves either (1) still firmly convinced of its aptitude notwithstanding the experiences we may have had of its playing us false, or else (2) doubting and distrusting it *on account of those experiences, i.e. positively*. This latter unfortunate attitude, of *real and positive* doubt may, perhaps, be a psychological possibility. But a real and *negative* doubt in the sense described is surely a psychological impossibility.

There is, however, another state of mind which may, perhaps, be called a "*negative* doubt"; but it will be a negative and *methodic* or *simulated* doubt, not a real suspension of assent, not a real abandonment of spontaneous conviction; and it is the state of mind really described both by Mercier and by Jeannière. We may be spontaneously convinced, certain, that a given judgment is true. But we may see at the same time that there are difficulties against it, reasons on the other side. Jeannière applies this to the aptitude of our minds to discover truth : "Qui negative dubitat," he writes,[1] "de valore facultatis suae habet validas rationes cur ei diffidat [serious reasons for distrusting it]. Attamen, ex una parte, hae rationes, non sunt sat firmae, ut eum impediant quominus suam facultatem pro recte conformata certo teneat [as Newman says somewhere, 'a hundred difficulties don't make one doubt'] ; at, ex altera parte, *sat firmae sunt ut eam impellant ad certitudines suas crisi subjiciendas*, seu ad quaestionem ponendam : numquid id quod verum teneo est verum ? quaenam certitudines sunt verae ?" That is, the inquirer holds for certain that his mind is capable of reaching truth, and goes on to make this certitude reflex and reasoned by a reflective analysis in which he will examine the difficulties. To make the matter clearer the author continues[2] : "In *negative* doubt, there are real reasons, serious reasons even, for doubting, but they are not decisive. [Hence they do not *succeed* in making the inquirer doubt ; and if they did his doubt would be real *and positive*.] Consequently in negative doubt the certitude which is the object of the doubt, and on which the inquiry is going to centre, remains ; he does not despair of it, on the contrary he is confident that he will be able to justify it before the bar of reason. Pending the completion of the justifying process he continues to allow himself to be guided by his certitude. . . . The negative doubt becomes positive, if on examination, the reasons for doubting prove steadfast and unanswerable, at least subjectively." This makes quite clear the attitude described by Jeannière as "negative doubt"; and it is likewise the attitude which we believe Mercier to have described by the same title. It is the proper attitude for the critical inquirer ; but if it be called "negative doubt" we must remember that it is not a *real* doubt but a *methodic* or *simulated* doubt, *i.e.* the open-minded questioning attitude of one prepared to discuss and examine difficulties against his spontaneous certitude.

---

runner of knowledge, but hardly a *means* to knowledge or a *method* of reaching knowledge.

[1] *Op. cit.*, p. 110.   [2] *Ibid.*, n. 1.

Nevertheless Jeannière describes it as a " real" doubt,[1] alleging that in regard to the objectivity of certitude in general a simulated doubt is impossible inasmuch as here the person "doubting" "cannot divide himself as it were into two persons, the one doubting [*i.e.* inquiring], the other suggesting the elements of solution. These latter in fact are logically non-existent at the commencement of critical research and cannot be given *a priori*."[2] We must confess that these remarks seem to us unconvincing. The "elements of solution" are the facts of consciousness on which the person reflects. They were given to him in his past experience and grounded his spontaneous certitude. They are present to him when he commences to reflect on them. There is no question of logical proof, but only of psychological analysis. Why can he not on the one hand retain his spontaneous conviction as to the real objectivity of his past assents, and on the other hand proceed to investigate critically all the facts that can be adduced whether for or against that conviction?

While holding that the doubt in question is a "real" doubt, Jeannière also holds that it can be (and indeed must be) *freely willed, deliberately assumed*.[3] We have understood a real doubt to be a real *abandonment* of assent on account of positive reasons against it, or a real *inability* to elicit an assent through lack of reasons. In this sense it cannot be put on or off at will like a garment. What Jeannière—and Sentroul,[4] whose terminology he adopts—appear to have in view is a *suspension* of assent which would not be an *abandonment* of assent, an attitude wherein the spontaneous assent is really retained but deliberately held in abeyance for the purpose of investigation. This is the attitude we, too, have in mind. But we do not think that such a suspension of assent merits the title of "real" doubt.

Now since, as we have seen, our spontaneous convictions are not all necessarily true (16), it can happen in the case of an individual conviction that the *methodic* doubt, with which we started to re-examine it, may possibly become, in the process of re-examination, a *real* doubt or uncertainty (p. 32, n. 2)—on account of newly discovered reasons which appear to militate against the conviction. *But simultaneously with the doubt becoming real the spontaneous conviction is destroyed.* It is replaced by the real doubt or uncertainty; and this may in turn give place to a reasoned conviction that our former conviction was erroneous,— to a certitude opposed to the original spontaneous conviction. Or the state of real doubt may persist, for want of sufficient grounds for an assent to either side of the contradictory. Or it may give place to a more or less probable opinion of the truth of one side. Finally, even when the original spontaneous conviction was really and objectively true, it may be temporally or per-

[1] *Op. cit.*, pp. 112-14.   [2] p. 113, n. 1.   [3] p. 114.

[4] *Doute "méthodique" et doute "fictif*," by MGR. SENTROUL, in the *Revue des sciences phil. et theol.*, July, 1909,—quoted by JEANNIÈRE, *op. cit.*, pp. 112, 114 n.

manently replaced by a real doubt,—since the human mind in considering the grounds of its assents is not infallible.

Real doubt, then, is a doubt that is for the time forced upon us, *i.e.* it *cannot* occur except as a result of our thinking that the grounds for our previous conviction (if we had such) are not really sufficient to warrant that conviction, and it *must* necessarily occur as soon as we do really think so. When it does occur and is really present, so far from being a means, it is in itself an obstacle, to our reaching truth with certitude. In so far as we are under its sway we have not truth, and it is only in the measure in which we can dispel it that we can attain with certitude to truth about the question with which it is concerned. Methodic doubt is not forced upon us ; it is freely entertained, and as a method or means of reaching a reasoned or philosophic certitude.

29. LEGITIMATE USE AND LIMITS OF METHODIC DOUBT.— About this methodic doubt we have now to ask whether or in what measure it is legitimate as a method of testing critically our spontaneous assents and beliefs in epistemology ; and especially, about what judgments or classes of judgments is it possible to doubt methodically.

That such a doubt has been employed, and successfully employed, in regard to individual judgments both in the sciences and in philosophy, as a method of investigating and demonstrating the truth of those judgments, is a matter of undeniable historical fact.

The method of indirect proof, or *reductio ad impossibile*,[1] employed by Euclid to demonstrate certain theorems in geometry, is an example of it : for such proof starts from the freely conceived *supposition that the theorem in question is not true.*

Aristotle recommends this method of procedure at the commencement of the Third Book of his *Metaphysics*. In order to reach a definite solution of any question, he says, we should commence by doubting, by inquiring into all the difficulties involved in it, the ἀπορίαι, the *pros* and *cons* of the question. And not only does he use this procedure in regard to particular truths in the special sciences. He also recommends us to use it in regard to *truth in general* when we are concerned, as we are in philosophy, with truth in general.[2]

---

[1] *Cf. Science of Logic*, i. pp. 337-54 ; ii. pp. 233, 328.
[2] " Est autem attendendum quod . . . consuetudo Aristotlis fuit fere in omnibus libris suis, ut inquisitioni veritatis vel determinationi praemitteret rationes emergentes.

Again, we find it employed by St. Augustine in his dialogue with Evodius where he discusses the reconciliation of human peccability with the moral goodness of the endowment of man with free will. "He who has endowed us with free will is an All-Perfect Being above all reproach," observes the saint. "I believe all that," replies Evodius, "but as I do not understand the matter let us investigate it *as if it were uncertain.*" [1]

Any one who is familiar with the philosophical and theological literature of the mediæval Schoolmen will know that this is *the* method *par excellence* employed by them in their investigations. He will find them always formulating the judgments whose truth they wish to establish, *in the form of questions*, and proceeding to accumulate as difficulties or objections all the grounds they are aware of, which would seem *to render those judgments doubtful or even to prove them false ;* and only after having done this will he find them setting forth the reasons *for* the truth of the judgments in question, and then finally solving the difficulties. What is this procedure but the methodic doubt we have been describing? When, for instance, St. Thomas Aquinas inquires, in the First Part of the *Summa Theologica :* "Utrum anima humana sit aliquid subsistens ? Utrum anima humana sit incorruptibilis ?" he does not *really* doubt that the human soul is a substance, and is incorruptible. He has an *habitual, firm* conviction that the human soul is a substance, spiritual, immortal, etc. But he wishes deliberately to consider these judgments—for the time and for his purpose—*as if they were doubtful.* And he does so in order that he may freely and impartially examine all that can be urged for and against the truth of these judgments, in order thus to bring out fully and clearly the intrinsic grounds and reasons on account of which these judgments are to be accepted with reasoned certitude as really and objectively true. We have here, then, the complex state of mind which is characteristic of methodic doubt, the attitude of habitual certitude combined with an actual freely entertained interrogative or questioning attitude.

Sed in aliis libris singillatim ad singulas determinationes praemittit dubitationes : hic vero simul praemittit omnes dubitationes, et postea secundum ordinem debitum determinat veritatem. Cujus ratio est, quod aliae scientiae considerant particulariter de veritate : unde et particulariter ad eas pertinet circa singulas veritates dubitare : sed ista scientia sicut habet universalem considerationem de veritate, ita etiam ad eam pertinet universalis dubitatio de veritate : et ideo non particulariter, sed simul universalem dubitationem prosequitur."—ST. THOMAS, *in III. Met.*, lect. I.

[1] *De Libero Arbitrio,* Lib. II., cap. ii.—*apud* MERCIER, *op. cit.*, p. 70.

About what classes of judgments is it possible and necessary to conceive this methodic doubt?

To answer this question let us first recall the fact that it is possible to entertain a *real* doubt [1] about such judgments, and only about such judgments, as to which we think that we have not sufficient grounds and motives to warrant a certain or firm assent : about such judgments the attitude of *uncertainty* is not only possible but right and proper, whether this attitude be a mere negative doubt arising from absence of grounds on either side, or a positive doubt arising from equality of grounds on both sides, or a more or less probable assent arising from preponderance of grounds on one side. And, of course, this attitude of *real* uncertainty about a judgment serves the purpose of investigating the truth or falsity of it equally well with a mere methodic doubt.

We can have a *methodic* doubt in the strict sense only about judgments which we really believe to be true. The question now is, *Can* we, or *ought* we to, entertain a methodic doubt about *all* such judgments? It is obvious that as long as we really believe them to be true we cannot entertain a *real* doubt about them. First, then, *ought* we, or is it *necessary* for us, to conceive a methodic doubt about *all* our spontaneous convictions without exception? Well it seems that we ought at least to *try to do so*. And the reason is that *ex hypothesi* we are embarking on the task of critically re-examining *all* our spontaneous belief and convictions, *all* our supposed knowledge, in order to see whether or how far it will stand the test of such critical reflection and emerge into reflex or philosophical certitude. And hence we must *try* to adopt the *questioning attitude* towards *all our assents without exception*.

But *can we succeed* in taking up this questioning attitude towards *all* of them? Is it physically (or psychically) possible to do so? Let us see. With regard to what we have called our freely formed convictions (11) there seems to be no difficulty. Neither is there with regard to mediate judgments [10(3), (4)], the cogent evidence for which is not here and now present to the mind, nor with regard to judgments accepted on extrinsic evidence [10 (5)]. All these we can regard as questionable for the purpose of reviewing critically the grounds of our assent to them. But what about trying to question, by methodic doubt, those

[1] *I.e.* an attitude of *real uncertainty*. *Cf.* p. 32, n. 2, above.

convictions which we have described as irresistible (11) or as immediately evident [10 (1), (2)]? Is it possible for me, I will not
say to doubt *really*, but even to adopt the questioning attitude of
treating and considering *as if they were doubtful*, such judgments
as " Two and two are four," " I am writing," " The sun is now
shining," " The same thing cannot be both true and false " ?
Well, I may *try* to suppose that " Two and two are perhaps not
four," or to ask " Are two and two four ? " But I find the supposition forthwith stifled, and the question forthwith answered in
the affirmative, by the very presence of the thought of these
numbers in my mind. I may try to doubt that I am writing, to
treat the judgment " I am writing " as questionable ; but I find
that, try as I may, I cannot. While basking in the full blaze of
the Summer sun at noonday I may try to treat the question " Is
the sun here and now shining ? " as serious ; but I cannot, for the
question answers itself. And so on

Why can we not treat such judgments as if they were doubtful ? Because *the immediate and cogent evidence of their truth is
actually present to our minds.* And for this same reason we do
not *need* to treat them as doubtful, to doubt them methodically.
We have recourse to the plan or method of regarding a judgment
as doubtful only in order to *demonstrate* it, *i.e.* to bring before
our minds the grounds for its truth ; but in the case of cogent,
self-evident judgments those grounds are already present to the
mind.

Hence it would appear that while we may legitimately try
to make this simulated or methodic doubt *universal,* we cannot
really succeed in doing so.

Yet this does not appear quite satisfactory, nor is it indeed
the last word on the question. For, as we have seen (25), it is
quite possible and legitimate to doubt methodically about the
capacity of the mind to discover any truth,—and that it is even
necessary to do so, inasmuch as this capacity has been denied by
many and needs to be investigated. But does not this methodic
doubt about the *capacity* of the mind involve—*de jure* and *de facto*
—a similar methodic doubt about *all* the cognitive *acts* of the
mind, and therefore about the real objective validity or real
truth-value of the irresistible and self-evident judgments just referred to ?

We seem, therefore, to have reached mutually contradictory
conclusions : that there are certain classes of judgments (*viz.* im-

mediately evident or self-evident judgments) which we cannot hold as questionable, or regard as if they were doubtful, even though we may try to do so ; and that we can, as a method, take up this attitude towards *all* judgments without exception. The contradiction, however, is not real but apparent. For "the possibility of questioning them, or regarding them as if they were doubtful," refers in the two alternatives to two distinct aspects of the judgments in question.

What is really unquestionable about those self-evident judgments is *first*, the consciously experienced mental fact that our assent to them is compelled. I am compelled to think that " two and two are four," that " I am writing," that " the sun is shining," etc. It would be *impossible* to regard this fact as questionable, for it is unquestionable, it is one of the data of our inquiry,—a fact of consciousness. It would also be *meaningless and absurd* to hold it as questionable, to doubt methodically about it : the only reason for doing so would be in order to verify it, but it does not need verification, for it is an experienced fact. *Secondly*, this too is unquestionable, beyond the possibility even of methodic doubt, and beyond all need of methodic doubt : the fact that we believe spontaneously that assent to such self-evident judgments gives us a hold on reality, puts us into possession of truth about reality.

Now when we say that it is impossible and superfluous to doubt methodically about self-evident judgments, what we mean is that it is impossible and superfluous to doubt methodically that they are mental facts which we spontaneously consider as putting us into possession of real truth. That and no more. And when Descartes observed that he could not doubt in any way, really or methodically, about his own existence as revealed in the fact of his actual thinking—" *Cogito ergo sum*,"—he really allowed this at least : that he could not doubt in any way about such self-evident judgments *considered as mental facts to the representative or truth-character of which his assent was spontaneously compelled*,[1] for as such they were part of what constituted his very thinking itself.

But now, consistently with all this, is it not possible to doubt methodically, to regard as questionable, the validity of this very truth-claim itself, even of those self-evident judgments? Note

---

[1] Did he also recognize and admit the *real objectivity* of the intuitive judgment in question ?   *Cf. infra*, §§ 31, 96.

that we say to doubt *methodically*, not really. And we answer that it is certainly possible to do so. We may go farther and say that it is necessary to do so ; for the nature and validity of this very truth-claim of self-evident judgments are among the chief problems of epistemology : and how can we investigate them without doubting methodically the validity of this truth-claim ? Two and two are indeed four ; but while I am spontaneously convinced that these numbers, " two " and " four," and all numbers generally, are not exclusively subjective products of my mental activity (23, *a*), but reveal extramental reality, that the necessity of two and·two being four does not arise exclusively from the constitution of my mind (*ibid., b*), that my assent is not compelled by purely subjective propensities, etc. (*ibid., c*), may I not hold these convictions of mine as open to investigation in order to vindicate them against the objections and attacks of subjectivism? I am indeed writing ; but while I am convinced that this judgment informs me of the real existence of a material pen, ink, and paper independently of my perceiving them (*ibid., a*), may I not, for the purpose of justifying this conviction, regard it as questionable, *i.e.* doubt it methodically? And so of the judgment that " the sun is shining," and of all other self-evident judgments, whether they be abstract or concrete, whether the immediate evidence for them be of the intellect or of the senses.[1]

We see then that it is indeed possible to extend our methodic or simulated doubt, even to self-evident judgments. But in regard to these latter what we may hold as questionable is not their existence as mental events of the cognitive order, or the fact that our assent to them is compelled, or the fact that we spontaneously believe them to give us a genuine insight into extra-subjective or extramental reality : under these aspects they are beyond all possibility and need of methodic doubt or questioning. What we may and must doubt methodically is *their significance* in relation to reality, or in other words the validity of our spontaneous conviction that they do give us a genuine insight

---

[1] *Cf.* JEANNIÈRE, *op. cit.*, p. 118 : " It is objected [against the possibility of a universal methodic doubt] that there are propositions . . . which I am forced to admit, nay, which I must admit in the very fact of denying them verbally. Of course ; but are these propositions objective ? Does the fact that I am forced to admit them prove anything ? Is this psychological necessity a mark of objectivity ? I don't know, I doubt it and *consider it worthy of investigation* (= negative doubt)."

into reality. And finally it must be borne in mind that this doubt is only a methodic or simulated doubt, not a real doubt.

In criticizing the doubt formulated by Descartes, Mercier [1] clearly expresses the view that a genuinely methodic doubt cannot be universal. "The expression ' universal methodic doubt ' is," he says, " self-contradictory. If the doubt is methodic it leaves room for certitude and supposes this latter in its habitual state ; if it was universal [with Descartes], striking the very faculty itself in its root, it must have been real." And a methodic doubt, as explained, is contrasted with a real doubt and cannot be itself real. On the other hand, Jeannière teaches that the methodic doubt with which we approach the critical investigation of knowledge, can be and must be universal, must extend to all our spontaneous convictions without exception.[2] Yet both authors are in substantial agreement as to the *universality* of the interrogative or questioning attitude of mind in which the inquirer must approach the problems of epistemology. What they very properly reject as an unlawful and impossible method is the Cartesian attitude of universal and *positive* doubt which would really destroy all spontaneous convictions and induce absolute scepticism. And they are agreed that it is both possible and necessary to extend a methodic doubt, *which will not destroy these convictions*, even to *self-evident* judgments ; recognizing, however, that in the case of these latter judgments the methodic doubt—which concerns their *real objectivity*—commences to give place to reflex certitude as soon as we commence to reflect on the grounds of our spontaneous assent to them.[3]

The " doubt " which it is lawful and necessary to employ as a method is rightly described as a *universal, simulated* doubt.

Such a doubt is, of course, lawfully applicable to judgments based on authority no less than to those based on intrinsic evidence, to the assents of faith no less than to the assents of science. The former no less than the latter have to be justified before the bar of reflecting reason : only if they can be so justified is religious faith a *rationabile obsequium*, a "reasonable service".[4] The believing Christian cannot, of course, compatibly with his belief, entertain a real and positive doubt about the fact or the contents of the Christian Revelation ; but he may lawfully adopt the inquiring attitude of methodic doubt in regard to them. The Christian apologist has to do so ; he has to *examine* his religious beliefs, to *investigate* the grounds of their credibility, to meet objections and discuss difficulties, so that he may *see* with reflex, reasoned, philosophic certitude, that the objects of his religious beliefs are such that they *can* be and *ought* to be believed. *Non crederem*, he should be prepared to say with St. Thomas,[5] *nisi credendum esse viderim*. But to examine, interrogate, explore, discuss one's religious beliefs is not to sacrifice or abandon them. And should the Catholic inquirer, in the course of this process, encounter what appear to him to be sufficient reasons for conceiving a *real* doubt about anything which he thinks himself bound as a Catholic to believe, his

[1] *Op. cit.*, § 34, pp. 71-4.
[2] *Op. cit.*, pp. 112-14. He also describes the doubt in question as a " real " but " negative " doubt. For criticism of these epithets, *cf. supra*, § 28.
[3] JEANNIÈRE, *op. cit.*, pp. 112-13. *Cf. infra*, § 32.   [4] Rom. xii. 1.
[5] *Apud* JEANNIÈRE, *op. cit.*, p. 151 n.

duty is to persevere patiently, reverently, humbly, reconsidering his own mental estimates, judgments, reasonings, etc., on all the relevant issues, in the confidence that in due time the difficulties will disappear.

30. DESCARTES' EMPLOYMENT OF REAL DOUBT AS A METHOD.—We have seen already (25-6) that if *per impossibile* a *real* doubt were to become *universal*, as it would, for example, were it to extend to the very capacity of the mind to attain to any truth, it would *eo ipso* paralyse thought and render all investigation impossible. Descartes seems to have seriously misconceived the method of critical investigation by his mode of employing doubt as a method. The doubt he actually employed was a *real* doubt, a doubt entertained, as he said himself, "for very strong and well-weighed reasons,"[1] a positive doubt, therefore, which, so far as it went, destroyed of necessity his hitherto spontaneously entertained conviction or certitude in regard to the judgments so doubted. In trying to push this real doubt as far as possible he claimed that he could and did include in it even the simplest and most self-evident judgments, those based on the immediate testimony of the senses and those which impose themselves irresistibly on the intellect.

The *possibility* of doubting *really* about the ordinary interpretation which men put upon the *testimony of their senses* may indeed be admitted :[2] it is at least intelligible : whether it is prudent or justifiable is another question.

[1] " Pour des raisons très fortes et mûrement réfléchies "—1re *Méditation*, ix. In undertaking thus to subject his spontaneous convictions to a *real* doubt, as a method for testing them, and to make this doubt universal if possible (*e.g.* by doubting the very aptitude of his mind to discover any truth), Descartes expressly exempted from the scope of his investigation the truths of faith, the moral and religious teachings of Christianity. He saw, of course, that as a Catholic, as a believer in revealed religion, he was not at liberty to foster a *real* doubt about the truths of his faith. But it is regrettable that he did not see the necessity of seeking for a method whereby they too could be critically investigated and justified; or, in other words, of showing that just as the certitude of science is justified on grounds of *evidence*, so the certitude of faith is justified on grounds of *credibility*. His failure to do so prompted the inference that religious belief is in no way *rationally justifiable*, and fostered the unfortunate tendency to make all religious belief a matter of the heart, the will, the emotions, etc.—a tendency which culminated in Kant's distinction between the *speculative* and the *practical* reason.—*Cf.* JEANNIÈRE, *op. cit.*, pp. 144, 149-50.

[2] I can and do doubt, he writes, " that I am here sitting at the fire . . . holding this paper in my hands . . . deliberately stretching out my hand and feeling it with my other hand," etc. (1re *Méditation*, ix., 14-15). And among the reasons he gives (*ibid.*, *cf.* 6me *Méditation*, ix., 61) is that " I remember having been often deceived when asleep by similar dream illusions ". He did not doubt that he had these experiences, whether sleeping or waking. What he did doubt was whether it

But how Descartes could have doubted really, seriously, and positively such judgments as that "two and three added together will always make five, or that the square will never have more than four sides . . . or even simpler judgments than these if such can be imagined"[1]—that indeed has been a puzzle to many of those who try to follow and piece out the sequence of his thought. For he claimed to have successfully included in this *real* doubt *all* immediate judgments of the ideal order [10, (2), (3)], including even the *Principle of Contradiction* itself.

Some would hold that Descartes was here the victim of what we may call a psychological illusion: that he only imagined, or wrongly persuaded himself, that he was really doubting judg ments which he did not really doubt, and which he could not have really doubted, inasmuch as it is psychologically impossible really to doubt such judgments.[2] And they hold further that if he did really doubt such judgments he was doing such violence to his reason, *by thus resisting cogent evidence,*[3] that if he had yielded, or as long as he yielded, to this real doubt, his power of thought was utterly paralysed and all investigation rendered meaningless. What meaning, they ask, can rational investigation have for a man who really doubts the *Principle of Contradiction,* and thus seriously thinks that the same identical judgment can be both true and false? And to prove that Descartes did not really doubt such a judgment as the *Principle of Contradiction,* though he professed (and perhaps imagined) that he did seriously doubt it, they point out how, inconsistently with his professions (and perhaps persuasion) of real doubt, he never ceased for a moment *to utilize* the *Principle of Contradiction* (and other immediate judgments of the ideal order), *to think* and *judge* and *reason* and *investigate* according to it, *on the basis of its being really true.* So that the real doubt which Descartes tried to make universal, and in which he thought he had succeeded in embracing absolutely every opinion, belief, and conviction, right up to the ultimate fact by which alone he thought his doubt was for the first time successfully resisted,—the fact of his own exist-

---

is possible to justify the distinction between dreaming and waking experiences, and more especially whether or how it is possible to justify our belief that the waking experiences reveal to us an extramental reality. We believe that a real doubt about this possibility is unjustified. But this position of ours has to be established. Obviously the whole topic is one for legitimate *methodic* doubt and investigation.

[1] *Discours de la Méthode,* 4me partie, vi., 32.

[2] *Cf.* MERCIER, *op. cit.,* § 41, p. 85.   [3] *Ibid.,* § 30, p. 63, n. 1.

ence as revealed in his own actual doubting, " *Cogito ergo sum*,"
—did not in effect and in reality embrace all that Descartes
thought he had involved in it: for it left untouched and un-
assailed not alone the "ultimate fact" of his own existence as
thinking or doubting, but also the *Principle of Contradiction*, and
indeed all immediately evident judgments of the ideal order:
which judgments Descartes, notwithstanding all his professions
of real doubt, never for a moment hesitated to act on, and to
make use of, in his speculations. This line of interpretation and
criticism is intelligible and suggestive as far as it goes, but it does
not get quite to the bottom of the matter.

When Descartes professed that he really doubted these ideal
judgments, in what sense did he understand them? What sense
or meaning of them could he have really doubted? We have
distinguished above (29) between such judgments as mental
events, as what we may call compulsory mental syntheses of
intra-mental or intra-subjective objects (20), and the significance
of such judgments as claiming an extra-subjective or real objectivity, as giving a genuine insight into reality and thus embodying *truth*. Now it is scarcely credible that Descartes could
have really doubted that such judgments are indeed compulsorily
formed and assented to by the mind, at least as mere mental
syntheses of which he, the thinking subject, was conscious, and
of which every thinking subject is conscious: two and two are
necessarily conceived as four by every sane thinking subject:
two and two are necessarily four *in* and *to* the thinking subject
or mind; nor is there any reason to believe that Descartes did or
could think otherwise.[1] But he could really doubt, and may have
really doubted, whether this necessary mental synthesis of
" 2 + 2 = 4," and other similar syntheses, gave him any insight

---

[1] *Cf.* MERCIER, *op. cit.*, § 50, pp. 102-3 : " The real problem of certitude centres
in our discovering whether the state of certitude has for adequate cause an irresistible propensity of the thinking subject, or is, on the contrary, objectively *motived*.

" Of course there are primordial propositions which it is impossible to deny,
inasmuch as their denial implicitly involves their affirmation : such, for instance, is
the principle of contradiction. But the sceptic is not concerned to contest such
facts of consciousness. The real question between him and ourselves is not whether
we experience assents that are spontaneously irresistible and psychologically undeniable, for he admits that we do and that they form the very data of the problem.
The question is to determine the cause of these assents, to find out whether the undeniable necessity of affirming such or such a spontaneously certain proposition is
wholly caused by the constitution of the thinking subject, or is due to the determining influence of an objective cause." *Cf. supra*, § 23.

into anything other than his own subjective thought-process itself.

Possibly this important distinction, which was afterwards made explicit by Kant, may not have been explicitly before the mind of Descartes.[1] But at all events it suggests a sense in which the latter could have *really* doubted the *objective truth* of those immediate judgments of the ideal order.[2] And anyhow it is here imperative to inquire in what sense Descartes did understand those ideal judgments *when he continued*, as he did, *to make use of them ;* and furthermore to inquire whether, or how, or where, he passed from the mere consciousness of his own thinking and doubting, from the mere *cogitatio* as a fact of purely subjective awareness, to the assertion of anything extra-subjective or real.

31. CRITICISM OF DESCARTES' DOUBT.—In examining these points we are less concerned to get at the real thought of Descartes than to get a clear view of the issues raised.[3] It is evident that if Descartes accepted and utilized these immediate ideal judgments only as subjective mental syntheses,[4] while really doubting that they had any valid extra-subjective or real reference, and at the same time regarded the whole content of his mental experience, the whole domain of thought which he tried to interpret in accordance with them, merely and exclusively as the phenomenon of his own subjectivity, as the thought or *cogitatio* of himself as *subjectum cogitans*,[5]—then the intuition [6] of him-

---

[1] Hence some critics of Descartes, aware of the importance assumed by this distinction through the influence of Kant, are at a loss to determine whether Descartes understood the "content of the clear and distinct idea" (which he propounded as the supreme criterion of truth) in the subjective or in the objective sense. *Cf.* ZIGLIARA, *Logica Critica* (54), iv. ; (65), ii., iii. JEANNIÈRE, *op. cit.*, pp. 153-4. The same question arises in regard to evidence itself as a criterion of truth.

[2] And of course it raises in an acute form the old question : What is *truth ?* On the subjectivist assumption that such mental syntheses of abstract concepts or thought-objects represent or reveal nothing but the thinking subject's own subjectivity, would the necessity (and consequent universality) of such syntheses or judgments deserve the title of *truth ?* If the mind is shut up in a system of concepts evolved from its own subjectivity, and is not conformed to a system of reality, is there, or can there be, *truth ?* *Cf.* § 17, above.

[3] It would be beyond our present purpose to explore and criticize the inconsistencies of *all* the steps in Descartes' "method". For a fairly full treatment of the subject, *cf.* MERCIER, *op. cit.*, §§ 30, 31, 34, 39-42 ; JEANNIÈRE, *op. cit.*, pp. 138-58.

[4] And as "true" merely in the sense that they impose themselves compulsorily on the mind as subjective syntheses necessitating assent,—a very questionable use of the terms *true*, or *truth*.

[5] In "cogitans" Descartes included *all* conscious processes : "dubitans, intelligens, affirmans, negans, volens, nolens, imaginans quoque et sentiens "—2*me* *Méd.*

[6] The "*Cogito ergo sum*" of Descartes is not an inference. It is, he tells us, the formulation of an intuition : "I myself, the thinking, doubting subject, exist". It

self as an existing, thinking, doubting subject, could have revealed
to him only a subjective, phenomenal content, what Kant afterwards called the "empirical *Ego*," which would be not at all
anything *objectively real*, not at all the "real *Ego*".[1]   Furthermore, if he accepted and utilized them only in the subjective sense,
and really doubted about their giving him any information concerning anything distinct from his own subjectivity, in other words,
about their real objectivity and truth,—what right had he to
claim anything more than the same *purely subjective significance*
for his judgment " I exist," " *Cogito ergo sum* "?   What right had
he to assert *this* judgment not merely as a subjective mental
phenomenon, but as objectively and really true,—seeing that,
considered as a mental synthesis compelling assent, it manifests
precisely the same cogent claims to assent, neither more nor less,
which the immediate ideal judgments manifested?[2]   Both the

is a judgment which purports to attribute a predicate " exist " to a subject " I "; but
as such it goes much farther than one's mere awareness of one's conscious processes.
The mere consciousness, which is the "indubitable fundamental fact " for Descartes,
asserts nothing; the judgment which is an interpretation of it purports to assert a
known objective reality and to predicate actual existence of this reality; and in this
sense it embodies, like all judgments,—and embodies as objectively true and applicable to reality—such ideal principles as the *Principle of Identity* and the *Principle
of Contradiction*.   If Descartes really doubted the real objectivity and truth of these
principles, how could the judgment "I exist" have transformed for him the mere
subjective awareness into a knowledge of objective reality?   *Cf.* MERCIER, *op. cit.*,
p. 94, § 46.

[1] *Cf.* MERCIER, *op. cit.*, p. 84 (§ 40); MAHER, *Psychology*, p. 267.

[2] " Truths," says BALMES (*Fundamental Philosophy*, Bk. I, chap. vi., § 65), " are
of two kinds, real and ideal.   We call facts, or whatever exists, real truths.   A real
truth may be expressed by the verb *to be*, taken substantively, or at least it supposes
a proposition in which this verb has been taken in this sense: an ideal truth is expressed by the same verb taken cópulatively, as signifying the necessary relation of
a predicate to a subject, abstracting it, however, from both.   *We are*, that is, *we
exist*, expresses a real truth, a fact.   *Whoever thinks exists* expresses an ideal truth,
for it does not affirm that there is anyone who thinks or exists, but that if there is
anyone who thinks, he exists.

" Take any real truth whatsoever, the plainest and most certain fact, and yet
we can derive nothing from it if ideal truth comes not to fecundate it.   We think,
we exist, we feel; these are indubitable facts, but science can deduce nothing from
them; they are particular, contingent facts . . . [and] have not of themselves any
relation with the order of science, nor can they be elevated to it if not combined
with ideal truths.   Descartes, when he brought forward the fact of thought and existence, driven as he was by his attempt to raise a scientific edifice, passed unawares
from the real to the ideal order.   *I think*, he said; and had he stopped here he
would have reduced his philosophy to a simple intuition of consciousness; but he
wished to go farther, he wished to reason, and then of necessity availed himself of
an ideal truth: *whoever thinks exists* " (*ibid.*, § 68).   What Balmes calls here " real
truths " are interpretations of what we have described (19) as "objects of awareness," and what he calls " ideal truths " (*cf.* 10) are truths which he understands as

" *Cogito ergo sum* " and any such immediately evident judgment as the *Principle of Contradiction*, or "two and two are four," [1] must stand or fall together ; or rather they must be accepted or rejected *in the same sense*. It would be against reason to accept the former as revealing objective reality to the knowing subject, and the latter merely as revealing states or phases or products of the mind's own subjectivity, but not as revealing objective reality.

Mercier interprets [2] Descartes as claiming that the fundamen-

revealing necessary relations *in objective reality*. The presence of an object to a conscious subject is itself a mere " brute " fact, so to speak. It is the interpretation of it as an existing reality, and existing as known, as object, that is a *real truth*. Our knowledge of real truths about *other existences* is dependent on our knowledge of the real truth *of our own existence*, and reaches us through this latter knowledge. But we cannot assert the " self," of which we become aware in all conscious activity, to be real, or to exist really, without asserting *the reality of the object* revealed through this awareness ; for we become aware of the thinking subject or self, not as a subject, but as an object, and only by making it object (*cf.* 8). I can assert that " *I, the thinking subject,* exist " only because I have made that " *I, the thinking subject* " an *object* of my awareness. Therefore if I announce it as revealing to me an object which is *real* I can do so only because (*a*) I believe that the very fact of the " *I the thinking subject* " being an *object* of my awareness *implies its real existence*, implies that I can predicate of it the substantive verb "exist" ; and because (*b*) I believe that the principle of contradiction is true of objective reality. That is to say, I recognize the *objective and real* validity of my thought in asserting (*a*) a real truth (my own existence) because of the presentation of a concrete object (the empirical or experienced *Ego*) to my consciousness, and in asserting (*b*) an *ideal* truth (the principle of contradiction) because of the presence of an abstract relation of objects to my intelligence. It was only on condition of thus recognizing the objective and real validity of thought that Descartes could have utilized the intuition of his own existence as a principle from which to infer anything (*cf.* JEANNIÈRE, *op. cit.*, pp. 154-5).

But perhaps the " object " of which I, the thinking subject, become aware in adverting to my own thinking, and which I spontaneously take to be, or to reveal, the real thinking subject, is not, or does not reveal, the real thinking subject, the real self at all ? In other words, perhaps the " object "-self, or the " known " self, is not really identical with, or really representative of, the " subject "-self or the " real " self, but is only a subjectively formed and subjectively coloured mental substitute of the latter ? And similarly, perhaps the other " objects " of which I, the thinking subject, become aware, and which I spontaneously take to be, or to reveal, realities other than my real self, are not, and do not reveal, such realities, but are only subjectively formed substitutes of these latter ? This is the doubt raised by Kant, the grounds of which must be duly examined.

[1] Or, indeed, any such immediate judgment of the *real* order as " I am writing," " the sun is shining," etc. For the difficulty arising in these cases from the similarly cogent character of the evidence in *dreaming* as in *waking* is dissipated by the undeniable fact that we can distinguish between dreaming and waking, and so correct the illusion. This difficulty against sense evidence will be considered at a later stage. Indeed the very fact that we can recognize illusions as illusions solves the apparent difficulty arising from illusions.

[2] And rightly ; for there is no doubt that Descartes regarded the intuition of the *Ego cogitans* as revealing the *real Ego*, and not merely a phenomenal content, a mental or subjective product, beyond which the real *Ego* must remain for ever concealed and unknowable.

tal intuition of the *Ego* in its thinking or doubting process is an intuition of the *Ego* as an objective reality ; in other words, as claiming the cogent evidence for the judgment " I exist " to be sufficient ground for asserting this judgment as a valid cognition or interpretation of a *reality* presented to the consciousness of the knowing subject. And he argues unanswerably [1] that if Descartes really doubted about the *objective and real truth* of other immediately evident judgments, he should if he were consistent doubt similarly about *the objective truth-claim* of the judgment " I exist," as distinct from the purely subjective sense in which it expresses the mere mental fact of awareness, and not the subject's *knowledge of any reality as object.* But Descartes did not doubt that the judgment " I exist " gave him true knowledge of objective reality. Therefore he was inconsistent in doubting that the *Principle of Contradiction* (which is involved in that judgment), and other similar self-evident principles, gave him true knowledge of objective reality.

Mercier sums up his charge of inconsistency against Descartes in this conditional form : " *If,* while you see that two and three are five, or while you will deliberately to stretch out your hand and feel it, it were possible for you to doubt the testimony of your consciousness, *a pari,* when you are conscious of doubting and existing, *it would be possible for you to doubt* the objective reality of your doubt and of your existence " [2]   In this *argumentum ad hominem* Mercier rightly understands Descartes' doubt about such judgments as " two and three are five," as bearing on the *objectivity* of these judgments, *i.e.* their character *as representative of reality*, and he infers that *a pari* Descartes could, and should if he were consistent, doubt about " the objective reality " of his own existence. Mercier here accepts, and argues on, Descartes' assumption that at least in the intuition of our own existence our minds *can and do attain to a knowledge of objective reality :* the assumption which Kant afterwards called into question. He points out very properly indeed that Descartes assumed too much in assuming that this intuition of our existence is an intuition of the self as " an immaterial substance, without any admixture of the corporeal ".[3] But in arguing against Descartes he recognizes,

<hr/>

[1] *Op. cit.,* § 39, pp. 80 *sqq.*   [2] *Op. cit.,* p. 81.
[3] *Ibid.,* p. 84. Intuition does not reveal the nature, but only the existence, of the *Ego*, and reveals this only *in and through the acts* of the *Ego*. And the *Ego*, thus revealed in the concrete, is the *human Ego*, a complex *datum* in which reason-

with the latter, the *real objectivity of human thought* at least in the intuition of one's own existence.

His argument against Descartes is that if in this case the thinker gets *a true knowledge of reality*, so does he likewise in the case of other immediately evident judgments; if the cogent character of the evidence makes it impossible to doubt about the objective truth of the knowledge reached in the former case it must have the same effect in the latter, for psychologically the evidence is cogent in all the cases. The cardinal error of Descartes was that he "wrongly interpreted the testimony of his own consciousness".[1] "Descartes' first mistake was to regard at any stage as doubtful ideal propositions and [experienced] facts the evidence for which irresistibly compels assent at every stage. It is not merely the proposition ' I, the thinking subject, exist' that presents this character of cogent evidence: no proposition, whether of the ideal or of the real order, which is free from all complexity, can present itself to the mind without irresistibly determining our assent to it." [2]

Now it is quite lawful thus to argue that since Descartes admitted that he could not doubt the judgment " I exist" to be true *in its objective sense of revealing reality to the knowing subject*, neither should he (or could he really) have doubted other equally clear and cogent judgments to be true *in this same sense of revealing objective reality :* inasmuch as the evidence is—psychologically—equally cogent in all such cases. For Descartes admitted *the real objectivity of human thought* in the first case, and Mercier urges *the cogency of the evidence* in all cases *as a mark* of this *admitted objectivity of thought,* and as adequate rational ground for assenting to all judgments endowed with it as *objectively and really true, i.e.* as revealing to the knowing mind *reality as it is.*

But, as we pointed out above (30), it is at least conceivable that a person would accept *all* such judgments as compulsory mental syntheses, and then,—pausing to inquire whence comes

ing alone can bring to light the existence of an immaterial or spiritual principle. Descartes' assumption was therefore not merely excessive but also erroneous. And if he erred by excess Kant appears to have erred by defect in interpreting the content of this same intuition. For Kant the intuition of the self does not in any way reveal the *real* self, but merely a stream of subjective phenomena. The permanent, abiding, self-identical something which gives this stream a conscious unity, and which we (wrongly as Kant holds) think to be the *real* self or *Ego,* is only a transcendental condition which thought necessarily presupposes for having intelligible experience of any sort.

[1] *Op. cit.*, p. 83.   [2] *Ibid.*, p. 86.

this cogency and what is the nature of the terms synthesized (23),—would perhaps conclude that the cogency came *from the subject himself,* or that the terms of the synthesis were to such a degree *subjective products* of the mind's activity that we can never know whether the synthesis reveals *reality as it is.* This is the attitude to which Kant gave expression,—an attitude which reveals a fundamental real doubt about the real objectivity of human thought in all its processes. We shall have to see later whether it is legitimate to entertain such a fundamental doubt as a real doubt about the real objectivity of knowledge ; or whether it is possible, by assuming provisionally' as a spontaneous conviction that *the object of knowledge is reality*—" *Objectum intellectus est* ENS,"—to show that this conviction is well-grounded, and indeed involved in the very conception of knowledge itself. Our main task, as against the philosophy of Kant, and against subjectivism in general, will be to show that the cogent self-evidence of a judgment is an adequate vindication of its *real objectivity,* that the spontaneous conviction we entertain just on this point precisely can be shown by critical reflection to be so involved in any intelligible conception of the very nature of thought and knowledge that the rejection of this conviction would paralyse thought and make the process of cognition wholly meaningless. But what we are just now concerned to point out is that to assume spontaneously that cogent evidence is an adequate mark of real objectivity is just one particular way of assuming spontaneously *that our minds are capable of attaining to really objective truth.* Now Mercier lays down very clearly the doctrine that at the outset of critical investigation we have no right to take this latter spontaneous conviction *as a reflex certitude,* or as being itself beyond the pale of critical investigation.[1] Nevertheless, at this very stage, and before he has established (against Kant and subjectivism generally) that "cogent self-evidence is a mark of *objective truth,*" he takes this spontaneous conviction and uses it in arguing against Descartes. And this procedure is perfectly justifiable, because Descartes *admits the conviction both as a spontaneous conviction and also as an unquestionably valid reflex certitude.* Hence if Mercier is using the conviction *as a spontaneous conviction* his argument has a provisional value which Cartesians should recognize ; and even if he is using it as *a reflex and un-*

---

[1] *Op. cit.,* §§ 56, 59, pp. 111-12, 119. *Cf. supra,* § 28.

questionable certitude (*i.e.* in arguing *ad hominem*), Cartesians by admitting it as such should accept its logical consequences.

32. WHAT SORT OF DOUBT IS LAWFUL REGARDING THE REAL OBJECTIVITY OF SELF-EVIDENT JUDGMENTS?—It may be asked, however, whether we can legitimately assume at the outset (except as an *argumentum ad hominem* against one who admits it), not merely as a spontaneous conviction, but as a reflex, reasoned certitude, the judgment that " Evidence is an adequate mark or test of objective truth " ?   It would seem that we cannot, at least as regards evidence in general.   Speaking of the aptitude of the mind to discover objective truth, Jeannière says that " even if this aptitude were evident, nevertheless antecedently to critical inquiry it is not yet clearly established whether evidence is a test of truth, inasmuch as it is by such inquiry that we seek a test ".[1]   The same author contends that *de facto*, at the outset of our inquiry, this aptitude is not evident, and that, even if it were, a reasoned and reflex certitude on this point would be useless, inasmuch as the aptitude, not being infallible, does not always secure us from error, and reflection alone can decide in which of its acts it attains to objective truth, and under what conditions.[2]   But the evidence in favour of this aptitude is cumulative and gradually borne in upon us by experience of our cognitive activities.   It is not like the cogent self-evidence of ideal judgments such as " 2 + 2 = 4 ".   Perhaps we can and ought to assume, not merely as a spontaneous conviction, but as a reasoned, reflex and unquestionable certitude, the judgment that " cogent self-evidence is an adequate test of objective truth " ?   It is clear that *if* we accept such a judgment as " 2 + 2 = 4 " as *objectively true*, as giving us *an insight into reality as it is*, and *if* we claim *reflex certitude* for it *in this objective sense* merely because we have tried to doubt it and failed on account of the cogency with which our assent is compelled,—*then* we are *eo ipso* claiming that in and through our reflex certitude of the objective validity of this assent we have also reflex certitude *that our mind*, in this (and every other similar) act of assent to a cogently self-evident judgment, *does actually attain, and is therefore capable of attaining, to objective truth*.   This point of transition from spontaneous to reflex certi-

---

[1] " Etiamsi aptitudo mentis esset evidens, ante inquisitionem reflexam nondum distincte constat utrum evidentia sit criterium objectivitatis : quaeritur sc. criterium " (*op. cit.*, p. 106).

[2] *Ibid.*, p. 107, Arg III.

tude in regard to such judgments is of the most extreme importance in view of the doubt raised by Kant as to the bearing of
their *cogency* on their *real objectivity.* Jeannière says that the
aptitude of the mind to reach objective truth is not evidently revealed in any single specific act of *spontaneous* assent: not even
in our assent to " 2 + 2 = 4 ". And the reason he gives is that
spontaneous assent always rests on such a merely *direct* and *confused* apprehension (of the grounds of assent) as will leave room
for possible error. Hence, he continues, even such judgments
cannot be affirmed " with a certitude that is certainly objective "
until the grounds of assent are made explicit by reflection.[1]
Very well, then ; let us reflect on our spontaneous assent to such
judgments. It does not need much reflection to make us aware
that the grounds of our assent are *intellectually cogent.* Will
mere advertence to this fact of introspection convince us that our
spontaneous assent was " certainly objective " ? Will it convince
us that the judgment to which we assent is not merely a compulsory mental synthesis but a synthesis which *reveals objective reality
to us ?* Well, the answer seems to be that such reflection will at
least *make a beginning* in transforming our spontaneous assent
to such a judgment as *objectively true* into a reasoned, reflex assent ;[2] and consequently in corroborating our spontaneous conviction that our minds are capable of attaining to knowledge of
objective reality, and transforming this assent also into a reflex
and reasoned certitude.

Such, apparently, is the attitude which Mercier adopts when,
in arguing against Descartes, and explaining the condition of
mind in which we find ourselves at the outset of our critical investigation, he asserts that in regard to immediately or cogently
evident judgments our unsuccessful attempt to doubt about them
gives us *eo ipso* a reasoned certitude *about their real and objective
truth.*[3] He knows very well, at this initial stage of the inquiry,

---

[1] "   hinc affirmari nequeunt cum certitudine certo objectiva nisi fuerint ad
cognitionem distinctam adducta. Hoc autem fit inquisitione reflexa " (*ibid.*, p. 107).

[2] Thus JEANNIÈRE says that the methodic doubt which we ought to attempt in
regard to their objectivity—" ne uno quidem momento durare poterit "—cannot last
a single moment (*op cit.*, p. 112).

[3] " In regard to truth in general, to all truth, it is both natural and lawful *to attempt a universal doubt* " (*op. cit.*, p. 115). " But the effort to doubt everything will
fail. We shall see in the course of our investigation [especially where he deals
with Kantism] that this is really so " (*ibid.*, p. 117). Then having pointed out that
mediate judgments, being demonstrable, may be doubted really or methodically, and
that analysis of them leads us back to immediately evident judgments, which are

that reasons for doubting their *real and genuine objectivity* will be urged by Kant and by extreme subjectivists; but he retains his spontaneous conviction that the mind can reach a true knowledge of objective reality, and that it does so in these assents to self-evident judgments; he finds this spontaneous conviction corroborated by his first acts of reflection on the grounds of these spontaneous assents; he hopes to be able to show in due course that none of the difficulties raised against the real objectivity of knowledge are sufficiently serious to raise a real doubt about it; and in showing this he will gradually render his spontaneous assents *fully* reflex, reasoned and philosophic.

33. THEIR REAL OBJECTIVITY NOT A MATTER FOR LOGICAL DEMONSTRATION, BUT FOR INTUITION THROUGH REFLECTIVE ANALYSIS.—It is important to bear in mind the significance of Mercier's claim that the intuition of self-evident judgments is an *insight into objective reality*, and not merely into the character of the subjective thinking process.   He rightly observes that such judgments are incapable of demonstration and that they do not need demonstration inasmuch as their cogency renders them indubitable.   Kant, however, would admit this, and nevertheless

indemonstrable, he asks what should be our attitude in regard to these latter. Observing that with Aristotle and St. Thomas we should *try* to doubt them, he continues that should this effort succeed, " in other words if a universal [and real] doubt could even for an instant take possession of the mind, as a reasoned attitude, it would be all over with certitude.   For the doubt of that instant would either persist the next instant or it would not.   If it persisted for this second instant, and so for subsequent instants, scepticism would manifestly have triumphed.   If *per impossibile* it did not persist, *i.e.* if a proposition which at one instant revealed itself as doubtful were to reveal itself the next instant in similar circumstances as certain, then too certitude would be no less effectively compromised.   For why trust the second judgment rather than the first ?   A faculty which, in exactly similar circumstances, would elicit contradictory acts would be unworthy of credence ; reflection, the sovereign arbiter, should pronounce as suspect and receive as doubtful all the depositions of such a faculty " (*ibid.*, pp. 116-17).   " There are propositions whose terms are such that their comparison necessarily reveals their agreement or disagreement, and that with a clearness which leaves no place for any doubt ; the moment at which our intelligence conceives the two terms must therefore inevitably synchronize with the moment at which their relation reveals itself and (by doing so) irresistibly compels the enlightened and unshakeable assent of the mind.   Hence, in the domain of reflection the initial attitude of the mind is *certitude* " (*ibid.*, p. 117).   " Critical investigation cannot set out from a universal doubt, for there is not a single instant when the elementary notions are present to the reflecting mind without their manifesting themselves to it in their evident objectivity " (*ibid.*, p. 88).   From these extracts we gather that Mercier here asserts, in anticipation of his polemic with the philosophy of Kant, that the cogent character of immediate evidence is a ground which rational reflection will declare to be an adequate ground for our spontaneous conviction that our minds are capable of attaining to *an objectively valid knowledge which reveals reality as it is.*

there is a sense in which he has doubted them: he has doubted that they give us an insight into reality as it is, and this is an expression of his general doubt about the capacity of the speculative reason to reach any knowledge of things as they are in themselves. How can this doubt be met? What has Mercier to oppose to it? He has the spontaneous conviction of mankind that the human mind can, and in assenting to such judgments does *de facto*, gain a true and certain knowledge of objective *reality*. But can the groundlessness of Kant's doubt be *demonstrated?* Or, in other words, can it be *demonstrated* that the human mind, in assenting to such judgments, gets a grasp of *reality* as its object? Manifestly it cannot be *directly demonstrated* to one who really doubts it. For such a one all our demonstrations will be stricken with the same doubt as the axioms in question, will be confined within the same mental sphere of "*subjective* objects" (20) as these axioms themselves, and will, therefore, necessarily fail in their purpose of convincing him that the mind can and does transcend its own subjectivity to know objective reality. For ourselves, too, such demonstrations, if attempted, would not and could not really *demonstrate* that the mind can know objective reality, for they would presuppose and be based upon our spontaneous conviction that the mind can do so. The only way, therefore, of transforming this spontaneous conviction (that the object known in self-evident judgments is *reality*) into a philosophical certitude, is to reflect on our cognitive processes and convince ourselves by an analysis of them that in the very nature of knowledge the truth of this spontaneous conviction of its real objectivity is involved. In working our way towards this reasoned certitude we shall have to examine the doubts raised by all subjectivist theories, in the hope of showing that they are based on groundless assumptions and defective analyses. Thus we retain throughout our spontaneous conviction that the object of knowledge is *reality as it is in itself,* and we justify this conviction, not by demonstrating it, but by exercising our cognitive faculties reflectively on the nature of cognition itself, and observing that in this reflective process their findings corroborate and justify that spontaneous conviction.

This, as we understand it, is Mercier's method of approaching Kantian and subjectivist theories in his *Critériologie.* And we wish to emphasize it because we believe it has been thought by some that in rejecting what he describes as the attitude of *excessive dogmatism* [1] he undertook to *demonstrate directly* the *real objectivity* of self-evident judgments, and therein also the power of the mind to attain to a certain knowledge of *objective reality*. But, on the contrary, he held that the self-evidence of such judgments reveals their *real objectivity*, that when our spontaneous belief in this real objectivity is examined critically under a methodic doubt (29) it is borne out by reflection on their self-evidence, and that this process of reflection is not a process of *demonstrating* but of *observing* ("*constater*"), of "judging the tree by its fruits ".[2] So far from holding that the *aptitude* of the mind to discover objective truth about reality could be *really* doubted, he clearly taught that such a doubt would paralyse critical research ; and while he held that it could be the object of a *methodic* doubt he taught with unmistakable clearness that the aptitude thus methodically doubted could not be demonstrated directly, that our spontaneous belief in this aptitude can be rendered reflex and reasoned only by an inquiry into the cognitive *acts* of the mind, and finally that the objective validity even of these acts themselves, *i.e.* their character as revealing and representing *reality* to our minds, cannot be *demonstrated*, but must be *apprehended, observed, perceived*, by our eliciting them under the scrutiny of introspective analysis.[3]

---

[1] *Op. cit.*, §§ 44-54, pp. 89-109. *Cf. infra*, § 35.

[2] " On jugera l'arbre à ses fruits " (*ibid.*, p. 88).

[3] " Just as I can know that my stomach can digest food without having first made a microscopic and chemical study of its mucous membrane or an analysis of its fermenting and digestive juices, so I can attain to truth and know that I attain to truth without having explored the intellectual *faculty* whereby I attain to truth. I have a very simple and natural way of informing myself on the digestive power of my stomach, and that is by letting it digest : if it does digest it must be presumably because it is capable of digesting ! So, too, I have only to let my intellect function spontaneously on the cognition of principles and facts. . . . If I can observe that I have assents or certitudes which are motived, that I have cognitions endowed with the character of objective evidence, then, from having seen my mind *at work*, from having observed its aptitude reveal itself *de facto* in its *act*, I shall have the right to affirm that aptitude of my mind to discover truth. Thus the aptitude [*i.e.* philosophic certitude about it] will not be a *postulate* logically anterior to any and every certain judgment, but will be an inference based on the fact that we are conscious of eliciting motived judgments."—MERCIER, *op. cit.*, p. 108.

" To solve the critical problem our reflex certitude must surely have objective validity; otherwise such validity could not be observed. To find gold in a mine, the gold must be there; that the stomach may digest, it must be capable of digesting. But it does not follow that we must *logically* presuppose the objective validity of certitude, that we must postulate this validity. Let us explore the mine; let the stomach function . . . in other words, let us reflect and *observe. Let us observe* ['*Constatons* '] : it is thus we . . . escape the vicious circle. . . . The mistake of certain authors is that they have failed to grasp the force of this '*constatons* '. They imagine that there is question of a *rational* act in the strict sense [*i.e.* a *logical demonstration*], and not of a simple process of observation; they see a work of reason, an inference, where there is really question only of a sort of psychological experimentation that is *sui generis* and irreducible, and which we have described as *observation* ['*constatation* ']."—JEANNIÈRE, *op. cit.*, p. 108, n. 2.

While fully endorsing the justice and reasonableness of the attitude illustrated in these passages we may add just two observations by way of comment. The *first* is that a *logical demonstration* of the aptitude of our faculties would indeed involve

Nor was he unaware that all these reflex critical investigations concerning the mind's spontaneous assents were themselves cognitive acts, in the real and objective validity of which he was all the time spontaneously believing (*cf.* 25). It is precisely because this spontaneous belief must be retained throughout, under peril of real and universal scepticism, that it is impossible strictly to demonstrate the real and objective validity of *any* of the mind's cognitive acts : the validity of the acts whereby it reaches *mediate* judgments depends on the validity of its apprehension of the *immediate* judgments from which the former are inferred ; and that the mind attains to genuine knowledge of reality in judgments which are immediate or self-evident cannot be *demonstrated* either, but it does not need to be demonstrated, for it can be *seen, observed*, by reflection on the nature of the evidence which compels us to assent to them as *manifestations of reality* to our minds.   All discussion of the considerations raised by subjectivist theories must, therefore, be in the nature not of a formal or logical demonstration that true knowledge is objectively real, but rather of a careful analysis of the grounds and motives of our assent to judgments, an analysis which will convince us that our judgments can—and do, when formed in accordance with the dictates of reason—reveal to our minds objective reality as it is : a result which can be achieved by showing the groundlessness of subjectivist attacks on the spontaneous convictions in question, and, indeed, not only their groundlessness but the ambiguities and inconsistencies whereby alone they escape such suicidal issues as solipsism and universal scepticism.

In our inquiry so far we have been suggesting that the subjectivism which

---

a sort of *petitio principii*, inasmuch as its conclusion should be " Therefore we are *philosophically* certain that our faculties can attain to truth," while its demonstrative force would depend on our previously assenting to the judgment, " We are *spontaneously* certain that our faculties can attain to truth '.   If, therefore, we reached the desired conclusion we should have done so not through the *logical* force of the process as a demonstration, but through the reflex insight which it would give us, as a *psychological* process, into the objective validity of our cognitive acts.   But granted that the reflective process is not a logical demonstration, that it is a process of *introspective observation*, it must be borne in mind that *even so* it can give us a reasoned, reflex, philosophic certitude that our minds can attain to a knowledge of objective reality, only on the condition that we do not at any stage of the process *really and positively* doubt, or really abandon our spontaneous conviction, both that our faculty of introspective observation is capable of revealing to us, and that our acts of observation are actually revealing to us, objective reality as it is.   Once doubt *really and positively* about the validity of the acts (and a *similar* doubt about the validity of the faculty would, of course, extend to the acts), and hopeless universal scepticism is the result (*cf.* MERCIER, pp. 116-17 ; *supra*, § 25).

The *second* observation is this : From the fact that knowledge is *sui generis* (6) no similes drawn from any other human process can *perfectly* illustrate the problem of knowledge.   The simile of letting the stomach digest would be perfect *if* digestion (and not cognition) were the process by which the stomach could discover whether its digestion were satisfactory or not.   Digging for gold in the mine would be a perfect simile, *if* the digging itself (and not the mind's cognition) were the process which determined the satisfactory character, or otherwise, of the digging.   It is by cognition we judge the validity of every other process ; while cognition itself is the only process which has to determine the scope and limits of its own validity : an inevitable fact which makes epistemological inquiry so delicate a matter.

doubts or denies that the mind in knowing can transcend itself to attain to
reality as it is, and the Kantism according to which the mind constructs the
"objects of knowledge" by somehow transfiguring reality with its own subjective factors,—are theories which in effect render knowledge of reality impossible, and the distinction between truth and error unintelligible.   But
those theorists repudiate this charge and contend that the mind certainly
has knowledge ; that in and through its judgments, necessary and contingent,
it sees and knows whole domains of mental objects ; and that in their theories
the distinction between truth and error is quite intelligible.   And obviously
there must be *some* sense in which they believe their thoughts, judgments,
reasonings and speculations to be validly representative of something beyond,
or something more than, their own individual subjectivity : to escape from
solipsism.   They cannot offer their speculations to the public, discuss and
argue epistemology with their fellow-men, unless they believe these latter to
be *in some sense* really and truly there.   Kant, for instance, must have spontaneously believed in the validity of his own introspective analyses, which resulted in the *Critique of Pure Reason*,—but of course he believed in its
validity only in the sense in which he understood "validity," *i.e.* as mentally
objective or phenomenal validity.   The *Critique* claimed to vindicate the
position that speculative knowledge can be valid only in this phenomenal
sense.   And since the *Critique* itself is not only a work *on* the speculative
reason, but also *of* the speculative reason, it follows that the conclusions of
the *Critique* could not consistently have been—and indeed were not *de facto*
—put forward by their author as giving either himself or those of his readers
who accepted them any insight into the *extramental* or *mind-independent
reality* of its subject-matter, but only into the phenomena supposed to be produced by this subject-matter in their minds.

Thus we see that subjectivists have arrived at conceptions quite different
from ours as to what "knowledge" is, what the "validity" or "truth" of
knowledge means, what "reality" is "in itself" and "in relation to the subject or process of cognition".   And in discussing with them the question
whether our conceptions or theirs are borne out by impartial introspective
analysis of the data, not the least difficulty is that of securing a common
understanding as to the meaning to be attached to the terms used in the discussion : for the tendency of the objectivist will be to use such terms in their
ordinary dictionary meaning, and of the subjectivist to use them in the much
more restricted meaning they naturally assume in his theory.   The whole of
the present preliminary discussion—as to the data and method of critical investigation, the proper attitude of mind in which to approach it, and the defining of a common platform for arguing with the subjectivist—has for its sole
object the enlightenment of the student as to what are the real problems at
issue.   It will help him to avoid those vexatious misunderstandings which so
easily arise from ambiguity in the use of terms.   But in discussing the real
problems with the sceptic, the idealist, or the subjectivist, this preliminary
question need not be raised *ex professo*,—and indeed should not be raised *ex
professo* owing to its peculiar subtleties.   Rather we should commence directly
with some of the admitted data of the problems, and endeavour to show that
an impartial analysis of those data bear out the spontaneous conviction that
men can and do attain to some certain knowledge of *reality as it is in itself.*

34. INCONSISTENCIES CONSEQUENT ON EXCESSIVE DOUBT.—
Assuming, as we safely may, that Descartes believed the intuition
of his own existence to give him *objective truth* about reality, and
that when doubting the truth of immediately evident judgments
what he really doubted was whether they gave him a similar *insight into objective reality*, we can see that his fundamental mistake was *to push real doubt too far*. It is undeniable that his
intention was not sceptical but dogmatic, not to undermine
human certitude but to vindicate it. But in effect he undermined
it,—that is, for himself and those who adopted his method. If
he and his disciples did not become universal sceptics, this was
not because of the " method " but in spite of it, and at the cost
of many inconsistencies.

For example, it was inconsistent really to believe in the objective truth of the judgment "I exist," and at the same time
really to doubt the objective truth of the *Principle of Contradiction* and other equally evident judgments. Again, when he
proclaimed that he could not really doubt his own existence because he had a "clear and distinct idea" of it, he could not, and
indeed did not, fail to see that he had an equally clear and distinct idea of "two and three being five," and other such judgments, which he had just really doubted because of the bare
possibility of his being the victim of some Malignant Power,
some "*Dieu trompeur*," rather than the creation of an All-wise
and All-truthful God. Hence he felt and admitted the need of
vindicating the trustworthiness of his criterion, the "clear and
distinct idea," by showing that it came from an All-truthful God.
"Without the knowledge of these two truths," he wrote,[1]—"that
God exists and cannot deceive,—I don't see how I can ever be
certain of anything." And so he proceeded to prove the existence of God—from premises of which, on his own admission, he
could not be certain except on condition of his already knowing
his criterion of the "clear and distinct idea" to be valid (which
he could not know without knowing of the existence and truth-
fulness of God),—and by the aid of the principles of Identity,
Contradiction, and Causality, which he had rejected as doubtful![2]

Of course it is not for emphasizing the indubitable character
of the truth of his own existence, as revealed in his own thinking
and doubting, that Descartes deserves reproach ; nor was he the
first to emphasize the point. St. Augustine had emphasized it

---

[1] IIIme *Méditation*, n. 34-6.   [2] *Cf.* JEANNIÈRE, *op. cit.*, pp. 147-8, 144-5.

centuries previously, and to excellent purpose, against the scepticism of the later Academicians.[1] And St. Thomas repeatedly drew attention to the indubitable self-revelation of the *Ego* in the process of thinking.[2] Rather it was for not emphasizing the equally indubitable character of a multitude of other judgments.

Doubt, as already observed, in so far forth as it is *real*, is the negation of certitude. This, however, is not saying that real doubt is always an obstacle to the attainment of reflex certitude ; wherever it is reasonable the prudent investigator has no option but to embrace it. Real doubt, however, is not necessary, or even useful, as a method. It is not necessary, for in order to reach a reasoned, or reflex, or philosophical certitude, all that is needed is the interrogative attitude involved in the *simulated* or *methodic* doubt which is consistent with the retention of spontaneous certitude. Nor is it useful, except indirectly, and as a means of warding off error by the suspension of our assent where the real and sufficient grounds of assent are not present. In such cases it is necessary and commendable, where assent would be unjustifiable and dangerous. As compared with error, real doubt is certainly the lesser of two evils.

But Descartes, and many philosophers since his time, seem to see something particularly commendable in the attitude of real doubt as compared with that of assent or belief or conviction. As a matter of fact it is both lawful and commendable to doubt really when we think there are sufficient reasons for doubting really; but to doubt really while the reasons for conviction appear to us to be adequate is neither lawful nor commendable, for it is unreasonable. The attempt to fix and fasten our attention *exclusively* on the grounds *against* our spontaneous convictions, while ignoring the grounds *in favour of* them,—and to do this with a view to reaching a state of *real* doubt about them,—is to adopt a prejudiced attitude at the outset of critical investigation. It is unfair to our faculties and reveals an unreasoning distrust of them. By all means let us use them cautiously and scrutinize them closely in their processes, but let us do so impartially. What reason is there for thinking that the shorter, surer, or safer

[1] " For the truths I proclaim I fear not the arguments of the Academicians. ' Perhaps you are deceived' they say to me. But if I am deceived I exist. He that does not exist is not deceived; hence even if I am deceived I exist."—*De Civitate Dei*, xi., 26. *Cf. De Trinitate*, xv., 21.

[2] " Nullus potest cogitare se non esse cum assensu : in hoc enim quod cogitat percipit se esse."—*De Veritate*, Q. x., art. 12.

passage from spontaneous to reflex certitude is that which leads through *real* doubt? None whatever, but rather the contrary. We therefore repeat what we have already remarked, that the reasonable initial attitude for those who undertake the critical study of human knowledge and certitude is to retain *all* their spontaneous convictions, and in the process of revision to reject gradually those and those only that may be found to have been groundless.

The homely simile in which Descartes [1] compares the mind at this initial stage of inquiry to a basket containing good and bad apples may here be helpful to the student. The *object* is to sort the apples, retaining the good and rejecting the bad, but the *problem* is to distinguish between the good and the bad ; for *ex hypothesi* all *seem* good : all our convictions *seem* certitudes (16). And the right *method?* Well, Descartes' attempt to doubt *really* about *everything* has been compared to the procedure of emptying all the apples, good and bad alike, out of the basket, for the purpose of picking back only the good ones ; but by doubting *really* even *about the capacity of his mind* to reach any certitude, he is accused of having *thrown away the basket* as well as the apples. This rough and ready simile is in its broad lines justifiable as applied to Descartes' method, but it must not be pressed too far, for it will not fit in with the details of the criteriological problem.

Two difficulties of the latter are fairly obvious : (*a*) Would not the process of going over all our convictions individually be interminable? This may be overcome in practice, so far as a general study of certitude is concerned, by taking the convictions *in classes*(10). And (*b*), By what test are we to discern the true from the false? This is the problem of the criterion of truth.

But we have not yet done with the question of method ; and if this preliminary question seems tedious our only apology must be the imperative necessity of approaching the main problems with clear conceptions as to what it is exactly we have to investigate, and what exactly are the data and the legitimate assumptions of such investigation.

35. THE OPPOSITE MISTAKE : EXCESSIVE DOGMATISM.— We have seen (4) that throughout the Middle Ages and down to the time of Descartes no serious doubt was raised about the power of the human mind to gain some degree of genuine insight into *reality as it is in itself,* or into the function of evidence as reveal-

[1] *Resp. ad VII. objectiones.*

ing reality to the knowing mind.   When, therefore, such doubts were seriously raised it is not surprising that philosophers who did not share them, but regarded them as groundless and un-reasonable, should have been somewhat at a loss as to how ex-actly they should meet and deal with such sceptical tendencies. This was the case with scholastic philosophers in particular, though not with them alone.   Anyhow, some scholastic philosophers, in their concern to defend the foundations of human certitude, appear to have singled out from among men's spontaneous convictions a certain small number of the more fundamental or primordial ones, and to have claimed that these cannot be legitimate subject-matter for any sort of doubt or of critical investigation whatsoever.   Thus Tongiorgi [1] and Palmieri,[2] two professors of philosophy in the Gregorian University at Rome during the pontificate of Leo XIII., taught that a " first *fact*," *viz.* the real existence of the Self or *Ego*, a " first *principle*," *viz.* the *Principle of Contradiction*, and a " first *condition*," *viz.* the *aptitude of the human mind to discover objective truth about reality*, must be exempt from, and presupposed by, all critical investigation into the scope and limits, the objectivity and truth, of human knowledge.[3]

Of course no objection can be taken to our retaining these three assents, from the commencement of our investigation, *as spontaneous convictions*.   But we retain many others in the same way.   The three mentioned are indeed fundamental in the sense that they are implicitly asserted in *all* our judgments.   The "first fact" and the "first principle" are among those self-evident judgments the *subjective or psychological cogency* of which we can-not doubt, even methodically, and the *real objectivity* of which is

---

[1] *Institutiones Philosophicæ*, Vol. I., Pt. II., chap. iii., nn. 425-6.

[2] *Inst. Philos.*, Th. V., pp. 136-8.

[3] Cf. RICKABY, *First Principles of Knowledge*, chap. x., pp. 169-76. BALMES, in his *Fundamental Philosophy* (Engl. tr. by BROWNSON, 2 vols., 1880) had already singled out in an analogous sense " truths of consciousness, necessary truths, and common-sense truths "—Vol. I., Pt. I., § 147, p. 94. Cf. MERCIER, *op. cit.*, § 48, p. 97. We need not examine the contention of Descartes that all philosophical truth must be reasoned out deductively from some *one* principle which would thus be the source of all truth and the basis of all certitude, his " principle " being the *Cogito ergo sum* (cf. MERCIER, *ibid.*, §§ 44-6). SPINOZA likewise (" *Ethica more geometrica demonstrata*," 1677), and FERRIER (*Institutes of Metaphysics*, 2nd ed., 1856), and other mathematically minded speculators, have attempted the task of deducing all truth by abstract logical reasoning from some one or some few " principles ". Such, too, is the pretension of the Hegelian Dialectic. But the data of human experience are far too complex and varied to admit of being brought under, and deduced from, and explained by, any one single principle. Cf. RICKABY, *op. cit.*, chap. vi., 7, pp. 115-16.

also borne in upon us from the outset, and ever more and more fully the more we reflect (under an attempted methodic doubt) on the nature of their evidence; but they are not the only self-evident judgments that present these characteristics.[1] The "first condition" must of course be assumed as a spontaneous conviction; it may not be *really* doubted; and even when it is methodically doubted it *begins from the very outset to be transformed into a reasoned certitude* by the reflective process whereby we see [2] that

[1] "What are the immediate propositions whose self-evident truth irresistibly compels the assent of the mind from the very outset? How many are they? . . . There are certainly more of them than one, as Descartes thought; there are certainly more of them than three, as Tongiorgi thought; the real number of them is undetermined: some of them are of the *ideal* order, *principles*, *axioms*; others are of the *real* order, truths of *immediate experience* or *intuition*."—MERCIER, *op. cit.*, p. 118.

[2] We have already remarked (33) that this reflective process is not a process of logical inference or demonstration. And if it be called a *demonstration* the student should be reminded of the special sense in which this term is used in the context. Thus DONAT (*Critica*, p. 29—*apud* JEANNIÈRE, *op. cit.*, pp. 107-8) writes: "Actus reflectentis valor objectivus tunc, quando inquisitio instituitur, utique supponi debet non quidem logice sed ontologice, *i.e.* valor hic *adsit* oportet sed non *primo cognosci* debet. Intellectus vero proprietas [*i.e.* its aptitude for truth] eo ostenditur, quod intellectus ex actibus ad ejus naturam concluditur. . . . Attamen haec demonstratio . . . ab aliis demonstrationibus eo differt, quod consequens non quidem stricte logice supponi, *i.e.* prius cognosci debet, attamen quod de eo serio dubitari non licet, quin praemissae eo ipso dubiae evadant." "*De eo serio dubitari non licet*," *i.e.* we must not *really* doubt the aptitude of the mind, or in other words lose or give up our spontaneous conviction that the mind has this aptitude; but we may and must adopt the open-minded, inquiring attitude in regard to it. This latter attitude is not a "*serious* doubt" in the sense of being a real doubt; but it is serious as a method, serious in the sense of being seriously and deliberately adopted, and not from mere frivolity or caprice, but with a grave and serious purpose. This methodic doubt or inquiring attitude JEANNIÈRE calls a *negative* doubt; and Mercier also, observing, however, that it differs from other negative doubts in this that it is deliberately invoked as a method or law of procedure to which the mind must submit itself (cf. § 28). But JEANNIÈRE, taking objection to Donat's terminology (*ibid.*, p. 108, n. 1), seems to suggest that this doubt about the aptitude of the mind should be real. "The criteriologist," he says, "does not merely act as if he doubted, he doubts; and his doubt is as universal as it can be. The moment a single certitude [*i.e.* spontaneous conviction] has been discovered to have been false, all may be found to be false . . . unless indeed all are not similar, and this is precisely what he has to discover." But having discovered one or more "certitudes" to have been false, he must, if he retains the others, remain spontaneously convinced that all his "certitudes" are not similar; the possibility that they may be all false is not a reasonably sufficient ground to make him really doubt, or in other words to destroy his spontaneous trust in, the aptitude of his mind; and in order to secure reflex certitude on this point all that is necessary is an open-minded inquiry into the *aptitude* by reflection on the *acts*. The obsession of the mind by a real doubt about its own aptitude is indeed an unfortunate possibility (25, 26), but so far from being a necessary ordeal for every inquirer on the path to philosophic certitude, it is a contingency in which the only hope for its victim is to shake off the paralysing obsession and proceed to use his mind in reflecting on its own cognitive activities.

As a matter of fact, however, the sentences just quoted from JEANNIÈRE must

the cogent evidence for immediate judgments reveals these as *objectively true*, as *giving us an insight into reality.*

It is probably because (*a*) the *objective truth* of the three primary convictions in question cannot be strictly demonstrated, because (*b*) methodic doubt about their *real objectivity* begins to disappear so promptly from the very outset of critical reflection and give place to reasoned certitude about them, and because (*c*) critical reflection has been often half-unconsciously in operation *before* we address ourselves *ex professo* to a systematic inquiry into the grounds of knowledge in general,—it is, we believe, under the influence of these facts, that the authors in question have set up for these "three primary truths" the claim that even at the very outset of critical investigation they cannot be doubted even methodically but must be assumed as reflex, reasoned, and unquestionable certitudes.   But, then, by the very fact that these authors discuss the difficulties raised by Kant and subjectivists generally against the *real objectivity* of evidence, by the very fact that they endeavour to show the unreasonableness of entertaining a real doubt about the aptitude of the mind to discover truth, they are *in practice* employing methodic doubt no less than Mercier himself, who takes exception to their apparent denial of its lawfulness in theory.[1]   And, moreover, he himself maintains that a *reflex and reasoned conviction* of the *real objectivity* of self-evident judgments at least *begins* to be borne in upon us *from the very commencement of our reflective analysis.*   For when he says in reference to them that "the initial attitude of the mind, *in the domain of reflection*, is certitude," [2] he apparently means a certitude which, from being previously perhaps only spontaneous, has with the first effort of reflection become reasoned and philosophic.

be read in the light of other extracts (cf. § 28), from which it appears that the "*negative* doubt" which he, with Mercier, advocates as a necessary method, is in effect not a real doubt, not destructive of, or incompatible with, the spontaneous conviction that the mind is capable of discovering truth.   But a "doubt" that is compatible with spontaneous conviction can hardly be called with propriety a "real" doubt.   As a *doubt*, it is not real ; as an *inquiring attitude* (which is all that it really means) it is of course real, in the sense of being adopted with a serious purpose.

[1] Possibly, too, their main concern being to repudiate a *real* doubt, they may not have appreciated the function of a mere methodic or simulated doubt, especially as the doubt employed by Descartes, and which afterwards came to be called "methodic," was in fact a real doubt, and very different from the doubt used by Aristotle, St. Thomas, etc. (28, 29), and which alone is genuinely "methodic".

[2] *Op. cit.*, p. 117 ; cf. § 32, above.

So that after all the difference between his attitude and theirs is more apparent than real.

It is indeed undeniable that the authors in question seem to forestall, as it were, subjectivism of every sort, by pointing out in advance not only that the *real objectivity* of the judgments " I exist," and "the same thing cannot be and not be," is not logically demonstrable and must be *seen* by reflection from the start, but also by pointing out that in this intuition of their real objectivity there is also seen from the start *the aptitude of the mind to discover objective truth*. But just as Mercier does not refuse to discuss the difficulties of subjectivism though he too asserts in advance that the cogent evidence of immediate judgments is a mark of their real objectivity, so neither do these authors even though they proclaim in advance that the aptitude of the mind to discover objective truth must be theoretically postulated as unquestionable, and assumed and acted on throughout all discussion of subjectivist difficulties.

And as a matter of fact all criticism of subjectivist theories must resolve itself into showing in one way or another that those theories involve such defective analyses of what all admit to be the *data* of critical investigation,—*viz.* men's spontaneous thoughts, judgments, assents, convictions, etc., *as mental facts,*—such defective analyses of these data as necessarily issue in contradictions and absurdities which do violence to man's rational nature as well as rendering knowledge impossible and all distinction between truth and error unintelligible. It is of comparatively little importance whether such criticism begins afar off, as it were, and by anticipation, or at close quarters with subjectivism.

But it must begin somewhere ; and the manner in which some scholastic writers approach the task conveys the regrettable impression that they consider subjectivism in general to be so self-evidently absurd as to need no criticism : an attitude which subjectivists are inclined to interpret as an unworthy evasion of a real problem. Of course it is not evasion of the problem, but only fair comment on the nature of it, to point out that the real objectivity of thought, in forming self-evident judgments whether of the ideal or of the real order, cannot be strictly demonstrated. But it will scarcely be regarded as satisfactory either by the disciples of Descartes, Malebranche, Locke, Berkeley, Hume, or Kant on the one side, or by the impartial student who desires to defend the real objectivity of knowledge on the other side, to find scholastic writers defending this objectivity by a mere appeal to the spontaneous dictates and persuasions of sound common sense.[1] This appeal, which is of course in reality a perfectly proper appeal to the verdict of reason itself on the nature and significance of *immediate evidence*, nowadays needs to be confirmed and supplemented by a careful psychological analysis which will show that the difficulties raised by subjectivism are based on a faulty and incorrect interpretation of cognitive processes.

Another fact worth noting in the present connexion is that besides the capacity of the human mind to attain to a genuine and objective knowledge of reality, there are involved in the very possibility of knowledge, in any intelligible conception of knowledge, or at all events in the universally prevalent and accepted notion of what knowledge is (*cf.* 6), many other fundamental judgments,—whether we call them "postulates," "assumptions," "beliefs," or by any other title,—which on the one hand are neither themselves immediately evident like axioms such as "two and two are four," nor logically demonstrable from any self-evident truths or axioms, and which on the other hand must be implicitly accepted as true and cannot be seriously doubted or denied without involving the utter destruction of all knowledge. That the real world is not a chaos—that reality is intelligible—that nature is uniform—that human minds are in the main similar, and have similar experiences,—are examples of what we mean. In fact one chief purpose of epistemology is to bring to light such fundamental convictions and to show their bearing on the possibility of knowledge. And the reason why the history of philosophy presents so many divergent and conflicting theories both as to the nature of knowledge and as to the nature of reality is because investigators have differed so much in regard to the assumptions and postulates they claim and accept as valid principles or starting-points, rather than in their reasonings from such principles.[2] It is in estimating aright the value and significance of those fundamental assents that a prudent fidelity to the voice of our rational nature, dictating to us what is reasonable, counts for so much. And since this voice is really articulate in those spontaneous convictions that are common to the race (15), it is not surprising that speculators who have daringly deviated from such convictions have arrived at so-called "theories of knowledge" which are rather theories of something that is not knowledge at all (*cf.* 6) : theories in which "knowledge," "truth," "error," "reality," no longer mean what men generally have understood by such terms, but express new and fanciful conceptions to which these speculators have attached these terms.

Real doubt about everything prevents investigation even from starting. Nor can reflection, once started, make any progress otherwise than by rendering some one or some few spontaneous convictions philosophic, and placing it or them beyond even methodic doubt. Hence the natural and

---

[1] *Cf.* JEANNIÈRE, *op. cit.*, p. 155, n. 2.
[2] *Cf. Science of Logic*, ii., pp. 142 (§ 231), 322-7.

even painful anxiety of the critical philosopher to get some firm and unshake-able foothold from which to start. Scholastic philosophers are not alone in claiming certain "primary" judgments or principles, from which, and in the light of which, they may proceed to interpret the data which they have to in-vestigate, *viz. the whole consciously experienced domain of which they are aware*[1] : for it must be remembered that these data themselves are only "brute facts," so to speak ; and the faculty of reflection has imperative need to get immediate possession of some judgments, some rational principles, which will make *knowledge, i.e. interpretation* of those data, possible. *All* philo-sophers, in fact, have to make up their minds about some judgments which they will not *question* but *utilize* in investigating the nature and limits of human knowledge. But they do not all choose the same "primaries". To give just one example, we find a modern author who is not a scholastic claim-ing, in a very suggestive work on epistemology,[2] that three certitudes must be accepted as underlying and involved in all knowledge, these three certitudes having for their respective objects the existence of the *self*, of *other selves*, and of *the world*: "I am, and I know that I am ; other men are, and I know that they are ; the world is, and I know that it is ". Whether or not such a starting-point is justifiable, at all events it embodies a very decisive assertion of the *real objectivity* of knowledge, *i.e.* of the view that what presents itself in the process of cognition, as object to the knowing subject for interpretation, is *real* (20-22). The author is well aware that all three certitudes have been seriously questioned, for he continues : "They are never called into question *except sometimes in psychology and philosophy or metaphysics :* a strange ex-ception *the occasion and meaning of which we must consider in due order*".[3] So he is prepared to examine and discuss the doubts. "At present," he adds, "it suffices to point out that no one really and sanely doubts their certitudes ['these certitudes'? or 'their certitude'?] as existing facts or realities : what is doubted is rather the common interpretation of the facts. Certainly we do not know *what* we are, or *what* the world is—except to a very small and dim extent. All this, however, has to be considered more in detail."[4]

Of course no one, not even the most extreme subjectivist, doubts them "as existing facts or realities " if by this we mean merely "facts of the know-ing subject's own awareness ". But suppose it be really doubted whether these three "objects of awareness " (19)—the individual Self or Mind, other Selves or Minds, and a Material Universe—are or reveal realities distinct from the subjective process of awareness itself, or whether if so these realities are as they are represented in the cognitive process, or wholly and unknow-ably otherwise,—how is such a doubt to be dealt with ?

We cannot *logically disprove* such a doubt or denial of the real objecti-vity of knowledge by *strictly demonstrating* such real objectivity. We may indeed show that our knowledge of other minds as objective to our own is dependent on our knowledge of a material universe as objective to our own mind ; and we may, by an analysis of sense perception, show that the indi-

[1] We regard such formulation of the "data " as less ambiguous than the more usual formula " facts of consciousness ".

[2] *Knowledge, Belief, and Certitude*, by FREDERICK STORRS TURNER (London, 1900), Bk. I., Part I., ii., p. 62.

[3] *Ibid.*, italics ours.   [4] *Ibid.*

vidual mind is brought into cognitive contact with a material universe that is really distinct from, and really other than, the individual mind itself. We intend to do this : and the considerations that will emerge from our analysis will, we hope, help to convey reflex certitude about the real objectivity of knowledge to the impartial reader.

But whether they will have the same effect on the subjectivist is another matter. If on mature reflection he still balks at the bugbear of "transcendence" (19), and so refuses to believe that his sense perception establishes cognitive contact between *his own subjectivity* and *a real world distinct from the latter*, it is hardly likely that he will be convinced by our employment of the Principle of Causality to prove that the world perceived by the senses is *really* objective to, and other than, his perceiving mind : for if mature reflection on the immediate evidence of sense perception fails to convince him that by means of this process he is made aware of realities that are other than, and distinct from, and independent of, the subjective perception-process which he identifies with his individual self, can we wonder if a like reflection on the immediate evidence of intellectual thought,—evidence so cogently presented to his mind in such abstract, axiomatic judgments as the Principles of Identity, Contradiction and Causality, or the principles of mathematics,—will likewise fail to convince him that the objects revealed to him in these judgments are objective *realities*, distinct from and independent of his subjective thought-process, and not merely " objectivated" modes of his own subjectivity ?

Mercier [1] thinks that it is from the latter domain—of abstract and necessary ideal judgments—that the mists of subjectivism should first be dispelled, by an analysis which will show that the cogent intellectual evidence of immediate judgments in this domain reveals them as *manifestations of reality* to the knowing subject, and therefore as of universally valid application to *all* reality ; and he thinks that *by the aid of those ideal principles*, thus established as true of *objective reality*, the difficulties raised by subjectivism against *sense perception* as revealing a real, external, material universe, can *then* be more easily and effectively dissipated (22). The question of the *order* in which the two domains should be explored, that of the senses and that of the intellect, with a view to vindicating the real objectivity both of sense perception and of intellectual thought, seems to us a matter of comparatively minor importance ; the really important task being to show the groundlessness of subjectivism in both domains alike.

[1] *Op. cit.*, § 25, pp. 45-50.

CHAPTER IV.

UNJUSTIFIABLE ISSUE OF THE INQUIRY: SCEPTICISM.

36. ORDER OF PROBLEMS. — Reverting to the problems raised in a previous chapter,[1] we might choose in the first place to expound the solutions we ourselves regard as the right solutions, *viz.* those offered by scholasticism, and then proceed to examine and criticize erroneous and defective theories. But in its main lines the scholastic theory is nearer to what we may call the common-sense interpretation of facts, and is therefore easier to grasp, than most of the other theories. It is by the negative process of eliminating these that the mind of the student will be prepared for the positive considerations on which the scholastic theory is based. Hence we consider it preferable to commence the inquiry into the *objectivity of knowledge* by a brief review of scepticism, next to deal with modern English subjectivism, then to examine the *apparent* objectivism of Kant's philosophy, and finally the *real* objectivism of the scholastic theory ; and this will be a gradual movement from extreme error in the direction of truth.[2]

We shall also endeavour to establish in the first place the objectivity of the *nexus* or synthesis established in the act of judgment, especially in judgments of the ideal order (10), between the mental objects or terms compared (the subject and predicate) ; then to show that these conceived objects (or " objective concepts ") themselves are really representative of the conscious data of sense intuition ; and finally to show that sense perception is a valid apprehension of reality as it is.

It is customary with scholastic writers to adopt a division of the whole investigation into two departments which have been described as *General* and *Special* Epistemology (or Criteriology) respectively [3] ; the object of the former

---

[1] Chap. ii., especially § 23.   [2] *Cf.* JEANNIÈRE, *op. cit.*, p. 201, n. 2.
[3] MERCIER recognizes this distinction and deals only with *General* Criteriology. JEANNIÈRE likewise adopts it and deals with both departments. Soo, too, are both departments included in the *Criteriology* of the *abridged edition* (English trs., 2 vols., by T. L. and S. A. Parker: London, Kegan Paul, 1917) of the Louvain *Cours de Philosophie.*

being to vindicate the possibility of certain knowledge in general, and that of the latter to investigate more in detail the scope and limits of this certain knowledge by an examination of its various sources : consciousness, memory, sense perception, intellectual intuition, deduction, induction, etc. The inconvenience of such an arrangement arises from the fact that the possibility of certitude in general cannot be fully and effectively vindicated against the detailed difficulties of sceptical theories without a detailed analysis of the sources whence such difficulties arise,—except, indeed, by anticipating, to some extent at least, the results of such special analysis, and thereby rendering some repetition inevitable.[1] But for the student repetition is not an unmixed evil ; and there are advantages in getting first a general survey of the principles of solution, and then supplementing this survey by special investigation of the main sources of our spontaneous convictions.

Among those, then, who have sought a solution of the problems of knowledge and certitude some have relied on the verdict of human reason or intellect (*Intellectualism*). Others have declared that the solution must be determined ultimately not by reason but by an appeal to one or other of a variety of non-intellectual motives—utility, sentiment, instinct, moral needs, supernatural aids, etc. Among the former some have taught that the last word of human reason reflecting on the problems is that they are insoluble. This is scepticism.

37. FORMS OF SCEPTICISM.—*Scepticism* (σκέπτομαι, *I inquire*), as an attitude of mind, is an overweening, excessive inclination to doubt. This may betray itself in the form of *practical* scepticism or *speculative* scepticism. By the former we mean an habitual attitude of practical distrust of one's natural powers, a constitutional or induced state of *pusillanimity*, an inability to make up one's mind, an irksome state of indecision, often combined with an inclination to act on mere impulse. This is mainly a morbid condition of the will and of the executive faculties, and can be cured only by an appropriate disciplinary regime of the will and the general character.

Speculative or *intellectual* scepticism is the attitude of one who doubts and distrusts the validity of his cognitive acts, his beliefs and convictions. When this attitude arises not so much from a serious study of the truth-value of knowledge as from a temperamental indifference to its truth or falsity it has been called *Dilettantism* in philosophy. The pursuit of esthetic

---

[1] Two of the main problems postponed for full discussion by JEANNIÈRE to Special Criteriology, *viz.* the validity of intellectual concepts (the " universals " question) and the validity of sense perception, are treated by MERCIER in his *Critériologie Générale*.

pleasure in contemplating all sorts and varieties of views and opinions, in flitting from one to another and resting in none, in passing through life without any fixed beliefs or ideals,—is allowed to stifle the pursuit of truth. This is unfortunately a widely prevalent attitude.[1] Brought up in an atmosphere of religious indifferentism, unequipped with any fixed standards of ethical values, educated into the morbid intellectual habit of a fickle freedom of thought, there are multitudes of men who have no reasoned beliefs on the great problems of life simply because they have never seriously tried, or felt any pressing need or desire, to search for such beliefs. This is perhaps the most dangerous, and certainly the most hopeless, form of scepticism, inasmuch as its victim feels pleased rather than pained at his unconcern for the truth. It is not, however, with this form of scepticism that we can hold any philosophical discussion ; but with intellectual scepticism in the stricter sense of a *reasoned* or *philosophical* doctrine according to which the *objectivity of human knowledge is and must remain doubtful.*

Of this again we may distinguish two forms, the one a purely imaginary and unreal form called *absolute* or *subjective* scepticism, the other a real and actual form called *relative* or *objective* scepticism. The former would be a (barely conceivable) state of doubt about absolutely everything, including the facts of consciousness, the real existence of thought and the thinker, the distinction between waking and sleeping, etc. No sane man has ever *de facto* entertained such a doubt. The real and historical forms of scepticism are forms of *objective* scepticism : recognizing the existence of spontaneous convictions as subjective facts of consciousness some philosophers have seriously doubted the validity of these cognitive states and processes *as representative of any reality beyond themselves.* Despairing of the power of the individual mind to reach beyond itself and attain to an insight into reality, these philosophers, while recognizing and acting on the practical need to use their spontaneous convictions as guides in the ordinary affairs of life (15), have maintained at the same time that there is no sufficient ground for believing that knowledge can solve any of the real problems relating to the origin, nature, and destiny of man and the universe.

[1] Not only in France, where it owes its prevalence in great measure to the enervating influence of RENAN (*cf.* JEANNIÈRE, *op. cit.*, p. 121 n.), but in all European and English-speaking countries wherever the Christian Faith has been on the wane.

The student will do well to remember that it is a *reasoned* and *real insight* into the nature of things, and more especially into the solution of the great, ultimate problems raised by reflection on human experience, that sceptics have been at pains to declare unattainable; that they do not deny to knowledge a certain practical, working utility for the guidance of life, but only that it gives us any *speculative* insight into the real nature and significance of the facts of mental experience.

And here again we may distinguish scepticism into *universal* and *partial* according as the sceptic doubts about the validity of *all* his convictions from whatsoever source (10); or only about those derived from some particular sources, while admitting the possibility and the fact of a reasoned certitude from other sources. Thus, for example, *Fideism* doubts the validity of any natural knowledge apart from the aid of supernatural faith; *Rationalism* doubts the validity of alleged revealed truth; *Positivism* doubts the validity of all knowledge of the suprasensible domain; *Kantism* doubts the validity of knowledge reached by the speculative reason; etc., etc. Most of the sceptical theories of modern philosophy are *partial* scepticisms; that is to say, their propounders, while doubting or denying the validity of knowledge derived from some sources, themselves claim to have attained to philosophical certitude through some other source or sources. And although all (objective) *scepticism* is some form or other of *subjectivism*, still it is the latter term that is more commonly applied to *modern* sceptical theories and tendencies, while the term *scepticism* is rather regarded as descriptive of *ancient* theories.

Finally, scepticism is a theory of *knowledge* (*logical*) rather than a theory of *reality* (*ontological*). The sceptic as such does not *deny* that God, or the soul, or a domain of spiritual reality exists (which would be atheism or materialism), but only that such can be known with reasoned certitude (agnosticism, positivism). If, therefore, a speculative sceptic were to believe in the real existence of God, or the soul, or a spiritual domain of being, he should admit that he holds such belief not as a reasoned conviction, but through custom, instinct, inherited mentality, or some other rationally inexplicable influences.

38. ITS MAIN HISTORICAL MANIFESTATIONS.—A. *Among the Ancient Greeks and Romans.*—In the pre-Socratic period (fifth century B.C.) *Protagoras,* starting from the teaching of

Heraclitus (4), taught that objective, absolute truth is unattainable; that all truth is relative to the individual knower; that what *appears* to him is true *for him ;* that "Man is the measure of all things". This was an erroneous, because an over-emphatic, assertion of the dependence of knowledge on the nature of the mental factor, in reaction against the crude speculations which had attempted to solve the riddle of the universe without paying any attention to the nature of the knowing mind. Similarly *Gorgias*, starting from the teaching of Zeno the Eleatic, is said to have contended (*a*) that nothing existed (presumably, nothing beyond the individual thought process); (*b*) that if anything existed it could not be known ; and (*c*) that even if it could be known the knowledge of it could not be communicated (through want of an indubitable common measure between mind and mind).

In the post-Socratic period *Pyrrho* (365-275),—on the testimony of his disciple *Timon* (325-235)—is said to have taught that sense knowledge can give us no reliable insight into things *as they are in themselves* because of their perpetual flux and instability, or even into things *as they appear to us* inasmuch as our senses often deceive us ; nor can reason give us certitude because arguments are always forthcoming *for* and *against* every contention ("*antinomies*"); therefore the right course is to *suspend our assent* (ἐποχή), and so attain to that equable tranquillity of soul (ἀταραξία) which is man's highest good. We have here an ethical thesis, a positive *practical* teaching, based on universal speculative doubt. This *Pyrrhonism* was revived in the first century B.C., in the form known as *Neo-Pyrrhonism*, by *Aenesidemus*, who defended it in ten "tropes" or *rationes dubitandi ;* by his contemporary, *Agrippa*, in five similar "tropes"; and a century later by the Roman physician, *Sextus Empiricus* (A.D. 150), who recapitulated and developed the doubts of Pyrrhonism in his voluminous writings, especially in his *Hypotyposes Pyrrhonianae* and his *X Libri contra Mathematicos*[1] [= dogmaticos]. The five tropes of Agrippa are as follows: (1) The conflicting views of philosophers ; (2) the relativity of all sense representations ; (3) the inevident character of the

---

[1] The other available ancient sources of information on Scepticism are: DIOGENES LAERTIUS, *De Vitis Philosophorum Antiquitatis ;* PLATO, *Theaetetus ;* ARISTOTLE, *Metaphysics ;* ST. AUGUSTINE, *Contra Academicos* and *Epistola ad Dioscorum.*

statements put forward as principles by the dogmatists; (4) the infinite regress in demonstrating, at once unavoidable and impossible; (5) the unavoidable *diallelus* (ὁ διάλληλος τρόπος, δι' ἀλλήλων) or *circulus vitiosus* in demonstration. Although these extreme sceptics rejected even the "probability" of the Academicians as a speculatively justifiable basis of conduct, it is clear that their preoccupation too was mainly ethical, for while they denied that philosophy is in any sense a system of speculative knowledge (αἵρεσις), they contended that it is a practical art of living (ἀγωγή) inasmuch as it counsels the guiding of life according to the individual's subjective conscious impressions.

The second Platonic Academy under *Arcesilaus* (316-241) adopted the view that since there is no available test of certitude, and *an appearance of probability* is the highest attainment of speculative reason, our judgment must remain suspended (ἐποχή). The third academy, under *Carneades* (219-129), contended that while certitude is unattainable, whether by the senses or by reason, nevertheless there are among men's subjective representations some that are sufficiently *probable* to serve as a basis for the proper conduct of life (*probabilism*). Under the influence of these systems, *Cicero* (106-43) believed that on all the great problems of life man must be content with probability.

B. *In Modern Times.*—It is clear that the ancient theories just mentioned, while doubting the objective validity of knowledge, recognized spontaneous convictions as facts of consciousness, and also admitted the reasonableness of acting on them as if they were objectively certain.

In the Middle Ages men universally admitted the objective validity of certain knowledge, and the power of the mind to attain to such knowledge (4).

The dawn of the Renaissance, however, with its cult of pagan antiquity, led to a recrudescence of ancient forms of scepticism. During the sixteenth and seventeenth centuries many continental writers revived the old *rationes dubitandi*. The most noted names are those of the French essayist, MONTAIGNE (1533-92 : *Essais*); CHARRON, a French priest (1541-1603 : *De la sagesse*) ; SANCHEZ, a Portuguese physician (1562-1632 : *Quod nihil scitur*) ; HUET, bishop of Avranches (1632-1721 : *De la faiblesse de l'ésprit humain*, published posthumously 1723, and for a time considered spurious); PASCAL, a French philosopher (1623-62 : *Pensées ; Lettres provinciales*) ; BAYLE, a French writer (1647-1706: *Dictionnaire historique et critique*).   Those writers, however, are not sceptics in the sense of adopting the *negative* attitude of the ancient sceptics, that assent should remain suspended, that no judgment should be affirmed or denied.   While doubting the capacity of the *intellect* or *reason* to reach truth, and contending that the *purely intellectual grounds* within the reach of natural reason are insufficient for certitude, most of them endeavour to base certitude on non-intellectual grounds, intrinsic or extrinsic, such as " reasons of the heart," supernatural grace, divine revelation,[1] etc.   By proclaiming the incapacity of natural and unaided human reason to discover truth, they hoped to vindicate more fully the efficacy and the necessity of the Christian Faith and Revelation.[2]   This is a form of dogmatism rather than scepticism.

Of this union of utter intellectual scepticism with a blind clinging to religious belief we have a striking and pathetic illustration in the writings of THEODORE JOUFFROY (1796-1841 : *Mélánges philosophiques*).   " We consider scepticism invincible," he writes,[3] " because we regard it as the last word of reason on itself."   " That we believe is simply a fact.   But are we justified in believing what we do believe? . . . That is a problem which the mind cannot help raising. . . . But from the fact that reason raises this doubt about itself, does it follow that reason can settle it ?   The *vicious circle* is too glaringly manifest.   If reason can so doubt itself as to feel the need of a control, clearly it cannot trust itself to exercise this control."[4]   " Nevertheless belief is a universal necessity.   We believe simply because we must."   Hence he concludes that at the basis of all our beliefs there lies " an act of faith, blind but irresistible, in the capacity of the mind to discover truth ".[5]

All those modern theories of knowledge which reject the appeal to intellect and seek to base human certitude ultimately on grounds that are not intellectual, are of course sceptical in tend-

---

[1] " As for the scepticism of Pascal, Huet, de Lammenais, it is rather a controversial weapon, an apologetic method, for leading men to the Christian faith, which is, in their view, alone capable of securing to the human mind the tranquillity and certitude for which it yearns."—LAHR, *Cours de Philos.*, *apud* JEANNIÈRE, *op. cit.*, pp. 127, 242.

[2] *Cf.* PASCAL'S *Pensées*, §§ 6, 7.   [3] *Mél. philos.*, p. 219.

[4] *Préface aux Œuvres de Th. Reid.*, t. i., p. clxxxv.

[5] *Cf.* MERCIER, *op. cit.*, pp. 176-7 (§ 80) ; JEANNIÈRE, *op. cit.*, p. 110, n. 1; p. 128, n. 1.

ency and in effect, though they may be dogmatic in intention :
an assertion which we hope to justify in the sequel.

The English subjectivism which received its impetus from
LOCKE (1632-1704) culminated in the thoroughly sceptical
phenomenism of HUME (1711-1776). And the " critical " philosophy of KANT, which was intended as a reaction against this
thoroughgoing scepticism, really fails to rescue human certitude
from the shipwreck of subjectivism (4).

But all these modern theories of knowledge have a constructive as well as a destructive side. On their destructive side they
restate all the considerations urged by the ancient sceptics to show
that certitude cannot be justified on grounds of reason. Rather,
however, than rest in universal doubt, they then attempt, on their
constructive side, to defend certitude in spite of reason, as it were,
by basing it ultimately on individual or social utility, or biological instincts and impulses, or sentiment and feeling, or ethical
and religious needs. They even think that they are erecting the
most effective barrier possible against scepticism by thus placing
the basis of certitude in a domain where they believe it will be
necessarily free from the corroding influence of the purely speculative reason. But however well-intentioned such constructive
efforts may be, we hope to show in due course that they necessarily fail in their purpose ; for, after all, the question " What
grounds of human knowledge and certitude are to be considered
satisfactory ? " must be asked and answered by man's speculative
reason. In this matter reason is the last and highest court of
appeal : which, however, is not saying that we are to believe only
what is *intrinsically evident*, but rather that we are to believe only
what is at least *credible, i.e.* what it is *reasonable* to believe. And
of this, what faculty is to judge, if it be not the faculty of reason ?

At present, however, we are concerned only with the destructive or sceptical side of such theories. And of course the real
refutation of the arguments urged against the capacity of the
mind to discover objective truth about reality will consist in the
whole critical analysis which will go to show that this capacity is
an undeniable fact. If, then, we consider here very briefly a few
of the main considerations urged by sceptics, our purpose will be
firstly, not to show that these considerations have *no* weight, but
to point out that while they are sufficiently serious to prompt an
investigation of the whole problem of certitude they are not sufficiently serious to render such investigation hopeless at the outset

(*cf.* 26) ; and *secondly*, to call attention to a few *ineffectual* ways of meeting the difficulties of sceptics.

39. CRITIQUE OF SCEPTICISM.—The arguments urged by sceptics do not show that reasoned certitude is unattainable.

A. The multitudinous errors and contradictions which have always prevailed in human beliefs show that the human mind is utterly unreliable.

Reply.—The existence of *errors* is an undeniable fact. But this does not prove that error is inevitable or that the human mind is essentially deceptive. If there were no available test of truth, no means of distinguishing truth from error, then indeed scepticism would be the only reasonable attitude to adopt ; but it is not evident, and sceptics have not proved, that there is no such test available. The fact of error only proves that the whole matter needs investigation ; and the very contention of sceptics, that errors have been recognized as such, is an implicit admission that there is an available test (26). The same applies to the existence of *contradictions*. Moreover, in regard to these latter it is undeniable that they do not extend to *all* our spontaneous convictions. There are spontaneous convictions that are irresistible (11); and all agree that they are irresistible. On this point there are no contradictions, but universal agreement; though, of course, contradictory views are held as to the significance of this fact.

B. But it is urged that from the very nature of the case reason can discover no satisfactory criterion of truth. Sceptics argue thus : " Either there is a valid criterion of truth or there is not. On this point as on all others *we* suspend our assent and say simply that we do not know. And *you* cannot show us that there is such a criterion. For by what consideration or argument can you show it? Whatever consideration you make use of, we need a criterion to test the value of such consideration ; for we cannot accept the consideration as convincing without having first submitted it to a criterion. Hence you have first to convince us of the validity of this latter criterion. And so on *ad infinitum :* unless you try to convince us by means of a criterion which we have not accepted, which is *begging the question.*" Or, to transfer the difficulty from the particular debate between sceptic and dogmatist, and to apply it to the possibility of objective knowledge, of demonstration or proof in general : " To judge of the real objectivity of our subjective or mental cognitive states we need a judging instrument or apparatus; to test the validity of this latter we require proof; to test the validity of this proof we need an instrument; and there we are on the wheel. As the senses cannot settle the question for us, being themselves full of uncertainty, we must have recourse to reason; but no reason can prevail without another reason : and there we are, driven back *ad infinitum*."[1]   This is the old difficulty of the *diallelus*.

Reply.—The whole argument is based on an equivocation. It assumes that the criterion of truth, the "instrument judica-toire," must be always and necessarily extrinsic to, and distinct from, the judgment of whose truth it is the test.   But since we have the power of reflecting on our judgments, what if we find that some judgments contain *in themselves, and inseparable from themselves,* a characteristic which is the test, and which we re-cognize to be the test, or criterion, of their own truth : so that by one and the same intuition we see the *truth of the judgment,* and *simultaneously,*—not antecedently or subsequently or by a dis-tinct judicial act,—the *validity of the criterion?*   If this be so,—and we hope to show that not all criteria are extrinsic to the judgment tested,—then we avoid both the *petitio principii* and the *endless regress.*   Of course if we fail to convince the sceptic that any of the judgments to which he admits he is forced to assent by psychological necessity, reveal on analysis a character which is at once a criterion or index of their real objectivity and truth, and at the same time a justification of that criterion, then we must only leave him in his scepticism.[2]

---

[1] MONTAIGNE, *Essais,* L. II., chap. xii. : " Pour juger des apparences que nous recevons des subjects, il nous faudrait un instrument judicatoire; pour verifier cet instrument, il nous fault de la demonstration; pour verifier la demonstration, un in-strument : nous voylà au rouet.   Puisque les sens ne peuvent arrester notre dispute, étant pleins eulx-mêmes d'incertitude, il fault que ce soit la raison; alcune raison ne s'establira sans une autre raison : nous voylà à reculons jusqu'à l'infiny."

[2] Sceptics do not deny the existence of spontaneous convictions as states of con-sciousness.   They admit, moreover, in practice and provisionally, for the sake of discussing the whole problem of knowledge, the competence of their reason to carry on a discussion.   JEANNIÈRE suggests this *argumentum ad hominem* against such disputants : " You grant that you really know your sensations, your conscious states; you see that in regard to them you know things (*viz.* subjective states) as they really are, and that this knowledge is objective in the sense that it attains to *that which is.* Therefore you admit *de facto* that it is possible for the mind to see that it attains to true knowledge.   If the *diallelus* were valid you could not be certain even of your states of consciousness " (*op. cit.,* p. 132, n. 1).   Now an *argumentum ad hominem* is an argument based on your adversary's admissions.   But do *all* sceptics admit that they know their own states of consciousness *as these are in themselves?*   Kant

C. Even the knowledge men think they have does not extend to all things : men are admittedly ignorant of many things. But all things are so inter-related and interdependent that ignorance of any single item or fraction of reality involves ignorance of the whole, just as knowledge of any one item would necessarily imply knowledge of the whole. Seeing, therefore, that we do not know *all* reality it follows that we *really know* nothing.[1] As Hegel

Reply.—(1) This difficulty cannot consistently be urged by the sceptic, for it implies that the objector *accepts* a certain view of reality *to be true, viz.* the view that reality is so knit into one system that we cannot know any part without knowing the whole. (2) Apart from that, however, the difficulty is based on the unproven and false assumption that knowledge, to be true, must be *comprehensive, exhaustive* of its object. *De facto* there is a kind of knowledge, the most perfect conceivable,—the comprehensive intuition which is the property of the Divine Intelligence, —which sees reality in this way, which sees " each in all and all in each ". But if *human* knowledge cannot attain to this ideal, —and, with all due respect to the Hegelian view of explanation, according to which " nothing can be known rightly, without knowing all else rightly," [2] it *cannot* attain to such an ideal,—it does not follow that it may not be true as far as it goes. Insight into reality need not be exhaustive in order to be genuine. Provided we possess reliable tests of truth we can draw the line between what we know and what we do not know, and thus avoid error. Our duty is, therefore, to seek for such tests or criteria.

D. Perhaps we are the sport of some Malignant Power by whom we have been endowed with faculties that are of their

certainly would not ; he holds that our knowledge of our conscious states is subject to the same law as all other knowledge is (according to his theory). We know them, he would say, as states of the " *phenomenal*," *empirical* mind, or self, or Ego, *i.e.* as products of subjective factors or forms with an unknown " datum " or " content " furnished by the transcendental, or real, or " noumenal " *Ego ;* but whether they are genuinely representative of the transcendal or real *Ego* and its real states—that we can never know. How far this position can be met by the contention that at least as regards conscious awareness of our own mental states there is no room for the distinction between these latter " as they are in themselves " and " as they appear to us "—we shall examine later, when we come to ask whether the general Kantian distinction between phenomenon and noumenon really serves the purpose for which it was invented. It may turn out that the distinction in question only substitutes for the difficulty of " transcendence " (in knowing objective reality) an equally grave difficulty against the possibility of knowing even phenomena!

[1] *Cf.* PASCAL, *Pensées*, Art. i. So also MONTAIGNE, SANCHEZ, etc.

[2] BOSANQUET, *Logic*, p. 393. *Cf. Science of Logic*, ii., § 257, p. 242.

nature deceptive.   We have already dealt with this curious fancy (26).

E. When sceptics object *a posteriori—i.e.* apart from all *a priori* difficulties—that they have themselves examined the problem of certitude ; that they have failed to find any rational basis therefor; that the criteria brought forward by dogmatists appear to them to be insufficient ; in particular that the " evidence " to which scholastics appeal as the ultimate and sufficient test of truth is really no test at all, inasmuch as " evidence " itself needs to be sifted and tested,[1]—we can only reply that if they are as modest as they must be presumed to be sincere they will allow that others may possibly succeed where they have failed.   We may also suggest that they reconsider the whole problem, and see especially whether they have rightly understood the claims put forward by scholastics on behalf of " evidence ".   This is the only reasonable way to deal with scepticism.   But there are mistaken ways of dealing with it, and ineffective arguments urged against it : a few of which we may now indicate.

A. It is a mistake to think that the sceptic, by virtue of his very attitude of doubt, contradicts himself, or puts himself outside the pale of rational discussion.   Of course if a sceptic were so foolish as to maintain positively and dogmatically, as a thesis, this self-contradictory proposition : " I am certain that nothing is certain " ; or to doubt the very existence of his own spontaneous convictions as subjective facts of consciousness ; or if he refused to admit as valid, at least provisionally and for purposes of discussion, the self-evident principles involved in all rational judgment and reasoning, such as the principle of contradiction,— then indeed it would be equally foolish to attempt to argue with him.   But such a type of sceptic is purely imaginary.[2]   The flesh-and-blood sceptic of history admits spontaneous certitudes as facts of consciousness, recognizes these as the *data* for discussion, and is willing to discuss and argue in accordance with the logical principles of inference.   He doubts about the objective validity of his spontaneous certitudes ; and even this position of his, *viz.* that " all objective certitude is doubtful," he holds not as being itself objectively certain, but as a *subjective persuasion* of his, about the objective certitude of which he claims to know nothing.

[1] HOBBES has said somewhere that " the inn of evidence has no sign-board ".
[2] *Cf.* MERCIER, *op. cit.*, § 36, pp. 76-7.

B. It is often urged against scepticism that it flagrantly contradicts "common sense" and must therefore be rejected. If by "common sense" is here meant the spontaneous, unreflecting belief of mankind, the sceptic will admit the antecedent, but will deny the consequent. And in fact the philosopher has no right to set up this spontaneous voice of mankind as an ultimate court of appeal, but rather to analyse it and see what real value can be attached to its dictates. If on the other hand "common sense" be understood to mean the reasoned verdict to which careful reflection on our cognitive processes leads, then the sceptic will deny the antecedent. And the only way to establish the antecedent will be *to examine the whole problem by reflection.*

C. Scepticism is opposed to man's natural appetite or craving for knowledge. Nature prompts man not to doubt but to believe. Man is by nature a dogmatist, a believer in the possibility of truth. Scepticism is unnatural. Natural cravings that are universal must have aptitudes corresponding to them. Hence the universal yearning of man for knowledge implies in man the capacity or aptitude to attain to knowledge.

The sceptic's reply to this line of argument is that while he quite recognizes and feels the natural craving, he fails to see that it can be satisfied. He doubts that the mere existence of a universal natural craving or appetite implies the existence of the capacity to satisfy that appetite. He observes that men have many cravings which they cannot satisfy, and that, for all he knows, the "human machine" may be a hopeless failure.

D. Scepticism is of course incompatible with the Christian religion, and undermines the foundations of faith; and the spread of scepticism among the masses, like the spread of free thought and religious indifference, leads to a regrettable lowering of moral standards.

But it is obviously useless to urge these considerations as refutations of scepticism. The question for the philosopher is not, "What happens to faith and morals if scepticism prevails?" but, "Is scepticism defensible on grounds of reason?" Is it, or is it not, the reasonable attitude for the mind to adopt in regard to the problem of certitude?

PART II.

INTELLECTUAL KNOWLEDGE : JUDGMENT.

CHAPTER V.

NECESSARY JUDGMENTS: ENGLISH SUBJECTIVISM.

40. OBJECTIVITY OF THE NECESSARY NEXUS ASSERTED IN IMMEDIATE JUDGMENTS OF THE IDEAL ORDER.—In an earlier section (10), in which we classified the judgments in which our supposed knowledge is contained, it was pointed out that our certitude about the universal conclusions of science whether deductive or inductive (*ibid.*, 3, 4),—and indeed about the immediate judgments of sense perception (*ibid.*, 1), and judgments based on testimony (*ibid.*, 5),—depends on the validity of what we called "immediate judgments derived from analysis and comparison of abstract ideas" (*ibid.*, 2), or, again, immediate judgments "of the ideal order".[1] These latter, therefore, are of supreme importance ; and the first question we have to examine in regard to them is the question whether the mind, in effecting the synthesis between subject and predicate, and assenting to this synthesis or *nexus* as obtaining *necessarily* and therefore *universally*, is determined to do so by what we may call a purely psychological or subjective necessity, however this may be explained, or rather by the compelling influence of an *intuitively apprehended* or *seen* connexion between the two thought-objects themselves which stand as subject and predicate of the judgment.

Let it be noted that we confine the inquiry to *immediate* judgments of the ideal order, *i.e.* those commonly called axioms or first principles, and described by the scholastics as *propositiones per se notae non solum in se sed quoad nos et omnes ;* [2] in other

---

[1] *Cf.* MERCIER, *op. cit.*, § 120, p. 285 ; JEANNIÈRE, *op. cit.*, pp. 203-4.

[2] *Cf. Science of Logic*, i., § 86. All *necessary* judgments, *i.e.* judgments in which a full analysis of subject and predicate reveals a *necessary nexus* between these terms, were held by the scholastics to be *analytic* and were described as *per se notae in se, i.e.* knowable by rational analysis of the notions involved. All the con-

words, to judgments whose terms are so simple as to be intelligible to all people of normal mental development. Such, for example, are the Principles of Identity and Contradiction ; the Principle of Causality ; the elementary truths of mathematics like " 2 and 3 are 5," " The whole is greater than its part," " Two straight lines cannot enclose a space"; the principles of ethics, like " Veracity is morally right," " Lying is morally wrong," etc.

Next, we are not inquiring here into the origin, nature, or significance of the *concepts* or *thought-objects* compared as subject and predicate in any such judgment, or whence or how they become present to the mind, but only into the *nexus* affirmed or denied between the concepts compared. Under what influence does the mind assert a necessary and universal connexion between subject and predicate? And we purpose to examine first the answers given by English Subjectivism, mainly as represented by John Stuart Mill (1806-1873) and Herbert Spencer (1820-1903),—the associationist and the evolutionist solutions as we may call them respectively.

41. SUBJECTIVE NECESSITY THROUGH ASSOCIATION.—The view represented mainly by Mill comes to this, that the individual mind effects the synthesis between subject and predicate of any such necessary judgment, *not* because it is demanded, and seen to be demanded, by anything appertaining to, or belonging to the nature of, these concepts or thought-objects themselves as present to the mind, *but* because the latter, in virtue of a law of its own constitution, the law of association of mental states by contiguity in experience, has grown so accustomed to think of a given predicate, *e.g.* " five " whenever it thinks of a given subject,

clusions of mathematics are of this kind. These, however, are not self-evident, because their terms are complex. But the terms of the axioms or first principles from which they are derived by demonstration are so simple that such axioms or first principles are within the reach of all. Thus, St. Thomas writes : " Quaelibet propositio, cujus praedicatum est de ratione subjecti, est immediata et per se nota quantum est de se. Sed quarundum propositionum termini sunt tales quod sunt in notitia omnium, sicut *ens* et *unum*, et alia quae sunt entis inquantum ens. Nam ens est prima conceptio intellectus. Unde oportet quod tales propositiones non solum in se sed etiam quoad nos, quasi per se notae habeantur ; sicut quod *non contingit idem esse et non esse*, et *totum est majus sua parte*. Unde et hujusmodi principia omnes scientiae accipiunt a metaphysica, cujus est considerare ens simpliciter et ea quae sunt eutis."—*Post. Anal.*, I., l. 5. And he also points out that the cognition of such principles varies with the development of the individual mind : " Intellectus principiorum consequitur naturam humanam quae aequaliter in omnibus invenitur . . . et *tamen* secundum majorem capacitatem intellectus unus majus vel minus cognoscit veritatem principiorum quam alius ".—*Summa Theol.* IIae. IIae., Q. V., a. iv. ad 3.

e.g. "two *plus* three," that it is unable to dissociate these objects. The objects just happen to have been uniformly associated in this way in the course of our sense experience. The necessity of the judicial *nexus* is therefore a purely *subjective, psychological* necessity. It is simply an inseparable, irresistible association of objects which, so far as they themselves are concerned, might have been related quite otherwise had our uniform sense experience been otherwise. The ."feeling of necessity" with which such mathematical and metaphysical axioms are affirmed is a product of mental association of conscious states uniformly experienced in *de facto* contiguity with each other. Hence all the information really conveyed by such judgments is just this and no more, that our minds *de facto* have always experienced certain conscious states or objects (which we therefore connect as subjects and predicates) as uniform co-existences or sequences. Such judgments do not at all inform us that there is any *essential* or *ontological* or *absolutely necessary* connexion between such objects. The experienced conjunction of such objects is a mere factual co-existence or sequence. By a subjective law of association the mind transforms this into a necessity which it (groundlessly) regards as absolute, as holding good beyond all actual experience, and for all possible experience. "In distant parts of the stellar regions,"[1] lying beyond experience, "it would be folly to affirm confidently" that any general or universal judgment holds as valid. "We should probably be able to conceive a *round* square as easily as a *hard* square or a *heavy* square, if it were not that in our uniform experience at the moment when a thing begins to be round it ceases to be square, so that the beginning of one impression is inseparably associated with the departure of the other. . . . We cannot conceive two and two as five, because an unseparable association compels us to conceive it as four. . . . And we should probably have no difficulty in putting together the two ideas supposed to be incompatible (*e.g.* round and square, etc.), if our experience had not first inseparably associated one with the contradictory of the other."[2] "The reverse of the most familiar principles of arithmetic and geometry might have been made conceivable even to our present mental faculties, if those faculties had co-existed with a totally different constitution of external nature."[3]

---

[1] Mill, *Logic*, III., chap. xvi., § 4.

[2] *Ibid., Examination of Sir W. Hamilton's Philosophy*, 2nd edit., pp. 68-9.

[3] *Ibid.*, pp. 85-6, note—*apud* Ward, *Philosophy of Theism*, i., p. 42 n. The student will bear in mind that " external nature " is reduced by Mill's subjectivism

From such extracts as these, and they could be multiplied if it were necessary, it is clear that according to Mill the only influence which the concepts or thought-objects can have in producing such judgments lies simply in this that *de facto* they come before the mind in a certain order and that therefore within the limits of conscious time-and-space experience wherein this order is found to prevail, and no further, we are justified in asserting that " 2 + 2 = 4," " the whole is greater than its part," etc., etc. It is only for the *nexus* of *fact* that there is a (mentally) *objective* ground, and even this ground lies not in the nature of the mental objects themselves, but only in the order of co-existence or sequence in which they happen uniformly to present themselves in consciousness. But when we pass to assert a nexus of *necessity*—that " 2 + 2 *must be* 4," etc.—the influence which determines us to do so is a *purely subjective influence*, a tendency arising *from the constitution of our own minds*, an influence which deceives us if we think that the *nexus* which it prompts us to establish (*e.g.* between " 2 + 2 " and " 4 ") is an *absolute* necessity, valid for all minds and for all reality.

In all immediate judgments of the ideal order, therefore,—including the axioms of mathematics,[1]—the synthesis effected

to " present sensations *plus* permanent possibilities of sensations " (*cf. Science of Logic*, i. pp. 149-50 ; *Ontology*, pp. 220, 334).

[1] HUME, who explained our belief in causality as due to custom (*cf. Ontology*, pp. 370 n., 385), and to whose influence is largely due the adoption, by subsequent English philosophers and psychologists, of the laws of " association of mental states " as the ultimate explanatory factors of all knowledge, himself appears to have hesitated about the capacity of his theory to give a satisfactory explanation of the necessary character of *mathematical* judgments. " All objects of human reason and inquiry," he writes (*Inquiry Concerning the Human Understanding*, vol. iv., p. 32 *sqq.*), " may naturally be divided into two kinds, to wit, *relations of ideas* and *matters of fact*. Of the first kind are the sciences of geometry, algebra, and arithmetic, and, in short, every affirmation which is either intuitively or demonstratively certain. *That the square of the hypotenuse is equal to the square of the two sides*, is a proposition which expresses a relation between these two figures. *That three times five is equal to the half of thirty* expresses a relation between these numbers. Propositions of this kind are discoverable by the mere operation of thought without dependence on whatever is anywhere existent in the universe. Though there never were a circle or a triangle in nature, the truths demonstrated by Euclid would for ever retain their certainty and evidence." This passage is unexceptional. But unfortunately he held that such judgments, in so far as they are understood to affirm *necessary* connexions, are results of a customary mental association begetting a merely *psychological* and *subjective* necessity in the *nexus* asserted ; and that they are true, or applicable to the objects present to the mind in sense-consciousness, *only approximately :* " When geometry decides anything concerning the proportions of quantity, we ought not to look for the utmost precision and exactness. None of its proofs extend so far. It takes the dimensions and proportions of figures, justly, but roughly, and

between subject and predicate is, in so far as it asserts an *absolute necessity*, a purely subjective synthesis ; and is, for all we know, invalid beyond the domain of the uniformly experienced facts of consciousness.

Now, however the " necessary " character which we recognize in such judgments is to be explained, it is certainly not satisfactorily explained by this theory of mental association. Nor do we purpose examining it in detail, for it is no longer seriously supported [1] by philosophers. We will merely indicate a few reasons to show the falsity of the thesis that "in immediate judgments of the ideal order the mind asserts a necessary connexion between subject and predicate *because it is compelled by a subjective tendency or law* to associate inseparably objects uniformly perceived or imagined together in fact ".

(1) If the subjective mental tendency to associate inseparably thought-objects uniformly experienced together could account for the necessity of the relation established between subject and predicate in ideal judgments, then wherever objects are uniformly experienced together they should exhibit the necessary connexion characteristic of such judgments. But in innumerable cases they do not. Therefore it is *not* owing to the influence of any subjective associating tendency we assert such necessary judgments.

The minor premiss might be illustrated indefinitely. For example, we have *always* experienced together and associated " snow " and " white," " fire " and " burns," " sugar " and " sweet," " wood " and " floats," etc. Yet we do not assert or believe that " snow *must be* white," " fire *must* burn," etc., by the absolute necessity whereby " the whole *must be* greater than its part," " 2 + 2 *must be* 4," etc. ; but on the contrary we can quite easily conceive snow not being white, fire not burning, etc., without

with some liberty. Its errors are never considerable, nor would it err at all did it not aspire to such absolute perfection" (*Treatise on Human Nature*, p. 350). This is a logical conclusion from the sensism which explains the *necessary* character of all mental synthesis of objects as a *subjective* necessity, a product of subjective associating factors in the mind itself, and as therefore not grounded in, or applicable to, the mind's objects as such. It really denies, therefore, that the necessary character of ideal judgments is in any sense objective. Hume dealt in a similar way with the Principle of Causality, and all other " necessary" judgments ; and it was this thorough-going destruction of the claims of science to objective and necessary truth that prompted Kant to inquire anew into the sense in which such judgments are objectively valid.

[1] For exhaustive criticisms of it, *cf.* WARD, *Philosophy of Theism*, vol. i. ; MERCIER, *op. cit.*, § 127, pp. 299-315 ; MAHER, *Psychology*, 4th edit., pp. 283-6.

any such absurdity or self-contradiction as that involved in " 2 + 2 *not* being 4 ".

(2) On the other hand, if the necessity of the connexion asserted between the subject and predicate of judgments of the ideal order were a purely subjective, psychological necessity, begotten of an irresistible or inseparable association of objects in consciousness, then such necessity could only manifest itself between any given subject and predicate *after a long experience of repeated associations of these latter.* But as a matter of fact it often manifests itself the first time such a pair of objects are presented to the mind, " by mere consideration of the ideas," and without any repetition of experiences ; nor is the necessity of the connexion strengthened in the least by repeated subsequent experiences, as it should be were it produced by a tendency generated and strengthened by repetition of experiences. Therefore the necessity of the synthesis is not due to a mental tendency to associate inseparably objects uniformly presented together in consciousness.

To illustrate the minor premiss, take such mathematical judgments as " three times five is equal to the half of thirty " or " $x + 1 + y - 1 = x + y$," or " two quantities each of which is equal to a same third quantity are equal to each other ". Even had we never experienced a concrete case of these connexions, still the first time we apprehend clearly and compare the objects related in these judgments we apprehend and assert the connexions to be *absolutely necessary.*[1]

Mill misinterprets the function of experience in regard to ideal judgments. The function of experience is, as we shall see later, to present through the senses and imagination the concrete instances from which the intellect obtains the thought-objects compared in such judgments, and perhaps also instances of their concrete connexion.[2] Nor can mere experience,—however protracted, uniform, and uncontradicted,—of the actual co-existence or sequence of two objects in consciousness ever furnish an *adequate objective ground* for asserting an *absolutely necessary nexus,* an absolute " *must* be," between them as subject and predi-

---

[1] DR. WARD thus sums up the two arguments given above : " that which I have *never* experienced, I regard as *necessary ;* that which I have habitually and unexceptionally experienced, I regard as *contingent.* Most certainly, therefore, mere constant uniform experience cannot possibly account, as Mr. Mill thinks it does, for the mind's conviction of self-evident necessity " (*op. cit.,* p. 49).

[2] *Cf.* CAJETAN, *In Anal. Post.,* L. II., c. 13,—*apud* MERCIER, pp. 307, 308 n.

cate. Mill really recognizes this ; and hence claims that the necessity in question is purely psychological and subjective,—the outcome of an associative tendency of the mind.

42. SUBJECTIVE NECESSITY THROUGH EVOLUTION.—The peculiar weakness of Mill's position lay in the attempt to account for the necessity of the *nexus* in ideal judgments by ascribing it to the operation of the associating factor *during the very limited experience of the individual mind.* This defect *evolutionist* writers have sought to remedy by postulating the operation of this tendency, and the transmission and solidification of its results by heredity, throughout the indefinite past ages during which the human intellect is supposed to have been gradually evolved from lower and non-rational forms of life.

" In its present garb," writes Maher,[1] " the theory claims to possess the combined merits of the hypotheses of *innate ideas*, of *a priori forms of thought*, and of *inseparable association*, while it escapes their deficiencies. Mr. Herbet Spencer is the leading advocate of the new form of the old creed. In his view, axiomatic truths both scientific and moral, are products of experience extending back through the history of the race. The so-called necessities of thought have been produced by association, working not merely through the short life of the individual, but away back through the millions of generations of ancestors which have intervened between man and the original protozoa. Mental associations contracted in the experience of each individual modify his organism. These modifications are transmitted by heredity, and appear in the offspring as mental tendencies or predispositions. They continue to accumulate and increase in every successive generation, until the intellectual deposit takes final shape as a *necessary law of thought* or a *form* of the mind. Space, time, causality, duty, are complex notions which have been elaborated during the long ages of ancestral experience. 'They have arisen from the organized and consolidated experience of all antecedent generations . . . till they [*i.e.* the mental acquisitions embodied in nervous modifications] practically became *forms of thought*, apparently independent of experience '."

The apparent advantage of thus allowing a practically indefinite lapse of time for the play of association to " evolve" the necessary judgments in question, is more than counterbalanced by the disadvantage that the hypothesis which thus tries to account for their necessary character is *of its very nature unverifiable.* In attempting to account by evolution for the origin of the notions, and to assign as the determining cause of their *necessary* synthesis a subjective mental disposition wrought and strengthened by association, and transmitted by heredity, Spencer is

[1] *Psychology*, 4th edit., p. 286,

" removing the question from the region of rational discussion and situating it where proof and disproof are alike impossible. This, however, is hardly an excellence which the empiricist can admire. The only criterion which he recognizes is that of experience. Now there is no theory, however wild, that has yet been broached on the subject—not even that of the ante-natal existence of the soul, conjured up by Plato—which is more utterly beyond the possibility of scientific proof than the new doctrine . . . geology and palæontology may throw light on the anatomic structure of the earlier forms of animal life, but their mental endowments cannot be deduced from fossil remains. Consequently, any hypothesis put forward as to the character and growth of the notions of space, time, causality, and morality in the alleged transitional species of past ages is as much outside the pale of science, as are the habits and customs of the natives of Sirius." [1]

Then, there is also the *unproven* assumption that evolution was steadily and uniformly *in one direction ;* for only such could plausibly appear to account for an evolved mental necessity. And there is the *false* assumption that the human mind was evolved from non-rational forms of conscious life. Moreover, it must not be forgotten that when Spencer speaks of " environment" and a " cosmos " generating mental dispositions through " organic experience," he can mean by the " environment " and " cosmos " only a *set of conscious states,* a *bundle of muscular feelings.* And if, despite his adoption of the subjectivist assumption that the mind can know only its own states, he postulates an extramental unknowable energy, infinite and eternal, he still maintains, nevertheless, that the necessary syntheses described by him as evolution-products have no corresponding necessities, and reveal no necessary characteristics, in the hypothetical " eternal energy " itself.

It is important for the student to note those points though they refer to Spencer's account of the origin and real significance of the *notions* or *thought-objects* compared, rather than to the main question under discussion, *viz.* Under what influence, subjective or objective, does the mind establish a *necessary synthesis* between such notions? Spencer's solution of this question is that we synthesize them simply because our mental constitution has been so evolved that we cannot help doing so : not by reason of anything seen in the nature of the thought-objects themselves, not on account of any necessary relation apprehended by the mind to exist between them, does the mind synthesize them, but simply because it is determined by its own constitution to

[1] *Psychology*, 4th edit., p. 287.

do so. The necessity of the *nexus* is, therefore, purely subjective and psychological, not objective and ontological,—a necessity arising from the inability of the mind to dissociate such objects or conceive the opposite relation between them. To all this we may reply as follows :—

(1) *Quod nimis probat nihil probat.* The theory proves too much. If it were true that the necessity which characterizes ideal judgments is a product of accumulated ancestral experience, there is no reason why such necessity should not be found to characterize such judgments as "fire burns," "wood floats," "sugar is sweet," "day follows night," etc., etc.,—inasmuch as the connexions in these judgments must have been the subject-matter of a uniform ancestral experience stretching indefinitely backward. Yet such judgments are apprehended as *contingent*, not *absolutely necessary.* On the other hand, the theory does not prove enough; for we recognize an absolute necessity in such judgments as "$7 + 5 = 3 + 9$," or "equilateral triangles are equiangular," although, as Maher observes, the occasions on which such objects were "found to be conjoined in experience cannot in the pre-mathematical age have been very frequent"[1]

(2) It is plainly a psychological misinterpretation of the necessary character of the *nexus* in ideal judgments to attribute this necessity to a subjective incapacity of the mind to break the *nexus* or conceive its opposite,—whether such incapacity be set down to the operation of custom, association, or evolution. There are, no doubt, irresistible associations which are due to instinct, heredity, habit, memory, belief, etc. The child cannot dissociate or separate the feeling of terror from the sensation of darkness. I cannot revisit the scene of a particular event without recalling it. The ancients could not conceive the antipodes to be inhabited owing to their habitual experience of bodies falling *downwards*, and their habitual belief that at the antipodes *downwards* would mean *off* or *away from the surface* there. Similarly, it is argued by Mill, Spencer, etc., we believe that "the whole must be greater than its part," "$2 + 2$ must be 4," etc., because an inseparable association of those predicates with their subjects renders us unable to separate them or to conceive their contradictories. But the testimony of consciousness itself protests against the alleged parity. When heredity, instinct, habit, memory, association, etc., connect mental states for us, we *do*

---

[1] *Psychology*, 4th edit., p. 289.

not see how the process takes place or *why it connects those states as it does.*

"When I pronounce the word 'orange,'" writes Piat,[1] "the image of the fruit occurs to my mind, and inversely the image or perception of the fruit recalls the name. But why this mutual recalling? I know not; or what I do know about it I know only by inference: I reflect that since two ideas regularly recall each other there must be some bond of connexion between them. But that is all. I don't see that bond of connexion, as I see a colour . . .; I only infer that it must be there: it is an unknowable thing, like the dishonoured *vires occultae* of the ancients, or like the substances which empiricists think they can dispense with."

But when I connect "2 + 2" with "4," or "the whole" with "greater than its part," surely it cannot be said that I do not see *why* the connexion is there, but only infer that, since the connexion is there, it must have a reason which is hidden from and unpenetrable to me.

As a matter of fact when objects of thought are conjoined in virtue of a mental tendency or disposition begotten by repeated experiences of their simultaneous co-existence or immediate sequence in consciousness,—whether our own or our ancestor's consciousness,—such conjunction must ever remain *at most* a *connexio facti* which the mind is *instinctively impelled* to make; it can never become a *connexio juris*, so to speak, *i.e.* a connexion seen to be absolutely necessary from the nature of the objects, by the mind contemplating those objects.

We might well leave the verdict on the question to the testimony of the student's own consciousness were it not that a closer analysis of this whole matter of the "necessity" of ideal judgments and the "inconceivability of their opposite" will help us to compare subjective or psychological necessity with objective or ontological necessity, and will lead naturally to a consideration of the Kantian theory of *a priori* mental forms. We will therefore examine it a little more fully.

43. THE TEST OF INCONCEIVABILITY.—According to Mill and Spencer the necessity of the *nexus* in a judgment means simply the *inconceivability of its opposite*, of its negation or contradictory. But this inconceivability, continues Mill, is always subjective, variable, and relative to the individual's experience.

---

[1] *La vie de l'intelligence,* in the *Revue neo-scolastique,* 1910, p. 346,—*apud* JEANNIÈRE, *op. cit.*, p. 169, n. 1.

It furnishes no reliable test that the *nexus* asserted to be " necessary" is absolutely necessary beyond the limits of experience. For example, the judgment that " the antipodes are inhabitable " was inconceivable to the ancients because they had always associated " antipodes " with " uninhabitable ". Hence, as we saw, Mill really denied that any *absolutely* necessary *nexus* between objects of thought is ascertainable by the human mind.

Spencer, however, apparently improved on Mill's position by claiming that the mental disposition to which the " inconceivability " is due has become, through ages of evolution, part and parcel of the very constitution of the mind itself; that when we ask ourselves *why* we hold certain judgments to be *necessarily* true, *e.g.* why " the whole is *necessarily* greater than its part " we find ourselves answering that it is necessarily so because *we cannot conceive it to be otherwise*, or, in other words, because our *mental constitution is such* that we *are forced to think it that way* and are *unable to think it otherwise ;* that, therefore, this test of the " inconceivability of the opposite " is the supreme and ultimate test of the surest knowledge, and the strongest motive of the highest certitude attainable by the human mind. Spencer, of course, recognized that what this test really determined according to his theory was the supposed *underlying uniformity of experience :* it was for him a *psychological test* of this latter ; while it was this latter uniform experience,—stretching back through indefinite ages,— which, by generating our cognitive tendencies and dispositions, determined for us what judgments appear to us as *necessarily* true.

Now from this position a very serious consequence immediately follows. It is this : that such a psychological inconceivability can, according to Spencer's own account of its genesis, never be absolute. For, the number of actual ancestral experiences (whether by *perception* or by *imagination*) in favour of a given *nexus* of ideas, being always *finite* (n), and the number of possible experiences (whether favourable or unfavourable) being *infinite* (∞), there is no *nexus* whose contradictory should not be infinitely more probable than the *nexus* itself, since the fraction representing the probability in favour of the *nexus* $\frac{n}{\infty}$, is always zero whatever be the magnitude of the finite n.

On Spencer's own principles of mental evolution our cognitive faculties depend on a cerebral organization which is indefinitely modifiable by evolution. " Hence," as Fonsegrive argues,[1] " the

---

[1] *La causalité efficiente*, pp. 47-52,—*apud* MERCIER, *op. cit.*, p. 320 n.

associations which depend on the actual organization of our brains are modifiable. But if we know that our actual associations are modifiable, their negation is no longer inconceivable. Therefore the associations reputed to be 'inconceivable' are not inconceivable, and their negation, which is proclaimed impossible by the evolution theory, becomes necessarily possible."

Spencer would of course point out that the *nexus* or association of thought-objects has become so indissoluble *de facto* that it is a psychological necessity for the human mind as at present constituted to link them together; although, no doubt, man's mental constitution *might* have been so evolved as *not* to have made such "inseparable" and "necessary" associations as *e.g.* "2 + 2 = 4," and *may* become so modified after the lapse of long ages of evolution that it may perhaps become capable of dissociating them, and thinking *e.g.* "2 + 2" as not being necessarily "4". And when it is pointed out that this so-called "indissoluble" association is, therefore, not an index of the *absolutely* necessary truth of such judgments, but only an indication that they are necessarily true *relatively to the actual constitution of the mind;* or in other words that it really makes them *contingent* judgments indicative of the manner in which the mind is actually compelled by its constitution to interpret what is given to it objectively, rather than of the nature of this objective *datum* itself, —Spencer admits these consequences, holding that all knowledge is inevitably relative to, and variable with, the evolving constitution of the knowing mind; that the mind can pronounce no synthesis of its objects to be *absolutely* necessary, that by no judgment can it gain an insight into the *absolute* nature of its objects, *i.e.* the nature they have apart from the subjective interpretation which it is forced by its own constitution to put upon them. In a word, absolute truth is unattainable.

The fact is that the necessity of the *nexus*, or the inconceivability of its opposite, as explained by Spencer, reveals merely *the mode of our subjective interpretation* of the supposed reality which is presented to our minds and which we interpret by such a synthesis of notions; but that it does not and cannot reveal to us anything concerning the mode in which the *datum* or reality so interpreted by us *really is*.[1]

---

[1] The question we are discussing is whether the *nexus* between subject and predicate (in immediate ideal judgments) is made owing to the compulsion of a subjective mental tendency or disposition, or by something in the nature of the thought-objects

The whole theory, then, would seem to issue in this, that while such necessary judgments are necessarily what they are for the human mind *in its present stage of evolution,* a time may come when some or all of them may not appear necessarily so for it, when the whole would not appear necessarily greater than its part, etc. ; and, furthermore, that if our minds had been constituted or evolved otherwise than they are supposed in the theory to have been, " 2 + 2 " might not appear necessarily " 4 " for them ; and finally that, for all we know, there may actually be minds, or at least there could be minds, for which " 2 + 2 " would not be necessarily " 4 ".

44. RELATIVE AND ABSOLUTE INCONCEIVABILITY.—Now the startling character of the conclusion just indicated is certainly calculated to set the student thinking as to what is really meant by the *necessity* of ideal judgments and the *inconceivability* of their opposites. He will ask—Is it not, at all events, one of the spon‧ taneous convictions of mankind that when men say " The whole *must be* greater than its part," " 5 + 7 *must be* 12," " Whatever happens *must have* a cause," etc., they mean that these judgments *must be* so, *absolutely* and *for all* minds? that when men say the negation, the contradictory, of any such judgment is *inconceivable,* they mean *absolutely* inconceivable by *any* mind? Do they not mean—or *do* they mean ?—that the necessity of the connexions

demanding this *nexus.* We are not yet inquiring as to the origin and significance of these thought-objects themselves. Now when we say that in the theories under criticism the *nexus* is compelled by *subjective* mental tendencies, and not by any-thing in the nature of the thought-objects compared, we are aware that these mental tendencies are explained as being produced through the influence of environment either on the individual (according to Mill) or on the race (according to Spencer). And is not this influence *objective ?* Yes ; it is objective to *sense consciousness, i.e.* it belongs to an order of mental objects which could not possibly produce such a mental disposition or tendency as would account for the *absolutely necessary nexus* of the ideal judgment. Therefore the theory which attributes this *nexus* to the in-fluence of such a mental disposition or tendency (however generated) either makes the *nexus* in question *subjective* by failing to assign the proper *objective* cause which would really account for its absolutely necessary character (*viz.* the nature of the *abstract thought*-objects compared) or else it makes the *nexus* objective (to sense consciousness) only by *mis-interpreting* its character of *absolute* necessity, *i.e.* by sacrificing its essential character and representing it as a merely contingent and factual connexion. And, moreover, the objectivity-to-sense, allowed by subjectivists, we shall discover to be an apparent, not a real, objectivity. At present we are only criticizing defective explanations of the nature and grounds of the *nexus* between subjects and predicates of ideal judgments. And our criticism is purely negative : the positive explanation of the necessary character of the *nexus* will be given below (chap. viii.) ; but the criticism of defective theories, especially those of Spencer and of Kant, inevitably raises the questions : Whence do these abstract thought-objects come ? How does the intellect get them ? What do they signify ?

between such thought-objects is wholly independent of the subjective structure or constitution of men's minds, and must hold
good for any and every conceivable mind? And when the
student comes to compare the necessity which the intellect apprehends in such judgments with the necessity whereby organic
feelings and states of sense consciousness are what they are, he
will get further food for reflection. For he will find this latter
sort of necessity to be dependent on his subjective constitution
as a conscious being, in a manner in which the former necessity
apparently is not dependent on the constitution of this intellect.
Here are a few passages which reveal typical illustrations of this
remarkable distinction :—

"In my present mental and bodily constitution," writes Maher,[1] "I am
necessarily pained by extreme heat or cold. I am forced to feel certain tastes
as agreeable or the opposite ; and I cannot *imagine* sensations afforded by
a different set of faculties from those with which man is endowed. But reflection tells me that the necessity or incapacity is subjective. The facts
might be reversed. On the other hand, in contemplating the proposition that
two things which are each equal to a third must be equal to each other, I am
conscious not merely that I must believe this truth, like any contingent experience, but also that it must objectively and necessarily be so : that it can
never be reversed." . . . "We do not apprehend the necessity of an axiom
from any blind incapacity or negative limitation of thought ; on the contrary,
it is the translucent self-evidence of the truth itself which extorts assent. We
may in our present constitution be *necessarily* pained by extreme cold or heat,
we may *necessarily* relish honey, or enjoy the scent of the rose, yet that these
things are necessarily so for all consciousness we do not judge ; but, that two
things each equal to a third are equal to each other, we not only necessarily
affirm, but affirm *as* necessarily holding *for all intelligence*. Assent to self-
evident axioms is, then, not a blind instinct due to habit either inherited or
acquired, but a rational apprehension of intelligible relations objectively
true."[2]

A little reflection on the meanings attached in ordinary usage
to the terms "necessary" and "inconceivable" will bear out
these passages,—though not without leaving something to be
explained.

(*a*) What is unperceivable by the senses, and therefore un-
picturable by the imagination, is often said to be "inconceivable" Thus to a person born blind, colour is "inconceivable"
in this sense. He has, and can have, neither the percept nor the
imagination image of colour. And though it can hardly be said
with propriety that he can have no *concept* of colour, no notion of

---

[1] *Op. cit.*, p. 285.   [2] *Ibid.*, p. 288 ; *cf.* pp. 160-2.

VOL. I.   11

what the term *means*,—for he can learn that it signifies a domain of human experience of which he is unfortunately deprived,— still we may say that he can have no positive concept of what this experience is.   The same is true of the deaf with regard to sound, and generally of people destitute from birth, whether wholly or partially, of the use of any of the senses, in regard to the corresponding domain of sense experience.   And, extending this, we may say it is possible that if we had other senses in addition to those we have, new domains of sense experience would be opened up to us ; or if we had senses different from those we have, our corresponding sense-experiences would be different from our actual sense experiences ; but having only the senses with which we are actually endowed we " cannot *imagine* sensations afforded by a different set "[1] of senses.   We know that some species of the lower animals have the senses of sight, smell, hearing, etc., much more highly developed than these are in man : for all we know they may, perhaps, have kinds of sense experience which man has not : at all events it is possible. When, therefore, we say that our sensations are *necessarily* what they are, and that to us other sensations are *inconceivable*, the *necessity* is plainly *subjective* in the sense of being *relative* to the actual constitution of our sense faculties, and the *inconceivability* is plainly *negative*, *i.e.* due to the *want* or *absence* of a cognitive faculty of a certain order, or in other words to a subjective limitation or incapacity of our minds.   Now, granted that we have senses of a certain kind, the consequent *necessity* of having corresponding *kinds of conscious sense experience* is very different from the *necessity* of the *relation* which we find to obtain between the abstract thought-objects compared in an axiomatic judgment such as " $5 + 7 = 12$ ".   There the mental object is an individual *concrete sense percept ;* here it is an *intelligible relation* between *abstract intellectual concepts.*   There the necessity is subjective, *i.e.* conditioned by the constitution of the subject's sense faculties ; here it is objective, *i.e.* seen to arise from, and belong to, the nature of the compared thought-objects.   So, too, the " inconceivability" of a sensation or sense-percept for which we have no corresponding sense faculty, is obviously subjective, due to the absence of such a faculty ; but the "inconceivability" of " $7 + 5$ " being other than " 12,"—well, at least men spontaneously judge and believe that it is *not* due to their not having

---

[1] *Cf.* MAHER, *supra.*

other sorts of intellects for which the relation of "$7 + 5 > $ (or $<$) 12" might be a possible object; but that it is due to, and is in fact only an alternative statement of, the *absolute, objective* necessity of the relation expressed in the judgment "$7 + 5 = 12$". And indeed it is plain that for any and every conceivable intellect whose experience includes *the consciousness of such abstract thought-objects as those compared in immediate ideal judgments*, the necessity of the relations between such thought-objects must spring from the nature of these latter and not from any subjective inability to conceive other relations between them.

But the question still remains : How do such abstract thought-objects come into our conscious experience endowed with such characteristics : a question which, as we shall see, Kant solves in such a way as to make it appear that it is the mind itself that gives its objects these characteristics, and that as a consequence the contemplation of them does not give the mind any insight into reality as it is in itself.

(*b*) What is *incredible* is often loosely described as "inconceivable". Here there is no question of inability to picture a certain object in the imagination, but of inability to accept a suggested judgment as true. If I say that "a race of horned horses" is "inconceivable,"[1] I mean not that I am unable to imagine a horned horse, or consider it impossible for such a being to exist, but simply that owing to the total absence of any evidence that such a being does exist I am unable to believe, or accept as true, the statement that such beings do exist.[2] But when I say that a square circle is inconceivable I mean something very different. I mean that while I can think the object "square" and the object "circle," I cannot think a single object which would be both square and circle, and I cannot admit as true the judgment that there are such objects, because *I see positively* that such an object is *impossible*, and that it is for this reason, and not from any subjective limitation of my intellect, that such an object is *unthinkable, inconceivable*.

Again, a suggested judgment may be inconceivable, in the

---

[1] *Cf.* MAHER, *op. cit.*, p. 284.

[2] I know that a substance called water is *conceivable* because I know it to be *possible*, and I know it to be possible because I know it *actually exists*. I know that it is a chemical compound of two gases, hydrogen and oxygen, in certain proportions, expressed in the symbol H_2O. Is a substance compounded of hydrogen and oxygen in *other* proportions, expressed symbolically H_2O_3, conceivable or inconceivable? possible or impossible? I do not know enough about the nature of the objects, oxygen and hydrogen, to say whether it is or not. *Cf. Ontology*, § 15, p. 83 n.

sense of incredible, to a person, because that person sees it to be objectively incompatible with certain other judgments which he holds to be objectively true. Thus the suggested judgment that "the antipodes are inhabitable" was "inconceivable" in this sense to many of the ancients. Why? Because they saw it to be objectively incompatible with certain other judgments which they—erroneously as it so happened—held to be objectively true, *viz.* the judgments that everywhere throughout the universe unsupported bodies fall in the same direction, and that therefore at the antipodes bodies would *fall away from* the surface of the earth. That is to say, the inconceivability was relative and subjective because it sprang from a persuasion or belief which was subjective because erroneous, because not objectively true. The "inconceivability" of the earth moving round the sun is of exactly the same kind, relative and subjective, *i.e.* it is inconceivable to people who see it to be incompatible with another judgment which they erroneously hold to be true : the judgment that "Whatever appears to be moving is really moving,"—which is a subjective, because an erroneous, generalization from experienced facts.

Now it will be observed that both of the examples just given are judgments of the *real* or *existential* order, that neither of them is an immediate judgment, but that the judgments with which they are incompatible are also judgments of fact, and that the former were held to be "inconceivable" because the opposites of the latter judgments were held to be inconceivable. But in what sense *are* these opposites "inconceivable" : "Gravity does not act in the same direction everywhere"; "The real motion of one body relatively to another is not always as it appears to the senses"? They are inconceivable in the sense in which *their* opposites are "necessary". And to whom can the judgments "Gravity acts in the same direction everywhere," "Motion is always really as it appears," be "necessary" judgments? Only to those for whom a uniform though limited experience has associated subject and predicate so strongly that in the absence of contrary experience they feel impelled to disbelieve in the separability of those notions. But this is plainly a relative and subjective necessity which a possible objective experience could destroy. They are contingent judgments, generalizations, and as it so happens illicit generalizations, from contingent, experienced facts.

But now let us turn to immediate judgments of the ideal order. It is possible indeed that a person may err in deducing remote conclusions from these. And hence he may erroneously regard the contradictory of such a conclusion as positively inconceivable, as absolutely unthinkable. But that is because he thinks his (erroneous) conclusion to be objectively and necessarily true. The inconceivability there is relative and subjective because the necessity of the conclusion is subjective, not objective. The judgment he regards as absolutely inconceivable is absolutely conceivable because objectively possible. But in regard to the apprehension of *immediate* ideal judgments the normal human mind cannot be mistaken, for the thought-objects compared are not complex but so clear and simple as to be within the reach of all. Hence we pronounce the judgment " The whole is greater than its part" to be necessary, *not* because its contradictory is inconceivable; but rather we pronounce its contradictory inconceivable because itself is necessary ; and we pronounce itself to be necessary *objectively, absolutely*, because we see positively that the nature of the thought-objects present to our minds makes this relation necessary for any and every conceivable mind.

There is, therefore, for the human mind a domain of abstract thought-objects between which there arise relations that are absolutely necessary. The fact that there is such a domain has a very deep significance, of which we shall have more to say later. But the extent and limits of the domain are unexplored. There are specific cases in which some people pronounce a suggested relation to be absolutely inconceivable and impossible, while others, holding that this alleged inconceivability is only subjective and relative in the case of those who maintain it, themselves hold the relation to be conceivable and possible. A probable explanation of this would be, perhaps, that under the ambiguity of language the contending parties are contemplating different thought-objects. Thus, some hold the judgment, " Space can be finite," to be positively inconceivable, while others hold not only that " Space can be finite " but that *de facto* " Space *is* finite ". Of this particular thought-object we shall have more to say in the sequel.[1] Or again, when Newton propounded his theory of universal gravitation under the form of *attraction*, the Cartesians held such attraction to be impossible, inconceivable. Why? Because they *assumed* that for interaction between bodies spatial contact, mediate or immediate, is absolutely necessary, and that the theory advocated interaction (by way of " attraction") through empty space without an intervening medium.

[1] The term *space* is ambiguous ; or rather the confusion is easy between the abstract thought-object, the *phantasma* or imagination image, and the concrete sense-intuition. There is an analogous divergence of view among philosophers as to whether an actually and simultaneously existing multitude of sense-objects can be infinite.

Now the inconceivability at once disappears *either* if a *medium* for the inter-action be assumed, *or* if such a medium be not regarded as really necessary, *i.e.* if matter can act *in distans*. We know that physical scientists have accepted the former alternative by the hypothesis of an *aether* pervading all space. But if interaction between bodies be not supposed to require contact, mediate or immediate, then " not only does *actio in distans* become conceivable but the negation of its possibility becomes inconceivable ".[1] As a matter of fact we know too little about the nature of space, matter, and action, to be able to say whether bodies can interact *in distans* (*i.e.* without a material medium) or not ;[2] just as we know too little about the nature of matter to say whether such a substance as H_2O_3 is possible or not.[3]

From the examples examined under (*a*) and (*b*) above it will be clear that when the relation between subject and predicate in a judgment is based upon uniform experience of their association in consciousness, and when the feeling of the " necessity " of that relation rests upon such accumulated experience, whether in-herited or acquired, such necessity is never absolute and irrever-sible, nor is the inconceivability of its negation absolute. It is in vain, therefore, that Mill appeals to such cases to argue that the necessity of immediate ideal judgments is of the same kind ; for there is no parity: the necessity of these does not rest on experience or on any subjective tendency to extend an experi-enced relation of fact beyond the range of experience.

Nor does it follow, as Mill contends, that if the relation between such ob-jects is not based on experience, such objects,—and the sciences, such as mathematics, which deal with their relations,—are *unreal ;* for even although such abstract thought-objects are not realizable *as such* in the concrete domain of sense experience, they are, as intrinsic possibilities, objective to intellectual thought and no mere subjective fictions or creations of thought ; and as such they constitute a domain of objective truth. But this will be explained later when we come to deal with the origin, nature, and significance of such ob-jects ; when it will be shown, as against Positivism, that the human mind is not confined, in its knowledge of objects, to the domain of *sense* experience.[4]

Spencer, too, confused that which is *imaginable* through a subjective limitation or absence of faculty, and that which is *incredible* owing to incompatibility with subjective associations, persuasions, or assumptions,—both of which characteristics have to do solely with facts of sense experience and with *real* or *exis-tential* judgments concerning such facts : judgments which are of their very nature *contingent*,—he confused those kinds of incon-

[1] MERCIER, *op. cit.*, p. 314.
[2] *Cf.* Ontology, § 104, pp. 395-6.
[3] *Cf. supra*, p. 163, n. 2.
[4] *Cf.* MERCIER, *op. cit.*, pp. 314-5.

ceivability with the characteristic of positive and absolute intellectual inconceivability which is concerned exclusively with
judgments of the *ideal* order, judgments about abstract objects
of thought : an inconceivability which, so far from indicating any
inability of the intellect, is always a positive pronouncement of
this faculty that a suggested relation between such objects is
absolutely impossible.

45. IS EXPERIENCE OF ABSOLUTELY NECESSARY RELATIONS
BETWEEN THOUGHT-OBJECTS CONDITIONED BY SUBJECTIVE
MENTAL FORMS?—The student will bear in mind that our
analysis so far has had the *negative* aim of showing that the
necessity of the *nexus* in immediate judgments of the ideal order
is not subjective : that it cannot be satisfactorily explained by
attributing it to subjective mental associations or dispositions
generated by the sense experience whether of the individual or
of the race. And before we offer the explanation which will show
this *nexus* to be objective in the genuine sense of being grounded
in the nature of the abstract thought-objects as such, we have to
examine the Kantian theory which also makes the *nexus* really
subjective by the contention that the thought-objects themselves
present these necessary relations because they get their nature,
and are what they are, by being formed or moulded by certain
subjective intellectual factors which are set down as the necessary
antecedent conditions, on the part of the intellect, for its having
such objects of experience at all.

In examining Spencer's theory we encountered the suggestion that those abstract objects of intellectual thought have their
nature conditioned by intellectual dispositions evolved by the
gradually accumulated and inherited experience of the human race.
But we saw that such empirically acquired dispositions cannot
account for the *absolute* necessity which is characteristic of ideal
judgments. In recognizing the impossibility of grounding this
necessity on repetition of experience Kant had a clearer perception of the truth than Mill or Spencer. Neither, however, will
Kant's own account of this necessity and its grounds be able to
stand the test of critical analysis.

CHAPTER VI.

NECESSARY JUDGMENTS : KANT'S THEORY EXPOUNDED.

46. GENERAL OUTLINE OF KANT'S THEORY OF KNOWLEDGE. —Just as in offering the scholastic account of the necessity and universality of judgments of the ideal order, we shall find it necessary to outline very briefly the other parts of the scholastic theory, so we must here give a broad outline of the whole Kantian Epistemology, in order to render intelligible his account of the grounds and validity and scope of necessary and universal judgments.

Born at Königsberg in 1724, Kant received in youth a distinctly religious training which was fostered and deepened by his study of the writings of Leibniz. But the influence of Jean Jacques Rousseau and the French Revolution proved an effective solvent to his religious faith and led him to a purely rationalistic conception of the Christian Religion. His early philosophical training was in the system of Leibniz and Wolff as expounded by Knutzen in Königsberg about 1740. This system had divorced metaphysics from the natural sciences and the knowledge derived from sense-experience.[1] Relying on supposed innate ideas and principles, especially on the Principle of Sufficient Reason, it sought to explain the world *a priori* and deductively as the work of a Sovereign Intelligence. It was too exclusively intellectualist, dogmatic, and *a priori ;* and Kant soon grew dissatisfied with its conclusions. Meantime his training had received a distinctly scientific bent by acquaintance with the masterly discoveries of such men as Leibniz and Newton in the domains of physics and mathematics. And his study of Hume's *Treatise on Human Nature* had convinced him of the impossibility of grounding the validity of knowledge on the empirical principles of Locke and the English school.[2] While he was *Privatdocent* in Königsberg University, from 1755 to 1770, he had been seeking a *via media* between rationalism and empiricism. The latter year, when he became Professor there and published his Inaugural Dissertation, *De mundi sensibilis atque intelligibilis forma et principiis,* divides what we may call the anti-critical from the critical stage of his thought. He now purposed to face afresh the three great questions : What

[1] *Cf. Ontology,* vii. p. 21.
[2] *Cf.* WINDELBAND, *History of Philosophy* (tr. by TUFTS), p. 537, n. 4. The following dates will help to fix Kant in relation to his predecessors : Locke died in 1704, Leibniz in 1716, Newton in 1727, Wolff in 1754, Hume in 1776, Rousseau and Voltaire in 1778.

can we know ? What ought we do ? and, What have we to hope for ? The answer to the first question was already foreshadowed in the *Inaugural Dissertation.* After eleven years the first edition of his first great work, the *Critique of Pure Reason* ("*Kritik der reinen Vernunft*"), appeared in 1781, a second and somewhat modified edition appearing in 1787. The general argument of the work had meantime appeared in briefer form in the *Prolegomena to any future Metaphysic* ("*Prolegomena zu einer jeden künftigen Metaphysik*") in 1783. Those works contain his verdict on the first question. His answer to the second is contained in the *Critique of Practical Reason* ("*Kritik der praktischen Vernunft*," 1788) and in the *Foundations of the Metaphysic of Morals* ("*Grundlegung zur Metaphysik der Sitten,*" 1785). Recognizing the tripartite division of all mental states into knowledge, feeling or emotion, and appetition or conation, and having dealt with the first and third in the two Critiques just mentioned, he published in 1790 the *Critique of Judgment* ("*Kritik der Urtheilskraft*") in which he analysed the sentiments of *beauty* and *order*, the *esthetic* and the *teleological* judgment. The *Critique of Judgment* is thus a pendant or supplement to the other two Critiques. The answer to the third question, suggested by the *Critique of Practical Reason*, and embodying Kant's philosophy of religion, is contained in a work published in 1793 under the title *Religion within the Limits of Pure Reason* ("*Religion innerhalb der Grenzen der blossen Vernunft*"),—a work which "provoked the hostility of the orthodox, and was the occasion of a reprimand from the Government of East Prussia ".[1] It grounds all religion "not on proofs of the speculative order, but on the *practical need* we experience of regarding the moral law as the expression of a Divine Will, and hence of believing in a God as the author and sanction of the moral order ".[2] Kant lived a studious and secluded life at Königsberg ; he never travelled ; he had little appreciation of art, but he evinced a deep sympathy with Nature in all her moods, professing ever an unbounded admiration for "the starry sky above him and the moral law within him ". He died in 1804.

Kant recognized the existence of judgments that are necessary and universal. He found that such judgments give us valid knowledge in the mathematical and physical sciences, *i.e.* where they are exercised upon the data of sense experience. He was struck by the apparently indisputable truth of such judgments in those sciences, as contrasted with the eternally controversial and dubitable character of so-called metaphysical principles and truths.[3] These, he concluded, are invalid, and do not give us *knowledge*, because they transcend actual and possible sense experience ; they have no empirical content to which they can be applied, and without an empirical content there is no *knowledge*.

---

[1] TURNER, *History of Philosophy*, p. 528.   [2] MERCIER, *op. cit.*, p. 233, § 104.
[3] *Cf. Critique of Pure Reason*, Introd. to 2nd edit., tr. by MAX MÜLLER, 2nd edit., 1900, pp. 724-6; Preface, *ibid.*, p. 692. All subsequent references are to the paging of this (2nd) edition of Müller's version.

The knowledge attained by the human understanding (" *Ver-stand*") in the physical and mathematical sciences is a valid knowledge of *appearances* or *phenomena*. ·When the human understanding has unified, as far as possible, the data of actual and possible sense experience, the human reason (" *Vernunft*"), in a higher, metaphysical effort, tries to transcend actual and possible sense experience by *thinking* the totality of its phenomena as conditioned by a reality itself unconditioned and lying beyond all possible experience.[1]   Reason thinks this absolute and unconditioned reality in three forms: as the unconditioned condition of all the phenomena of internal experience it is the *Soul* (the noumenal or real *Ego*) ; as the unconditioned condition of all the phenomena of external experience it is the *World*, the *Universe*, the *Cosmos ;* as the unconditioned condition of all that is conditioned it is *God*, the *Absolute*.[2]   But when reason is thus forced to think these three ideas, the " psychological," the " cosmological," and the " theological," its thought is not *constitutive*, productive of new and further *knowledge*,—for through lack of all possible empirical content these ideas cannot constitute objects of *knowledge ;*—its thought is here only *regulative* of knowledge already acquired.   These three objects of pure reason are *normative ideals* whereby the mind is constrained to seek a higher unification of the phenomena which alone are objects of knowledge.   Being beyond sense experience these objects of pure reason cannot be objects of knowledge.   Pure reason is forced to *think* them, to contemplate them ; but it cannot *know* them to be real, as, indeed, neither can it know them to be unreal.[3]

[1] " The thinking, which is determined by the categories [of the understanding], puts the data of the sensibility into relation with one another in such a way, that every phenomenon is *conditioned* by other phenomena ; but in this process the understanding, in order to think the individual phenomenon completely, must needs *grasp the totality of the conditions* by which this particular phenomenon is determined in its connexion with the whole of experience.   But in view of the endlessness of the world of phenomena in its relation to space and time, this demand cannot be fulfilled.   For the categories are principles of relation between phenomena ; they cognize the conditionality or conditional character of each phenomenon only *by means of other phenomena*, and demand for these again insight into their conditional nature as determined by others, and so on to infinity.   Out of this relation between understanding and sensibility result for human knowledge *necessary and yet insoluble problems ;* these Kant calls Ideas, and the faculty requisite for this highest synthesis of the cognitions of the understanding he designates *Reason* in the narrower sense." —WINDELBAND, *op. cit.,* p. 548.

[2] *Cf. Critique,* pp. 271-2.

[3] Although " all speculative knowledge is limited to objects of *experience*," still " it should be borne in mind, that this leaves it perfectly open to us to *think* the

Metaphysics, therefore, in the sense of a scientific knowledge of the suprasensible, is impossible; for the objects of scientific knowledge must have an empirical or sensible content, and these ideas have no such content.

But if we cannot attain, by the exercise of *speculative reason*, to a *scientific knowledge* of the suprasensible or metaphysical, we can attain, by the exercise of *practical reason*, to a firm *personal belief* in the moral law, human freedom, personal immortality, and God's existence, as realities.[1] Science, with which speculative reason is concerned, and which is confined to sense experience, is *non-moral*: it can have nothing whatever to say about the fact of moral duty, or about religion, which is based exclusively on this latter. It has been, says Kant, a disastrous mistake to try to make morality and religion matters of science. Is there a moral law? Is man free? Is the soul immortal? Is there a God? Speculative reason pronounces these problems to be beyond the domain of scientific knowledge, of scientific proof or disproof: its attitude towards them must be that of simple *agnosticism*; at most it can *think* such objects as possibilities, but it cannot pronounce either for or against their reality. We can attain to them not by way of *scientific knowledge* through the *speculative reason*, starting from the data of sense, but only by way of *personal belief* through the *practical reason*, starting from the dictate of ethical duty, the *categorical imperative* revealed in our moral conscience. Thus Kant thought to render a signal service to humanity by removing morality and religion from the domain of science and from the consequent corroding influence of scientific doubt; by placing the foundations of religion in the domain of

same objects as things by themselves, though we cannot *know* them. For otherwise we should arrive at the absurd conclusion, that there is phenomenal appearance without something that appears."—*Critique*, p. 698. *Cf.* WINDELBAND, *op. cit.*, pp. 547-8: "For if we should deny the reality of things in themselves, 'all would be immediately resolved into phenomena,' and we should thus be venturing the assertion that nothing is real except what appears to man or to other sensuously receptive beings. But this assertion would be an assumption completely incapable of proof. Transcendental idealism must, therefore, not deny the reality of noumena; it must only remain conscious that they cannot in any wise become objects of human knowledge" (*cf. ibid.*, pp 699-700). *Plato III*

[1] "But after all progress in the field of the supersensuous has thus been denied to speculative reason, it is still open to us to see, whether in the practical knowledge of reason *data* may not be found which enable us to determine that transcendent concept of the unconditioned which is demanded by reason, and thus, according to the wish of metaphysic, to get beyond the limits of all possible experience, by means of our knowledge *a priori*, which is possible to us for practical purposes only."—*Critique*, pp. 695-6.

moral conscience ; and by cutting off all possibility of interaction or communication between those two domains of human experience.[1] Man has an invincible belief in the dictate of moral conscience. This implies, as postulates, human freedom, personal immortality, and God's existence. These postulates, which speculative reason *thinks* as ideas, and points to as possibilities, but cannot *know* as realities, practical reason attains to as real, not by way of speculative or scientific knowledge but by way of subjectively and personally certain belief. Thus, human experience, taken in its totality—including scientific knowledge, metaphysical ideas, moral and religious beliefs—has two distinct starting-points : *sense data*, the subject-matter of scientific knowledge ; and the *categorical imperative* of conscience, the basis of moral and religious beliefs. Metaphysics finds no basis in science ; were it based on science it would be powerless to attain to the real ; but fortunately, while failing to come into *scientific* contact with the real, it attains to the real through *belief,* by way of the practical reason revealing the postulates of the moral conscience.

To sum up then : The universal and necessary judgments of mathematics and physics have won the unanimous assent of mankind ; those of the traditional metaphysics have not. Why have they not ? Because, while using the principles and methods of those sciences, they purported to attain to universal and necessary judgments which were claimed to embody scientific know-

---

[1] " I am not allowed therefore even to *assume,* for the sake of the necessary practical employment of my reason, *God, freedom,* and *immortality,* if I cannot *deprive* speculative reason of its pretensions to transcendent insights, because reason, in order to arrive at these, must use principles which are intended originally for objects of possible experience only, and which, if in spite of this, they are applied to what cannot be an object of experience, really changes this into a phenomenon, thus rendering all *practical extension* of the pure reason impossible. I had therefore to remove *knowledge* in order to make room for *belief.* For the dogmatism of metaphysic, that is, the presumption that it is possible to achieve anything in metaphysic without a previous criticism of pure reason, is the source of all that unbelief, which is always very dogmatical, and wars against all morality.

" If then it may not be too difficult to leave a bequest to posterity, in the shape of a systematical metaphysic, carried out according to the critique of pure reason, such a bequest is not to be considered therefore as of little value. . . . The greatest benefit, however, will be that such a work will enable us to put an end for ever to all objections to morality and religion, according to the Socratic method, namely, by the clearest proof of the ignorance of our opponents."—*Critique of Pure Reason*, Preface to the 2nd edit., pp. xxx and xxxi (tr. by Müller, pp. 700, 701). *Cf. Prolegomena to any Future Metaphysic,* § 60. Kant never worked out the projected *Metaphysic of Nature* which was to follow the *Critique of Pure Reason,* as the *Metaphysic of Morals* followed the *Critique of Practical Reason.*

ledge of the suprasensible. But this is impossible; for those principles and methods can yield a valid universal and necessary knowledge only of the appearances or phenomena presented by what is given in sense-intuition. A metaphysical *knowledge*, which would be scientific because necessary and universal, of that which transcends actual and possible sense experience, is an illusion. A metaphysic of the suprasensible, constructed by the speculative reason, after the manner in which this faculty reaches scientific knowledge of the phenomena given in sense experience, must necessarily be *sceptical, agnostic,* because the ideas it reaches, having no empirical content, cannot yield *knowledge.* But while the metaphysic constructed by the *pure reason*, thus issues in *speculative scepticism*, the metaphysic constructed by the *practical reason* on the basis of the categorical imperative of conscience, is, from this standpoint of belief, dogmatic: it is *moral dogmatism.* If man is forced by his speculative reason to *think* God, the soul, freedom, duty, immortality, etc., as ideas, but is frustrated by the very constitution of this faculty, and by the only principles and methods it can command, from ever *knowing* those as realities, he can, nevertheless, through his practical reason attain to a firm subjective persuasion or belief in them as realities. For there is a fact of supreme import which, while outside the domain of sense intuition and therefore beyond the possibility of *knowledge*, both as to itself and its implications, is yet an indubitable fact of consciousness and furnishes the ground of an irresistible *belief* in the *reality* both of itself and of its implications. This fact is the dictate of duty in the moral conscience, and its implications are the reality of a soul endowed with freedom, responsibility, and personal immortality, and the existence of God as the author and sanction of the moral order.

With the supremacy here vindicated for the practical reason over the speculative, and with its correlative isolation of belief from knowledge, we shall have to deal later. Our present concern is to examine Kant's account of the necessity and universality of the scientific judgments formed by the speculative reason, with a view to seeing whether the grounds he offers for these characteristics are satisfactory or tenable. For this purpose we shall have to set forth in greater detail the part of his theory which deals with them, and then, laying aside for subsequent treatment certain very important problems raised by the theory —as to the nature of the objects compared in such judgments, and the manner in which the mind gets them—to fix our attention exclusively on his account of the necessary and universal *nexus* involved in such judgments.

47. NECESSARY AND UNIVERSAL JUDGMENTS DESCRIBED AS "A PRIORI".—The aim of Kant, in his *Critique of Pure Reason*, is to explore the power of the human reason in general, in its speculative employment, with a view to ascertaining the domain and limits of the knowledge to which it can attain; and particularly to see whether, in this employment, it can attain to a knowledge of *reality*, especially of any reality transcending *actual and possible sense experience.* He takes his stand on the fact that the physical and mathematical sciences contain judgments which are necessary and universal and impose themselves on all human minds. Whatever *knowledge* may be, these judgments contain knowledge. And he wants to find out what is *knowledge*, what it is *to know.*

"That all our knowledge begins with experience there can be no doubt. For how should the faculty of knowledge be called into activity, if not by objects which affect our senses and which either produce representations by themselves, or rouse the activity of our understanding to compare, to connect, or to separate them : and thus to convert the raw material of our sensuous impressions into a knowledge of objects, which we call experience. In respect of time, therefore, no knowledge within us is antecedent to experience, but all knowledge begins with it.

"But although all our knowledge begins with experience, it does not follow that it arises from experience. For it is quite possible that even our empirical experience is a compound of that which we receive through impressions, and of that which our own faculty of knowledge (incited only by sensuous impressions) supplies from itself. . . . It is therefore a question . whether there exists a knowledge independent of experience, and even of all impressions of the senses ? Such *knowledge* is called a *priori*, and distinguished from empirical knowledge, which has its sources a *posteriori*, that is, in experience. . . . We shall . . . understand by knowledge a *priori* knowledge which is *absolutely* independent of all experience, and not of this or that experience only. Opposed to this is empirical knowledge, or such as is possible a *posteriori* only, that is, by experience.[1] Knowledge a *priori*, if mixed up with nothing empirical, is called *pure.* Thus the proposition, for example, that every change has its cause, is a proposition a *priori*, but not pure : because change is a concept which can only be derived from experience. . . .

[1] This meaning attached to the phrases a *priori* and a *posteriori* is a distinct departure from the meaning previously accepted in philosophy. By a *priori* knowledge was understood knowledge derived by reasoning from *cause* to *effect*, from *ground* to *consequent*, from universal principles to their particular applications; and by a *posteriori* knowledge, the knowledge of causes through their effects, the knowledge reached by induction, the knowledge of laws derived from consideration of facts. And this usage is still common outside Kantian philosophical literature. *Cf. Science of Logic*, ii., §§ 254-6.

Now experience teaches us, no doubt, that something is so or so, but not that it cannot be different . . . experience never imparts to its judgments true or strict, but only assumed or relative universality (by means of induction). . . . If, therefore, a judgment is thought with strict universality, so that no exception is admitted as possible, it is not derived from experience, but valid absolutely *a priori.* . . . If . . . strict universality is essential to a judgment this always points to a special source of knowledge, namely, a faculty of knowledge *a priori.* Necessity, therefore, and strict universality are safe criteria of knowledge *a priori*, and are inseparable one from the other. . . . That there really exists in our knowledge such necessary, and in the strictest sense universal, and therefore pure judgments *a priori*, is easy to show. If we want a scientific example, we have only to look to any of the propositions of mathematics ; if we want one from the sphere of ordinary understanding, such a proposition as that each change must have a cause, will answer the purpose ; nay, in the latter case, even the concept of cause contains so clearly the concept of the necessity of its connexion with an effect,[1] and of the strict universality of the rule, that it would be destroyed altogether if we attempted to derive it, as Hume does, from the frequent concomitance of that which happens with that which precedes, and from a habit arising thence (therefore from a purely subjective necessity) of connecting representations."[2]

These opening passages from the Introduction to the *Critique of Pure Reason* show how Kant understands the phrase " *a priori* knowledge," and also that he distinguishes between the relative necessity and universality of inductive generalizations and the strict, absolute necessity and universality appertaining to certain other judgments. And the last sentence shows how he clearly recognized Hume's account of strictly necessary and universal judgments, basing these on habit or custom begotten by reiteration of sense perception and its products, as destructive of the scientific or necessary character of these judgments by making this necessity subjective. We shall have to watch, however, what Kant means by "experience," and by a "faculty of knowledge *a priori*". As against Hume, and in common with Plato, Aristotle, and the tradition of centuries, he recognized the existence of judgments which transcend the subjective, changing, contingent conditions of the individual mind and reveal something absolutely necessary and universal. Failing to find in *experience,* or in any habit psychologically engendered by experience *as set forth by Hume,* a satisfactory explanation of the necessity and universality which he saw to be obviously characteristic of certain scientific

---

[1] Rather, " the concept of a happening, an event, a contingent being, contains so clearly the concept of a connexion of dependence on a cause ". *Cf. infra*, §§ 64-6. -

[2] *Critique,* pp. 715-17.

judgments, he sought now to make these characteristics on the one hand independent of anything *given* in experience, and on the other hand independent of anything *produced* in the individual mind through experience, by attributing them to forms or functions genetic or productive of these characteristics, and which must be conceived as belonging to the mind as a faculty of "*a priori* knowledge," and thus rendering the experience which we have (with its *necessary* and *universal* judgments) possible.

48. THOSE OF THEM THAT AMPLIFY OUR KNOWLEDGE CLAIMED TO BE "SYNTHETIC-A-PRIORI". — Looking at the various judgments in which our knowledge is supposed to be contained, Kant first distinguishes between *judgments of perception* and *judgments of experience*. The former, such as "I feel cold," "I have a toothache," embody a subjective, personal experience which is beyond the control of others and cannot be an object of science. When on the contrary I say "The sun heats the earth" my judgment asserts, between the sun and the earth, a relation which is not personal to me, but common to, and verifiable by all : a relation which is *necessary, universal, objective*, and therefore *scientific*. It is a *judgment of experience*.[1] By saying that the relation is "objective," Kant means simply that it is necessary and universal. This, as we shall see more fully, is what he *means* by the term "objective".

Next, among judgments of experience he distinguishes between those that are based solely on experience, and in which the predication is *posterior to*, and grounded in, experience,—*a posteriori* judgments,—and those in which the predication is grounded in something wholly independent of, and logically or rationally *prior to* experience,—*a priori* judgments. The former are scientifically unimportant inasmuch as even when they are universal, such as, "all bodies are heavy," the universality is only "empirical," and "arbitrary," not strict or absolute.[2] It is the latter, what he calls the "*a priori* judgments," all of which have strict and absolute universality and necessity, that need to have the grounds of these characteristics clearly brought to light.

[1] "In the judgment of experience the spatial or temporal relation is grounded by a category, a conceptional connexion, whereas in the mere judgment of perception this is lacking. Thus, for example, the succession of two sensations becomes objective and universally valid when it is thought as having its ground in the fact that one phenomenon is the cause of another."—WINDELBAND, *op. cit.*, p. 544.

[2] Nevertheless inductive generalizations have a sort of "necessity," the explanation of which is supremely important. *Cf. Science of Logic*, ii., Pt. IV., chap. iii. and iv.

The former judgments are *synthetic* as well as *a posteriori* that is to say, the information given by the predicate about the subject is something over and above what is contained in the concept of the subject itself, and has to be sought in the total experience whence we derive our concept of the subject ; it is something conjoined or synthesized with, or added on to, this latter.   But such judgments tell us simply what was or is actually in experience : they can never tell us what *must* be for *all* actual and *possible* experience.   The mere uniform recurrence of a conjunction between a subject and a predicate in the domain of intellectual thought can never inform us that they *must* be conjoined for all intellectual thought.

This, however, is precisely what absolutely necessary and universal judgments tell us.   And how is this to be explained ? Perhaps all such judgments are *analytic* in the sense that the predicate merely gives the whole or part of what is found by rational analysis to have been involved in the very concept of the subject itself, so that in virtue of the *Principle of Identity* all such judgments must be necessarily and universally what they are, inasmuch as they are all expressions of the absolutely necessary principle that " every thing is itself".

Now Leibniz had held that this is so ; that all judgments whether of the ideal or of the real order are reducible by analysis to the Principles of Identity and Contradiction ; that *all* science is built up analytically, by a purely deductive " drawing out" of what is implicitly contained in our innate intellectual conceptions both of the possible and of the actual or existent ; that our minds, demanding by their constitution a " sufficient reason " for everything whether possible or actual are forced to conclude that everything whether possible or actual *must be* what it is, because they are forced to conclude that the universe must be the work of an All-Wise and Omnipotent Being whose " sufficient reason " for creating the universe can only have been that it is the best and therefore the only universe possible, and therefore could not be other than it is ; so that *all* our knowledge is *necessary* in its character, seeing that it unfolds the implications of innate conceptions which could not be other than they are : " Verum est affirmatum, cujus praedicatum inest subjecto.   Itaque in omni propositione vera affirmativa, necessaria vel contingente, universali vel singulari, notio praedicati aliquo modo (manifeste vel tecte) continetur in notione subjecti ; ita ut qui perfecte intelligeret notionem utramque quemadmodum eam intelligit Deus, is eo ipso perspiceret praedicatum subjecto inesse." [1]

This account errs by excess, making all our judgments necessary. It explains why the human individual, whose own existence is contingent, conditioned by limits of time and space, and subject to change, can intellectually apprehend objects and relations that transcend all such conditions and appear to be what they are eternally, immutably, necessarily,—by the assertion that both the knowing mind or individual and the known object or reality are *necessarily* so constituted by the Self-Existent, Eternal, Necessary Being.

But Kant saw that, apart from many questionable assumptions involved in this explanation, it contradicts the plain fact that *not all* our necessary and universal judgments are *analytic* in the sense that the predicate is already implicitly contained in our concept of the subject; that not all scientific knowledge is the product of an analysis of our conceptions in accordance with the Principles of Identity, Contradiction, and Sufficient Reason. He observed that an analysis which would merely extract predicate-concepts from subject-concepts that already contained them does not really amplify our knowledge : it "gives us a great deal of knowledge which, though it consists in no more than in simplifications and explanations of what is comprehended in our concepts (though in a confused manner), is yet considered as equal, at least in form, to new knowledge. It only separates and arranges our concepts, it does not enlarge them in matter or contents." [2] Judgments that are analytic in this sense are merely *explicative* or *illustrating* judgments ; they are not *ampliative* or *expanding* judgments.

But, now, beyond this comparatively unimportant class of judgments that are analytic in the sense explained, there is still the vast and really important class of judgments that are absolutely necessary and universal, and yet whose predicates are not to be found in an analysis of their subjects. How and why is it that we can assert such judgments? It is here that Kant, seeking a *via media* between the rationalism of the school of Leibniz and the empiricism of Hume, missed the true *via media* which accounts for the *nexus* in such judgments by a wider analysis of our concepts than that just described,—a process guided and determined

---

[1] LEIBNiz, *Opuscules et fragments inédits*, publi hed by COUTURAT, pp. 16-17,— *apud* MERCIER, *op. cit.*, p. 236.

[2] *Critique*, pp. 4, 5 ; cf. *ibid.*, p. 8.

by the influence of the *reality given* to the mind,[1]—and found the misleading *via media* of *a-priorism*, which ends in a subjectivism no better than the empiricism of Hume. For, according to Kant, such judgments are in no sense analytic, in no sense derived from an analysis and comparison of what is given in our concepts. They are, he holds, *synthetic* in the sense that like the *a posteriori* judgments of experience they give us new knowledge which we had not even implicitly antecedently to our forming them ; but unlike the latter, being necessary and universal they are not grounded *a posteriori* by anything *given* to the mind, in or through experience (for what is given in experience can explain only what *is*, not what *must* be); they can be grounded only on something which we must conceive to belong to the mind, the judging or synthesizing faculty, *prior to*, and as an indispensable condition of, the very possibility of constructing such judgments or syntheses : in a word, such judgments are *both* synthetic *and a priori*, "*synthetic-a-priori*".

Analytic judgments, in which the predicate-concept is derived by analysis from the subject-concept, are indeed necessary and universal, but they do not give us any new knowledge, and their necessity and universality are grounded in the necessity and universality of the Principle of Identity, in accordance with which this analysis must be conducted.[2] Synthetic judgments do expand our knowledge by inter-relating and synthesizing into fuller and richer concepts those concepts which we possess antecedently to the synthesis. When the ground for thus synthesizing such concepts is *experience*, the syntheses are *a posteriori* judgments, and the knowledge yielded by those *a posteriori* synthesis can never be *necessary* or *universal* knowledge : such syntheses reveal only *contingent* relations of *fact*, limited to *actual* experience. When, therefore, judgments establish a *necessary* and *universal* relation between a subject-concept and a predicate-concept not contained already in the former, not only must such judgments be synthetic, but the synthesis must be grounded in, and produced by, something other than experience ; and this "something other than experience" must be conceived to be some synthesizing factor or factors appertaining to the constitution of the mind

---

[1] *Cf. infra*, chaps. viii., ix.

[2] But how or why can the human mind, which is itself *contingent, individual, limited* as to existence in time and space, apprehend *any* principle, even the analytic *Principle of Identity*, as *absolutely necessary, immutable, eternal, universal*, etc. ? The question, in this form, apparently did not suggest itself to Kant.

itself as a faculty of necessary and universal knowledge, and belonging to the mind *a priori*, *i.e.* as a prerequisite condition for the mind's being able to form such necessary and universal judgments.

49. EVEN CONCEPTS, REGARDED AS "OBJECTIVE," *i.e.* AS NECESSARILY AND UNIVERSALLY VALID, ARE CLAIMED TO BE " SYNTHETIC-A-PRIORI ".—And not only are such *a priori* synthesizing factors of the mind required for the formation of such necessary and universal *judgments* as amplify the knowledge already contained in our concepts, but such factors are required for the formation of our *concepts* themselves :[1] the proof of this being that we can *think* the *data* of experience only by synthesizing these under certain forms by the application of which these *data* appear as *necessarily and universally* such or such ; for since experience cannot present its *data* as *necessarily and universally* such or such, the forms which make these data so appear must be *pure forms* (*i.e.* non-empirical, unmixed with any empirical *datum*), belonging to the mind *a priori*, or as a condition for our so apprehending the *data* of experience. Thus, for example, whatever is given in experience is apprehended *necessarily and universally* as being a *substance*, or an *accident*, as *in space* and *in time*, as a *cause*, as an *effect*, as a *whole* or a *part*, as *one* or *many*, etc.[2] Therefore for the formation of those concepts, whereby we interpret the *data* of our experience to be *necessarily* and *universally* what we conceive those data to be, there must be in the mind *a priori* factors or forms which give necessity and universality to those concepts regarded as valid for all minds, or as necessarily imposing themselves on all minds.[3] When Kant holds such *concepts* to be *necessarily* and *universally* valid he means that they can not merely be *thought* as *logically* possible or free from self-contradiction (which he apparently regards as no index to their being in any sense independent of the individual mind), but that they can be *known* as " objective realities " or " real pos-

---

[1] *Cf.* PRICHARD, *Kant's Theory of Knowledge*, p. 162 ; *Critique*, p. 64 : " as far as their contents are concerned no concepts can arise analytically "

[2] *Cf. Critique*, Introd. to 2nd edit., p. 718.

[3] Many of our complex concepts are reached through a series of judgments whereby we add on notes successively to a simpler concept. When we assert the validity, or objective validity, of such a *concept*, we really assert the objective validity of those anterior judgments, or of the implicit judgment that the concept in question is not a mere subjective product of our individual thought-activity, but a mental insight into something objective, something that can impose itself on other minds. *Cf. Science of Logic*, i., §§ 79, 80, 123, 124. *Infra*, chap. xii.

sibilities " : from which it is obvious that the " knowing " implies an *assertion* or *judgment* in reference to the concept.[1]

Every judgment is an act both of analysis and of synthesis, an *actus componendi et dividendi*. But this has reference to the comparison of subject and predicate.[2] Kant uses the term *synthesis* in this accepted sense as the *conscious* assertion of an identity between subject and predicate in an affirmative judgment. But it is unfortunate and not a little confusing that he uses the same term, in reference to the formation both of concepts and of judgments, and even of sense intuitions, in a quite distinct and very technical sense (peculiar to his own theory) in which it signifies the function whereby the mind *unconsciously* applies a *pure a priori* form or category to a *datum*, and thus *constitutes* " experience " by *constructing* an *object* of *knowledge*.[3] For Kant, the *data* of scientific, *i.e.* universal and *necessary* knowledge, get their *objectivity* from the mind itself, simultaneously in point of time with conscious experience itself, but by a function whereby the mind, by applying to the *data* of experience its own *a priori* forms, makes such conscious experience possible. Thus only can the mind make its experience *objective, i.e.* an experience embodying *necessary* and *universal* judgments, by synthesizing its data through relations which are *necessary* and *universal* because they are the product of relating factors which belong to the very constitution of the mind, which are brought to experience *a priori*, and which thus constitute experience.

50. ANALYSIS OF A PRIORI CONDITIONS OF KNOWLEDGE IN SENSIBILITY AND IN UNDERSTANDING.—Thus the necessity and universality which cannot be explained by the empiricism of Hume on grounds of experience, or by the rationalism of Leibniz on grounds of analysis, finds its explanation in the *a priori* forms whereby the mind synthesizes the data of experience.

[1] " In order to *know* an object," he writes (*Critique*, p. 698 n.; *cf. ibid.*, p. 789), " I must be able to prove its possibility, either from its reality, as attested by experience, or *a priori* by means of reason. But I can *think* whatever I please, provided only I do not contradict myself, that is, provided my conception is a possible thought, though I may be unable to answer for the existence of a corresponding object in the sum total of all possibilities. Before I can attribute to such a concept objective reality (real possibility as distinguished from the former, which is purely logical), something more is required. This something more, however, need not be sought for in the sources of theoretical knowledge, for it may be found in those of practical knowledge also." By regarding the concepts in question, therefore, as valid, as necessary and universal, and therefore " objective " for knowledge, Kant regarded as requisite something more than their mere thinkability, which " something more " must in any case take the form of an implicit judgment or assertion that they are not mere products of the individual thinker's mind. " Validity," or " objective validity," or " necessity and universality " can in fact have no meaning except in reference to a *judgment* or *mental assertion* about the *significance* of some *datum* or fact or state of consciousness. *Cf.* also Kant's view that " in the mere concept of a thing no sign of its existence can be discovered ".— *Critique*, p. 183; PRICHARD, *op. cit.*, p. 309, n. 2.

[2] *Cf. Science of Logic*, i., § 78

[3] *Cf.* WINDELBAND, *op. cit.*, p. 515.

But in order to yield *knowledge* these *a priori* forms must be applied to *empirical data*.   Such data are yielded in physics by direct sense perception, and in mathematics by the constructive imagination ; but in metaphysics the *a priori* forms do not and cannot yield knowledge for there are no sense data here to which we can apply them.

According to Kant, therefore, *to know scientifically,—i.e.* through necessary and universal judgments, or through concepts which impose themselves with a like necessity and universality on all minds,—means to *synthesize the concrete data of sense-perception under a priori mental forms* which make these *data objective* by inter-relating them in ways which impose themselves necessarily and universally on all minds.

These *a priori* forms Kant calls *transcendental ;* and the *Critique of Pure Reason*, the aim of which is to bring them to light and discover their function in knowledge, he calls a *transcendental* critique.   The term, Kant assures us, does not designate that which *lies beyond the reach of experience* (and which might be called *transcendent*),[1] but that which is a prerequisite, on the part of the mind, to make experience possible.   It does not denote a relation of knowledge to things, but a relation of knowledge to the faculty of knowledge.   The *Critique* is therefore an inquiry into the *a priori* or *transcendental* conditions of the possibility of knowledge.   The first portion, which analyses the *a priori* conditions of *sense perception* is called the *Transcendental Esthetic ;* the second portion, which analyses the *a priori* conditions of *intellectual thought* is called the *Transcendental Logic ;* and this is subdivided into the *Transcendental Analytic* and the *Transcendental Dialectic*, the former treating of the *a priori* concepts which can give us *knowledge* by their application to an empirical datum, and the latter showing that the attempt to extend the application of these forms beyond the domain of sense intuitions, to the domain of the suprasensible where they have no possible empirical content, fails to elevate thought into objective knowledge.[2]

[1] As opposed to *immanent* or " confined within the limits of possible experience ".   A principle which tends to transgress those limits is called by Kant *transcendent*.   And his contention is that all the principles which pure reason can legitimately employ are *immanent*, that the use of them to *transcend* experience leads to the illusions of metaphysics.   *Cf. Critique*, pp. 240-1.

[2] *Cf. Critique*, pp. 49-50.   These three sections bring to light respectively (1) the pure *a priori intuitions of sense* (Space and Time) which render possible the

51. THE A PRIORI FORMS OF SENSE INTUITION.—Kant commences to work out his general theory in detail by the following observations :—

"Whatever the process and the means may be by which knowledge reaches its objects [Gegenstände], there is but one that reaches them directly, and forms the ultimate material of all thought, *viz.* intuition [Auschauung]. This is possible only when the object is given, and the object can be given only (to human beings at least) through a certain affection of the mind [Gemüth]. This faculty (receptivity) of receiving representations [Vorstellungen] according to the manner in which we are affected by objects, is called sensibility [Sinnlichkeit]. Objects therefore are given to us through our sensibility. Sensibility alone supplies us with intuitions [Auschauungen]. These intuitions become thought through the understanding [Verstand] and hence arise conceptions [Begriffe]. All thought therefore must, directly or indirectly, go back to intuitions, *i.e.* to our sensibility, because in no other way can objects be given to us. The effect produced by an object upon the faculty of representation [Vorstellungsfähigkeit], so far as we are affected by it, is called sensation [Empfindung]. An intuition [Aushauung] of an object, by means of a sensation, is called empirical. The undefined object of such an empirical intuition is called a phenomenon [Erscheinung].

"In a phenomenon I call that which corresponds to the sensation its *matter;* but that which causes the manifold matter of the phenomenon to be perceived as arranged in a certain order, I call its *form.* Now it is clear that it cannot be sensation again through which sensations are arranged and placed in certain forms. The matter only of all phenomena is given us *a posteriori;* but their form must be ready for them in the mind [Gemüth] *a priori,* and must therefore be capable of being considered as separate from all sensations.

"I call all representations in which there is nothing that belongs to sensation *pure* (in a transcendental sense). The pure form therefore of all sensuous intuition, that form in which the manifold elements of the phenomena are seen in a certain order, must be found in the mind *a priori.* And this pure form of sensibility may be called the pure intuition [reine Auschauung]. Thus if we deduct from the representation of a body what belongs to the thinking of the understanding, *viz.* substance, force, divisibility, etc., and likewise what belongs to sensation, *viz.* impermeability, hardness, colour, etc., there still remains something of that empirical intuition, *viz.* extension and form. These belong to pure intuition, which *a priori,* and even without a real object [wirklichen Gegenstand] of the senses or of sensation, exists in the mind as a mere form of sensibility." [1]

Isolating sensibility from "everything which the understanding adds by means of its concepts" on the one hand, and separ-

necessary and universal knowledge embodied in *mathematics;* (2) the (twelve) *a priori concepts or categories of the understanding,* which render possible the necessary and universal knowledge embodied in the rational science of *Physics;* and (3) the (three) *a priori ideas of the reason,* to which the futile attempt to reach a knowledge transcending all possible experience, leads in *metaphysics.*

[1] *Critique (Transcendental Esthetic),* pp 15-17.

ating from the "empirical intuition" thus isolated, "all that belongs to sensation [Empfindung]" on the other, Kant discovers (in the course of the *Transcendental Æsthetic*) "as principles of *a priori* knowledge, two pure forms of sensuous intuition, *Space* and *Time*"—the former rendering possible external sense perception and the latter rendering possible perception of the mind's own internal states.

52. CONCEPTION AND JUDGMENT. A PRIORI FORMS OF THE UNDERSTANDING.—He then proceeds, in the Introduction to the *Transcendental Logic* thus to outline the function of the understanding and its concepts in relation to the intuitions of sense :—

"Our knowledge springs from two fundamental sources of our soul [des Gemüths] ; the first receives representations (receptivity of impressions— Eindrüke), the second is the power of knowing an object through these representations (spontaneity of concepts). By the first an object is *given* to us, by the second the object is *thought*, in relation to that representation which is a mere determination of the soul. Intuition therefore and concepts constitute the elements of all our knowledge, so that neither concepts without an intuition corresponding to them, nor intuition without concepts, can yield any real knowledge.

"Both are either pure or empirical. They are empirical when sensation, presupposing the actual presence of the object, is contained in it [them ?]. They are pure when no sensation is mixed up with the representation. The latter may be called the material of sensuous knowledge. Pure intuition therefore contains only the form by which something is seen [etwas ange-shaut wird], and pure conception [reiner Begriff] the form only by which an object is thought [des Denkens eines Gegenstandes überhaupt]. Pure intuitions and pure concepts only are possible *a priori*, empirical intuitions and empirical concepts *a posteriori*.

"We call *sensibility* the *receptivity* of our soul [Gemüths], or its power of receiving representations whenever it is in any wise affected, while the *understanding*, on the contrary, is with us the power of producing representations, or the *spontaneity* of knowledge. We are so constituted that our intuition must always be sensuous, and consist in the mode by which we are affected by objects. What enables us to think the objects of our sensuous intuition is the understanding. Neither of these qualities or faculties [Eigenschaften] is preferable to the other. Without sensibility objects would not be given to us, without understanding they would not be thought by us. *Thoughts without contents are empty, intuitions without concepts are blind* [" Gedanken ohne Inhalt sind leer, Auschauungen ohne Begriffe sind blind "]. Therefore it is equally necessary to make our concepts sensuous, *i.e.* to add to them their object in intuition, as to make our intuitions intelligible, *i.e.* to bring them under concepts. These two powers or faculties cannot exchange their functions. The understanding cannot see (vermag nichts anzuschauen), the senses cannot think. By their union only can knowledge be produced."[1]

It appears, therefore, that the function of the understanding as *cognitive*, as a faculty *of knowledge*, is to apply to the pheno-mena or representations already synthesized in the empirical sense intuitions through the forms of *space* and *time*, certain *a priori* forms, *concepts* or *categories* of the understanding itself; thus to synthesize further the intuitions by means of the con-cepts; and thereby to think the results of these latter syntheses as *objects*, or in other words to *know* them to be for all minds

---

[1] *Critique* (*Transcendental Logic*), pp. 40-1. Kant drew a sharp contrast be-tween the "receptivity" of sense and the "spontaneity" of understanding, and ascribed exclusively to the understanding the function of making representations "objective," *i.e.* necessary and universal, by means of its pure *a priori* concepts. (The representation achieved by the empirical intuition and which he calls a "pheno-menon" he refers to as the "*undefined object*" of such an empirical intuition," *op. cit.*, p. 16.) But the sensibility is also, on his own showing, a synthesizing function whereby a raw material, a manifold of sense impressions, visual, tactual, etc., is arranged, ordered, unified by the mental forms of space and time. It is these two forms, moreover, that render possible the necessary and universal judgments of mathematics,—of pure geometry (*space*) and of arithmetic (*time*),—judgments which he represents as belonging to *sensibility*, and which he treats in the Transcendental *Æsthetic*, as being apparently independent of the categories of the understanding. Hence Kant is said by some to have recognized later a power of spontaneity, of mak-ing representations "objective," *in the sensibility*. "Earlier, sensibility and under-standing were set over against each other as receptivity and spontaneity; but space and time, pure forms of the sensibility, were indeed the principles of the synthetical ordering of sensations, and thus belonged under the general notion of synthesis, *i.e.* spontaneous unity of the manifold" (WINDELBAND, *op. cit.*, p. 538, n. 4). The fact is, however, that he recognized the co-operation of sensibility and understanding as essential to attaining objective knowledge; nor did he really break with the uniform philosophical tradition that knowledge is contained formally only in the act of judg-ment, and that this act is an act of the understanding. But judgment or interpreta-tion inseparably accompanies not only conception but also sense perception or sense intuition. It was his view of the latter as a "synthesis of matter and form," which prompted him to speak of the judgments of *mathematics* as "judgments of the *sensi-bility*": for he had conceived the judging function of the understanding to be also such a synthesis. (*De facto* neither the intellectual concept nor the sense percept or intuition give *knowledge* till the mental representation in each case is *asserted* mentally, by an act of judgment, to be validly significant or representative of reality). But Kant really recognized that the space-and-time sense intuitions are not objects of knowledge until they are *judged* (or "synthesized" under pure concepts) by the understanding. Consequently the judgments of mathematics, which he treats in the Transcendental *Æsthetic*, since they contain "objective" knowledge, are judgments of the understanding, no less than the physical and metaphysical judgments with which he deals in the *Transcendental Logic*: an implication which "is really incon-sistent with the existence of the *Æsthetic* as a distinct part of the subject dealing with a special class of *a priori* judgments" (PRICHARD, *Kant's Theory of Knowledge*, p. 35).

necessarily and universally as they thus appear to each individual mind which operates these syntheses.

Kant proceeds next to isolate the understanding from the sensibility and to discover in it all the *a priori* forms, concepts, or categories by the application of which to the empirical intuitions of sense it thinks these as objects, or asserts them to be objective, *i.e.* necessarily and universally what they are. The understanding cannot know intuitively, but only discursively, *i.e.* by the synthesizing function of "arranging different representations under one common representation "[1] By this he means, apparently, "different subjects under one predicate concept ". For he proceeds :—

The only use which the understanding can make of these concepts [2] is to form judgments by them. As no representation, except the intuitional, refers immediately to an object,[3] no concept is ever referred to an object immediately

[1] *Critique*, p. 56. For a clear and searching criticism of the whole passage, *cf.* PRICHARD, *op. cit.*, chap. vii. p. 146 *sqq.* ; chap. viii. p. 162 *sqq.*

[2] *Pure* or *empirical* concepts ? From the context, apparently *empirical*. *Cf.* PRICHARD, *op. cit.*, p. 29, n. 1. But how are *empirical* concepts formed ? By the application of a *pure* or *a priori* concept to an empirical sense intuition. Is this function of synthesis or application a conscious act of judgment ? The intellectual process of forming universal concepts has always been called *conception*. Kant reduces "all acts of the understanding " to "judgments " (*cf. infra*). This enables us to understand how he can discuss the "objectivity " or "necessity and universality " of *concepts*, for he can do so only in reference to an implicit judgment—a "judgment of *reality* or *existence*" : "*This is* so-and-so"—which he must hold to accompany the formation or conception of the universal concept (49). This implicit judgment is or may be conscious. But the synthesis of the *a priori form* with the sense intuition is not, in Kant's theory, a *conscious* process. *Cf.* WINDELBAND, *op. cit.*, p. 545. To this we must return later. Of course this Kantian account of conception as a synthesis of the sort described is untenable. *Cf. infra*, chap. xii.

[3] Kant's use of the term "object" ["Gegenstand "], a term of such primary importance in his theory, is extremely confusing. By "representation " ["Vorstellung "] he means what is present to us, what we are aware of, in any conscious state. It may be a relation between two empirical concepts, as in the judgment "all bodies are divisible ". But each of these is itself a representation [a "Vorstellung "], consisting of the synthesis of some *pure* concept of the understanding with an empirical sense intuition. And it is this synthesis (of formal and material elements) that is an "object" in the technical sense of imposing itself necessarily and universally as such on our minds. The empirical sense intuition itself is also a representation consisting of the synthesis of a pure intuition-form (Space or Time) with a sensation-matter : which synthesized mental *product* is also *object* (or can become an *object* by being *thought* under a pure concept of the understanding) and "is called phenomenon" ["Erscheinung "] (*Crit.*, p. 16). It is not the "given " sensation-*matter* that is "object"; it is the empirical intuition (*i.e.* matter *plus* form) that is "object," and it becomes "object" only by being thought by the understanding through some pure or *a priori* concept "in relation to that representation *which is a mere determination of the soul* " ("als blosse Bestimmung des Gemüths," *ibid.*, p. 40). In the process of empirical sense intuition the *sensibility receives* "representations " (or "mere determinations of the soul "), while in the processes of intellectual conception and judg-

but to some other representation of it, whether it be an intuition, or itself a concept. A judgment is therefore a mediate knowledge of an object, or a representation of a representation of it.   In every judgment we find a con-cept [the predicate] applying to many, and comprehending among the many one single representation [the subject] which is referred immediately to the object.   Thus in the judgment that all bodies are divisible, the concept of divisible applies to various other concepts, but is here applied in particular to the concept of body, and this concept of body to certain phenomena of our experience.   These objects therefore are represented mediately by the con-cept of divisibility.   All judgments therefore are functions of unity among our representations, the knowledge of an object being brought about, not by an immediate representation [as in sense intuition ?], but by a higher one, comprehending this and several others, so that many possible cognitions are collected into one.   As all acts of the understanding can be reduced to judg-ments, the understanding may be defined as *the faculty of judging.*   For . . . the understanding is the faculty of thinking, and thinking is knowledge by means of concepts, while concepts, as predicates of possible judgments, refer to some representation of an object yet undetermined.   Thus the concept of body means something, for instance, metal, which can be known by that con-cept.   It is only a concept, because it comprehends other representations, by means of which it can be referred to objects.   It is therefore the predicate of a possible judgment, such as, that every metal is a body.   Thus the functions of the understanding can be discovered in their completeness, if it is possible to represent the functions of unity in *judgments.*[1]

If then the function of the understanding is *to judge, i.e.* to relate among themselves and so to unify the syntheses effected by the imagination [Einbildungskraft] among the manifold repre-sentations of our empirical time-and-space intuitions, and if it does this by synthesizing those representations, through the schemata of the imagination, under pure *a priori* forms of its own, it will be possible to discover *all* these forms by examining all the possible *modes of judgment* which have been brought to light in Logic by analysis and classification of judgments.   And as

ment the *understanding produces* " representations," which, although " mere deter-minations of the soul," it *thinks* as *objective, i.e.* as phenomena or mental appear-ances which are necessarily and universally such for all human minds.   It is in virtue of the *a priori* element that the product of the synthesis has this " objective " or " necessary and universal " character.   The subjectivism of this whole position will be examined later.   Here we want merely to note that Kant sometimes uses the term " object " as if he meant by it the material as distinct from the formal ele-ment of knowledge, what is (always and avowedly supposed by him to be) given to the mind, as distinct from what is contributed by the mind, in knowledge.   But this meaning is not legitimately admitted by his theory ; for according to the theory we can *know* as an " object " only the mental representation, the " phenomenon," which latter does not and cannot represent the *matter* contributed, the extra-subjective or extramental, the " noumenon " or " thing-in-itself ",

[1] *Critique, ibid.,* pp. 56-7,

judgments are classified in Logic on the four grounds of *Quantity*, *Quality*, *Relation*, and *Modality*, yielding three modes of judgment on each basis, so we can conclude that according to the following twelve forms of judgment the understanding contains the following twelve *a priori pure concepts* or *categories* :—

Forms of Judgment.		Categories.	
(*a*) QUANTITY.		(*a*) QUANTITY.	
(1) Singular	This S is P	(1) *Unity.*	
(2) Particular	Some S is P.	(2) *Plurality.*	
(3) Universal	All S is P.	(3) *Totality.*	
(*b*) QUALITY.		(*b*) QUALITY.	
(1) Affirmative	S is P.	(1) *Affirmation.*	
(2) Negative	S is not P.	(2) *Negation.*	
(3) Infinite	S is not-P	(3) *Limitation.*	
(*c*) RELATION.		(*c*) RELATION.	
(1) Categorical	S is P.	(1) *Substantiality.*	
(2) Hypothetical	If A is B, S is P.	(2) *Causality.*	
(3) Disjunctive	S is either P or Q.	(3) *Reciprocity.*	
(*d*) MODALITY.		(*d*) MODALITY.	
(1) Problematic	S may be P.	(1) *Possibility.*	
(2) Assertoric	S is P.	(2) *Existence.*	
(3) Apodictic	S must be P.	(3) *Necessity.*	

The artificial and unsatisfactory character of this deduction of the " categories " has been so universally recognized that it calls for no comment here. The traditional logical classification of judgments on the fourfold basis of quantity, quality, relation, and modality, has really no connexion with Kant's account of the judgment. For Kant the unity effected by the judgment is a synthesis or unification of manifold representations under a common concept ; and the analysis of such an act should have led him merely to the conclusion that there are " universals," or concepts, or categories, but could not have revealed to him what these are : since the bare " form " of a " universalizing " process cannot yield "kinds " of universalizing.[1] But if the judgment whose "forms " are classified in the traditional Logic be regarded as a process of synthesizing, it is a synthesizing or unifying not of manifold particulars under a universal, " but of the two conceptions which constitute the terms of the judgment ".[2]

The fact that while the Aristotelian categories are a classification of *concepts* (used as *predicates* in our judgments), the Kantian categories appear to be rather a classification of *judgment-forms* or *modes of relating*, finds its explanation in Kant's view that the formation of the (empirical) concept itself, including the process of " thinking " the latter as " objective," involves the

[1] *Cf.* PRICHARD, *op. cit.*, pp. 150-2.

[2] *Ibid.*, p. 152. The author sums up his criticism of Kant's " Metaphysical Deduction of the Categories " (*op. cit.*, chap. vii.) with this observation : " Judgment, as Kant describes it, does not involve the forms of judgment borrowed from Formal Logic as its essential differentiations ; and these forms of judgment do not involve the categories " (*ibid.*, p. 160).

synthesizing or relating the elements of a given manifold under a unifying form and judging the product to be "objective," *i.e.* to be necessarily and universally such for all minds.[1]

53. THEIR APPLICATION IN MATHEMATICS AND PHYSICS.—

Kant next goes on to show, in the course of the *Transcendental Analytic*, that by the application of the categories of the understanding to the time-and-space intuitions of sensibility we can form certain synthetic-*a-priori* judgments which give us a valid insight into Physical Nature *as a phenomenon*, inasmuch as this phenomenon, in the very process whereby we apprehend it as an object, is made to conform to the *a priori* laws of our understanding.

He had *assumed* the truth of necessary and universal mathematical judgments, and had inferred therefrom the nature of their objects, *viz.* that these must be mental phenomena, conformed to the *a priori* forms of time and space in the mind itself. It was probably the self-evidence of mathematical judgments that had led him to take them as a starting-point; for "as we directly apprehend their necessity they admit of no reasonable doubt".[2] But in his treatment of Physics as compared with Mathematics we find some significant differences

Physics needs besides its mathematical basis (sense intuitions and their mathematical, time-and-space relations) a number of general principles of connexion between things. These principles, such as that every change must have a cause, are synthetic and come into consciousness in and through experience; but being necessary and universal they are in the understanding *a priori ;* and by means of them we think Nature as a systematic whole of phenomena on which we impose the *a priori* categories of our understanding. The necessary and universal principles which emerge from an analysis of the categories, and which form the principles of a *Metaphysics of Nature*, can, moreover, be applied to this system of Physical Nature only by a mathematical formulation reached " through the empirical conception of *motion*, to which all occurrence and change in Nature is theoretically to

---

[1] Kant maintained that " all apprehension involves on the part of the mind the relating to one another in various ways of the elements of what is apprehended ; if the elements were not so related they would not be elements of one object ; and they cannot be related except the mind at the same time relates them, since relation exists only for consciousness."—JOSEPH, *Introduction to Logic*, p. 48. For remarks on the Kantian categories, *cf. Science of Logic*, i., § 77, pp. 150-3.

[2] PRICHARD, *op. cit.*, p. 24.

be reduced. At least, science of Nature, in the proper sense, reaches only so far as we can employ mathematics: hence Kant excluded psychology and chemistry from natural science as being merely descriptive disciplines." [1]

Thus, physical science, for Kant, would be applied mathematics, mechanics, dynamics, statics, kinetics, etc., as illustrated, *e.g.* in astronomy; and he apparently claimed for its laws the same sort of necessity and universality as for the truths of pure mathematics. The significance of this will be apparent when we find him giving as illustrations of such "necessary and universal" laws of physics the judgments "that in all changes of the material world the quantity of matter remains always unchanged: or that in all communication of motion, action and reaction must always equal each other".[2]

Another remarkable difference is that

"the general principles underlying physics, *e.g.* that every change must have a cause, or that in all change the quantum of matter is constant, appeared to Kant in a different light [from those of mathematics]. Though certainly not based on experience they did not seem to him self-evident. Hence in the case of these principles he sought to give what he did not seek to give in the case of mathematical judgments, *viz.* a proof of their truth. The nerve of the proof lies in the contention that these principles are not merely in-volved in any general judgment in physics, *e.g.* 'All bodies are heavy,' but even in any singular judgment, *e.g.* 'This body is heavy,' and that the validity of singular judgments is universally conceded. Thus here the fact upon which he takes his stand is not the admitted truth of the universal judgments under consideration, but the admitted truth of any singular judgment in physics. . . . At the same time the acceptance of mathematical judgments and the proof of the *a priori* principles of physics have for Kant a common presupposition which distinguish mathematics and physics from metaphysics. . . [They] are true only if the objects to which they relate are phenomena. Both in mathematics and physics, therefore, it is a condition of *a priori* knowledge that it relates to phenomena and not to things in themselves. But just for this reason metaphysics is in a different position; since God, freedom, and immortality can never be objects of experience, *a priori* know-ledge in metaphysics, and therefore metaphysics itself, is impossible. Thus for Kant the very condition the realization of which justifies the acceptance of mathematical judgments and enables us to prove the principles of physics, involves the impossibility of metaphysics." [3]

The *Transcendental Analytic* reaches the result "that the understanding *a priori* can never do more than anticipate the form of a possible experience; and as nothing can be an object of experience except the phenomenon, it follows that the understanding can never go beyond the limits of sensibility,

---

[1] WINDELBAND, *op. cit.*, p. 546.   [2] *Critique*, p. 722.
[3] PRICHARD, *op. cit.*, p. 25.

within which alone objects are given to us ". . . .[1] "All our representations are no doubt referred to some sort of object,[2] and as phenomena are nothing but representations the understanding refers them to a *something*, as the object of our sensuous intuition, this something being, however, the transcendental object only. This means a something equal to x, of which we do not, nay, with the present constitution of our understanding, cannot know anything."[3]

54. THE "ILLUSION" OF METAPHYSICS.—Kant accordingly proceeds in the *Transcendental Dialectic* to lay bare what he calls the transcendental illusion ("Schein") of the knowledge of the suprasensible, supposed to be obtained by the employment of the categories beyond the domain of sense intuition in *Cosmology, Rational Psychology*, and *Natural Theology*. In Cosmology he claims that the extension of the four classes of the categories beyond the domain of experience inevitably leads us to these four *antinomies*, or pairs of mutually contradictory theses and antitheses :—

(*a*) *Thesis :* The world must have a beginning in time and be limited in space. *Antithesis :* The world is eternal and infinite.[4]

(*b*) *Thesis :* Matter is divisible into ultimately indivisible or simple atoms. *Antithesis :* Matter is indefinitely divisible.[5]

(*c*) *Thesis :* Besides the necessary causation of Nature there is a causation that is free. *Antithesis :* Necessary causation prevails universally to the exclusion of freedom.[6]

(*d*) *Thesis :* There exists an absolutely necessary Being belonging to the world either as a part or as a cause of it. *Antithesis :* There nowhere exists an absolutely necessary Being, either within or without the world, as the cause of it.[7]

Such are the self-contradictory results of attempting to determine, or to know, by means of the categories, the *something*, the thing-in-itself, to which we are forced by thought itself to refer the phenomena of our spatial or external sense intuitions.

Similarly, *Rational Psychology* is involved in a series of *paralogisms* in attempting to infer the substantiality, simplicity, spirituality, and immortality of the soul or mind or *Ego* from the phenomena of our internal or temporal sense intuitions. For the understanding has no intuitive knowledge; it understands

---

[1] *Critique*, p. 201.

[2] But the representations themselves are the "objects". For ambiguity of this term, *cf. supra*, p. 186, n. 3.

[3] *Ibid.*, p. 204.   [4] *Ibid.*, pp. 344-5.   [5] *Ibid.*, pp. 352-3.

[6] *Ibid.*, pp. 362-3.   [7] *Ibid.*, pp. 370-1.

only discursively, by a successive series of syntheses of mental phenomena into "objects". These syntheses imply a synthesizing function, a real, unconditioned "transcendental unity" of all our apperceptions, a supreme unifying factor which we are forced to think as the *real Ego*, but which is devoid of empirical content, and is therefore an unknowable x, a noumenon. The idea of it has a merely *regulative* value for investigating the phenomena of mental life, the sum-total of the conscious representations which constitute the *empirical Ego*. "I think" is a mere logical function of all judgments. Of itself it can yield no knowledge: for the "I" is a mere empty form and not an actual or even a possible object of knowledge; no category, substance or any other, is applicable to it, for it is devoid of empirical content. Therefore all efforts to designate or determine in any way the real *Ego* involves the paralogism of confounding the latter with the empirical mental phenomena to which alone the categories of the understanding are applicable.

In the domain of *Natural Theology* Kant endeavours to show in a similar way that all theoretical proofs of the existence of an Absolute Being (which pure reason is forced to think as an "*ideal*") are sophisms which involve an illegitimate application of the category of causality beyond the domain of possible experience.

Kant believed that those antinomies and contradictions arose in metaphysics owing to the traditional assumption that in knowledge the mind is conformed to things as its objects. He thought the secret of the progress made by mathematics and physics lay in the assumption that in their domain the objects of knowledge are made to conform to the mind's ways of thinking them.[1] And he suggested making the experiment of a similar "Copernican revolution" in metaphysics, to see if it too would fare better on the assumption "that the objects must conform to our mode of cognition,"[2] than it had previously fared on the opposite assumption. The reversal, he believed, enables us to understand the possibility of synthetic-*a-priori* knowledge and to demonstrate certain laws which lie at the foundation of nature, *e.g.* the law of causality; but it also involves what is for metaphysics a "startling result," *viz.* "the impossibility of going with it be-

---

[1] *Cf. Critique* (Pref. to 2nd edit.), p. 690 *sqq.* The contention of Kant here is ably criticized by PRICHARD, *op. cit.*, p. 10 *sqq.*
[2] *Critique, ibid.*, p. 693.

yond the frontier of possible experience, which is precisely the most essential function of metaphysical science "[1]—to deal with God, freedom, immortality, etc. This very consequence, however, *viz.* the impossibility of a scientific metaphysics, really serves to vindicate the assumption that in knowledge objects must conform to our way of representing them and must therefore be phenomena, not things in themselves ; and to disprove the opposite assumption that knowledge conforms to objects as things in themselves. For it is this latter assumption that involves metaphysics in unavoidable contradictions ; and it is the former assumption that clears up the contradictions by showing them to be due to a confusion of phenomena with things-in-themselves, or in other words, to an attempt on the part of metaphysics to apply to the latter the laws that govern only the former :—

"That which impels us by necessity to go beyond the limits of experience and of all phenomena, is the *unconditioned*, which reason postulates in all things by themselves, by necessity and by right, for everything conditioned, so that the series of conditions should thus become complete. If then we find that, under the supposition of our experience conforming to the objects as things by themselves, it is *impossible to conceive* the unconditioned *without contradiction*, while, under the supposition of our representation of things, as they are given to us, not conforming to them as things by themselves, but, on the contrary, of the objects conforming to our mode of representation, that *contradiction vanishes*, and that therefore the unconditioned must not be looked for in things, so far as we know them (so far as they are given to us) but only so far as we do not know them (as things by themselves), we clearly perceive that, what we at first assumed tentatively only, is fully confirmed."[2]

Thus in the attempt to apply the law of causality beyond the domain of possible sense experience metaphysics was equally forced to the mutually contradictory conclusions that "necessary causality is all-pervading," and that "there must be a free or unconditioned cause" :—

"I should not then be able to say of one and the same being, for instance the human soul, that its will is free, and, at the same time, subject to the necessity of nature, that is, not free, without involving myself in a palpable contradiction : and this because I had taken the soul in both propositions, in *one and the same sense*, namely, as a thing in general (as something by itself) as without previous criticism I could not but take it. If, however, our criticism was true, in teaching us to take an object in two senses, namely, either as a phenomenon, or as a thing by itself, and if the deduction of our concepts of the understanding was correct, and the principle of causality applies to

---

[1] *Critique* (Pref. to 2nd edit.), p. 695. [2] *Ibid.*, p. 695.

things only if taken in the first sense, namely, so far as they are concepts of experience, but not to things as taken in their second sense, we can without any contradiction think of the same will when phenomenal (in visible actions) as necessarily conforming to the law of nature, and so far, *not free*, and yet, on the other hand, when belonging to a thing by itself, as not subject to that law of nature, and therefore *free*. Now it is quite true that I may not *know* my soul, as a thing by itself, by means of speculative reason (still less through empirical observation), and consequently may not know freedom either. . This, however, does not prevent me from *thinking* freedom. .   " [1]

So the recognition that *knowledge* is confined to phenomena, and that consequently a scientific or speculative metaphysic is an illusion, solves the antinomies, and thus prepares the way for the practical reason to build up a metaphysic of *belief* in the reality of God, freedom, and immortality on the basis of an ethical intuition of duty or moral obligation.

55. THE "COPERNICAN REVOLUTION".—Now it is interesting to note that the so-called "Copernican revolution," which is supposed to have led to these results is not justified, as Kant believed it to be, by a consideration of the procedure in mathematics. Progress in mathematics is not due to any conscious assumption that its objects conform to our way of thought, but to a procedure whereby we draw, for example, or imagine a certain figure, *see* certain necessary relations to obtain within it as such, and conclude that they must necessarily hold good for all possible cases of it. In concluding thus we see that all possible cases must conform to the necessary relations or laws thus discovered by our minds ; but this by no means involves that these laws are mental laws, or that objects must conform to the mind, but rather that they must conform to their own nature as seen by the mind.

And if this procedure be applied to an object of metaphysics, such as the soul, it implies that we should, through perception, imagination, and thought, gain an analogous insight into its nature, an insight which would enable us to see, for example, that, having such a nature, it is necessarily free, spiritual, immortal, etc. Progress in metaphysics would therefore depend on our capacity to gain such an insight into the object (*e.g.* the soul) as would involve the discovery of certain necessary properties and relations in that object, and the consequent formulation of certain necessary and universal judgments concerning it. Nor could this capacity for progress be in the least influenced by our

[1] *Critique* (Pref. to 2nd edit.), p. 699.

consciously regarding the necessary relations so attainable as *mental* laws or consciously supposing that the object, by always and necessarily verifying these laws, or conforming to these laws, is thereby being "constructed" by the mind itself, so as to conform to "mental laws".[1]

Furthermore, Kant's contention that objects must be conceived as having to conform to the mind is not *really*, but only *verbally*, a "Copernican revolution" of the ordinary view that in knowledge the mind must be conceived as having to conform to objects. For in the ordinary view "objects" mean things and events that are independent of the mind in the sense that they exist and happen independently of our knowledge of them, and that in knowledge our ideas are made to conform to them. And the real contrary of this view would be that our ideas exist first, and that objects, *i.e.* things or events, coming into existence afterwards, must in doing so adapt themselves to our ideas. But this seems absurd, inasmuch as we always think of the existence or reality of objects as the presupposition of our knowing them, and not the existence of the knowledge as a presupposition of the existence of its objects. Now Kant *appears to avoid* this absurdity, and makes the view that "objects conform to knowledge" plausible, only by attaching a new and different meaning to "object," *viz.* by making it designate something which, like knowledge itself, is within the mind, and which he calls a "phenomenon". The terms of the conformity are, therefore, not the same as in the ordinary view, for with Kant the conformity is between two realities within the mind, and not as in the ordinary view between knowledge within the mind and a reality outside the mind. Hence his view is not really a reversal or "Copernican revolution" of the ordinary view that we know objects or things independent of or outside the mind by bringing our minds into conformity with these. And, in fact, his conclusion is that we do not and cannot know things in themselves (*i.e.* what is meant by "objects" in the ordinary view) at all. Hence he should have said, not that the ordinary view puts the conformity in the

---

[1] "Success or failure in metaphysics would therefore consist in success or failure to see the necessity of the relations involved. Kant, however, makes the condition of advance in metaphysics consist not in the adoption of a certain procedure but of an assumption, *viz.* that objects conform to the mind. And it is impossible to see how this assumption can assist what, on Kant's theory, it ought to have assisted, *viz.* the study of God, freedom and immortality, or indeed the study of anything."— PRICHARD, *op. cit.*, p. 13.

13 *

wrong way, but that we should not speak of such conformity at all, inasmuch as he holds objects, in the sense of things in themselves, to be unknowable.[1]

Another and final point worthy of note, before we pass from the exposition of his theory, is the following. He misstates the general problem of knowledge by representing it as a difficulty which the existence of necessary and universal judgments presents to the ordinary view that in knowledge the mind is conformed to objects that are independent of it ; and the solution he reaches shows that he misstates it.

By asking, How can the mind discover a *necessary and universal* law about such objects, a law which is valid beyond actual experience of them? he insinuates that *empirical, a posteriori* judgments present no parallel difficulty, inasmuch as these rest on actual experience[2] of the objects, and are thus conformed to the objects in the very process by which they arise. But this is not so unless we assume that in actual sense experience we apprehend objects or things as they are in themselves. But *the validity of perceiving is as serious a problem as the validity of thinking.* The general problem of the relation of mind to things concerns *empirical, a posteriori* judgments as well as necessary judgments ; and Kant could confine the problem to the latter only by ignoring the relation of mind to things in the former.

And the solution he reaches shows that he misstated the problem in appearing to confine it to necessary judgments : for his solution is that while *both* classes of judgments are valid of *phenomena, neither* class is valid of *things in themselves,* or, in other words, that of things in themselves we can know neither general laws nor particular characteristics.

The general problem which Kant had in mind, and which he really solved in the agnostic sense just indicated, was of course

---

[1] *Cf.* PRICHARD, *op. cit.*, pp. 15-16.

[2] With Kant "experience" always implies the presence of a *sensuous* element in consciousness. "The point of the word 'experience' is that there is direct apprehension of some individual, *e.g.* an individual body" (PRICHARD, p. 3). "The existence of *a posteriori* synthetic judgments presents no difficulty. For experience is equivalent to perception, and, as we suppose, in perception we are confronted with reality, and apprehend it as it is. If I am asked 'How do I know that my pen is black or my chair hard?' I answer that it is because I see or feel it to be so. . . . I appeal to my experience or perception of the reality to which the assertion relates. My appeal raises no difficulty *because it conforms to the universal belief that if judgments are to rank as knowledge, they must be made to conform to the nature of things,* and that the conformity is established by appeal to the actual experience of things." —*Ibid.*, p. 7 (italics ours).

that of the relation of our cognitive states in general to reality
as their object; but in stating the problem he confounded it with
another and distinct problem which does not concern this relation,
but, assuming it to be there, asks, What is it that makes the
objects of knowledge, or things, or reality, *necessarily and universally* conformable to certain laws of connexion which the mind
discovers therein?—(1) What is it that makes all conceivable
cases of plane triangles necessarily and universally conformable
to the *absolutely* necessary and universal law of having their
interior angles equal to two right angles? (2) What is it that
makes all conceivable cases of living organisms conformable
to the *contingently* necessary and universal law of having their
origin from antecedent organisms,—the biological law, *omne vivens
ab ovo*, or *omnis cellula ex cellula?* Kant found the solution of
this special problem in his solution of the former, *viz.* by declaring
that in knowledge the relation of conformity is not between the
mind and reality but between the mind and its own phenomena,
or mental appearances: for, he argued, if the " objects " of knowledge are constructed by the mind according to constructive
principles whereby the mind can thus determine what its possible
experiences will be, it is then intelligible that in knowing it can
legislate, as it were, or consciously apprehend laws to which
objects must necessarily and universally conform. But, as we
shall see, this solution solves nothing. For it is necessary to distinguish two kinds of necessity and universality, absolute and
conditional or contingent, as illustrated by the two examples
just given. The problem raised by the latter is that of the grounds
of our belief in the *Uniformity of Nature*,[1] a problem which Kant
does not specifically distinguish from that raised by the former.[2]
And we shall see presently that his attempt to account for the
absolute necessity and universality of the *nexus* in what he calls
synthetic-*a-priori* judgments, by seeking the origin of this necessity in *a priori* mental forms, only deprives such judgments
of all real knowledge-value, while it either makes their necessity
subjective and relative to the *de facto* structure of the human mind,
or else declares its real or ontological basis to be unknowable.

56. THE INFLUENCE AND THE ISSUES OF KANT'S TEACHING.
—In the preceding sections (46-55) we have endeavoured to give

---

[1] *Cf. Science of Logic*, ii., §§ 223-6.
[2] Neither does PRICHARD, whose criticism (*op. cit.*, pp. 12-22) we have substantially followed in the text.

a general outline of Kant's Theory of Knowledge. The theory has had a profound influence on subsequent speculation. The doctrine embodied in the *Critique of Pure Reason* and in the *Prolegomena* was developed into a system of *Idealistic Monism* by FICHTE (1762-1814), SCHELLING (1775-1854), and HEGEL (1770-1831).

Kant had described the *matter* of knowledge as "given from without," and had pronounced it to be as a thing in itself *unknowable*. Fichte observed that there is no reason to suppose that the matter of knowledge does not lie *within* the subject, like the form, and emerge into consciousness with the latter in the process of cognition. Both the matter and the form of knowledge lie in the *One Absolute Reality* which is the *Transcendental or Absolute Ego*, and which by opposing itself to itself as "object" to "subject" evolves itself into partial and evanescent "consciousnesses," each of which is an individual human mind.[1] Thus men are but aspects of the *Absolute Ego ;* and man's highest duty is self-renunciation and the merging of his personality in the *Absolute Ego* according to the law of Universal Love.

Schelling did not, like Fichte, subordinate object to subject, or absorb the former in the latter. Subject and Object, Spirit and Nature, are but two aspects of one ultimate, self-identical reality, the *Absolute,*—which, from its indeterminateness, was described by Hegel as "the night in which all cows are black".

Hegel himself gave "subject" a logical primacy over "object". But thought and its object are one reality. Antecedently to all antithesis of subject and object is the Absolute, which is Thought or Idea, and which by a purely rational, logical, necessary process of evolution, becomes subject and object, spirit and nature, ideal and real. He worked out a most elaborate philosophy of Absolute Idealism which has also exercised a profound influence on modern thought.

Apart from the line of development represented by those three names there were other currents set in motion by Kantism. Perhaps the main influence of Kantism has been exerted by the destructive or sceptical side of its teaching. Kant taught that reality is in itself unknowable. What right had he, therefore, to postulate the *existence* of a reality beyond or independent of the mere content of the individual conscious state?[2] It is notorious

[1] *Cf.* MERCIER, *op. cit.,* §§ 145-6, pp. 398-401. JEANNIÈRE, *op. cit.,* p. 38.
[2] *Cf.* MERCIER, *op. cit.,* § 144, pp. 395-8.

that he postulated it in virtue of a "transcendental" use or application of the principle of causality, an application condemned as invalid by his own theory. Even his disciples were prompt to note this inconsistency in regard to a most grave and crucial problem in his theory; and were not slow to proclaim utter agnosticism as the logical goal of the effort of human reason to explore its own capacity. Nor was it consistent of Kant to postulate the *existence* of a noumenal reality, and to proclaim impossible any knowledge of its *nature*, for if a necessity of thought forces us to recognize its existence, why should we yield so far to this necessity of thought, and refuse to yield to it when it forces upon us inferences in regard to the nature of the reality? And as a matter of fact Kant did inconsistently accept and work upon assumptions in regard to the *nature* of the noumenal reality : for he spoke of it *in the plural*, as *things*-in-themselves, thus implicitly admitting its manifoldness, implicitly identifying it with bodies in space,[1] and implicitly ascribing a distinct noumenal reality to individual men : assumptions as to its manifoldness which were soon swept away by the monism of Fichte, Schelling, and Hegel.

Again, the chasm he created between knowledge on the one hand and ethical and religious belief on the other, proved disastrous to both alike.[2] No doubt many sincere thinkers among his disciples have sought to emphasize the fact that Kant never doubted the power of the mind to grasp reality, and that while he took from the speculative reason the power to *deny* reality, no less than the power to affirm it, he accorded to the practical reason the power to *attain to* reality ; and they have loyally tried to build up a moral and religious metaphysic on the dictate of ˙duty. But other no less sincere thinkers have seen the futility of such an attempt. If I can *know* nothing about the nature of reality I cannot know whether it is one or manifold, whether, therefore, I myself as known to myself, and other men as known to me, are mere phenomena of an unknowable reality, or are each a distinct reality. When, therefore, Kant builds up a system of ethical and religious " beliefs " for *me* and for *others*, on the basis of a dictate of duty revealed in *our* consciences, I cannot help reflecting that this dictate of my conscience is also a *datum of my*

---

[1] *Cf.* PRICHARD, *op. cit.*, pp. 32, 77, n. 2.
[2] *Cf.* MERCIER, *op. cit.*, § 143, pp. 392-5, for comparison of the two *Critiques*.

consciousness,[1] that therefore it is no less phenomenal than my own *empirical* self and the other *empirical* " selves " or men, which (according to the theory) are the only " selves " I can know of ; nor can I help concluding that beliefs built on such a " phenomenal" basis, and entertained *by* phenomena *about* phenomena, cannot possibly secure for me as a real being a *genuine*, if only personal, contact with reality.[2]   Moreover, if the last word of my reason, reflecting on the really supreme questions concerning my own nature and destiny, were that my will dictates to me that I am to believe personally in *that which I cannot know to be true*, *viz.* that God exists, that I am His creature, endowed by Him with freedom, responsibility, immortality,—is it reasonable or natural that I as an intelligent being should or would shape my life according to the dictate of a blind faculty to believe in the reality of that whose reality I must at the same time hold to be problematic and unknowable?   Such a faith would not be the *obsequium rationabile* of true Christianity ; and the history of the gradual disintegration of the many nominally Christian forms of "belief" in modern times bears eloquent testimony to the feebleness of faiths that are based not on reason, but on the quicksands of personal feelings, emotions, and impulses.[3]

[1] *Cf.* MERCIER, *op. cit.*, § 143, p. 394.   [2] *Cf.* JEANNIÈRE, *op. cit.*, p. 193 n.

[3] The fact is that Kant's theory, taken as a whole, is a sort of intellectual solvent : by profoundly misconceiving and misstating the actual nature and manner of the mind's cognitive functions it tends to induce a morbid condition of intellectual vacillation and insecurity.   Its errors are the more dangerous because they are for the most part half-truths, deformations of the real truth.   Its wresting of such terms as "object," "objectivity," "truth," etc., to new meanings, after having repudiated their traditional meanings, and its not infrequent transitions from one meaning to another, give it a plausibility which may deceive the student until more mature reflection brings to light the ambiguity and confusion.

The whole theory involves positions incompatible with Catholic belief, as, for instance, the *metaphysical agnosticism* which proclaims that reality is unknowable, the *moral dogmatism* which denies an intellectual basis to faith and morals and places them on grounds that are non-rational, and the merely symbolic interpretation which is the only interpretation it can consistently give to the facts and doctrines of the Christian religion.

CHAPTER VII.

NECESSARY JUDGMENTS: KANT'S THEORY EXAMINED.

57. THE CASE FOR THE "CRITIQUE OF PURE REASON".—
As regards the general criticism of Kant's theory of knowledge, it is clear that such criticism may naturally fall under certain broadly distinct heads, corresponding with certain main positions in the general theory. For instance, the attempt to base human certitude concerning the solution of the supreme problems raised by human experience,—God, freedom, duty, religion, immortality, etc.,—*ultimately* on a dictate of the *practical reason*, must be examined separately in its proper place. Again, the distinction between *mental appearances* or *phenomena*, and *reality* or *things in themselves* or *noumena*, and the alleged impossibility of attaining to *knowledge* of the latter, can be best examined in connexion with the general problem of the validity of *sense perception*. The relation of intellectual conception to sense perception or sense intuition, and of the concepts of the understanding to the intuitions or perceptions of sense, is another distinct problem involving some account of the mode of transition from sense to intellect, from perception to conception and judgment,—the problem of universal ideas. It will be examined more fully later on, and here only incidentally in so far as it is involved in the theory whereby Kant seeks to account for the *necessity* and *universality* of the *nexus* revealed in certain judgments by representing the latter as *syntheses* of mental forms, which condition experience *a priori*, with what is "given" in this experience, and whereby these *data* are alleged to be raised to the *status* of mental or phenomenal "objects" of knowledge. The main considerations urged on behalf of the general doctrine of the *Critique* may be briefly summarized as follows.

The general thesis of the *Critique* is that the mathematical and physical sciences have progressed, while metaphysical science has failed, because it is only in the former and not in the latter that scientific, *i.e.* necessarily and universally valid, judgments fulfil the requisite condition for giving knowledge, *viz.* the synthesis of an *a priori* form with an empirical sense *datum* to constitute an object of knowledge ; and the *Critique* simultaneously claims to show that the scope of all scientific knowledge is restricted to phenomena and cannot extend to things in themselves. In bringing to light the essential conditions of scientific knowledge, and showing them to be such that scientific knowledge is possible in mathematics and physics, but impossible in metaphysics, the *Critique* is claimed to bear in itself its own vindication.

Moreover, on the one hand, the empiricism of Hume did not, and could not, satisfactorily account for the *necessary* and *universal* character of scientific judgments, inasmuch as these are not and cannot be grounded in sense experience. But, on the other hand, neither can these characteristics be explained by supposing, with Leibniz, that such judgments are derived by a purely rational process of *a priori*, deductive analysis from certain innate, necessary principles ; for analytic judgments are merely explicative and cannot extend our knowledge. Hence the real explanation lies in the *via media*, whereby such judgments are seen to be at once *a priori* and therefore necessary, and at the same time synthetic and therefore productive of new knowledge,—to be syntheses of *a priori* mental forms with empirical sense *data*.

And finally, the whole position is confirmed by a proof of complete induction, whereby Kant purports to bring to light all the necessary and universal principles of mathematics, physics, and metaphysics, and to show that all are synthetic-*a-priori* judgments.

These are the main lines on which the doctrine of the *Critique* is defended. What, now, are the main considerations that may be urged against its account of the characteristics of necessary and universal judgments?

58. A Priori Forms neither Essential nor Sufficient to Account for Necessary and Universal Judgments.— We may observe in the *first* place that it is not the only *via media* between the extreme *a priorism* of Leibniz which does indeed fail to justify the application of necessary judgments to the world of sense experience, and the empiricism of Hume which equally fails to account for the necessary character of such judgments. There is another *via media*, that of Scholasticism, which accounts for the characteristics of necessary and universal judgments, and that in a way which *does not sacrifice their real objectivity, or the*

validity of their application to the domain of suprasensible reality.[1]
Even, therefore, if Kant's theory offered a sufficient and satis_
factory explanation of necessary judgments we could not con_
clude its truth without first examining the alternative offered by
Scholasticism. But it does not even offer a sufficient and satisfactory explanation; and this is our next point of criticism.

In the *second* place, therefore, we say that Kant's theory, while
according only a nominal and not a real objectivity to necessary
and universal judgments, *either makes their necessity and universality merely relative, subjective and psychological, or else confesses
the real ground and explanation of these characteristics to be unknowable.* That the *objectivity* ascribed to such judgments is
intramental, and determined by subjective or mental forms *a
priori*, is manifest from Kant's own exposition. We merely note
this and pass to the question of their *necessity*.

Kant had rightly observed, against Hume, that mere habit or
custom, a mere psychological product of association of mental
states, or any mental factor subject to the vicissitudes of individual, personal existence, could not account for more than a
merely relative stability, a mere expectation of uniformity in the
nexus of judgments based on such factors. But if the *a priori*
mental forms, to which Kant attributes the necessity of the *nexus*,
belong to the mental structure or constitution of the *individual*
thinking subject, they can account no less unsatisfactorily for the
necessity of the *nexus* in question. For the individual thinking
subject, the individual man, is himself contingent, no less than
the rest of the world of his sense experience. Factors of his
mental constitution could, indeed, explain why *e.g.* two and two
would appear necessarily four *for him*, and for all other minds
constituted *similarly to his own*, because, namely, he and they,
in virtue of that *de facto* mental constitution, could not think or
judge otherwise. Just as mere sense experience can tell us that
a thing is *de facto* such or such, but not that a thing *must be* so
and *cannot be otherwise*, so a necessity of judging which would be
due to *a priori* mental forms would indeed show us that the mind
is *de facto* so constituted that it must judge in a certain way, *e.g.*
that 2 + 2 are 4, but it would not show us that the mind *must be*
so constituted, and *cannot be constituted otherwise*, *e.g.* so that it
could judge 2 + 2 to be something other than 4. In other words,

[1] *Cf. infra*, chap. viii.

such factors could account for a *de facto*, relative, psychological necessity in judgments. But they could not account for the wholly different sort of necessity and universality which our minds do undeniably apprehend in the relation between "two *plus* two" and "four," and in the similar relations revealed in all *absolutely* necessary and universal judgments. For it is notorious that *not only are we forced to think and to judge* these relations to be what they are, but also that we think and judge them to be what they are *for all conceivable minds*, however constituted or constructed. We see, no doubt, that of course *human* intelligence cannot think them to be otherwise, but we see further that *no intelligence* could think them to be otherwise; for we see that they *cannot be* otherwise, and that *this*, and no subjective limitation or constitutional incapacity of intelligence, is the reason why all intelligence must think them to be thus and not otherwise.

If, then, the *a priori* mental forms of the sensibility and understanding are to be taken as constitutional factors of the individual thinking human mind, they are just as powerless as Hume's "habit of expectation, begotten by custom," to explain a *nexus* whose necessity is not merely subjective and personal, but independent of subjectivity, impersonal, really objective, and thereby and not otherwise *scientific*. Hence, despite Kant's dogmatic intentions, and his retention of the terms "object" and "objectivity," his theory accords to scientific judgments a necessity that is no more than *subjective* and *relative*.[1]

As a matter of fact it does not in the least help to account for the absolutely necessary and universal validity of the relation apprehended in such a judgment to say that it is by the function of an *a priori* mental form we construct and represent in consciousness such a relation;[2] for whether the relation appertains

---

[1] Even on the assumption that there are other human minds constituted similarly to my own, minds which *must*, therefore, think these relations as I do (which "necessity and universality" are all that Kant means by "objectivity"), these characteristics of such judgments are still obviously relative to, and conditioned by, that mental constitution : which is precisely what we mean by a "subjective" or "psychological" characteristic. Moreover, according to Kant's theory, I can *know* of the existence of other men and minds (and indeed my own) *only as phenomena*, not as realities. And if the *a priori* forms are ascribed to human minds *as phenomena*, the whole theory of the *Critique* gives the *apparent*, not the *real* grounds of the necessity and universality of scientific judgments.

[2] In due course it will be shown that the analogous supposition that the *matter* of our knowledge, what is given in perception, is mental, in nowise helps to a solution of the problem either.

to what is *given to* the individual mind in judging,[1] or to what the individual mind *brings to* the judgment, it is clear that the *absolute, ontological* necessity of the relation apprehended can be neither identified with, nor explained by, the contingent, psychological necessity or law whereby the individual mind must apprehend that relation to be what it is. Supposing such a relation to be, as an object of knowledge, partly a *mental* construction or law, cannot account for the necessary character of the relation, inasmuch as the mind, being itself contingent, can, on reflection, apprehend no more than a relative, subjective necessity in any supposed product of its own cognitive functions.

The contention that the relation which we see in such a judgment is a law, or the manifestation of a law, of our own judging nature, will not account for the *absolute* necessity of such a relation, unless by "our own judging nature" we mean not the mind of the contingent, individual, personal *Ego*, but some necessary, universal, impersonal intelligence, transcending the limitations of individual consciousness,—such as was postulated by Fichte's transcendental idealism. This was the logical extension given by Fichte to Kant's "transcendental *Ego*," and it brings us to an interpretation of Kant's theory whereby it is contended that the theory really escapes the charge of subjectivism and relativism.

The interpretation is that though Kant set out to investigate the conditions on which the *human* mind (meaning his own mind, and the minds of other men, assumed by him as existing distinct from, and independent of, one another) can attain to necessary and universally valid truths (such as those of mathematics and physics), nevertheless the *a priori* mental forms which he professed to bring to light—as the necessary mental conditions for our having experience involving the apprehension of such truths —were, in virtue of his analysis, necessarily located by him not in our human minds *as known by* our human minds,—in other words, not in the "empirical *Ego*" of which alone each of us is conscious,—but in our human minds *as things-in-themselves,* as noumenal or real (and therefore *unknowable*): so that while the synthesizing functions of the forms are carried on (unconsciously) by the noumenal, transcendental, or real *Ego* or mind, it is only the *results* of these syntheses that can and do come into con-

---

[1] As Plato supposed; and as the scholastic theory supposes, without the implications of Platonism. *Cf. infra,* chap. viii.

sciousness as actual intuitions, conceptions, and judgments of the sensibility and the understanding.[1]   Now, according to this interpretation the ground of the necessary character of the relations apprehended in necessary judgments is, no doubt, removed from the contingent, individual human mind, and placed in "mind" as a noumenal, transcendental, real being or "thing-in-itself"; but unfortunately such interpretation has the twofold result *firstly*, of declaring this ground to be *eo ipso* unknowable, and *secondly*, of making the whole doctrine of the *Critique* self-contradictory.   For, a main conclusion of the *Critique* is that the *noumenal*, the *real*, is in itself and as to its real nature *unknowable;* but if so how can it be either possible or consistent for Kant to ascribe to it the *a priori* forms and their functions?   Hence we conclude that Kant's theory either assigns a ground which makes the necessity and universality of the judgments in question merely subjective, psychological, and relative, or else declares the ground of their necessity and universality to be unknowable.

59. SIGNIFICANCE OF THE "CRITIQUE": ITS THESES MUTUALLY DE-STRUCTIVE.—Kant's contention, of course, is that analysing human cognitive experience as we find it, and seeking an adequate explanation of it, we are forced by a *necessity of thought*, by a *necessity of our reasoning faculty*, to infer, as the only possible explanation of that experience, such *a priori* forms, such structure and functions, on the part of the mind (conditioning *a priori* the experience), as he has brought to light by his analysis.   But manifestly, if he holds that the results so brought to light constitute *knowledge* of the *real* nature of mind [2] as transcendental or noumenal, or as it is in itself, he

---

[1] This is commonly understood to have been Kant's meaning. *Cf.* WINDEL-BAND, *op. cit.*, p. 545 (italics ours): "In fact, the individual consciousness . knows itself to be bound in a way that is likewise valid for all others.   Only in this dependence consists the reference of thought to an object.   But if . . . the ground of the objective validity of the time (and space) relation can rest only in its determination by a rule of the understanding, it is on the other hand a fact that *the consciousness of the individual knows nothing of this co-operation of the categories in experience*, and that he rather accepts *the result of this co-operation* as *the objective necessity of his apprehension of the synthesis* of sensations in space and time."
"The production of the object, therefore, *does not go on in the individual consciousness*, but lies already at the basis of this consciousness; for this production a higher common consciousness must therefore be assumed, which comes into the empirical consciousness of the individual, *not with its functions but only with their result.*   This Kant termed in the *Prolegomena*, 'consciousness in general'; in the *Critique*, 'transcendental apperception,' or the 'I' [or 'self' or 'Ego']."
"'Experience' is accordingly the system of phenomena in which the spatial and temporal synthesis of sensation is determined by rules of the understanding. Thus 'Nature as phenomenon' is the object of an *a priori* knowledge; for the categories hold for all experience, because experience is grounded only through them."
[2] He has, of course, no right (on his own theory) to assume that reality consists of *minds*-in-themselves, any more than of *things*-in-themselves (in the plural).

contradicts his own theory. Since he holds that "what we think to be a necessity of things as they are in themselves is not [or, for all we know, need not be] a necessity of them," it "can just as well be urged that what we think to be a necessity of our perceiving [or judging] nature is not [or need not be] a necessity of it ".[1]

If, on the other hand, the doctrine of the *Critique* be that the *a priori* forms and their functions must be thought to belong to "consciousness in general," or the "transcendental apperception," or "transcendental *Ego*," and that this transcendental consciousness is indeed a "necessity of thought" for pure reason, but must be likewise for pure reason only a *mere logical function of judging and thinking*, and cannot be *known* by pure reason to be a *reality*,—then what meaning or significance have the conclusions of the *Critique?* Of what value are they as a body of knowledge? They purport to tell us what we necessarily think to be involved, on the part of the mind, in the cognitive experience of the mind ; and they also tell us that what we thus necessarily think to be so involved need not *really* be so involved in the nature of the real mind which really performs the judging and thinking ! They do not appear to be put forward as a system of judgments which we are to *believe*, for it is only what is derived from analysis of the dictate of conscience in the *Critique of Practical Reason* that is put forward with that sort of claim. Neither, apparently, are they put forward as a system of judgments claiming to constitute *scientific knowledge*,—unless we adopt the first interpretation given above and regard them as merely describing the individual human mind as a phenomenon, *i.e.* the "empirical *Ego*,"—for *all* "scientific knowledge " is (according to the theory) *only* of *phenomena*. But on that interpretation the *Critique* fails, as we have seen, to account any more satisfactorily than Hume's empiricism for the absolute necessity and universality of a certain class of our judgments.

We might pertinently ask whether the conclusions reached in the *Critique* are judgments which themselves conform to the conditions laid down in the *Critique* for a *scientific* judgment : Are they themselves syntheses of *a priori* categories of the understanding with empirical intuitions of the sensibility ?[2] The fact is, of course, that the conclusions of the *Critique*, and the reasonings by which they are reached, do not belong to a distinct and peculiar order of mental research, apart from those revealed in speculative scientific knowledge, or in practical belief. Throughout the *Critique* Kant uses in his reasonings the ordinary canons of logical inference, arguing from mental facts to mental conditions, from mental acts to mental faculties or powers, from the

Apart from the fact that his inferences,—from the mind's actual cognitive experience to what this presupposes on the part of the mind itself,—are faulty and based on defective analysis, the procedure of working back from actual experience to the postulates which make such experience possible, is sound and proper in principle. *Cf.* §§ 5, 26, *supra*. What he should have inferred, and what an accurate analysis of human cognitive experience in its entirety would have revealed to him, as really involved in it and presupposed by it, was what multitudes of philosophers before and since have inferred from it : the spirituality and immortality of the human soul, the freedom of the will, the existence of a Necessary Being as First and Final Cause of the Universe and Supreme Ruler of the physical and the moral order.

[1] PRICHARD, *op. cit.*, p. 63.

[2] *Cf.* MERCIER, *op. cit.*, § 144, pp. 393-4.

nature of effects to the nature of their determining causes. But he seems himself to have regarded the whole inquiry of the *Critique* as *sui generis*, as being quite distinct both from the procedure which (in mathematics and physics) yields *scientific knowledge*, and from that which (in the practical domain) yields *moral and religious belief*, and as yielding itself neither science nor belief, but rather an insight into the *pure a priori*, *transcendental* conditions which reason must verify in itself in order to have scientific knowledge.[1] This insight, supposed to be given by the conclusions of the *Critique*, would be itself a transcendental insight (a " Transcendental Logic," in its three parts, *Æsthetic, Analytic,* and *Dialectic*) into the nature of reason itself as a faculty of knowledge. But on this we must observe that according to the theory of the *Critique* itself no *a priori* judgment which is *pure* (to the exclusion of an empirical sense intuition which would make it scientific), or in other words, no *purely transcendental* knowledge, can *of itself come into consciousness* (for " conceptions without intuitions are empty ") ; hence if the conclusions of the *Critique*, as being concerned with the *pure a priori* structure and conditions of the mind, are themselves *purely a priori* and *purely transcendental* judgments, they tell us not what we can become conscious of in regard to such structure and conditions, but only what we must, by inference from the facts of consciousness, conclude as being necessarily there. And it was of course by such inference (from the facts revealed in consciousness as to our judgments in mathematics and physics) that Kant *de facto* reached his conclusions concerning the *a priori* conditions of scientific knowledge. But, furthermore, if the conclusions reached in the *Critique* were themselves *pure a priori* judgments, having themselves no empirical content, but were solely concerned with the *a priori* laws of the mind (as Kant must have held that they were, to avoid the other alternative of holding them to be concerned merely with the mind *as a phenomenon*, and therefore incapable of revealing its *a priori* laws), then neither does it appear how, on his theory, we could *ever become conscious of these conclusions themselves!* For these conclusions are judgments of the pure reason, and an empirical content is, on his theory, the only means of bringing down a judgment of pure reason from the transcendental domain of what is required *a priori* for such a judgment into the domain where such a judgment can be consciously formed.

Kant appears to have believed that pure reason can, without an empirical content, form conscious judgments about its own *a priori* conditions for knowledge, and that he was doing so in the *Critique ;* whereas he really was not doing so. He was not examining—nor could he consistently with his own theory examine, or formulate any conscious judgment about—the nature or structure of the faculty of pure reason in its *a priori* condition, or as independent of all actual and possible experience. But he appears to have

---

[1] The *Critique* is " a treatise on method [' Traktat von der Methode,'] not a system of science itself ['System der Wissenschaft selbst '] ; but it marks out nevertheless the whole plan of science [' den ganzen Umriss derselben '], both with regard to its limits, and to its internal organization. For pure speculative reason has this peculiar that it is able, nay, bound to measure its own powers, according to the different ways in which it chooses its own objects, and to completely enumerate the different ways of choosing problems."—*Critique*, Pref. to 2nd edit., pp. 22-3 (Müller, p. 696).

thought that such procedure was possible, and that he was actually employing it. Hence the ground he has left for his critics to accuse him of entertaining the absurd pretention that it is possible to seize on the pure forms of
thinking, emptied of all thinking experience ; and of setting himself a task
similar to "that of investigating a telescope, before turning it on the stars, to
determine its competence for its work "[1]

60. HOW THE FUNCTION OF "A PRIORI SYNTHESIS" IS
DESCRIBED AS PERMEATING JUDGMENT, CONCEPTION, AND
EVEN PERCEPTION.—We have shown so far that Kant's attempt
to account for the characteristics of necessary and universal
judgments is unsatisfactory, that the procedure in the *Critique* is
inconsistent, and that the general theory reaches the startling
conclusion that reality is in itself unknowable. But inconsistent
reasoning may possibly chance upon a true conclusion, nor is the
startling character of a thesis a proof of its falsity. We have,
therefore, to examine on their merits the grounds on which Kant
bases his conclusions ; and chief among these is the analysis which
purports to show that all necessary and universal judgments
which yield scientific knowledge are products of a mental *synthesis* of an *a priori* form with an empirical sense *datum*, in other
words, that they are *synthetic-a-priori*.

Judgments in which the predicate merely restates the whole
or part of what is already contained in the subject-concept, Kant
calls analytic ; and while recognizing that they are necessary and
universal he holds that they do not add to our previous knowledge, that their rôle is secondary in science, and that the process whereby we previously form such subject-concepts is the
really important process from the point of view of scientific
knowledge. And this latter process he holds to be an *a priori*
synthesis.[2]

We have seen (49, 52) that he explains conception, the process of forming (empirical) concepts, no less than judgment, as a
process whereby we synthesize an *a priori* category with a sense
intuition, and see the product to involve within itself necessary
and universal relations, and thus to be objectively valid. The
process which Kant calls conception therefore essentially involves
a judgment, *viz.* the judgment whereby the individual mind
asserts that what it is representing in consciousness is similarly

---

[1] An analogy used by DR. CAIRD (*Critical Philosophy of Kant*, i. 10), in reference both to Locke (*Essay*, i., 1, §§ 2, 4) and to Kant,—*apud* PRICHARD, *op. cit.*,
p. 3. *Cf.* MERCIER, *op. cit.*, §§ 144, 148.

[2] *Cf. supra*, § 49, § 52, p. 186, n. 2.

representable, so to speak, by all minds, *i.e.* is representable by
them necessarily and universally as a something belonging to,
and involved in, men's actual or possible experience, and as
being necessarily and universally for all what it is for each.
This implicit judgment is what scholastics call the " judgment of
existence or of *adequate* possibility," as distinct from mere *logical*
or *objective* possibility in the scholastic sense.[1] Conception as
such implies (for scholastics) only that its object is logically possible, free from self-contradiction, and the implicit judgment to
this effect. No doubt this implicit judgment involves the further
implicit judgment of *adequate* possibility, once we are convinced
that whatever is intrinsically, logically possible, is also extrinsically possible for God, and is therefore *adequately* possible. But
we must abstract from this in getting at Kant's meaning. He
does not explicitly distinguish between the adequate possibility
and the actual existence (at some point of time in men's possible
sense experience) of what is represented as objective in the
empirical concept. What we have to note is that conception as
he understands it implies more than the mere logical possibility
(or absence of self-contradiction) of what is conceived ;[2] it implies the adequate possibility of the latter ; and thus conception,
for him, *always* involves a mental assertion or *judgment* that
what is conceived is necessarily and universally, for all men's
possible sense experience, what it is represented by the individual mind to be.

It is important, and at the same time difficult, to get an accurate idea of what Kant meant by the function of *judgment* (52),
not only because of his practically identifying judgment with conception, but also because of his apparently identifying it even with
sense perception or sense intuition.[3] Particularly in dealing with

[1] *Cf. Ontology*, § 7.
[2] *Cf. supra*, § 49, p. 181, n. 1, for Kant's distinction between *thinking* the
logically possible, and *knowing* the *really* possible. " The possibility of a thing can
never be proved from the fact that its concept is not self-contradictory, but only by
being authenticated by an intuition corresponding to it " (*Critique*, p. 789). *Cf. ibid.*,
pp. 782 *sqq.* Speaking of the concept of the *noumenon* as a mere limiting concept,
Kant says: " I call a concept problematic, if it is not self-contradictory, and if, as
limiting other concepts, it is connected with other kinds of knowledge, while its
objective reality cannot be known in any way " (*ibid.*, p. 207). *Cf.* also *ibid.*, pp.
335-7, where Kant deals with the *possible* and the *impossible* as divisions of "the
concept of an object in general, taken as problematical, it being left uncertain
whether it be something or nothing ".
[3] *Cf. supra*, § 52, p. 185, n. 1. " In the *Prol.* § 13, Remark iii., Kant carefully distinguishes judgment from perception, but destroys the effect of the distinction by

the perception of space involved in geometrical judgments, he seems to identify judgment with perception, speaking of such judgments as *perceptive*,[1] and explaining how it is possible for "*perception* to precede the actuality of the object and take place as *a priori knowledge*".[2] On his own theory it is only the understanding that makes representations *objective, i.e.* necessary and universal, by the synthetic function of its categories, and so elevates them to the plane of "knowledge"; yet he endeavours to explain the necessity and universality of geometrical judgments, and to claim for them a "knowledge" value, by the factors and function of sense intuition alone, and without calling in the categories of the understanding.[3] Sensibility would thus be a power of apprehending, and perception an act of apprehending, *necessary and universal relations.* But this would be ascribing to sense the function that is peculiarly characteristic of reason or intellect.

The fact is, of course, that the function of judgment (or "interpretation") normally accompanies not only conception but also sense perception; that a perceptive or imaginative representation of spatial *data* always accompanies our geometrical judgments. But this concrete representation should not be confounded with the concomitant intellectual apprehension or intuition of *abstract spatial relations as necessary and universal*,—in which apprehension the geometrical judgment consists.

The fact that judgment or interpretation normally accompanies both conception and perception thus offers an intelligible explanation of Kant's tendency to confound the former with the latter functions. But when we come to ask ourselves what Kant meant by giving the supposed function of synthesizing *a priori* forms with empirical sense data the title of "judgment," we encounter another confusion. For the function of "judgment" or "judging"—in all its various forms (categorical, hypothetical, disjunctive; affirmative, negative; apodeictic, problematic; uni-

regarding the judgment as referring to what is relative to perception, *viz.* appearances."—PRICHARD, *op. cit.*, p. 100, n.

[1] *Prolegomena*, § 7.   [2] *Ibid.*, § 9, italics ours.

[3] According to PRICHARD (*op. cit.*, p. 35), "Kant afterwards points out that space as an object presupposes a synthesis which does not belong to sense "; and he adds, "this admission implies that even the apprehension of spatial relations involves the activity of the understanding". If, however, the *objectivity* of geometrical judgments cannot be accounted for by the sensibility alone, neither can their *necessity and universality*, which Kant identified with their objectivity. Yet he seems to have ascribed their necessity and universality to the function of the sensibility alone.

versal, particular, etc.),—has been traditionally understood to be an act whereby we *consciously* compare or relate some two simpler conscious representations and thus, of course, reach a more complex representation or mode of representing the content of the mental terms thus compared.[1]   And the new representation, arising from this act of comparison, has always been thought to be determined by, and grounded in, the *consciously apprehended characters* of the previous representations thus brought into relation with each other by the judicial act.   According to Kant's theory, on the contrary, while the function of forming *analytic* judgments[2] is indeed a process of *conscious* comparison (of previously formed concepts), the grounds of which are consciously apprehended by the mind ; and while *synthetic-a-posteriori* judgments are also *conscious* comparisons in which the determining ground of the (contingent) relation,—*viz.* the whole " experience from which " the concepts were " abstracted,"[3]—is also consciously apprehended ; the function of forming a *synthetic-a-priori* " judgment " (or " conception " of some representation mentally asserted to be " objective" or necessarily and universally valid as such for all minds) is so described that it appears to be itself as a process *unconsciously* performed—and, therefore, we may with justice say *instinctively* and *blindly* performed—by the mind : since the mind consciously apprehends *only the result or product* of the synthesis [4]

---

[1] *Cf.* PRICHARD, *op. cit.*, pp. 152-3. Kant confounds the function which he calls judgment, and which he describes as the unifying act of " arranging different representations under a common representation " [*i.e.* the act of bringing individuals or classes under a wider class concept], with the function of referring [and thus making " objective "] a perception to a supposed extramental reality which produces the latter (*ibid.*, pp. 147-9). Moreover, by calling the supposed *a priori* synthesis a " judgment " he confounds that supposed synthesis (which is, if anything, a unification of individuals under a universal) with the quite distinct synthesis or unification of two concepts, subject and predicate,—in which the act of judgment has been traditionally understood to consist (*ibid*, pp. 152-3). *Cf. Critique*, p 751.

[2] *I.e.* judgments in which, the predicate being pre-contained in the subject, the relation is *seen* to be necessary and universal.

[3] *Critique*, p. 719 : this " experience " being described as " itself a synthetical connection of intuitions " (*ibid.*).

[4] *Cf. supra*, § 58, p. 206, n. 1. The following qu te distinct functions are at various places confounded by Kant under the common title of judgment : (1) the conscious function of bringing an individual or individuals under a universal ; (2) the conscious function of comparing two conceptions as subject and predicate (or two simple judgments as ground and consequent) ; (3) the supposed function of making a sense intuition " objective " by referring it to a supposed noumenal cause of the sensation (*cf.* PRICHARD, *op. cit.*, p. 148) ; (4) the " transcendental " (and therefore presumably unconscious) function of synthesizing the manifold of a pure time-and-space intuition under a pure *a priori* concept of the understanding (*cf. ibid.*, c. vii., pp. 162-5).

(of " form " and " matter "), but not the process itself whereby the necessary and universal relation emerges into consciousness as a mental object, or the determining ground or reason of the characteristics with which it so emerges.

61. HOW THE NECESSITY AND UNIVERSALITY OF THE AP-PREHENDED PRODUCT OF THE SYNTHESIS IS SUBJECTIVE.—Now on this theory the complex representation resulting from the whole process is indeed seen by the mind to involve a necessary and universal relation between certain of its elements ; and the relation is " objective" not only in Kant's sense in which this term is taken to *mean* "necessary and universal," but also in the sense of being an *intra-mental* object (20) : it is something which the knowing mind or subject contemplates.   But the mind con-templating this relation as an object, does not see, and is not and cannot be conscious or aware of, the ground or reason of the necessity of the relation.   The mind is and must be unaware of the *motive* or *moving influence* which determines it to apprehend the relation as it does, *i.e.* as necessary and universal.   For that which determines the mind to this apprehension lies not in what is given to the mind to be interpreted through the apprehension, not in those elements of the total representation [1] which are really objective to the knowing subject in the sense of being given to the latter for interpretation, not in the content of the representation,—a content which the mind spontaneously takes to be real independently of itself, to be given to and not pro-duced by itself.   No ; what determines the mind to apprehend the object, *i.e.* the relation, as necessary and universal,—nay, what makes the relation necessary and universal,—lies in what is (sup-posed on the theory to be) contributed by the mind itself : for it is the *pure a priori* form, belonging to, and contributed to the total representation by, the constitution of the knowing subject : a determining factor of whose influence the mind in judging cannot

---

In the " *Metaphysical Deduction of the Categories*, the aim of which is to discover the conceptions of the understanding " (*ibid.*, p. 141), judgment is " treated as an act by which we relate conceptions " (p. 210) ; while in the " *Transcendental Deduction of the Categories*, the aim of which is to vindicate their validity, *i.e.* their applica-bility to individual things " (p. 141), judgment is " represented as an act by which we relate the manifold of sense in certain necessary ways as parts of the physical world " (p. 209).

[1] Whether this be a space-and-time sense intuition, thought as " objective," a so-called *synthetic-a-priori* judgment of the sensibility, or a conception or judgment of the understanding. The representations in question are of course not *pure a priori*, but empirical, *i.e.* syntheses of *pure a priori* forms with *empirical* matter or data.

be aware.¹ And hence the relation as apprehended is after all *subjective* in the very important sense that its necessity and universality are determined by what we may justly call the instinctive operation of unconscious factors lying on the subjective side of the whole " judging " or " knowing " process.

If, on the other hand, the total complex representation effected by the necessary and universal *judgment* were so to emerge into consciousness that the concepts compared in the judgment were seen to bring with them as a feature of their content the ground of the necessary and universal relation,²

¹ Since on Kant's theory reality is in itself unknowable it is manifestly inconsistent on his part to ascribe the necessity and universality of judgments about the phenomenal world, or the systematic order or arrangement we observe in phenomena (*i.e.* the Uniformity of Nature), to any principle or principles located in the *transcendental subject* or *Ego*, rather than to principles located in the *transcendental object* or *non-Ego*, or—what comes to the same thing—located in our conscious representations because of their relation to a transcendental and unknowable object. *Cf.* PRICHARD, *op. cit*, pp. 177-86. As a matter of fact, in the portions of the *Critique* in which he vindicates the validity of the application of the categories of the understanding to sense intuitions (*i.e.* in the " *Transcendental Deduction* " and in the " *Analytic of Principles* "), Kant *seems* to represent the necessity and universality of judgments about the phenomena of the physical universe as " objective," or grounded on principles *revealed in* this universe ; but we must remember that this so-called " objective " physical universe is, according to his theory, a domain of *mental representations*, and furthermore that the necessity of the judgments and principles referring to these representations comes to them from the *subjective* side,—from the *a priori* forms of the knowing subject or mind. Similarly, in a remarkable passage where Kant undertakes to refute " the *problematical* idealism of Descartes" (*Critique*, tr. MÜLLER, pp. 778-81 ; p. 705, n —*Cf.* PRICHARD, *op. cit.*, pp. 319-24) he uses an argument which, if it proves anything at all against Descartes, proves that self-consciousness involves an immediate awareness of *things in space*, not merely as (objective) mental representations or phenomena, but as *things in themselves*, or *realities independent of our minds*. The argument is that the possibility of self-consciousness implies a permanent. But this permanent cannot be anything internal to my mind, any perception or representation, for every such state can be apprehended only in relation to another permanent. Hence this permanent must be the *real* permanent (*viz. matter ; cf.* Remark 2, *Critique*, p. 780) to which external sense intuition is related. Kant, however, destroys the value of this momentary admission, so inconsistent with his general theory, by describing the " reality " of this " external " correlate of spatial sense intuition as resting " entirely on its being indissolubly connected with internal experience " (*ibid.*, p. 706, n.). The fact is, of course, that " the permanent " which is involved in self-consciousness, being a *real* permanent, is on Kant's theory unknowable, and that he has therefore no right to say whether it is the real *Ego* or the real *non-Ego*. His own theory makes it impossible for him to prove, against the *psychological idealism* of Descartes,—which he regards as " a scandal to philosophy " (*ibid.*, p. 705, n.),—that self-consciousness involves " the objective reality of external phenomena " (*ibid.*).

² Which Kant, unmindful of his theory, occasionally admits, as *e.g.*, when he allows the necessity of presupposing that phenomena have a mutual *affinity* (*Critique*, pp. 93, 100),—which affinity he gratuitously ascribes to the transcendental apperception effected by the noumenal (and unknowable) *Ego*, rather than to a real ground of the affinity in the transcendental *non-Ego*. *Cf.* PRICHARD, *op. cit.*, p.

then such a judgment could be properly described as *objectively evident :* it would be objective not only intra-mentally, but in the fuller sense of reveal-ing a characteristic of something given to the mind to interpret. Similarly, when the complex *concepts* which we use as predicates in our judgments have been reached by a series of antecedent judgments whereby we *consciously* syn-thesized simpler notes or concepts into more and more complex concepts, if each of these judgments by which we mentally announced such synthesis to be objectively valid—*i.e.* to be representative of real actualities or real possibilities of human experience—were grounded on *consciously apprehended* features of *what was given* to the mind in the processes of perception and conception, then the validity of such conceptions could likewise be properly said to be grounded on objective evidence. This is the scholastic position, which will be vindicated below.

And now, to what test are we to subject Kant's account of the necessary and universal judgment as a synthesis of an *a priori* form with an empirical *datum ?* Since he removes the whole mechanism and process of the alleged *a priori* synthesis from the domain of consciousness, teaching that only the finished product or result appears in this domain, and tries to vindicate the ex-istence and functions of the *a priori* forms by the contention that they are the *only* means of explaining the conscious product which we have in the necessary and universal judgment, it would be useless to argue (as against the theory) that there are no such *a priori* forms or syntheses because we are not conscious of any such.[1] However, even if a theory does not purport to be based on facts of consciousness, at least it ought not to contradict facts of consciousness. If, therefore, we can show that the mind, in forming necessary and universal judgments, and in forming the concepts which it uses as pre-dicates (and implicitly judging those concepts, when forming them, to be objectively valid), is determined throughout by the *consciously experienced influence* of *what is given to it* in perception and conception for its interpre-tation, and that Kant's theory of synthetic-*a-priori* judgment (and conception and sense-intuition) ignores and virtually denies the existence of this consciously apprehended objective, determining influence,[2] then the theory will have been weighed in the balance and found wanting.

219: "Since the manifold is originated by the [unknowable] thing in itself, it seems prima facie impossible [on Kant's theory] to prove that the elements of the manifold must have affinity, and so be capable of being related according to the categories".

[1] *I.e.* we may not appeal to the absence of *immediate* evidence in support of the theory. We have already argued that the *mediate* evidence, the various arguments and considerations, urged by Kant in support of it, do not show it to be the *only possible* explanation of the facts : the scholastic theory will be shown to offer a better explanation of them.

[2] Kant, no doubt, says that "geometrical knowledge, being based on *a priori* intuition, possesses immediate evidence, the objects being given, so far as their form is concerned, through their very knowledge *a priori* in intuition" (*Critique*, 1st edit., p. 87; MÜLLER, p. 73); and elsewhere he speaks of "the principles of the *mathe-matical* use of the categories" (*i.e.* the application of the latter to "the *intuition* of a phenomenon only"), in contrast with their *dynamical* use (*i.e.* their application to the *existence* of a phenomenon) as having "immediate evidence" (*Critique*, 1st edit., p. 160; MÜLLER, p. 131). *Cf.* § 53. But it must be remembered that the judgments to which he thus appears to accord the quality of self-evidence are not *objective* even

62. GRADES OF NECESSITY IN JUDGMENTS. SINGULAR
JUDGMENTS. VALIDITY OF CONCEPTS. THE PROBLEM STATED.
—It will be essential to distinguish between (necessary and universal) judgments in which both concepts, subject and predicate,
are abstract and universal, and are already implicitly asserted by
the mind to be objectively valid, and (singular) judgments in
which something that is represented as an (actual or possible)
individual occasions the representation of a universal concept and
is compared as subject with this latter as predicate. The former
judgments are concerned immediately only with the domain of
abstract concepts and their relations : they are judgments of the
ideal order (10). We can examine these separately, and see
whether they are "*a priori* syntheses" of the kind described by
Kant. The other (singular) judgments give rise to the problem
of the validity of universal concepts, or the applicability of the
latter to the intuitions of the senses ; and also to the question
whether the syntheses of simpler concepts or notes by which
complex concepts are formed (and pronounced to be representative of adequate possibilities or actualities of experience) are
determined by the subjective influence of *pure a priori* forms of
the understanding, as Kant would have it, or by the consciously
apprehended influence (called "objective evidence") of what is
given to the mind in forming them, as scholastics claim.[1]

in his own sense of being necessarily and universally valid in regard to the *existence*
of *phenomena*. They are "self-evident" only because the subjective, mental form
which enters into them is a *pure intuition* of the sensibility, not a *pure concept* of the
understanding. Mathematics yield "objective knowledge," in Kant's sense, only
through the synthesis of the pure concepts of the understanding with the space-and-
time intuitions, for by such syntheses alone do the latter serve to produce "objective
phenomena," or "Nature" as an object of experience. And these latter syntheses,
being determined by the instinctive, unconscious, subjective function of the pure
concepts of the understanding, cannot possibly be determined by that quality which
is understood by scholastics to be *given* with the total representation (in which the
judgment consists) and which scholastics describe as "objective evidence".

[1] Kant would of course hold that the apprehension of a subject-concept as "singular" already involves the application of a category (of "unity" in Quantity) to "the
undefined object of . . . an empirical intuition" (*Critique*, p. 16 ; *cf. supra*, p. 185,
n. 1). According to his theory *all* empirical *concepts* are formed by *synthetic-a-priori*
judgments, not excepting the concepts used in *a posteriori* judgments. Thus the
a posteriori judgment, "This body is heavy," presupposes a *synthetic-a-priori* judgment by which "heavy" is represented as an *attribute of a substance*, another by
which "body" is represented as a *substance having possible attributes or accidents*
(Relation : "substance and accident"), another by which a present "undefined
object of . . . an empirical intuition" is represented as a *singular object* or phenomenon ("unity" in Quantity) and as existing (Modality : "existence"). And
for *all synthetic-a-priori* judgments alike (when applied to empirical sense-intuitions)

Before taking some of the examples adduced by Kant as typical of *synthetic-a-priori* judgments in mathematics and in physics, it may be well to observe that he is sometimes accused of using the term *analytic* in too narrow a sense. But this is really only a minor question of the usage of words. Scholastics describe as " *analytic*" or "*per se* " judgments (" modi dicendi *per se* "), all judgments which are *in materia necessaria, i.e.* in which the mind can see a *necessary* relation between subject and predicate by a comparative analysis of both of these concepts into their simplest notes or elements, and *without an appeal to experience* for any information additional to that contained in the concepts so analysed.[1] The functions of the senses and the imagination are

he claims a uniform " objectivity " or " necessity and universality," which is supposed to constitute their scientific or knowledge value. Thus it would appear that provided no mistake is made in forming such *synthetic-a-priori* judgments and conceptions, the whole system of objective Nature, or the phenomenal universe, represented in such judgments and conceptions, *i.e.* in so far as it is object of scientific knowledge, is what it is, and exists as it does, for all human minds *by an absolute necessity whereby it could not conceivably be otherwise.* Thus the *physical* universe, as a scientifically knowable *phenomenon*, is endowed with *metaphysical* necessity ; and the *existential* judgment, or judgment of *existence* (" existence" meaning for Kant objectivity as a phenomenon in actual or possible sense experience : adequate possibility), is identified with the *essential* judgment or judgment of absolute, metaphysical *necessity.* From this position to the absolute idealism of Hegel the transition is easy ; nor is the position really altered by the distinction which Kant introduces elsewhere (*cf. Critique*, p. 145) between the first two groups of categories as " mathematical " and relating to the *nature* of phenomena, and the second two groups as " dynamical " and giving knowledge of *existence*, for this means *necessary* existence. (Of course Kant, holding that the phenomenal universe, as a whole, cannot be an object of possible experience, holds that no knowledge-judgment can be formed by the understanding about it. Although he will allow scientific or knowledge value to the judgments " This, and that, and the other, and any and every, actual or possible phenomenon or group of phenomena, are *caused*," he will deny all knowledge value to the judgment " The whole phenomenal universe is *caused*"). We have already noted a distinction (§ 55) between the absolute, metaphysical necessity of certain ideal judgments, such as those of pure mathematics, and the contingent, physical necessity of inductively established laws that involve the principle of the Uniformity of Physical Nature. We may add to these a class of generalizations which have a still lesser degree of necessity and universality—the generalizations of social science, based on the general uniformity of human conduct. So far from recognizing these distinctions, Kant's theory seems to imply that every single contingent fact or phenomenon (in human experience) which can become an " object " of " scientific " knowledge by being " related " to the mind as object of a *synthetic-a-priori* judgment or conception must be *eo ipso* necessarily and universally what it is judged or conceived to be, and that by a necessity so absolute than its opposite is inconceivable. It is important to note these serious implications of Kant's theory that the *a priori* synthesis alone gives scientific knowledge. The contention that the concept of anything as singular, unit, individual, implies a process of synthesizing an *a priori* form of the understanding with an unknown *datum*, and the further contention that all such *a priori* syntheses reveal only *mental appearances*, will be examined later.

[1] *Cf. Science of Logic*, i., §§ 85-90 ; MERCIER, *op. cit.*, § 117, pp. 270-3,—with extracts from ST. THOMAS, *In I. Anal.*, ll. 10 and 35 ; *De Anima*, Lib. ii., l. 14 ; CAJETAN, *In I. Anal.*, c. 3, and *In Post. Anal.*, c. 4 ; and SUAREZ, *Met. Disp.*, i., § 6, c. 27.

necessary in order that the intellect may abstract from the data of these faculties the concepts in question ; and in this sense the comparison of the concepts is not independent of sense experience.   But it is independent of the latter in the sense that it is not repetition of experiences that is the ground of the necessary relation apprehended in the judgment ; and with this Kant is in agreement.   When the judgment is absolutely necessary and universal, and when the predicate-concept is not contained in the definition of the subject-concept, scholastics hold that an analysis of *both* concepts, provided it be so prosecuted as to bring to light *not merely the definition* of each concept but all *the properties necessarily involved in*, and *necessarily following from*, these concepts (by an absolute necessity of thought [1]), will inevitably reveal a necessary relation (of identity or of incompatibility) between subject and predicate.   If we can show that this is really the case in those of Kant's examples which are really necessary judgments in the absolute sense (for not all his examples are such), then we shall have shown that the mind in forming such judgments is not operating an instinctive, subjectively necessitated synthesis, blind but irresistible, as demanded by Kant's theory ; but that it is apprehending in the light of the evidence of the concepts themselves an objectively revealed relation.   This, however, is not enough : for the further question must be asked and answered, How does the mind build up such concepts, *i.e.* concepts implying such properties that those of one concept are seen to involve *necessary* relations with those of another ?   For if *conception* be an *a priori* synthesis, the evidence just referred to—for the necessary relations between the products of conception—cannot be after all any more objective than these products themselves which are characterized by it.   If on the other hand the process of forming the concepts themselves can be shown to be *motived* and *guided* by *what is given* to the intellect through sense experience, rather than mentally necessitated by the unconscious functioning of *a priori* forms of the intellect, then the thesis that grounds necessary judgments on *objective evidence* will be fully vindicated.   And such a conclusion will be quite independent of the nomenclature we use in reference to these processes of judgment and conception, *i.e.* whether we call them processes of *analysis* or processes of *synthesis ;* for as a matter of fact *both* analysis *and* synthesis are involved in *each* process.   In regard to judgment, for example, there can be no *ignoratio elenchi* as to the class of judgments in question : they are necessary and universal judgments in which the predicate-concept is *not* disclosed by a *mere analysis of the definition* of the subject-concept.   Whether on that account we call the judicial process which terminates in the apprehension of a necessary relation between them a process of *synthesis*, or whether because this relation is revealed by a *deeper analysis*, penetrating to the properties of both concepts, we therefore describe the judicial process as one of *analysis*,—matters but little.   The crucial point is whether the process, however described, is a subjective, instinctive process of whose grounds we are unconscious, or is on the contrary a process of conscious comparison, the grounds or evidence or motives for which are consciously apprehended in what is given to the judging mind.[2]
Another point worthy of note, before going on to the examples, is this,

---

[1] *Cf. Science of Logic*, i., § 47, p. 83.
[2] And similarly in regard to conception, as will be explained later.

that Kant is said to have underrated the scientific value of judgments that are analytic in the narrower sense.[1] It is contended that even such judgments, besides clarifying our notions and helping to order and systematize our know-ledge (48), also help "to the intuition of relations grounded in them, and so to progress in knowledge ".[2] Kant's reply, however, would be that they can be ampliative only in the sense of making clear and explicit what was already contained at least in a vague and confused way in the subject-concept itself, and that it is always the *conception* of this latter (by an *a priori* synthesis) that really adds to our stock of scientific or objective knowledge. The point is of minor importance compared with his account of *all* concepts and of the *wider class* of necessary and universal judgments as *a priori* syntheses of mental forms with empirical sense *data*.

63. KANT'S CLAIM EXAMINED. A. MATHEMATICAL JUDG-MENTS. B. GEOMETRICAL JUDGMENTS. C. THE "PRIN-CIPLES" OF PHYSICS.—A. All mathematical judgments are synthetical. . . . At first sight one might suppose indeed that the proposition 7 + 5 = 12 is merely analytical, following, according to the principle of contradiction, from the concept of a sum of 7 and 5. But if we look more closely we shall find that the concept of the sum of 7 and 5 contains nothing beyond the union of both sums into one, whereby nothing is told us as to what this single number may be which combines both. We by no means arrive at a concept of Twelve by thinking of the union of Seven and Five ; and we may analyse our concept of such a possible sum as long as we will, still we shall never discover in it the concept of Twelve. We must go beyond these concepts and call in the assist-ance of the intuition corresponding to one of the two, for instance, our five fingers,   . and so by degrees add the units of the Five, given in intuition, to the concept of Seven. . .   That 5 should be added to 7 was no doubt implied in my concept of a sum of 7 + 5, but not that that sum should be equal to 12. An arithmetical proposition is, therefore, always synthetical."

The drift of this argument seems to be that in order to ap-prehend a necessary relation of equality between 7 + 5 and 12 I must go beyond the mere concepts of 7 and 5, call in the aid of the sense (or imagination) intuition of one of them, and add its contents gradually to the other concept in order to "see the number 12 arising before me";[4] and that therefore the judg-ment is *synthetic:* while, on the other hand, the necessity of the relation proves that the judgment must be an application (to sense intuitions of data that are potentially numerical) of an *a priori* mental law of relating sense data thus numerically.

But as against this it is obvious that if I have the concept of what a "unit" is, of what a "number" (or sum or collection of units) is, and of what each of the three definite sums, "five,"

[1] *Cf.* MERCIER, *op. cit.*, § 117, p. 274.   [2] *Ibid.*
[3] *Critique*, pp. 721-2.   [4] *Ibid.*

"seven," and "twelve," is,—in other words, if I know what each
of these terms respectively *means*, what the definition of each is,
—then I must see that the sum of the two collections, "seven"
and "five," is not merely itself *a sum or collection in general*, but
that it is precisely and *identically* the individual sum or collection
which I conceive as "twelve," and which I call "twelve". And
I see this from an analysis and comparison of the concepts. The
whole process is an analysis of concepts. "Five" is a definite
sum of units, *viz.* $(1 + 1 + 1 + 1 + 1)$; "seven" is another
definite sum of units, *viz.* $(1 + 1 + 1 + 1 + 1 + 1 + 1)$; their
sum is yet another definite sum of units, *viz.* $(1 + 1 + 1 + 1 + 1)$
$+ (1 + 1 + 1 + 1 + 1 + 1 + 1)$, which I see to be the identi
cal sum of units which I call "twelve," *viz.* $(1 + 1 + 1 + 1 + 1$
$+ 1 + 1 + 1 + 1 + 1 + 1 + 1)$. No doubt, when we count
we must use concrete sense intuitions or symbols or imagination
images to help us to compare the concepts abstracted from them.
But it is not the concrete symbols, or their juxtaposition in sense
intuition or imagination, that constitute or reveal the relation
which is apprehended as necessary and universal. Neither, however, is it a permeation of these (so to speak) by a supposed
mental relating-form or relating-function productive of such
necessity. It is, as will be explained later, the abstract character of the content of these intuitions as conceived by the
understanding.

B. Nor is any proposition in pure geometry analytical. That the straight
line between two points is the shortest, is a synthetical proposition. For my
concept of *straight* contains nothing of magnitude (quantity), but a quality
only. The concept of the *shortest* is, therefore, purely adventitious, and
cannot be deduced from the concept of the straight line by any analysis
whatsoever. The aid of intuition must, therefore, be called in, by which
alone the synthesis is possible.[1]

Here the contention is that the predicate belongs to a different category (quantity) from that of the subject (quality) and
cannot therefore be derived by analysis from the latter. But the
proposition, stated fully, reads, "The straight line, compared
with any other line, between two points, is the shortest distance
between such two points"; from which it will be seen that the
subject involves *three* categories, *viz. quantity* ("line"), *quality*
within quantity ("straight"), and *relation* within quantity ("compared with, etc."), and that the predicate contains the same three,

[1] *Critique*, p. 721,

viz. quantity ("distance"), *quality* and *relation* within quantity ("shortest"). Even, therefore, if the concept of "the shortest distance between two points," be not considered to give the *definition* of the concept of "straight line," it gives at least a property which is seen to be *necessarily involved* in the concept of "a straight line compared with any other line".

Of course the sense intuition of a three-dimensional spatial universe is required to yield the abstract concepts of volume, surface, line, point, distance, direction, etc. And if it be asked, How or why do we form such a concept of a "straight line" that as compared with other lines we see it to be necessarily identical with our concept of "shortest distance" between two points?—we reply, Because even if we do not say that this latter is what we *mean* by a "straight line"; even if, with Euclid, we mean by the concept of "straight line" a line "which reposes equally on its points," [1]—or, in other words, all of whose points bear *the same* relation *of direction* to its starting-point,—we see intuitively that a straight line, A———X, whose intermediate points involve all the same direction from A, is necessarily shorter than any other line, A————X, whose intermediate points, *a*, *b*, *c*, etc., involve many different directions from A. The concept of "straight line between two points" is the concept of the constant or uniform direction of the one from the other; and this is seen intuitively to involve less spatial relations of linear distance than a line not constant or uniform in direction. The relation between subject and predicate, in the proposition under consideration, is seen to be realized in any concrete perceptive or imaginative intuition of space. But the necessity of the relation is not grounded in the concrete sense intuitions; it is grounded in the concepts and revealed by their analysis; and it is necessary because the concepts present *in the abstract* what is given by the sense intuitions in the concrete.[2] The necessity

---

[1] Εὐθεῖα γραμμή ἐστιν, ἥτις ἐξ ἴσου ἐφ' ἑαυτῆς σημείοις κεῖται. For a fuller discussion of this point, *cf.* MERCIER, *op. cit.*, § 118, pp. 276-81, 309-10; also art. *Philosophy and Geometry* in the *Irish Ecclesiastical Record*, vol. xx. (Feb., 1906), pp. 100 *sqq.*

[2] Nor, as we shall see, is there any reason to suppose that any such spatial concept is "constructed," or presented to consciousness in imagination, by "presenting *a priori* the intuition corresponding to it," or that it is itself a synthesis of an *a priori* form of the understanding with a *pure* or *non-empirical* intuition of space. In a remarkable passage, where Kant, assuming the possibility of a *pure, a priori,* *non-empirical* intuition of space, explains how we "construct" geometrical concep-

of the relation, therefore, does not arise from any supposed *synthesis* of *what is given* in sense intuition with a mental *a priori* form whose function would be to produce such relations.

C. "*Natural science (Physica) contains synthetical judgments* a priori *as principles* . . . such as, that in all changes of the material world the quantity of matter always remains unchanged : or that in all communication of motion, action and reaction must always equal each other. It is clear not only that both convey necessity and that therefore their origin is *a priori*, but also that they are synthetical propositions. For in the concept of matter I do not conceive its permanency but only its presence in the space which it fills. I therefore go beyond the concept of matter in order to join something to it *a priori*, which I did not before conceive *in it*. The proposition is, therefore, not analytical but synthetical, and yet *a priori*, and the same applies to the other propositions of the pure part of natural science." [1]

Now if the first of those propositions formulates the chemical law connected with the name of Lavoisier, that " Throughout chemical changes the quantity of matter remains invariable," it is manifestly an *a posteriori* proposition, a generalization from experience, wholly devoid of the absolute necessity which characterizes *e.g.* the judgments of mathematics. If, however, it is meant to assert that " In whatsoever changes take place throughout the whole physical universe there is neither creation nor annihilation of matter," then the judgment is indeed a legitimate and probable physical hypothesis or systematic conception,[2] *a posteriori*, based upon experience, but likewise devoid of absolute necessity. And similarly of the other example : the law that " In all material, mechanical motions action and reaction are equal and opposite," is, in so far as it is verified, a physical law reached inductively or *a posteriori* from experience, based solely on experience, and likewise devoid of absolute necessity. We

---

tions, he appears to touch accidentally on the real ground of the necessity of geometrical judgments, *viz.* the abstract character of geometrical concepts. It is in the second of the following sentences (the first involves the impossible supposition of a pure, *a priori* perception, independent of experience and devoid of empirical content) : " Thus I construct a triangle by presenting the object corresponding to that concept either by mere imagination, in pure intuition, or afterwards on paper also in the empirical intuition, and in both cases entirely *a priori*, without having borrowed the original from any experience. The particular figure drawn on the paper is empirical, but serves nevertheless to express the concept without any detriment to its generality, because in that empirical intuition we consider always the act of the construction of the concept only, to which many determinations, as, for instance, the magnitude of the sides and the angles, are quite indifferent, these differences, which do not change the concept of a triangle, being entirely ignored."—*Critique*, tr. by MÜLLER, p. 573. *Cf.* PRICHARD, *op. cit.*, p. 52 n.

[1] *Critique*, p. 722.   [2] *Cf. Science of Logic*, ii., §§ 226-32, pp. 120-48.

have already drawn attention to Kant's confusion of the physical, contingent, conditional necessity of inductive laws, which are partial expressions of the general law of the *Uniformity of Physical Nature*, with the absolute necessity of the abstract principles of mathematics and metaphysics. No doubt, his theory, according to which the question of the "necessity" of any given judgment must be settled not by an appeal to consciously apprehended grounds of objective evidence which would disclose the nature of the *nexus* between the concepts compared, but rather by the allegation that we are forced to form the judgment by a subjective, unconsciously operating function of the mind,—such a theory naturally exposes the individual thinker to the danger of self-deception, of thinking that whenever a judgment seems to him to transcend the limits of men's actual experience, and to embody *some sort of* necessity, it must be due to the *a priori* function of a subjective mental form.

64. D. THE PRINCIPLE OF CAUSALITY AND METAPHYSICS. DOCTRINES OF KANT AND HUME.—Take the proposition that all which happens has a cause. In the concept of something which happens I no doubt conceive of something existing preceded by time, and from this certain analytical judgments may be deduced. But the concept of cause is entirely outside that concept, and indicates something different from that which happens, and is by no means contained in that representation. How can I venture then to predicate of that which happens something totally different from it, and to represent the concept of cause, though not contained in it, as belonging to it, and belonging to it by necessity? What is here the unknown x, on which the understanding may rest in order to find beyond the concept A ["all which happens"] a foreign predicate B ["has a cause"], which nevertheless is believed to be connected with it? It cannot be experience, because the proposition that all which happens has its cause represents this second predicate as added to its subject not only with greater generality than experience can ever supply, but also with a character of necessity, and therefore purely *a priori*, and based on concepts.[1]

We have here the main contention that the Principle of Causality is a synthetic-*a-priori* judgment. Kant's identification of the concept of "cause" with that of "absolutely necessitating cause" is illustrated by the following passage :—

Even the concept of cause contains so clearly the concept of the necessity of its connexion with an effect, and of the strict universality of the rule, that it would be destroyed altogether if we attempted to derive it, as Hume does, from the frequent concomitancy of that which happens with that which pre-

[1] *Critique*, Introd., pp. 7, 8.

cedes, and from a habit arising thence (therefore from a purely subjective necessity), of connecting representations.[1]

Finally, this necessity-and-universality-producing "rule," is a *pure, a priori* concept or form of the understanding ; and the *empirical* concept of cause,—to which it gives rise by *a priori* synthesis with the temporal connexion of sense-intuitions in the imagination (thus giving this connexion a *necessary order* whereby one representation is conceived not only to precede but necessarily to determine another),—is confined by the theory to *phenomena of sense experience.* Those two important points will be obvious from the following passage :—

> The objective relation of phenomena following upon each other remains undetermined by mere perception. In order that this may be known as determined, it is necessary to conceive the relation between the two states in such a way that it should be determined thereby with necessity, which of the two should be taken as coming first, and which second, and not conversely. Such a concept involving a necessity of synthetical unity, can be a pure concept of the understanding only, which is not supplied by experience, and this is, in this case, the concept of the *relation of cause and effect*, the former determining the latter in time as a consequence, the cause not being something that might be antecedent in imagination only, or might not be perceived at all.[2] Experience itself, therefore, that is, an empirical knowledge of phenomena, is possible only by our subjecting the succession of phenomena, and with it all change, to the law of causality, and phenomena themselves, as objects of experience, are consequently possible according to the same law only.[3]

Now it is true that the Principle of Causality is not *a posteriori* in the sense of being based on experience. But it is not true that its necessity cannot be explained by showing it to be grounded on an analysis of concepts derived from experience, or that to

---

[1] *Critique*, Introd. (2nd edit.), p. 717.   [2] *Cf. supra*, p. 176, n. 1.

[3] *Critique*, p. 755. *Cf. ibid.*, pp. 164 *sqq.* It is clear from those extracts that for Kant the empirical concept of cause is the concept of the *necessitating phenomenal antecedent* of an event, rather than the *efficient principle* of the latter ; and that the "necessity" he is really trying to explain is the physical necessity (which he misinterprets as absolute) attaching to the Principle of the *Uniformity of Nature*, and to physical laws, which are applications of the latter. It is the problem which Mill, consistently with his phenomenism, declared to be scientifically insoluble. *Cf. Science of Logic*, ii., §§ 219 (pp. 78-9), 224 ; *Ontology*, § 100. Kant similarly holds that we cannot *know* whether or not this law of necessary connexion between phenomena, which he calls the law or principle of causality, is validly applicable beyond the domain of actual and possible sense experience. With the Kantian confinement of "knowledge" to "appearances" we shall deal later. In the present context we examine merely Kant's contention that the Principle of Causality is a *synthetic-a-priori* principle. For an analysis of *Change* and *Efficient* Causality, and their implications, *cf. Ontology*, §§ 6-10, 97-8, 100-5.

explain its necessity we must have recourse to the hypothesis of an *a priori* mental form synthesized with the data of experience.[1] Hume, after reducing the necessity of the *nexus* (between the concept of "a thing happening" and the concept of "having a cause") to a mere psychological necessity, went so far as to declare that he could actually break the *nexus* in thought and think of a thing beginning to be without thinking of a cause or productive principle: "All distinct ideas," he writes, "are separable from each other, and as the ideas of cause and effect are evidently distinct, 'twill be easy for us to conceive any object as non-existent this moment, and existent the next, without conjoining to it the distinct idea of a cause or producing principle".[2] As a matter of fact it is impossible for us to separate the distinct ideas of cause and effect. Kant rightly recognized this inseparability, but wrongly sought the reason of it in a supposed *a priori* mental law of relation, when he could have rightly detected it in what is given in the empirical concepts themselves as compared with each other in the abstract by the understanding.

65. SCHOLASTIC ACCOUNT OF THE PRINCIPLE.—Let us first explain the principle, and the concepts which enter into it, in the sense in which they have been traditionally understood in scholastic philosophy.

The principle is not expressed *in its full amplitude* by the formula "whatever happens, or begins to exist, has an efficient cause"; for although "happening" or "beginning to exist" is for us the index to "being caused," it is not inconceivable that a thing could have existed indefinitely *a parte ante*, without a beginning in time, and yet have been always dependent on an efficient cause. It is not the concept of "temporal beginning" but the non-temporal notion of *contingency* that necessarily involves the notion of dependence of the contingent being on a cause. The proper formulation of the principle is, therefore, that "An existing contingent being, *i.e.* a being which does not exist by a necessity of its essence, which does not contain in the concept of its essence the sufficient reason of its existence, necessarily implies a cause of its existence" The absolute necessity of the principle, thus stated, can be seen from an analysis of its concepts. By a contingent existing being we mean a being which actually exists, and yet cannot account, by its own being or essence, for

---

[1] *Cf. Ontology*, § 100.
[2] *Treatise on Human Nature*, p. 381.   *Cf. Ontology*, § 98, p. 370 n.

its actual existence ; and by an efficient cause we mean a being which by its efficient influence causes such contingent being to exist, and to exist thus dependently on the former being or cause. A contingent being does not contain in its formal concept the note of actual existence. If, therefore, we conceive it as actually existing we cannot conceive it as existing *of itself*, in virtue of what is contained in its formal concept, for thus to conceive it would be self-contradictory : it would be to conceive what is formally the same thing as *not existing* and yet *as existing*,— which violates the principle of contradiction. If, therefore, we conceive a contingent being as actually existing, we must, in order to avoid self-contradiction,—or, in other words, in virtue of the principle of contradiction,—conceive it not now by itself but as being rendered actually existent through the causal influence of an extrinsic being, and as existing dependently on this latter. Thus, in virtue of the principle of contradiction, we are compelled, in conceiving a contingent being as actually existent, to conceive the latter as dependent on a cause, and so to conceive as absolutely necessary the principle of causality.

If we consider the principle in reference to the *beginning* or *coming into existence* of a being, the necessity of the principle is still more manifest from an analysis of the concepts ; for—Hume's authority notwithstanding—not only is it not "easy" for us, but it is absolutely impossible for us, to think *an absolute beginning from nothingness*, to think of a thing coming into existence without thinking of a " productive principle " of such existence. And why ? Because though the concept of a contingent thing or object (*i.e.* a thing which is not conceived as existing *necessarily*, in virtue of its essence) is the concept of something *absolute*, nevertheless the concept of such a thing *coming into actual existence* is a concept which is necessarily *relative*, and by the principle of sufficient reason necessarily refers us beyond the concept of the bare essence of that thing to the concept of a productive principle of the actual existence of that thing.[1]   The subject and predicate

---

[1] *Cf.* MERCIER, *op. cit.*, § 118, pp. 282-3 : " Suppose B, a contingent being, as actually existent. Since, *ex hypothesi*, it is contingent it can be thought of as non-existent. Nevertheless, suppose it in fact to exist. From the supposition either of two alternatives arises. Either we say that the essence B is, in the two states, formally and in all respects *the same being* : then we cannot avoid self-contradiction, for we assert that one being, *formally one and the same*, exists and does not exist : the contradiction is flagrant. Or else, we say that the essence B is not formally and in all respects the same in the two states : which is to say that from a first point of view

of the principle, though "distinct" concepts, are inseparable in thought, and they are inseparable in thought because they are seen, by analysis of their implications, mutually to involve each other. They are *seen* to be such because they *are* such; and they are such, not because an *a priori* form of the understanding makes them such, but because *reality* which they represent to the understanding in the abstract, and which is given in the concrete in sense experience, *is of such a nature.*

It is easy to anticipate, from the point of view of Kant's theory, the exception he would take to the exposition we have just given of the causal relation. He would say that while it may indeed represent what we *are forced to think*, it goes beyond the domain of what we *can know.* He would confine causality to the domain of the phenomenal and refer it exclusively to the

"transition from the not-being of a state into that state. . . . This arising . [he continues]¹ . . . is, therefore, mere change, and not an arising out of nothing. When such an arising is looked upon as the effect of a foreign cause, it is called creation. This can never be admitted as an event among phenomena, because its very possibility would break the unity of experience [note how he here supposes that 'thought,' if it is to give 'knowledge,' must be subordinated to sense experience and confined to the domain of the latter : because his own theory of the conditions required for 'thought' to yield 'scientific knowledge' demands such subordination and limitation]. If, however, we consider all things, not as phenomena, but as things by themselves and objects of the understanding only [which objects he gratuitously supposes to be devoid of all empirical content], then . . . they may be considered as

it is the essence simply and absolutely (*essentia nuda*), while, from a second point of view, the essence B is no longer considered alone but as subject to an influence beyond itself (*essentia quatenus substat influxui extrinseco*) : and so we escape contradiction, but only by affirming causality. For if the essence B exists only on condition of its being subject to an influence beyond itself, which makes it exist, then the existence of B depends necessarily on an efficient cause. In a word, we cannot deny the principle of causality without denying the principle of contradiction ; the principle of causality is analytic.

"But let us understand this aright. The principle is not analytic in Kant's narrow acceptation of this term. For the *predicate* of the principle, '*necessarily dependent on an efficient cause,*' is not contained in the essential concept of the subject, '*contingent being*'. The latter is an *absolute* term, the former a *relative.* But a predicate cannot be derived from an alien category ; the notion of a relative cannot be derived from the notion of an absolute, and hence the principle is not analytic in Kant's meaning of this term.

"When, therefore, we claim that the principle is analytic we mean that it is a proposition which expresses a relation that is knowable in itself and without recourse to information extrinsic to the terms of the proposition ; and the relation is knowable in itself because there is between the predicate and the essence of the subject a connexion which is intrinsically necessary."

¹ *Critique*, p. 168.

15 *

dependent in their existence on a foreign cause. Our words would then assume quite a different meaning, and be no longer applicable to phenomena, as possible objects of experience."

Passing over the gratuitous assertion that our "words" (and our concepts) "assume quite a different meaning" (supposed to be incapable of yielding "knowledge"), when used to represent *analogically* the suprasensible domain of reality (66, 74, 93), let us rather consider the principle of causality now on Kant's own ground, *i.e.* in reference merely to change in the domain of sense experience.

When what we apprehend as a causal change takes place among phenomena we *necessarily* refer the resulting state to the operative influence of a cause. Why? Let Kant himself state the problem :—

When a substance passes from one state a into another b, the moment of the latter is different from the moment of the former state, and follows it. Again, the second state, as a reality (in phenomena), differs from the first in which that reality did not exist, as b from zero ; that is, even if the state b differed from the state a in quantity only, that change is an arising of $b - a$, which in the former state was non-existent, and in relation to which that state is $= 0$. The question, therefore, arises how a thing can pass from a state $- a$ to another $= b$?[1]

66. INADMISSIBILITY OF KANT'S LIMITATION OF THE PRINCIPLE TO THE DOMAIN OF SENSE EXPERIENCE.—The obvious answer to the question is, of course, that the change from a to b can take place only under the real influence of some real and really efficient principle, productive of, and therefore capable of accounting to our intelligence for, the apprehended difference between b and a. We know it to be self-evidently impossible for *something actual* to arise *from nothingness*. And if this necessity of thought is not valid here in what it appears to disclose to us about what is given to us through our concepts, *i.e.*, about reality, not only is *all knowledge* impossible, but *all thought* is an illusion.

Let it be noted, at the same time, that while the principle of sufficient reason imperatively compels us to conceive a change or happening as implying a relation of essential dependence on a cause, or productive or efficient

---

[1] *Critique,* p. 169 : This is a fair statement of the problem, apart from the failure (which is immaterial to the point here at issue) to notice that, although a is "zero" in reference to the *actuality* of $(b - a)$, it is not zero in reference to the real *potentiality* of $(b - a)$; and to notice further that this potentiality of $(b - a)$ in a does not *adequately* account for the actuality of b ; and finally to draw the obvious inference from these considerations to the *necessary existence* of an *Uncaused First Cause* of all change in the universe of our experience. *Cf. Ontology,* §§ 10, 102.

principle, it by no means compels us to conceive this latter as being itself necessarily a thing or object of possible *sense experience*, but only as being *intelligible, i.e.* capable of being apprehended by the understanding, if not adequately at least faithfully, if not positively at least negatively and analogically, by means of our intellectual concepts, all of which have an empirical content because of the origin of all of them from the *data* of sense experience.

Kant, however, merely offers, as an answer to the question he proposed, an account[1] which purports to explain how the time succession of our conscious representations is transformed by an *a priori* function of the understanding into a series of "objective" phenomena wherein we conceive prior elements as necessarily determining, and posterior elements as necessarily determined, and thus think all phenomena distributively to be necessarily interrelated as causes and effects.[2] Instead of answering the question, How can a thing pass from one state ($= a$) into another ($= b$)? and appealing to the principle of sufficient reason for the necessary implications of such a fact, he appeals to that principle[3] to answer this other question: How is it that we think an event or phenomenon, b, as *necessarily* (and not merely *temporally*) presupposing, and necessarily determined by, some antecedent *event* or *phenomenon, a,* and *vice versa, a* as not merely preceding, but necessarily involving and determining, some subsequent or consequent, b?

But, now, is the alleged fact for which he thus seeks and assigns a "sufficient reason" really a fact? Is it a fact that we must think, or that the principle of sufficient reason forces us to think, of any empirical happening or event or phenomenon of sense experience (*viz.* "things represented in the state b"), as necessarily and universally determined by *another happening* or *event* or *phenomenon of sense experience* (*viz.* "things represented in the state a")? *It is not a fact.*[4] What the principle of sufficient reason obliges us to think is that every change (or transition from state a to state b) must have *a real productive principle*, whereby the change is accounted for, and rendered intelligible to

---

[1] *Critique*, pp. 169-72; *cf.* pp. 161 *sqq.*

[2] This supposed process of giving "objectivity" to our representations will be examined later. *Cf. infra*, § 93.

[3] *Ibid.*, p. 164.

[4] And *a fortiori* the principle does not oblige us to think of every event or phenomenon as *necessarily determining* some *subsequent* phenomenon or phenomena, —unless indeed we conceive it as actually and formally causing the latter, a notion which is not contained in the concept of an event or phenomenon as such.

us. It by no means obliges us to think that this latter principle must be itself *a phenomenon of sense experience*, but only that it must be *a reality* and have a *real connexion* (by way of efficient influence) with the caused phenomenon, and the latter a *real connexion* (by way of dependence) with the former.[1]

Nay, more, while it obliges us to think that whatever happens must *necessarily*—and that by an *absolute* necessity—have an efficient cause or productive principle, it does not by any means oblige us to think that whatever happens must have a *necessary* or *necessitating* cause,[2] *i.e.* a cause which by the fact of its real existence and by a necessity of its nature produces the effects which it does actually produce. It is only *a posteriori*, by actual experience, we can discover the nature of the causes which produce the phenomena of our experience. *De facto* we discover some of those to be *free*, *self-determining* causes, not themselves determined or necessitated either by their own nature or otherwise to produce the effects they do actually produce ; others we discover to be so constituted and so related with the whole system of the universe that they are determined and necessitated by their very nature and rôle in the universe to be *uniformly* and *necessarily* productive of the definite effects. But this uniformity and this necessity are by no means *absolute*, but *conditional, contingent, physical,* or *moral*, the ultimate grounds of which are quite different from those of the absolute, metaphysical necessity which characterizes such principles as the principle of causality or the principles of mathematics.[3]

That the phenomena of the physical universe are not only *efficient* causes in the sense of being really operative and productive of effects, but that they are even *necessarily* productive of, and *necessarily* connected with, these effects (which " necessity of connexion " is what is nowadays mainly meant and expressed by the phrase "*physical* causality"[4]): those are *a posteriori* judgments, based on experience. The necessity referred to is contingent and conditional, and the problem of accounting for it is that of discovering the ultimate grounds of our assent to the principles on which the induction of physical laws is based.[5] It is quite distinct from the absolute necessity which characterizes the judgment that "every change must necessarily have a pro-

---

[1] *Cf. Ontology*, §§ 102-4.   [2] *Ibid.,* § 99 (*d*); *Science of Logic*, ii., § 218.
[3] *Ibid.,* § 219 (p. 78), 224.   [4] *Ibid.,* § 218; *Ontology*, § 100.
[5] *Cf. Science of Logic*, §§ 224, 250, 256.

ductive principle or cause ".[1] The absolute necessity of this judgment has been shown by analysis to result from the implications of the concepts compared.

Nor can it be allowed on the one hand that the concepts, *in so far as they are empirical*, derive the necessity of those implications from an *a priori* form of judgment, and are validly applicable only within the domain of sensible or phenomenal antecedents and consequents (by synthesis of such form with sense *data*) ; or on the other hand that in claiming for them a valid extension to the domain of *the real*, whether sensible or suprasensible, we are using them as *pure concepts*, devoid of empirical content, and are therefore reaching, by means of them, what may indeed be " necessities of thought," but what cannot possibly be " objects of knowledge ". For none of the concepts with which we consciously deal in our judgments are *pure* concepts, or pure *forms of the understanding* in Kant's sense : all our concepts have an empirical content by reason of our abstracting them from the data of sense experience ; but none the less they can and do give the understanding a valid insight into the *existence* of objects that are suprasensible, and a genuine, if analogical and inadequate, insight into the *nature* of such objects.

Nor, finally, can we admit Kant's contention that such an insight is not "knowledge" but "illusion ". He himself admits that we *can* attain to a genuine insight into the existence and nature of the ultra-phenomenal or real, though only by way of subjective, personal belief, as a product of speculation on what he calls the data and postulates of the *practical reason ;* but as we have already observed, these data are likewise facts of conscious human experience, nor has Kant anywhere proved his assumption that the human mind has *two* ways,—distinct and incommunicable in their data, their processes, and their results,—of speculating and reasoning on the data of human experience in general.

[1] *Not* " Every change must have a *necessitating* (or ' physical ') cause," or " Every change must have a *phenomenal* (*i.e.* sensible or perceptible as distinct from suprasensible) cause " : neither of these propositions is true.

CHAPTER VIII.

NECESSARY JUDGMENTS : SCHOLASTIC THEORY.

67. In Necessary and Universal Principles of the
Ideal Order the Ground of the Judicial Nexus is Seen
to be In the Objects as Conceived : Objective Evidence.
—We have seen that Empiricism cannot account for the characteristics of necessity and universality apprehended by the mind
in judgments of the ideal order (40-44). At the opposite extreme
we found the equally unsatisfactory attempt of Leibniz to account
for those characteristics (48). And finally, we examined in detail Kant's endeavour to find a *via media* between these extremes
in the theory of the necessary and universal judgment as the
product of a mental function of *a priori* synthesis. We saw that
this theory is not the only *via media* (58); that it accords to the
nexus of such judgments only a spurious objectivity, and either
makes the *nexus* as subjective and relative as Empiricism does,
or else confesses the ground of it to be unknowable (61);
that it contains mutually destructive theses (59), and by using
each of the terms "judgment" and "synthesis" ambiguously,
confounds processes that are distinct from one another (60).
Moreover, examining the judgments instanced by Kant as typical
synthetic-*a-priori* judgments (63-6), we saw that in no single instance do they afford any ground for the view that the necessary
and universal *nexus* between subject and predicate is established
by an unconscious function whereby these concepts are combined
a priori into a complex representation,—the mind being conscious only of this product, but not of any reasons or motives for
the formation of it. At the same time we briefly contrasted with
the *subjectivism* of Kant's theory the *objective* character of the
alternative solution offered by scholasticism (61). And we incidentally called attention to Kant's confusion of different grades
of necessity in scientific judgments, when distinguishing the
problem actually under discussion, *viz.* that of the nature and
grounds of the judicial *nexus*, from the further problems, which

will be discussed later, concerning the *real* significance, and mode of formation, of the concepts themselves (62).

We have now to fix our attention once more on those necessary and universal judgments of the ideal order, *i.e.* on those of them that are principles, that are concerned with our simplest concepts, and to indicate the real reason why the mind apprehends the *nexus* in them as absolutely necessary and universal. The problem is that of the nature, significance and grounds of the *nexus* between two universal concepts as subject and predicate in the judgment. It is to be distinguished from the closely related problem concerning the nature and significance of the concepts themselves as compared with the concrete data of sense perception ; and from the further problem of the significance of these sense percepts or sense intuitions themselves (62).

The judgment is, as we have seen, a complex representative process whereby we *interpret* one thought-object as subject of the judgment (in judgments of the ideal order an abstract object) by identifying another (abstract) thought-object as predicate with it, or by separating the former from the latter (in the negative judgment). What is immediately apprehended by the judgment, therefore, the apprehended "term" of the act of judging, is a *relation* or *nexus* (of identity or non-identity) between two conceptually distinct thought-objects. Now why does the mind apprehend this *nexus* as absolutely necessary, and therefore as obtaining universally, between the compared elements in the judgments under consideration? In examining and rejecting Kant's reply to the question, for the reasons indicated, we have already suggested the true reply, *viz.* that the ground of the *nexus* lies *in the concepts themselves*, that through *analysis and comparison* of the concepts the *nexus reveals* or *manifests* itself to the intellect as obtaining necessarily and universally between the concepts ; or in other words that the *nexus* becomes *objectively evident* to the intellect, that the intellect *sees intuitively* and immediately the necessity of the *nexus*, and under the constraining influence of this objective evidence asserts and assents to the judgment.

Such is the thesis we have now positively to establish.[1]   It

[1] *Cf.* JEANNIÈRE, *op. cit.*, pp. 207 *sqq.* ; MERCIER, *op. cit.*, §§ 111-13, pp. 253-61 ; MAHER, Psychology (4th ed.), pp. 289-91. The thesis might be formulated in a variety of ways. For instance, seeing that the validity and certitude of all knowledge depend on the validity and certitude of the principles or immediate judgments

contradicts not only the Kantian doctrine according to which the *nexus* is the product of an unconsciously operating synthetic *a priori* function, unaccompanied and unsupported by any consciously apprehended reason or motive, but also all theories which would ground scientific knowledge and certitude ultimately on any instinctive, constitutional factor or function of the knowing subject.[1]

68. PROOFS OF THE THESIS.—And how is the thesis established? Obviously, only by appealing to the testimony of introspection as to what takes place when we form any such judgment. And since we have already had recourse to this procedure in examining Kant's solution (63-5) we can here afford to be brief.

I. When, therefore, I reflect on my spontaneous assent to such a judgment as that $7 + 5 = 12$, I observe the following facts : (*a*) that I affirm a *necessary* identity between predicate and subject ; (*b*) that I affirm the identity *after having seen it* intellectually through comparison of the concept of " 12 " with the concept of " $7 + 5$ " ; (*c*) that I affirm it *because I have seen it*. Moreover, I observe that (*d*) I see the necessary identity because I see that *the concepts necessarily involve such identity ;* that (*e*) I do not assert it until I see them involve it and then only because I see them involve it ; (*f*) that in order to see them involve it I analyse each concept into its simplest elements : the predicate into a total sum of units $(1 + 1 + 1 + 1 + 1 + 1 + 1 + 1 + 1 + 1 + 1 + 1)$ and the subject into two lesser sums $(1 + 1 + 1 + 1 + 1 + 1 + 1)$ and $(1 + 1$

of the ideal order, now under consideration, it is equivalent to the scholastic thesis that the *supreme criterion or test of true or genuine knowledge, and the ultimate motive of human certitude, is to be found in the intrinsic, immediate, objective evidence of first principles of the ideal order.*

[1] Of course it is natural to, or in accordance with the nature of, the intellect to assent to evident judgments. But to describe this natural function of the mind as " intellectual instinct " (cf. BALMES, *Fundamental Philosophy*, vol. i., §§ 155-6), and then to assign *this* as the *reason* of assent, is misleading. Besides the principles, however, of which there is question in the present context, there are undoubtedly numerous spontaneous convictions of mankind,—such as that the mind can discover truth, that an external universe exists, that nature is uniform, that under due and normal conditions human testimony is trustworthy, etc.,—convictions which have not the *self*-evidence of axioms on the one hand, nor admit of the rigorous demonstration of a theorem in geometry on the other, and which, nevertheless, reflection declares to be evidently *credible,* to be such that it would be *unreasonable,* intellectually imprudent and suicidal, to doubt them. If we call these, with the Scotch school, truths of " common sense," or ascribe our belief in them to an " intellectual instinct," we are free to do so provided we recognize that this " sense " or " instinct " does not act blindly, but rather that it reacts consciously to the influence of intellectually apprehended grounds or evidence seen and felt to be sufficient to warrant a certain assent to the judgments in question.

+ 1 + 1 + 1), whereby I see the former as a whole to be identical with the two latter as its constituent parts. On the one hand I see the parts of a whole ; on the other hand I see the whole itself composed of these parts. The identity, therefore, manifests itself to me : I affirm it because it manifests itself to me : it is there objectively revealing itself to my intellect ; and this objective manifestation of the *nexus* I call the *objective evidence of the truth of the judgment*.

Hence I am conscious that I form such judgments, that I apprehend relations between their constituent concepts, *because I see intuitively* these relations *objectively evident, objectively revealing themselves to me*. Hence I reject as false the assertion that I establish any such relation *without seeing why I do so;* that I synthesize mental terms or concepts *a priori* and *unconsciously* into a complex representation of which I become conscious as a necessary product or unity, without seeing why it is so. I reject such a doctrine as false because introspection convinces me that I *do* see the reason of my mental assertion of the *nexus*.

II. It seems hardly necessary to dwell upon the fact that my assent to the *nexus* is determined not by any unconscious mental function productive of the *nexus*, but by the nature of the thought-objects or concepts themselves as present to the mind. The thesis may, however, be confirmed by investigating the reason of the different states—doubt, opinion, certitude—through which the mind often passes successively in regard to the same judgment, and therefore in the presence of the same concepts. Take any *mediate* judgment of the ideal order, as, for example, that " Every number ending in 0 or 5 is divisible by 5," [1] or that " The three interior angles of a plane triangle are together equal to two right angles" [2] Why is it that at first I doubt, suspend my assent, inquire ? that in order to resolve the doubt I set myself to analyse the terms of the proposition ? that according as the analysis develops, revealing step after step in the demonstration, my mental attitude changes gradually from mere doubt into surmise, opinion, and finally absolute certitude? Why, if not because at first I do not *see* the *nexus*, then set myself to discover whether it *is really there* or not, and only assent to it *when* and *because* I *discover* it ? Why, if not because in other words it is the nature and law of my intellect only to assent to *that which is*, when I discover *that which is*, when *that which is manifests* itself to me, and *because* it

---

[1] MERCIER, *op. cit.*, p. 225.   [2] JEANNIÈRE, *op. cit.*, pp. 210-11.

manifests itself to me, and because *I know that* it manifests itself to me? ˙ Therefore my assent to the *nexus* is determined by my *apprehension, discovery, intuition* [1] of the *nexus* objectively existing and revealing itself to my mind.

If, on the other hand, it were the law of my mind, as Kant would have it, that in presence of two concepts [or the materials of two sense intuitions], *e.g.* "the three interior angles of a plane triangle" and "equal to two right angles," my assent to the necessary *nexus* were determined by the instinctive *a priori* application of a mental category, there is no intelligible reason why, when the matter is present, the application of the category should not take place automatically and forthwith, or why my intellect should pass through successive stages of suspense, inquiry, and assent [2] in reference thereto. "If," as Mercier argues,[3] "the assent of my intellect were determined not by the manifestation of the truth but by the constitution of the faculty independently of the manifestation of objective truth, this *succession* of states

---

[1] It is important to note that this intuition is a *fact* which no theory is at liberty to elude or ignore. *Cf.* COHEN, *Journal of Philosophy, Psychology, and Scientific Methods*, 1911, p. 541 (*apud* JEANNIÈRE, *op. cit.*, p. 211 n.) : "To the question: How can reason give us knowledge? we might answer simply that it does, and that there is no valid reason to suppose that it cannot do so. [Kant's theory notwithstanding;—which, though accepting mathematics as ' knowledge,' nay as the perfect type of knowledge, yet ascribes its judgments solely to the *sensibility*, and then inconsistently goes on to confine *knowledge*-value to syntheses effected by the categories of the *understanding*. *Cf. supra*, § 51.] We may perhaps indicate our answer more positively by saying that reason gives us knowledge in the same way in which ordinary sense perception does so, by presenting an object to us. A series of syllogisms involves a series of perceptions [*i.e. intellectual* perceptions or intuitions] on our part. The *therefore* of each syllogism expresses a perceived fact, *viz.* that the third proposition or conclusion follows from or is supplied by the two premises. This is just as much an ultimate fact as that a particular object looks red or tastes bitter. If my neighbour cannot see the redness of apple, or taste its bitterness, then there can be no further argument on the matter between us. [*Cf.* MERCIER, *op. cit.*, p. 254.] Neither can there be any further argument between us if he cannot see that the propositions, Socrates is a man, and, All men are mortal, imply, Socrates is mortal. . . .

"It is to be observed that this fact of implication is just as objective as the facts asserted by the premises. For it is because of the relations between the two premises, and not from the reasoner's arbitrary *fiat*, that the conclusion follows [—nor from an unconsciously, instinctively operating *a priori* mental form, supposed to *make* it follow]. The assertion that the propositions are mental [*i.e.* reveal only mental products, appearances, phenomena?] would not help us any, for it is obviously not true that any two propositions will imply a definite third proposition. It is because of what the propositions assert that the conclusion follows." And what they assert, and what the concepts imply, is not only *mentally objective* but also *real.—Cf. infra*, chap. ix.

[2] *Cf. infra*, § 91, where this consideration is developed. [3] *Op. cit.*, p. 256.

would be inexplicable. We could of course understand that in presence of the terms of *one* proposition the intellect would remain in doubt, while in presence of the terms of *another* proposition it would assent; but that *the same* matter and *the same* category could produce now doubt and again certitude—is simply unintelligible. Hence such a succession of intellectual states is incompatible with the Kantian theory."

III. As a further confirmation of the thesis let us compare the conscious states aroused in us by the exercise of the *intellectual* function of judging or interpreting with those aroused in us by the exercise of mere *sensibility*.

Through the impressions produced on our senses by objects, the latter *necessarily* make us aware of them *as they appear*, even when they appear to us otherwise than as they really are. A *straight* stick, plunged in water, *necessarily* appears to the eye *as bent ;* two *plane* pictures, seen through the stereoscope, *necessarily* appear as one *solid* object seen in perspective or relief; and so on. We can correct such illusions of course ; but it is by intellect we correct them, not by sense : the deceived sense can never correct its own deception. Or rather, we should say, it can never correct the error of the *intellect* judging *spontaneously* that such objects *are* as they *appear*. For it is really not the *sense* that deceives us : the sense always and necessarily reports the object, or brings it into consciousness, according to the actual concrete impression made upon the sense faculty in the actual concrete condition in which the sense organ happens to be,—and continues to report thus even after we have corrected the erroneous interpretation put upon it by the intellect judging spontaneously. Thus, in reporting to us how things appear, the function of the sense is always determined and necessitated by the nature of the actual concrete impression made upon it.[1]

But while sense is thus necessitated in revealing to us how things *appear*, intellect is not necessitated by the mere sense impressions in judging as to how things *are*. Our sense-awareness or sense-consciousness of how things appear is not *knowledge*, it only furnishes the materials of knowledge, the data for *interpretation*. Knowledge proper is knowledge of *how and what*

---

[1] The origin, in sense perception, of the distinction between the *appearance* of things and their *reality*, and the significance of the distinction as bearing on the possibility of certain knowledge concerning reality, will be investigated more fully below (chap. xx.).

things are ; it is attained only by judgment ; and judgment has for its immediate object the assertion of a *nexus* (of identity or non-identity) as real. Now in asserting this *nexus* the intellect is not determined by the mere presence of the terms of the relation (subject and predicate) in consciousness. Introspection assures us, from what takes place in the case of *mediate* or *demonstrated* judgments, that the intellect can abstain from asserting such a *nexus* until it has so analysed the terms of the comparison into their simplest elements that it *sees the nexus to be really there.* Moreover, after it has assented it can *reflect*, deliberately reconsider the matter of the judgment, deliberately withdraw its assent unless and until the objective reality of the *nexus* shines in clearly upon it and compels its assent. Thus, too, it can correct its first spontaneous judgment of a sense *datum* if that judgment were erroneous because too hastily formed according to appearances. By reflection it can apprehend that in the datum *as it appears* the grounds for asserting that judgment (as to what the datum *really is*) are not yet manifest, and it can suspend its assent until they become manifest : until then, but no longer, for by the clear and evident manifestation of the *nexus* the intellect is necessarily determined to elicit the judgment, to yield its assent. While, therefore, intellect is a faculty of " spontaneity " in the sense that it does not, like sensibility, merely make us passively aware of *how things appear*, through received impressions, but, by actively considering and interpreting the data thus received, judges how things really are, it is not a faculty of " spontaneity " in the sense intended by Kant, *i.e.* in the sense that its function is wholly determined by the thinking or judging subject : on the contrary, its function, though determined by the latter *as to its exercise* or application (*quoad exercitium actus*), is determined *objectively* (*quoad specificationem actus*) by the ontological truth or reality of the *nexus* apprehended through the judgment.

Moreover, when the intellect has before it two absolutely simple thought-objects revealing a necessary *nexus* of identity or incompatibility,—*e.g.* " Whatever happens has a cause," " Two straight lines cannot enclose a space," etc.,—and when it sees these objects to be absolutely simple, incapable of further analysis, then not only is it compelled to assert and assent to the *nexus*, but in doing so *it is infallible.* That is to say, in such circumstances it cannot be deceived as to the fact that the objective *nexus* is *really there.* If the intellect apprehends the objects at all it is conscious not merely that they *seem to it* to be necessarily related, but that they *are really* so related and that they cannot be otherwise. There is no room for error here any more than there is room for error in the mere simple conception of the objects themselves separately. Error can creep into conception only in so far as this is accompanied by a judgment, *i.e.* by the judgment (*a*) that the conceived object *actually exists*, or (*b*) that the conceived object is *intrinsically possible.* Now judgments of the ideal order belong to the latter class. And just as error can creep into the reasoning processes by which we derive remote conclusions concerning the mental relations of complex concepts, so error can creep into the processes by which we form complex concepts themselves by successive judgments whereby we synthesize simpler notes or factors to form a complex object which we judge to be intrinsically possible. But just as no error is possible in apprehending intellectually the absolutely simple, unanalysable objects of thoughts, such as being, unity, number, quantity, whole, part, straight line, space, cause, etc. ; just as we must apprehend them as they are, as objects of thought, as objective possibilities, as intrinsically possible, each involving in itself no mutually incompatible factors because each is only one factor and therefore intrinsically possible because conceivable, or else we do not apprehend them at all,—so too if we apprehend intellectually the self-evident *relations of necessary identity or incompatibility* between them, relations which constitute the *first principles or axioms of the ideal order,* we *must apprehend these relations as they really are,* or else not apprehend them at all : we cannot misconceive them : intellect is here infallible.

The thought-objects which enter into these principles are the factors from which all our complex concepts are formed. And if, as Kleutgen observes,[1] " reason were subject to error in the simple conception of these factors and their relations it could not reliably form complex concepts by reflection, or examine those formed spontaneously and indeliberately, and so all thought, spontaneous no less than reflex, would become impossible.[2] But intellect knows itself to be infallible in those primordial judgments ; error is possible only in regard to the complex or composite : simple, unanalysable objects we either do not apprehend at all, or else we apprehend them truly, as they are." Similarly St. Thomas says that since the essences of things are the proper object of the intellect this faculty " cannot be deceived *per se* in regard to the essence of any object of thought, though it may be deceived *per accidens* in

---

[1] *Philosophie der Vorzeit,* § 298.   [2] *Cf.* next argument, *infra.*

relating thought-objects in judgment and reasoning. And hence intellect cannot err in judgments which appear evident from the apprehended essences of the terms compared, as is the case in *first principles*. . . . But intellect may be deceived *per accidens* in apprehending the essences of complex thought-objects : not indeed from any organic defect as in the case of the senses, for the intellect is not an organic faculty, but from the judging processes subservient to the definition of the complex object. . . . Hence in the apprehension of simple thought-objects, where there is no judicial synthesis or composition of factors, we cannot fall into error, but [either apprehend these as they are, or] fail altogether to apprehend them." [1]

This constraining force of the objects of our thought upon intellect, this property they have of compelling intellect to apprehend them as they are, is what scholastics call *cogent objective evidence*.[2] It is clearly an objective motive or ground of assent, at least in the sense that is a property of the conceived objects themselves, and is as objective to the intellect as these latter are themselves ; and we hope to show later that these conceived objects or concepts are themselves objective in the sense of being *real*, of being discovered and not constructed by the activity of intellectual conception or thought.

IV. Finally, the very contention of all subjectivism or scepticism is itself an implicit avowal that it is the law of the intellect to be guided in its judgments only by evidence, by the revelation of ontological or real truth. For the contention is that when we reflect on our spontaneous convictions prudence dictates that we should suspend our assent. Why? Because we have not objective evidence for them. And how long? Until we have objective evidence for them,—even if that be indefinitely. But it is the same reason or intellect, obeying the same law, that *reflects* and *judges spontaneously*. The only difference is the extrinsic interference and direction of the will in the former case. Hence, as Mercier rightly argues,[3] "the admission that in the domain of reflection the intellect can suspend its assent and yield only to objective evidence, involves the conclusion that in its direct judgments also it can let itself be guided exclusively by the manifestation of the objective identity of subject and predicate, furnished spontaneously through sense experience. Accordingly,

[1] *Summa Theol.*, i., Q. 85, a. 6,—*apud* KLEUTGEN, *l.c.*
[2] The term " evidence " in the popular sense embraces evidence that is not cogent, and even evidence that is only apparent, as distinct from genuine or real. It will be investigated *ex professo* when we come to deal with evidence as the supreme criterion or test of truth.
[3] *Op. cit.*, pp. 258-9.

the power which subjectivists at least implicitly allow to reflecting reason they cannot logically deny to spontaneous reason ; and therefore by necessary inference they should conclude with us that certitude has for its determining cause an *objective motive* of assent : which is the very negation of subjectivism."

Those arguments show that our *spontaneous* certitude about self-evident judgments of the ideal order can be *justified by reflection.* Our assent to them is now seen to be not merely *psychologically* or *subjectively* necessary but to be grounded on *objective* motives, *i.e.* on motives seen by the intellect to be involved in the very nature of the objects revealed to us through the concepts compared. From this, moreover, we see that our spontaneous assents should not be rejected *a priori* merely because they are spontaneous (25-27). Those of them that are genuine are objective all the time : their objectivity is not *created* but *discovered* by critical reflection. And finally we see that in this critical revision of our spontaneous assents the intellect must allow itself to be guided solely by objective evidence, *i.e.* by the clear manifestation of objective reality.[1]

69. IN NECESSARY JUDGMENTS THE CHARACTER OF THE APPREHENDED " NEXUS " IS DUE TO A PROPERTY OF THE THOUGHT-OBJECTS OR CONCEPTS, *viz.* THEIR *"Abstractness".*—From the considerations just put forward the conclusion is inevitable that in immediate necessary and universal judgments of the ideal order the intellect discovers and apprehends intuitively a *nexus* which is objectively there between the concepts compared : which is another way of saying that the objects thus identified or discriminated are what they are necessarily and universally, and independently of our judging activity ; that it is not this activity which creates them or makes them to be such as they are.

But if, then, these conceived objects give rise on analysis to relations which are apprehended to be *necessarily* and *universally* valid in regard to such objects, and to be so independently of our judging activity, so that these relations characterize these objects themselves and not merely our mode of *judging* them, the question still remains : How are the *absolute* necessity and universality of these relations to be accounted for ? Manifestly these characteristics cannot appertain to any objects *as perceived through sense experience*, for they transcend the limits of sense experience. The

---

[1] *Cf.* JEANNIÈRE, *op. cit.*, pp. 213, 215.

necessity and universality in question are not empirical or *a posteriori*. They characterize objects not as perceived by sense but
as conceived by intellect. The question then is, why or how is
it that objects, as conceived, reveal such relations?

The answer is that the objects reveal those relations because
intellect, in conceiving them, apprehends them *in the abstract, i.e.*
divested of all the conditions of the contingent, actual, physical
existence whereby alone they can be data or objects of sense ex
perience. It apprehends them (in their essence or nature) as
being independent of the limitations under which, in their sensible, physical, material existence, they come into sense experi
ence : and because it so apprehends them it can and does see in
them properties, laws, relations, which characterize their essences,
which are not revealed by, or grounded in, sense experience
of their actual physical existence, but to which, nevertheless, as
characterizing their essences, their actual physical existence must
necessarily and universally conform. And it is our intellectual
intuition of these objects as involving such properties, laws, and
relations, that gives us the absolutely necessary and universal
judgment,—the judgment which is *a priori* in the sense that it is
not grounded in sense experience,—though not *a priori* (1) in the
sense that it must or can be formed prior in time to sense experience, or (2) in the sense of revealing not anything objective
or given to thought, but something that would be merely a necessary condition *ex parte subjecti cognoscentis* for having intelligible
sense experience.

Now we believe spontaneously that these abstract thought-
objects are real,[1] just as we believe that the data of sense perception are real : it is by means of the former that we interpret the
nature of the latter : it is by concepts we attain to a knowledge
of percepts. When we come to justify this spontaneous belief in
the reality of the abstract objects of conception we shall see how
the function of conception is conditioned and occasioned by the
function of perception : how intellectual conception implies on
the part of the intellect an *abstractive power*, or *faculty of abstraction*, called by scholastics the "active intellect," "*intellectus
agens*," whereby the intellect can apprehend, in and through the
concrete, individualized, and physically existent *data* of the senses
and imagination, modes or aspects of the *nature* of this empirically presented reality,—modes or aspects which reveal this reality

---

[1] For doubts, prompting *Conceptualism*, cf. *infra*, § 86.

in abstraction from the modes which condition its *actual physical existence* as revealed in sense experience.

The *abstractive* and *intuitive* character of intellectual conception or thought is thus the key to the characters of necessity and universality in judgments of the ideal order. The intellect *abstracts*, as its proper objects, from the concrete, individual data of conscious sensation and reflection, the reality which constitutes the essences or natures of these data : these essences or natures it *contemplates* in this condition of abstraction from the contingencies of their actual physical existence, an abstract condition in which they are static, changeless, self-identical entities : and thus it *sees* them to be characterized by properties and relations which, like themselves, are immutable, necessary, eternal, etc.

This explanation, however, involves certain positions which have yet to be vindicated, *viz.* (*a*) that intellect gets all its thought-objects in and through the concrete data of sense perception and reflection, that no ideas are innate ; (*b*) that what these thought-objects, or abstract and universal concepts, reveal to the mind is *really* in those concrete data ; (*c*) that in sense perception, through those concrete data *reality* is revealed to the mind. Moreover, even assuming those positions to be vindicated,—as we hope to vindicate them in due course,—it is not yet apparent how the abstractive character of thought can furnish an *adequate* explanation not only of the objective validity, but of the absolute necessity and universality, of judgments of the ideal order. Or, at all events, if the relations of absolute necessity and universality revealed in these judgments are characteristics *of reality*,—nay, even if they were characteristics only *of thought*,—then, even in this latter case, seeing that thought itself is a reality,—the bare fact of the mind's ability to apprehend such objects and relations ought at least to suggest the momentous conclusion that there is *some* reality,—at least thought itself or the thinking human soul,—which transcends the physical, sensible modes of existence in which the concrete data of sense are presented to consciousness. For, even though these abstract objects and their relations are not given to intellect except in and through external and internal sense experience and self-consciousness,—processes which reveal only individual things and events in their actual, concrete existing and happening,—nevertheless it is undeniable that the relations in question cannot be grounded in our sense experience of actual things and events. For sense experience (including memory) reveals only what *does* or *did exist* or *happen actually*, while the relations in question are apprehended by intellect as expressing what *must be*, as holding good *necessarily* and *universally*. Moreover, we spontaneously believe that whatever does exist or happen actually, whether within the domain of actual or possible sense experience or beyond this domain, must exist or happen *in accordance with what those necessary relations between our abstract thought-objects express ;* that nothing real can actually exist or happen otherwise than in conformity with those necessary principles which characterize the objects of intellectual thought ; that nothing which *is real* can contradict them : in other words, that those

16 *

absolutely necessary and universal judgments of the ideal order are *laws of reality*, laws to which whatever is *either actual or possible* must conform, laws which are partial expressions of the *nature* or *essence* of *reality*. If, then, the data revealed through sense are *actually existing realities*, the abstract objects revealed through intellectual thought, in the process of conception, must be actualized in those data, and must, in so far as we apprehend such abstract objects, reveal to us what is essential to those data as real, what constitutes their natures or essences as real, and what expresses the laws or principles of being, to which laws they, as real, must in the actual modes of their physical existence necessarily conform.

Now, if these spontaneous beliefs in the reality of the abstract, universal objects of *intellectual conception*, and in the reality of the concrete, individual data of *sense perception*, be justifiable, then reality as apprehended by *intellect* in the form of abstract thought-objects, grounding absolutely necessary and universal relations, must be *somehow* independent of the modes of concrete actual existence wherein that same reality reveals itself to *sense*. Not that the abstract objects of intellectual thought have, as such, an actual existence which would be wholly independent of, and apart from, the world of sense data, as some interpret Plato to have taught ; or that we have intellectual intuitions of them which are immediate and innate in the sense of apprehending these objects independently of sense perception and of the reflex consciousness which reveals the individual mind in its conscious processes. If these abstract thought-objects,—seen to be as such necessarily, universally, eternally, immutably, and indivisibly as intellect conceives them,[1]—were also *as such actually existent*, then indeed the characteristics of the absolutely necessary and universal principles of the ideal order would be adequately accounted for ; but in this Platonic theory of *Extreme Realism* the world of *sense experience* would be not only unexplained, inexplicable, unintelligible, unknowable, but would be even illusory and unreal. Our intellectual conception of reality in the form of abstract thought-objects is not independent of the sense perception and self-consciousness whereby these objects in their actual concrete modes of existence are apprehended by sense and presented to intellect. But although the actual existence of reality in modes wherein alone it is perceivable by sense, and its actual perception in such modes, form the *necessary condition* for the presentation of reality to the human intellect and for its apprehension by the intellect, nevertheless when reality is thus presented in sense data, intellect, apprehending these data as abstract thought-objects or real essences or natures, apprehends reality *in abstraction from the sensible modes of its actual existence*, apprehends reality as to *what* it is in itself, and therefore as to what it *must be*, if, or whenever, or wherever, it does actually exist.

Why, then, can the intellect form absolutely necessary and universal judgments about the things and events revealed through sense,—judgments which transcend sense experience, and to which it knows that the things and events of sense experience *must* conform ? Because these judgments, though they presuppose the sense experience whereby we apprehend sense data in their actual modes of sensible existence, are not grounded upon the actual

[1] *Cf. Ontology*, §§ 14-20, pp. 79-100.

existence of these data, but simply upon their *reality*, which, abstracted intellectually from their actual existence, intellect has conceived in the form of
abstract objects of thought ; and because these judgments reveal, and are
known to reveal, laws or principles expressive of the very nature of reality
as such,—laws, therefore, to which all reality, perceivable and conceivable,
must necessarily conform.[1]

These judgments do not assert that the abstract objects of conception
actually exist, but only that they are real, that they are essences objectively
revealed to intellect ; and although, as actually existent, the objects are apprehensible only in and through the data of sense, nevertheless, as essences,
or objective possibilities of existence, they are independent,—as to what they
necessarily are and necessarily involve in themselves, *i.e.* as to what they are
conceived by intellect to be,—as such, they are independent of the modes and
conditions of their actual existence in the domain of sense.

70. WHAT CAN BE INFERRED FROM THE CHARACTERISTICS
OF ABSTRACT THOUGHT-OBJECTS OR ESSENCES ? A DEBATABLE
QUESTION.—The reality which scholastics vindicate for objects of
intellectual conception as such, and which is identical with their
objectivity to thought,—or, again, with their intrinsic possibility
or intrinsic capability of actual existence,—or, again, in the case
of complex objects, with the compatibility of their constituent
factors,—and which is the ground of their conceivability, is, no
doubt, an *ideal* reality. That is to say, firstly, it is, as such, apprehensible not by sense but by intellect ;[2] and secondly, as such
it does not imply, but abstracts from, actual existence. By
calling it an "ideal" reality, do we, however, mean that it is a
creation or construction of the *subjectum cognoscens*, of the intellect that conceives it ? By no means.[3] Or that it is the product
of a synthesis of a mental or subjective factor with a "given" or
objective factor? Again, by no means.[4] As to its content it
is wholly given, wholly objective, to intellect : its content is
wholly presented to, and discovered, not constructed, by intellect.
The ideal reality of objects of intellectual conception, their reality
as possibilities of actual existence, is not a consequence but a
condition of their actual conception. The objects conceived by
human thought are real possibilities of actual existence not
because they are conceived or conceivable by human thought,

---

[1] *Cf. Ontology*, § 15, pp. 82-4.

[2] It is, as scholastics say, not " sensibile *per se*": *per se* and *in se* it is an
" objectum *intelligibile* ": it is " sensibile *per accidens* " only, inasmuch as it is really
one with its concrete modes of physical existence, which are " sensibilia *per se* ".

[3] This will be established later by refutation of *Conceptualism* in its various
forms.

[4] *Cf.* preceding note.

but conversely, they are conceived and conceivable by human thought as objects because they are first and in themselves real possibilities of existence.[1]

Thus, then, reality is given to us in certain modes of its actual existence whereby it forms the data of sense perception. Through sense perception reality is given to intellect in the form of thought-objects which it apprehends to be real, prescinding altogether from these perceptible modes of their actual existence as sense data. This ideal reality which we apprehend them as having, we see to be likewise independent of our own thought, to be not a mere logical entity, or mental product objectively present to our thought: inasmuch as we see that these thought-objects, together with the *necessary* relations which character-ize them,—relations of possibility or impossibility, compatibility or incompatibility,—are revealed to, and not produced by, our thought; or, in other words, that our thought-activity does not construct or create its objects. In what, then, does this ideal reality, this objective possibility of thought-objects consist? Be-sides the *actual* reality which they have in the data of sense, and the *presence* (20) which they have *to the human intellect conceiving them* in the abstract, have they any other being or reality?

Some philosophers, reflecting on the features of necessity, eternity, immutability, presented by these thought-objects and their relations, have contended that the intellect in apprehending them is apprehending intuitively the Necessary, Eternal, Self-Existent, Absolute Reality of the Divine Being, as Prototype and Exemplar of all contingent existences; that such thought-objects, as actualized in these latter and thus perceivable through sense, and as being in this condition contingent, individual, temporal, and mutable, could not possibly present the character-istics which our absolutely necessary and universal judgments re-veal in them; that therefore we apprehend intellectually the real natures or essences of sense data not through sense perception of the actual existence of these latter, but through a primordial and immediate intellectual intuition of the Absolutely Necessary and Eternal Being : the being that is first or fundamental in reality is

---

[1] *Cf. Ontology*, § 16, p. 86 ; § 18, p. 89. The doctrine in the text is of course in direct conflict with Kant's theory according to which the intrinsic possibility of a thought-object is no index of its reality, and its extrinsic possibility (involving its reality) would be its actual or possible presence in *sense* experience, so that the latter would be the source and standard of the real possibility of things. *Cf. supra*, § 49 ; *infra*, § 88.

also first in thought: *Primum ontologicum est primum logicum.* This form of extreme realism, which is obviously akin to Platonism, is known as *Ontologism.*[1] We shall see later why it is untenable.

Among Scholastic philosophers there are some who hold that since the whole order or domain of ideal thought-objects, conceived objectively by our intellects, reveals itself to our intellects as *real*, as independent of conception in the sense that it is discovered, not invented, by conception; and since, on the other hand, it also reveals itself as being *necessarily what it is*, independently of the actual existence of the sense data in which it is actualized, and in and through which it is presented to our intellects, nay more, as determining necessary laws of reality, to which laws these sense data in their actual existence must necessarily and universally conform, so that the actually existing contingent data of sense are dependent as to their natures or essences on the ideal objects of thought, rather than these being dependent, as to what they are, on the former;—since these ideal thought-objects are such, it follows that from their reality, thus revealed to our intellects objectively as independent both of perception and of thought, we can, nay must, *infer* the reality of a Self-Existent, Necessary, Immutable, Eternal, Absolute Intelligence, as the Prototype and Exemplar of those intellectually apprehended essences, and the ultimate ground of their characteristics of absolute necessity, immutability and universality.[2]

Others, on the contrary, hold that while these abstract thought-objects are undoubtedly real, the reality which they are seen by the human intellect to have is that which they *actually* have in the concrete data presented to the intellect in the processes of external and internal sense experience and reflection on its own (intellectual) activities; that the manner in which intellect apprehends these data,—*viz.* in abstraction from all the conditions of the actual experience in which they are presented to it,—adequately accounts for the characteristics of necessity, immutability, eternity, universality, etc., which they exhibit when considered in this abstract condition; and that, therefore, these

---

[1] *Cf. Ontology*, § 19, pp. 94-5. *Cf. infra*, § 80.

[2] *Cf.* DE MUNNYNCK, O.P., *Praelectiones de Dei Existentia* (Louvain, 1904, pp. 11-25, 46-7, 56-9, 75, *et passim*); LEPIDI, *Ontologia*, pp. 90-1 (*apud* DE MUNNYNCK, *op. cit.*, pp. 18-19), and *De Ontologismo* (Louvain, 1874); BALMES, *Fundamental Philosophy*; KLEUTGEN, *Philosophie der Vorzeit*, §§ 303-9, 476; and other authors referred to in our *Ontology*, § 18, p. 89.

characteristics furnish no legitimate ground for an inference to
the reality of a Supreme, Necessary, Eternal, Self-Existent Being.[1] According to this view, intellect would apprehend in the
actually existing concrete data of sensation and reflection beings
or realities which, though they have the *contingent modes of
existence* apprehended in sense experience, are as to their *real
essences* unattainable by sense and accessible only to thought.
Moreover, the characteristics of necessity, universality, immutability, etc., apprehended in these thought-objects and their relations really characterize the sense data of which these objects form
the natures or essences:[2] they cannot, however, be apprehended
in the sense data *by sense,* but only *by intellect ;* for while sense
apprehends its data merely in the actual modes of their physical
existence, intellect apprehends the essences or natures themselves
which have these physical modes of existence, and sees in them
properties, relations, laws, which are necessary, immutable, universal, etc., in the sense that, being characteristics of the essence
of reality, whatever is real, whatever is possible or actual in any
domain, perceivable or conceivable, must necessarily conform to
them.[3]

Whether the inference from the characteristics of abstract thought-objects
to the reality of a Necessary, Eternal Intelligence be legitimate or not, at all
events just as those who defend it as valid cannot fairly be charged with ontologism,[4] so neither can those who reject it as invalid be fairly charged with
equivalently denying to the human intellect the power of attaining to any
knowledge of objects transcending the domain of sense. To hold that from
the properties we apprehend in abstract objects of conception we can infer the
reality of a Necessary Intelligence as the ultimate ground of them, is very
different from identifying the former with the latter. So, also, to hold that
the properties of these thought-objects can be explained by the mode in
which the intellect apprehends them in the concrete data of sensation and reflection, is very different from holding that as modes of reality they are all
merely sensible, or incapable of modes of actualization which transcend the
power of sense and are apprehensible by intellect alone. For if, in the data
of sensation and reflection the intellect can apprehend reality, and modes of
reality,—such as " existence," " being," " substance," " quality," " action,"

[1] *Cf. Ontology*, §§ 13-20, pp. 75-100; MERCIER, *Ontologie*, pp. 40-49.

[2] *Cf. Ontology*, p. 92, n. 1 ; *Science of Logic*, i., pp. 161-2, 179-80; ii., 220.

[3] This power, whereby intellect apprehends, in the data of sense, realities that
transcend the physical, sensible mode of existence,—whereby it apprehends that
which has material, physical, time-and-space existence, apart from the conditions of
such existence, and as an abstract essence or thought-object,—points to the conclusion that the soul endowed with such a power must itself have a nature or essence
which is spiritual, which transcends the sensible mode of existence.

[4] *Ontology*, pp. 94-5.

" relation," etc.,—which it sees to be really and in their own nature capable of being actualized, and of actually existing, otherwise than as they actually exist in the domain of sense, then the power of intellect to transcend the domain of sense realities is vindicated. Nor can it be objected that by ascribing the characters (of necessity, universality, immutability, eternity, etc.) which intellect apprehends in the objects of conception, or rather by ascribing our intellectual apprehension of those characters, to the *abstractive* function of intellectual thought, we are thereby forced to admit that these objects, as thus apprehended, are not real, but mere subjective products of our thought-activity : just as we have contended that they must be if they get their characters from the application of *a priori* forms of the understanding to sense data. This objection we shall presently see to be groundless, when, in defending the reality of these thought-objects, we come to explain the nature of thought as abstractive. Suffice it to say here, by way of anticipation, that whereas in Kant's theory, on the one hand reality is from the very origin of cognition in sense perception *veiled off from* the mind as to its real nature, and possibly metamorphosed or disfigured both in perception and in thought, and on the other hand the characteristics of thought-objects are really rendered inexplicable by referring them to functions or forms in the (supposed) unknowable domain of the transcendental *Ego* (59) : in the scholastic theory on the contrary reality is *revealed to* the mind both in perception and in thought, and is not disfigured by our conception of it in the abstract any more than by our sense perception of it in the concrete. Moreover, the characteristics of our abstract thought-objects are explained by inferring from the reality of these latter the *suprasensible character of thought itself* and the spirituality of the human soul ; and by further inferring from the *actuality* of the mind and of the objects of its experience the Necessary existence of a Supreme, Self-Existent, Absolute First Cause as the Ultimate Ground of all actual and possible experience. It was not in denying that absolutely *necessary* and *universal* judgments can be grounded in *sense* experience that Kant erred ; or in turning for an explanation of these characteristics to *intellect ;* or in seeking such explanation in an analysis of the manner in which intellectual apprehension attains to its objects ; or even in concluding that its objects *are seen* to have these characteristics precisely because of the manner in which intellect is able to apprehend them. Where he erred was in thinking that intellectual conception is a *construction* of objects with these characteristics, by means of subjective factors or forms of transcendental and therefore unknowable origin (59), and that accordingly the objects thus subjectively constructed are not *real ;* whereas conception is in fact a *discovery* of objects which *are real*, and which *really have* these characteristics, and which are seen to have them precisely because this intellectual apprehension or discovery seizes in the abstract, and apart from the actual conditions of their concrete, physical, individual existence, realities, or real essences, which are revealed to sense only by reason of their being actualized and existent in these sensible conditions.

PART III.

INTELLECTUAL KNOWLEDGE : CONCEPTION.

ᴵᵛ CHAPTER IX.

ORIGIN AND VALIDITY OF CONCEPTS : MODERATE REALISM.

71. PROBLEM OF THE ORIGIN OF CONCEPTS.—So far we have endeavoured to explain and vindicate the doctrine that the *nexus* between the concepts compared in the mental act of *judgment* is *objective*, and that our assent thereto is based on grounds of objective evidence. Next comes the equally important question as to the nature, origin, and real significance of these *concepts* themselves. What is the nature of the process of *conception*, whereby we become intellectually aware of such abstract thought-objects, endowed with such characteristics, as we have been examining? What is the relation of these thought-objects to the process of conception? And what is their significance, their relation to reality?

As to the source or origin of them it is the general teaching of scholasticism that *no* concepts are *innate, i.e.* that there is no process of intellectual conception whereby the individual intellect would discover such abstract objects of thought in the intellect itself, so to speak, and independently of the conscious perception of concrete sense *data.* On the contrary, the conception of such thought-objects is dependent on, and conditioned by, conscious perception of sense data. The intellect gets all its objects *in and through sense perception and self-consciousness.* In this sense scholastics accept the aphorism, *Nihil est in intellectu quod prius non fuerit in sensu:* only through the actual exercise of sense perception, external and internal, and through the consequent process of reflex intellectual consciousness, are objects given to intellect. But they are far from attaching to the aphorism the meaning given to it by sensist and nominalist philosophers : that nothing can be conceived by intellect except what can be per-

ceived by sense: that intellect can know nothing of reality beyond the sensible, physical, material modes of its actual existence
as revealed in sense perception: that all intellectual conception,
judgment, and reasoning are but mental complexes, associations,
re-presentations of what is actually presented in sense. On the
contrary, they repudiate this practical. negation of intellect, this
reduction of all the mind's cognitive faculties to the level of
sense. And they hold that although the intellect gets all its
objects dependently on sense perception, inasmuch as it is this
latter that conditions and originates the functions of intellectual
thought,—conception, judgment, reasoning,—nevertheless it can
and does apprehend, in and through the data of sense, modes of
being or reality which are not in themselves really and objectively
conditioned by the actual existence whereby they reveal themselves in sense experience, but which abstract from, and transcend, this sensible mode of existence. Nay *all* the modes of
being which intellect apprehends in what is given in sense perception abstract from their actual existence as data of sense;
and are thus, as conceived, *immaterial negatively*, or *by abstraction*. Moreover, intellect has, in addition to the data of sense,
all the conscious mental activities *including intellectual thought
itself*, as data on which to reflect; and thereby it conceives or
apprehends modes of reality—*viz.* thought, volition, intellect,
will, personality, spirit, etc.,—which it interprets as being, even
in their concrete, actual existence, *unperceivable* by sense, *suprasensible, positively immaterial.* Hence, to emphasize this power,
which intellect has, of apprehending reality in modes transcending those of its actual, concrete, *sensible, perceptible existence,*—in
modes which characterize its *nature* or *essence* simply as *intelligible,*—scholastics subscribe to the qualification by which Leibniz
sought to correct Locke's aphorism and protect it from the misinterpretation of sensism, when he re-stated it: "Nihil est in
intellectu quod prius non fuerit in sensu, *nisi intellectus ipse*".

By means of external sense perception, scholastics teach, we
are made directly and immediately aware of something which we
interpret as *real*, as a *material* reality, extended, spatial, temporal,
manifold, endowed with various sensibly perceived qualities.[1]
By muscular and organic sensations we become aware of that
which we interpret as *our own real organism*, distinct from the
rest of the material universe. In all this there are involved also

---

[1] *Cf.* JEANNIÈRE, *op. cit.*, pp. 216, 219-22.

the functions of memory and association of our cognitive states and activities. Through self-consciousness we become aware of what we interpret as *real* cognitive activities of our own selves as *real* cognitive agents. We judge our own individual selves to be real beings in a world of distinct but similar human beings.

It will be noted that *sense perception*, sense awareness, or sense consciousness of *data* or objects, is accompanied throughout by the higher, *intellectual* function of *conception*, *i.e.* the intellectual apprehension of thought-objects, and that by means of these concepts we are constantly *judging* or *interpreting* the *data* of sense. Sense alone does not give us knowledge, but only the raw materials of knowledge. Our first spontaneous and scarcely conscious judgment is the judgment of *existence*, the judgment that "something *is*," the judgment which involves the concept of *actual being, actually existing reality.*

According as sense perception and consciousness furnish their real data the intellect is, however, not only conceiving the actual existence of these data and judging *that* they "are" or "exist". It is also conceiving *what* they are, or that in which their reality consists, *viz.* "substance," "body," "extension," "number," "space," "time," "life," "mind," "action," "change," "cause," "effect," "possibility," "actuality," "quality," "relation," etc., etc.; and is judging or interpreting *what* those *data* are, by means of these thought-objects derived from those data.

While thus exploring the nature of the reality that is given to us in external and internal sense perception, and in reflection on our own mental, cognitive activities, we judge that the actual mode of existence of material things, including our own body or organism, is extended or spatial, is mutable, successive, temporal; and also that our own individual selves, including our mind, the subject and agent of all our conscious states and activities, came into existence, began to be or exist in time, and are therefore contingent and caused like all the other immediate data of our cognitive experience. But reflection on our own intellectual and volitional activities, as revealed in consciousness, discloses these to us as activities of a higher order than material, physical, sensible events: we apprehend them as spiritual activities of a spiritual substance. We observe at the same time that by intellectual thought we apprehend absolutely necessary and universal relations among the objects of our concepts: the first principles of thought and being, the axioms of the sciences. By their self-evidence these force themselves upon our intellect; and, spontaneously accepting them as giving valid information about reality, we utilize them to prosecute as far as we can our interpretation of experience: even, perhaps, so far as to attain by means of them to a reasoned certitude concerning the reality of human freedom and responsibility, the immortality of the human soul, the dependence of man and the world on a Supreme Being, the First Cause and Last End of all contingent reality.

72. PROBLEM OF THE VALIDITY OF CONCEPTS.—But reflection on the grounds and validity of these processes of judgment and inference forces us to scrutinize more closely the process of intellectual conception and the nature of those abstract thought-objects whereby we interpret the data of sense perception and self-consciousness and infer therefrom the reality and existence of a domain of being which transcends the scope of sense perception and is apprehensible only by intellectual thought. Through this further scrutiny we can trace the relations between sense perception and intellectual thought. Sense and intellect are rooted in the same individual soul or mind. Sense, as we shall see, reveals reality to us; but intellect alone *knows* what is given through sense to be real, and alone *judges* it to be real. Moreover, by reflecting on our processes of sense perception, their nature, their scope, and their objects, we see and judge intellectually that reality is revealed through sense perception only in so far as it has actually the modes of existence which we conceive intellectually as the material, or physical, or sensible modes of existence, *i.e.* in so far as it is visible, tangible, audible, etc., and concretely individualized in space and time. But we are conscious that while by means of our external and internal senses (including the functions of imagination, sense memory, and mental association of sense perceptions), we apprehend reality in these *sensible modes* of its *actual existence*, we apprehend simultaneously, by the intellectual process of conception, in and through these perceived modes of its actual sensible existence, reality itself *as to what it is essentially*, and not only the reality of the data of sense perception, but the reality of our perceptive processes, and of ourselves the perceivers: all these we conceive intellectually as objects of thought, as realities which, in and through the given sensible modes of their actual existence, we apprehend as *essences*, *i.e.* as to *what they are*, and *in abstraction from* these modes of their *actual, sensible existence*. Not

of course that we thus apprehend *completely* their natures or essences. Far, indeed, from it;[1] but that we apprehend intellectually from the beginning, and in some small degree, *what they are*, by apprehending thus intellectually, and in the abstract, in and through those sense data, such conceived thought-objects as *e.g.* "being," "substance," "quality," "extension," "space," "time," "change," "motion," "cause," "effect," "action," "relation," etc., etc.

But *do* those abstract and universal thought-objects or concepts, which we thus employ as predicates to interpret the data of experience, give us in very truth a genuine knowledge of reality? In answer to this question the history of philosophy reveals a variety of conflicting and contradictory views: the *Nominalism* of sensist philosophers, who, confounding the concept with the imagination image, not only fail to account for the existence of necessity and universal judgments (40-45), but render the process of judgment wholly unintelligible; the *Conceptualism* which, regarding those abstract thought-objects as pure products of the mind's supposed constructive activity, must consequently deny the possibility of any valid intellectual knowledge of the individual data which make up the world of man's sense-experience; the post-Kantian *Absolutism* which, confounding concept with percept, identifying universal with individual, unifying subject with object of knowledge, substitutes for a reasoned analysis of human cognition a fanciful, pantheistic exposition of the universe as a logical evolution of the One and Sole Reality; and the *Realism* which, in various forms, asserts the *reality* of that which is intellectually conceived, or apprehended by thought.

The meaning of the question here at issue, *viz.* "Are the objects of our intellectual concepts *real?*" is this. It is by means of these concepts, by utilizing them as predicates in our judgments, by affirming or denying them of the subjects of these judgments,—in other words by identifying the objects of our concepts with the subjects of these judgments, and therefore ultimately with what is given to us in and through sense experience to interpret (or by separating those objects from these data in the negative judgment),—that we *interpret* what is given to us in and through sense experience, and thus attain to what we believe to be *knowledge of the real*. Now this implies not only that *the*

---

[1] *Cf.* JEANNIÈRE, *op. cit.*, p. 220, n. 2; p. 222, n. 1.

real is given to us in and through sense experience to interpret,[1] but also that the conceived objects whereby we accomplish this interpretation are also real. But are they? Or does not *conception* rather, perhaps, *mis*represent the real? Instead of revealing reality does not conception rather conceal it, cut it off from the possibility of our knowing it by casting between it and our minds a subjective or mental product which we erroneously believe to be real?[1] That is the question. It is known in the history of philosophy as the question of the significance or validity of " *Universals*," inasmuch as conceived objects are, as such, abstract and (potentially or actually) universal. Now what we believe to be the correct answer to the question is that which is known as the answer of *Moderate Realism, viz.* that our concepts represent what is given in and through sense perception; and that, inasmuch as sense perception also is a valid cognitive process, what is given in and through it *is real.*

The exposition and defence of Moderate Realism will involve some psychological analysis of the process of conception: for though the question of the *validity* of our universal concepts is distinct from that of their *origin* and mode of formation, still the two questions are practically inseparable: the conclusions we reach on the latter question must inevitably influence our views on the former.

There are some who hold that the *critical* question (*i.e.* of validity of concepts, etc.) should be kept quite distinct from, and be treated independently of, the *psychological* question (*i.e.* of their origin, formation, development, etc.). But such total separation and isolation of standpoints only leads to unreality in speculation. Moreover, the history of philosophy shows decisively that they have not been separated. For although philosophers have not always drawn the same inferences regarding the *validity* of intellectual thought from their conclusions regarding its *origin*, still they have never really treated the two questions in complete isolation from each other.

Maher, in his *Psychology*,[2] gives the following interesting " comparison of the evolutionist doctrine with other theories concerning the *origin* and *nature* of primary truths : A. The *Evolutionist* maintains (1) the existence of obscure innate ideas or cognitions, as (2) an *organic* inheritance, (3) from a *lower* form of life, (4) acquired by *sensuous* experience, during a vast period (5) and *therefore* of eminent validity within the field of possible experience : B. *Plato* upheld (1) innate ideas or cognitions, as (2) faint *spiritual* vestiges (3) of a *previous* life, of a *higher* grade, but (4) not derived from *sensuous* experience, and *therefore* of eminent validity : C. *Descartes* and *Leibniz* defended (1)

[1] Which will be established later, when we come to deal with sense perception.
[2] 4th edit., p. 286 n.

•

innate ideas or cognitions, as (2) *divinely* implanted in the mind (3) and *therefore* of eminent validity: D. *Kant* held (1) innate forms (2) antecedent to and conditioning *all* experience (3) and *therefore* subjectively *necessary* within the field of possible experience, but (4) of *no real* validity as applied to *things in themselves:* E. *Associationism* denies innate ideas of any form, and ascribes the *necessity* of these cognitions to the constant experience or the individual's own life.

73. THE PROCESS OF CONCEPTION ;[1] TERMS DEFINED.—By means of our sense faculties, internal and external, we are made aware of *individual things and events* of the material or sensible domain of experience; and of what are called the *sensible qualities* of matter. How this takes place will be examined later. Here we assume that the conscious states aroused in us by the operation of our external and internal senses, imagination, sense memory, sense consciousness, and sensuous association of concrete sense *data*, put us into real cognitive contact with real individual things and events of the material universe, including our own concrete conscious selves. Whatever is thus sensuously apprehended is characterized by concreteness, numerical individuality, spatial and temporal determinateness. On the other hand, whatever is apprehended by intellect, whatever is conceived, whatever is an object of thought, is characterized by its abstractness, by its isolation from the individualizing conditions of sensible existence, by its capacity for indefinite multiplication or realization in the domain of sense, by the fact that it is indefinitely *predicable* of individual sense data. As against Sensism and Nominalism, scholastic psychologists emphasize the opposition between the characters of the sense-percept and the imagination picture or *phantasma* on the one hand, and those of the intellectual concept or thought-object on the other ;[2] nor is there any need to labour the point here.[3] The question we have to consider is, how the intellect gets these abstract and universal thought-objects which we use as predicates of our judgments, and whereby we thus obtain *knowledge.* And it will make for clearness if at this stage we fix the meanings of the terms *conception, concept, universal.*

Conception is the name of a mental *process,* the process by

---

[1] For detailed treatment of this problem *cf.* MAHER, *Psychology,* chaps. xiii. and xiv.

[2] *Cf.* MAHER, *op. cit.,* chap. xii., pp. 235-8, 272-8 ; MERCIER, *Psychologie,* §§ 168-9 ; *Ontologie,* § 26 ; *Ontology,* § 14, pp. 79-82 ; PEILLAUBE, *Theorie des concepts,—passim.*

[3] *Cf. infra,* §§ 83, 84.

which we apprehend the thought-objects in question. Some-times, though rarely, it is used, as synonymous with *concept*, to signify the mental product, result, or term of this process. The process is of course always the individual process of an individual human mind, an individual mental event ; and as such of course it cannot be universal.[1]

The term *concept* needs more careful definition (with its looser synonyms, *notion, idea, thought*). By the process of conception there is produced in the individual intellect some mental result, product, modification, or term, which is of course as individual as the process itself. This psychic or mental modification in which the process terminates may be called a *concept* (or notion or idea or thought) ; and this is one meaning of the term *concept*,—what we may call its *subjective* meaning, or its meaning in and for psychology.

But by the process of conception and the effect wrought by this process in the intellect,—the *concept* in the sense just defined,— we have revealed to us, and apprehend or become aware of, an *object*, a thought-object or conceived object ; for conception is a *cognitive* process, and the resulting mental state or product, the concept, is a *means of cognition*. Now this *conceived object*, or *thought-object*, has also been called a *concept ;* and this is what we may describe as the *objective* meaning of the term, its meaning as a *cognitive* fact or factor, its meaning in and for epistemology. It recalls the etymology of the term,—"aliquid *conceptum*," "a *conceived* something," but the very application of the term to the conceived or apprehended or represented [2] object at once sug-gests inquiry as to the nature of this latter and its relation to the knowing subject on the one hand and to extramental reality on the other. The function and significance of this " object of awareness " (whether in conception or in perception) have yet to be investigated (20). In conception this thought-object or con-ceived object has sometimes been called the " *objective* concept " ("conceptus *objectivus*"), to distinguish it from the concept as psychic term or product of the conception process, the " *subjective* or *formal* concept " ("conceptus *subjectivus* seu *formalis*").

[1] When we think of the whole class of such mental processes or events, taking place in all men's minds, and give them a common class-name, *conception*, we are thinking of them as an abstract, universal thought-object.

[2] " Represented," not in the sense of pictured, but in the sense of *re*-presented, inasmuch as reality is " presented " in sense perception and imagination before it is apprehended by intellect.

The term *universal* (or *general*) is opposed to the term *individual* (or *singular*); and as applied to objects of cognition it means simply that which is "common to many," "applicable to many," "predicable of many". It is an adjective which, in reference to knowledge, is used very often as a substantive: as when we speak of "the significance of *universals*," "the validity of *universals*," "the controversy about *universals*". Obviously in such cases it is of the highest importance to be clear as to what the substantive is which is understood as qualified by the adjective "universal". This, in fact, it might be said, is in a certain sense the whole point in dispute in the "*universals* controversy"

There is of course no danger of misunderstanding when we use the terms *universal* and *singular* in reference to *language*. all are agreed that some logical terms (*e.g.* "Maynooth") are singular, and others (*e.g.* "college") universal or general. But we speak of the *concept* also, which is expressed by the general logical term, as *universal:* "universal concepts" is quite a familiar expression in philosophy. What does it mean? It does not mean that the concept as *product of the mental process* is universal: as an effect of the process of conception it is just as individual as this latter, or as the intellect in which it occurs. It is to the concept *in its objective meaning*, as revealing reality or representative of reality,—in other words, to the object immediately presented to the intellect through conception, to the immediate conscious term of our thought,—that we apply the adjective *universal*.[1] It is this mental object, this object of intellectual awareness, that we speak of as "a universal"; and the whole controversy about "universals," "universal ideas," or "universal concepts," is precisely about the nature and function and significance of these thought-objects in the process of intellectual cognition. Are they mere products of the knowing subject's cognitive activity, having no reference beyond themselves to the conscious data of sense or to (supposed) extramental realities? Are they themselves extramental realities apprehended by intellect through the process of conception? And if so, are they distinct and apart from the individual *data* which make up the domain revealed to us through our senses? Or do they constitute the reality of this domain? Is it *only* through the senses, or *only* through the intellect, or through *both alike*, that we get a genuine cognitive insight into reality as it is in

---

[1] And the same is true of the adjective *abstract*.

itself? These are some of the questions that have originated the
historic "controversy on universals".

Another important fact for the student to note is this, that
we have to deal with *all* universals, with all class notions alike,
with every single concept that can be used as a predicate in a
judgment; but that nevertheless a distinction can be drawn, as
regards their apprehension by the mind, between *complex* concepts,
formed by an intellectual synthesis of simpler compatible notes
or factors on the one hand, and these *simpler* and comparatively
unanalysable concepts,—including the root notions of all knowledge, the *ultimate categories* of thought and being,—on the other.
These latter are, of course, the more important from the point of
view of the validity of knowledge.

As we have already stated in various contexts (49, 60), the
process of elaborating complex concepts from simpler ones consists of a series of judgments whereby the factors are synthesized
as compatible, and judged, under the influence of objective
evidence, to constitute objectively possible or actually existing
realities.[1] If these factors themselves, these elementary thought-
objects, give us a genuine insight into the nature of reality, so
can the complexes formed from them. The former of these
theses will be established below (78), and the latter also independently (91).

74. ANALYSIS OF CONCEPTION. VARIOUS THEORIES. KANT
ON INTUITION.—We come now to the question of the manner
in which the intellect apprehends its objects in conception, particularly those widest thought-objects,—such as being, substance,
accident, quality, relation, quantity, unity, multitude, space, time,
change, action, causation, etc.,—which are the root-notions that
form the warp and woof of all our knowledge.[2] Influenced by
the profound differences between objects of thought and objects
of sense, many schools of philosophy, ancient and modern,—*e.g.*
Platonism, Cartesianism, Ontologism,—have espoused in one
form or other the theory of innate ideas, *i.e.* the view that some
at least of the objects of thought are apprehended by intellect
independently of sense perception and sense data: the intellect
would have a power of immediate intuition of such objects, these
objects themselves constituting the real extramental world (Plato),
or a world of mentally produced objects from which we would

---

[1] *Cf.* MAHER, *op. cit.*, pp. 294-303.   [2] *Cf.* MERCIER, *op. cit.*, § 131, p. 332.

infer the reality of the world of sense (Descartes), or finally the uncreated, divine exemplars according to which God has created the world of sense (Ontologism).

Now we believe that scholastic psychologists are right in rejecting such theories and maintaining that the intellect gets *all* its thought-objects by the operation of its own native power of abstraction on the data yielded by external and internal sense perception, combined with its power of observing its own cognitive activities. It is indeed quite true that *all* thought-objects as such are at least *negatively* immaterial or suprasensible in the sense of being abstract and potentially or actually universal; and it is true, moreover, that some of them are *positively* suprasensible in the sense that from their very nature, as apprehended by intellect, they are understood to have modes of existence transcending those of sense data (71). But even these latter thought-objects, —*e.g.* God, spirit, thought, volition, personality, freedom, responsibility, justice, and ethical concepts or thought-objects generally, —can be apprehended by intellect contemplating and reasoning from the data of sense-consciousness and introspection. That such thought-objects are not innate, that the intellect has not a direct intuition of suprasensible realities independently of the perception and imagination of individual sense data, is proved by scholastic psychologists against Platonism and Ontologism from a variety of considerations.[1] Of these we may mention two: (1) Thought, although not exercised through a bodily organ, is nevertheless dependent on the sense organs and the brain,—not intrinsically and subjectively, as if functioning by means of them like sense, but extrinsically and objectively, inasmuch as if any sense faculty (*e.g.* sight) is absent (as in those born blind) the individual can have no concepts or ideas of the corresponding domain of objects (*e.g.* colours): which shows that thought derives its objects from the data of sense.[2] (2) Thought, even when exercised on positively suprasensible objects, is always accompanied by sense-imagery; and the significance of this fact, as pointing to the sense origin of all our thought-objects, cannot be explained on any theory of innatism. There is an element of sense intuition even in our most spiritual thought-objects. Hence it is that the insight we get into a suprasensible domain of reality through such thought-objects does not give

---

[1] *Cf.* MAHER, *op. cit.*, pp. 253-5; 239-42.
[2] *Cf.* JEANNIÈRE, *op. cit.*, pp. 219-20.

us a proper and positive, but only an improper and analogical knowledge of the nature of such realities : before such thought. objects can be predicated of suprasensible realities they must be stripped of the limitations with which they are characterized in the data of sense ("*via negationis*"), and then affirmed of those suprasensible realities ("*via affirmationis*") as belonging to them in a higher manner into which the human intellect has no positive insight ("*via eminentiae*").

Nevertheless such knowledge is genuine, and faithful as far as it goes, though it is imperfect and inadequate. Kant is very insistent in emphasizing the view that of such (suprasensible) objects of thought we can have no genuine *knowledge :* because, as he contends, we can have knowledge only of objects of which we have *intuition*, but sense is our only faculty of intuition, and therefore we can *know* only such thought-objects as the intellect or understanding constructs by synthesizing its own *a priori* forms with elements of sense intuition : in thinking such objects as the Absolute or Unconditioned, the Soul, Freedom, Spirituality, Immortality, etc., the intellect has no element of sense intuition corresponding to the *a priori* forms it is attempting to use, and therefore it cannot *know* whether these objects are real or unreal, though it is forced to think them. In an important passage already quoted,[1] he says that there is only one mode of knowledge that reaches its object directly, in which " the object is given," and this one mode is sensibility : " Sensibility alone supplies us with intuitions. These intuitions become thought through the understanding and hence arise conceptions." If this meant that all objects of thought are apprehended by intellect in and through the data of sense-consciousness and introspection, no scholastic would take exception to it ; but we know how Kant has wrested the term *object* from its ordinary and obvious meaning, and how he regards all " objects " both of thought and of sense as partially constructed by *a priori* mental factors or forms. So, too, when he says " All thought therefore must, directly or indirectly, go back to intuitions, *i.e.* to our sensibility, because in no other way can objects be given to us," his language is in agreement with that of scholasticism. But if intuition, or intuitive cognition, is that in which the object is directly given to the cognitive faculty, may it not be the case that in intellectual conception the thought-object is given directly to the intellect in

---

[1] *Critique* (*Transcendental Esthetic*), pp. 15-17 : *supra*, § 51.

and through and with the object given to sense? If sense and intellect are faculties of the same individual mind, and if sense gets its objects intuitively under the influence of extramental reality, as Kant himself admits, may not intellect simultaneously apprehend *its* objects, after its own manner, having them presented to it through the channels of sense and in the very objects which sense apprehends after *its* peculiar and appropriate manner? This we believe to be the true alternative account of conception. It is an intellectual process of intuition,[1]—*abstractive* intuition whereby intellect apprehends in the abstract, and consequently as universal, objects which are given to sense as concrete and individual.

75. SCHOLASTIC THEORY OF ABSTRACTION.—In tracing the transition from sense to intellect, and the relations between the respective objects of sense and intellect, it is well to distinguish between facts and theory. The facts are revealed by introspection, and the most important among them are the following. By the operation of the external and internal senses, and by our consciousness of these cognitive activities, we are made aware of concrete, individual data or objects or phenomena,—things, events, sense feelings, sensible qualities, etc.—a conscious stream or manifold of impressions. Each of these we apprehend intellectually as an abstract thought-object, as an isolated aspect of the sense-manifold, and thus we gradually come into possession of a stock of abstract and universal concepts or thought-objects whereby we *interpret* the individual data of sense and acquire *knowledge* of what we believe to be the real universe or totality of things.

So much for the facts. Now inasmuch as these thought-objects are not innate, inasmuch as we identify them in judgment with the individual data of sense, it follows that the intellect must somehow apprehend them in the data of sense and as constituting the intelligible natures or essences of these latter. When, therefore, sense perceives its data in the concrete, intellect must simultaneously exercise a power of apprehending them in the abstract. So much at least is clear,—whatever account we may be able to

---

[1] Complex concepts are, as we have seen, elaborated by a series of *judgments*. The object apprehended by intellect in the act of judgment is always a *relation*. The self-evident judgments, or axioms, in which the relation is apprehended immediately and without the aid of other judgments, is also described as *intuitive*, to distinguish it from the judgment which is reached through the aid of other judgments and which is described as *mediate* or *discursive*.

give of the actual operation of this faculty of abstraction. Maher says that according to "some able scholastic psychologists . . . the operation is incapable of further analysis. Consciousness assures us that the intellect lays hold of the abstract and universal aspect in the concrete sensible phenomenon ; but we cannot penetrate beyond this ultimate fact." [1]

The schoolmen called this *abstractive faculty* of intellect the *Intellectus Agens,*—the νοῦς ποιητικός,—after Aristotle,—and endeavoured by an introspective analysis of the whole process of conception to trace the transition to the latter from the concrete individual percepts or imagination images of sense consciousness. The Averroïstic interpretation of Aristotle's teaching transformed the theory into a metaphysical doctrine known as monopsychism : the monistic view that individual human minds are participations of one single Intelligence common to all men. Moreover, certain scholastics seem to have identified the *Intellectus Agens* with the Divine Mind, or with a Supernatural Illumination of individual human minds by the Divine Mind in the act of intellectual cognition ; and much mystic writing of an ontologist tendency grew up around the theory during the Middle Ages. But apart from such exaggerations the theory itself is purely psychological and keeps close to all the facts revealed by introspection. Its main points are as follows :—

Intellect, like sense, is a passive faculty inasmuch as it is not always in act, not always consciously operating. It has therefore to be reduced from potentiality to actual operation by some appropriate motive force or stimulus. This actualization takes place simultaneously with the exercise of sense cognition. This latter results in the sense apprehension or sense awareness of some concrete individual sense *datum*. This *datum*, present to sense consciousness through the percept or *phantasma*, is, however, sensible, organic, material. Of itself it is incapable of determining the intellect to *its* appropriate operation ; for the intellect is a spiritual faculty, belonging to a higher domain than that of sense, and its operation is therefore an effect which transcends the causal influence of anything in the domain of sense. There must be, therefore, in the intellect itself a power of determining itself, on the occasion of actual sense cognition, to its own appropriate mode of cognition. By virtue of this abstractive faculty,

---

[1] *Op. cit.*, p. 304, where the author quotes HAGEMAN, PIAT, and MENDIVE as expressing this view.

or *intellectus agens*, there is produced in the understanding or *intellectus possibilis*,—*i.e.* in the intellect considered in its state of potentiality,—an appropriate *cognitional determinant*, a *species intelligibilis impressa*, an immaterial or spiritual modification whereby the understanding conceives or apprehends immaterially and in the abstract,—through an appropriate intellectual act or process and its product or term, the *species intelligibilis expressa*, or *verbum mentale*,—that which was given in sense consciousness in its concrete, numerical, space-and-time individuality. If it be asked why this abstractive operation takes place on the occasion of sense cognition, and why, being itself natural, instinctive, and blind, so to speak, it always issues in an activity which is specifically appropriate to that of sense, *i.e.* in an abstract concept of the individual *datum* actually present to sense, the answer is simply that sense and intellect are rooted in one and the same individual soul or mind, "which is so constituted that on the stimulation of the former the latter responds by a higher reaction of its own—somewhat as the appetitive faculty, which conceived as such is blind, tends towards an object apprehended by a cognitive faculty as good. In both cases it is the soul itself which acts through the faculty."[1]

Thus, then, for the conscious intellectual conception of any thought-object there is required the co-operation of a twofold cause or principle : on the one hand the presence in sense consciousness of an individual, concrete sense *datum* or *phantasma*, and on the other hand the abstractive power, on the part of the intellect, so to modify or determine itself by the *species intelligibilis impressa* that it apprehends in this individual *datum*, by means of the product or term of conception (the *verbum mentale*), the abstract thought-object which expresses more or less inadequately the essence or intelligible reality of the individual sense *datum*. We assume here that the sense *datum* makes us directly aware of *reality*.[2] And the mental product of conception, the *species intelligibilis expressa* or *verbum mentale* is the *medium* or *means* whereby we are made *intellectually* aware of the *thought*-object which is potentially in the sense datum, constituting the *reality* revealed to sense consciousness in this latter.

Intellectual cognition is an interpretation of reality by means of abstract thought-objects used as predicates in judgment.

[1] MAHER, *op. cit.*, p. 309.
[2] The validity of sense perception will be established later.

Reality is given through sense-data, and in these the intellect apprehends its abstract thought-objects. This does not imply that all intellectually knowable reality is merely material or sensible ; for, as we pointed out above (71, 74), intellect appre-hends, in the sense-data, modes of reality that transcend sense, and can infer from sense-data the actuality or actual existence of positively suprasensible or spiritual modes of reality. But it does imply that the concepts or thought-objects by which our intellect apprehends such suprasensible realities, being abstracted from sense-data and being primarily and properly representative of such data, do not represent suprasensible realities intuitively, ade-quately, and positively, but only analogically and inadequately.

Furthermore, the mental product of the conception process, the *verbum mentale*, the entire *intellectual* modification whereby the intellect is cognitively assimilated to the reality, *is not itself the object of which the intellect becomes aware*—just as we shall see later that the *species sensibilis expressa* is not the object of which sense becomes aware. It is that which gives the reality an *esse ideale*, which constitutes the reality present to intellect (20, 21).

What the intellect consciously apprehends, in and through the *verbum mentale*, is the object of the concept, the thought-object. If this thought-object be itself called the *verbum mentale*, this latter term is being used in its objective sense, synonymously with the objective sense of the term *concept* (73).

Now it would seem that what is made immediately present to intellect in conception must be *either* the mental modification itself (from which a real extramental object would be somehow inferred—by a process which, according to Kant and others, could never reveal to us this extramental object as it really is) ; *or* else the reality itself which has its real being outside[1] the mind, or independently of cognition, but is made present to the mind through the mental modification ; *or* else a mentally constructed object whose ultimate constituent factors are reproductions or representations of extramental reality, and in which construction, therefore, the intellect sees, or can see, without any pro-perly inferential process, this latter reality.[2] These alternatives appear to be exhaustive. All scholastics reject the first alternative as leading inevitably to subjectivism and agnosticism.[3] Those scholastics who adopt the third alter-

[1] As we have noted already, such terms as " outside," used in reference to intellectual cognition, have no local or spatial signification.

[2] Bearing in mind that intellect derives its objects from the domain of sense cognition, the alternatives in the text, and the subsequent observations, apply equally to sense cognition. *Cf. infra*, §§ 106, 107, 112.

[3] The assumption that in the act of cognition, whether sensuous or intellectual, what the mind immediately apprehends is only a phase or modification of itself, is

native rather than the second, would point out that, in opposition to the first alternative, it safeguards the objective validity of intellectual knowledge inasmuch as the thought-object constructed by, and present to, the intellect, is constructed by the latter *under the influence of the external reality*, is a mental reproduction of this reality, specifically and essentially so determined by the reality that it necessarily represents, and puts us into immediate intellectual contact with, the reality.[1]   And they prefer it to the second alternative because the object present to intellect is an absolute essence in the abstract, while the reality is individual and concrete : " In that mode of human intellectual cognition called *simple apprehension* [or conception], the object *present* is not identically *the thing which is* [or *exists*, *i.e.* the extramental or thought-independent reality].   The *thing which is* is singular ; the object present is an abstract nature in the absolute." [2]   But if this argument is intended to prove

at the basis not only of modern subjectivism but of the earlier forms of Grecian scepticism recorded and criticized by Aristotle. St. Thomas clearly saw this and often anticipated the assumptions of modern subjectivism by criticisms of which the following passage from the *Summa Theologica* (I., Q. lxxxv., a. 2) is typical : " Quidam posuerunt quod vires quae sunt in nobis cognoscitivae nihil cognoscunt, nisi *proprias passiones*, puta, quod sensus non sentit nisi passionem sui organi, et secundum hoc intellectus nihil intelligit, nisi suam passionem, scilicet, speciem intelligibilem in se receptam : et secundum hoc species hujusmodi est *ipsum quod intelligitur*. Sed haec opinio manifeste apparet falsa ex *duobus*. Primo quidem, quia eadem sunt, quae intelligimus, et de quibus sunt scientiae : si igitur ea, quae intelligimus, essent solum species, quae sunt in anima, sequeretur quod scientiae omnes non essent de rebus, quae sunt extra animam, sed solum de speciebus intelligibilibus, quae sunt in anima. . . . *Secundo*, quia sequeretur error antiquorum dicentium, omne quod videtur, esse verum ; et sic quod contradictoriae essent simul verae : si enim potentia non cognoscit nisi propriam passionem, de ea solum judicat . . puta, si gustus non sentit nisi propriam passionem, cum aliquis habens sanum gustum judicat, mel esse dulce, vere judicabit ; et similiter si ille, qui habet gustum infectum, judicet, mel esse amarum, vere judicabit : uterque enim judicabit secundum quod gustus ejus afficitur. . . . Et ideo dicendum est quod species intelligibilis se habet ad intellectum *ut quo* intelligit intellectus. . . . Sed quia intellectus supra seipsum reflectitur, secundum eandem reflexionem intelligit et suum intelligere, et speciem qua intelligit. Et sic species intellecta *secundario* est *id quod* intelligitur. Sed *id quod* intelligitur *primo* est *res* cujus species intelligibilis est similitudo."
[1] *Cf.* MAHER, *op. cit.*, pp. 51-4 ; 309-10.
[2] JEANNIÈRE, *Criteriologia*, p. 223 n. ; where he proceeds to quote with approval the following observation made by ROUSSELOT in his very acute and suggestive study, *L'Intellectualisme de S. Thomas* [p. xvii—after defining cognition as an "apprehension " or " taking possession " ("*captation* ") of being or reality] : " It is not necessary that this [apprehension] be immediate, that is, that the reality known by me be identically the idea [in the objective sense, the thought-object] which I have of it.   This indeed would be the highest ideal of intellectual apprehension of Reality : in the view of St. Thomas we attain to it only in two cases : in the intuitions of the actual *Ego* by its own self, and in the beatific vision."   Yet in regard to the former St. Anselm represents it as taking place through an image or representation of the self in the self : " Nulla ratione negari potest, cum mens rationalis se ipsam cogitando intelligit, imaginem ipsius nasci in sua cognitione ; imo ipsam cognitionem sui esse suam imaginem ad sui similitudinem, tanquam ex ejus impressione formatam " (*Monologium*, c. 33).   True, this may mean only that by the whole cognition process the mind is assimilated to the known reality.   At all events in all cases, not excluding that of self-cognition, the reality must become present as object to the knowing

that the entity which is present to the intellect as a thought-object, which has a mental presence or *esse ideale* there, is *really other* than the entity which has an *esse reale*, or a reality independent of thought, that the former entity is not really identical with, but is of course faithfully if inadequately repre. sentative of, the latter,—the argument does not seem to us to be con. clusive. For, as we shall see below (§ 76), the same reality which has or can have its mode of real being as a manifold of existing individuals *in rerum natura*, and independently of cognition, can be made present to intellect by the process of conception and the consequent psychic product or modification called the *species intentionalis*, or *verbum mentale*, or *esse ideale*. It is only this *mode of presence*, this *esse ideale* itself, or, in other words, the *abstractness* and *universality*, in which the reality is grasped by intellect,—it is this whole mental mode, and it alone, and not the *datum* which is endowed with it, that can properly be described as an "intellectual construction,"[1] a logical entity or *ens rationis*. Hence we prefer to hold to the second alternative given above : that the thought-object of which the intellect becomes directly aware in conception, the *concept* or *verbum mentale* in the objective sense (73),—which becomes immediately present to the intellect through the mental modification, through the concept or *verbum mentale* in the subjective or psychological sense,—is identically the real entity which has its own real mode of being or *esse reale* independently of cognition. Nor do we think that the scholastics who prefer to express their view in the language of the third alternative really mean that the object which the intellect consciously appre- hends in conception, and which is consciously present to intellect, is really other than the extramental reality : they certainly repudiate the view that what intellectual cognition apprehends is merely the mental state ; and when they describe the *verbum mentale* as "mirroring" or "representing" reality, or as that "in which" reality is "mirrored,"[2] they mean by the *verbum mentale* the mental process or state or product, and not something which is itself immediately apprehended as an object, and recognized as an image of something beyond itself, something extramentally real. The relation of the mind to the extramental reality in cognition will come up again for fuller con- sideration in connexion with sense perception.

• If the thought-objects apprehended by the intellect in and through its concepts, turn out to be real, to be aspects of reality, it would appear at first sight that, according to the theory of con- ception just outlined, reality is so directly revealed to the intellect

subject. *Cf. supra*, §§ 8, 20. No doubt, the individual physical reality, existing in external nature, cannot, in its physical reality, its *esse reale*, be *in* the mind ; but in this *esse reale* it can be *present to* the mind : it can be the object of which the mind is immediately aware—by means of the *species expressa* or *verbum mentale* con- sidered not as object of awareness but as a mental modification assimilating the mind to the object of awareness. *Cf. supra*, § 20, p. 79 n.

[1] *Cf.* MAHER, *op. cit.*, p. 250.

[2] Some of them describe the *verbum mentale* (metaphorically of course : in all such descriptions, applied to intellect, the concepts and terms are used analogically) as a *perfect* mirror, noting at the same time that a perfect mirror *would be itself invisible*.

as to preclude the possibility of error (22). But the possibility of error is really quite consistent with the direct and immediate revelation of abstract aspects of reality to intellect in conception. For it is only in judgments that error can occur. Now all judgments are either judgments of existence or judgments of essence: they either affirm or deny the actual existence or happening of some thought-object, or else affirm or deny the real and intrinsic possibility of some thought-object. Judgments of the former class can clearly be erroneous even though the apprehended thought-object be real, for though real it need not be actually existent. It is by series of judgments of the latter class that we form complex concepts, and here too the judgment may be erroneous; for the synthesis or complex judged to be intrinsically possible need not be really so, even though each of the simpler conceptual factors or thought-objects composing it may be itself possible.[1] Only in regard to the most elementary, axiomatic syntheses is the intellect infallible (67). But furthermore, and finally, our conception of the simplest, unanalysable thought-objects, even although it is invariably accompanied by the implicit judgment that these objects are real, cannot be said to be itself, and apart from this judgment, true or false. Conception and concepts may have *real objectivity*, inasmuch as the conceived object is—as we hope to show presently—real; but it is only the interpretation of these concepts that sets up between the mind and reality the relation we call truth or error (22).

76. REALITY OF OBJECTS OF CONCEPTION : MODERATE REALISM EXPLAINED.—The thought-object is, as we have seen, abstract. That is to say, it is devoid of all the time-and-space conditions and limitations which individuate the sense-object and make the latter a numerically singular or individual, concrete and incommunicable, datum of experience. That which is apprehended by sense in the individualizing conditions which we describe as "material" or "sensible" is apprehended by intellect in abstraction from these conditions,—in a state which, therefore, characterizes the object as "immaterial" (negatively) or "intelligible".

The *reason* of this is that the material reality, given in sense consciousness, must, in order to be apprehended by the intellect, be made present to the intellect,[2] and must, as thus present to the

---

[1] *Cf. Ontology*, § 15.
[2] *Cf.* St. Thomas, *Cont. Gentes*, L. IV., c. xi.: "Omne intellectum inquantum intellectum oportet esse in intelligente: significat enim ipsum intelligere ap-

intellect, be conformed to the *immaterial* or *spiritual* mode of
being of the intellect : according to the principle that whatever is
thus in, or present to, a knowing subject must assume the mode
of being of this latter, cognition being a sort of mental reproduc_
tion, in the knowing subject, of the known object.[1]

The *consequences* of this abstract character of the thought_
object are very important. The first of them is that, when it
is regarded in itself and as to its positive content, it is *neither
singular nor universal*, it is apprehended neither as *numerically
one, individualized, incommunicable* (as it is grasped by sense), nor
on the other hand as conceptually one but *common to many,
predicable of many* (as it is grasped by a subsequent reflective act
of the intellect formally universalizing it). A realization of this
fact is of the first importance towards a right solution of the
" Universals " problem. The beginner may find some difficulty
in realizing it. He will probably be puzzled by the reflection
that whatever is real must be either one or manifold, either singu_
lar or universal. But he can meet the difficulty by distinguishing
between what can *be* and what can *be thought*. Whatever about
the singularity or universality of being *as it really is,*—about
which more hereafter,—it is a simple fact of introspection that
being *as an object of thought* can abstract from both these characters.

"If you ask," says St. Thomas, "whether that nature (*humanity*, or
human nature considered in the absolute or abstract) can be characterized as
one, or as many, I answer that *it cannot be described as either* one or many,
because each of these attributes lies outside the concept of humanity, and
either can happen to be verified of it. For if plurality were essential to it, it
could never be singular, whereas it is singular as found, for example, in
Socrates. And similarly if unity were essential to it as conceived by the intellect then it would be numerically one and the same nature in Socrates

prehensionem ejus, quod intelligitur, per intellectum ". This is the application to
intellectual cognition, of the wider principle that *all* cognition implies the presence
of the known object to the knowing subject, and the consequent assimilation of the
latter to the former : " Omnis cognitio fit secundum similitudinem cogniti in cognoscente ".—*Ibid.*, L. II., c. lxxvii.

[1] " Cognitum est in cognoscente secundum modum cognoscentis, vel, Receptum
est in recipiente per modum recipientis."—St. Thomas, *Summa Theol.*, I., Q. 84, a.
7 (*apud* Kleutgen, *Phil. der Vorzeit.*, § 26, n. 1). *Cf. De Veritate*, Q. X., a. 4 :
" Modus cognoscendi rem aliquam est secundum conditionem cognoscentis, in quo
forma recipitur secundum modum ejus ". The relation of this *esse mentale*, or mental
presence, of the known object, to the *esse reale* or real being of the latter will be investigated presently.

and Plato, for example, and could not be multiplied in a multiplicity of individuals."[1]

And such a modern and non-scholastic writer as the late Professor James here adds his testimony to that of the prince of mediæval scholastics :—

"The conception [2] of an abstract quality is, taken by itself, neither universal nor particular. If I abstract *white* from the rest of a wintry landscape this morning, it is a perfectly definite conception, a self-identical quality which I may mean again ; but as I have not yet individualized it by expressly meaning to restrict it to this particular snow, nor thought of the possibility of other things to which it may be applicable, it is so far but a floating adjective."[3]

No doubt, being a definite object of thought, and having a definite content or meaning whereby it can be consciously distinguished from other abstract thought-objects, it may be said to have a conceptual or formal unity ;[4] but in its abstract, absolute condition, and as yet not consciously related by the intellect to the individual object or objects of sense, from which it was abstracted, or made an object of reflex intellectual contemplation, it can be truly said to be neither singular nor universal.

Now the thought-object, considered in this abstract condition as object of direct intellectual conception, has been called by scholastics the *direct*, or *metaphysical*, or *fundamental*, or *potential* "universal"[5] And when they say that "universals" are "fundamentally" in things or reality,—"*Universale est \ . . fundamentaliter in re*,"—they mean that it is this abstract thought-object which, as to its content, is *real*, or *in things independently of our thought*.

[1] "Si quaeratur utrum ista natura (natura *humana* considerata modo absoluto ut abstracta) possit dici una vel plures, *neutrum concedendum est*, quia utrumque est extra conceptum humanitatis et utrumque potest sibi (humanitati) accidere. Si enim pluralitas esset de ratione ejus nunquam posset esse una, quum tamen una sit secundum quod est in Socrates. Similiter si unitas esset de intellectu et ratione ejus, tunc esset una et eadem natura Socratis et Platonis, nec posset in pluribus plurificari."—*De Ente et Essentia*, c. iv.

[2] *I.e.* "concept" or "thought-object". *Cf. supra*, § 73.

[3] JAMES, *Psychology*, i., p. 473—*apud* MAHER, *op. cit.*, p. 294, n. 3.

[4] *Cf. infra*, § 81.

[5] The *species intelligibilis expressa*, or *verbum mentale*, "considered as the intellectual expression of the essence of the object abstracted from the individualizing notes which accompany it in the physical world is called the *direct*, or *potential* universal. It is not as yet an *actual* or *formal* universal concept. It prescinds alike from universality and individuality. It merely expresses in an indeterminate manner the essence of the object, omitting all individualizing conditions."—MAHER, *op. cit.*, p. 310,

The next important consequence of this abstract character of the object of conception is that, precisely because it is apprehended by intellect in the abstract, it is seen, by comparison with the corresponding individual sense-object (percept or imagination phantasm) which is simultaneously present in consciousness, to be not only in this latter object, and identical with it, and predicable of it, but *to be capable of indefinitely repeated realizations* in an indefinite multitude of other and similar sense-objects. By this act of intellectual reflection the object is apprehended to be potentially or actually "*common to many*," "predicable of many"; in other words it is *formally universalized.* When thus apprehended as susceptible of indefinite multiplication or realization in the domain of sense, the thought-object is called a *reflex*, or *logical*, or *formal* universal. And when scholastics say that "universals" are "formally" in the mind,—"*Universale est formaliter in mente,*"—they mean that the object of thought or conception considered *as a universal,*—*i.e.* as something common or communicable to, and realizable in, and predicable of, many things,—is only in the mind, and is, as such, not independent of thought. In other words, it is *because* the object is a *thought*-object, *or* in virtue of its being present to intellect, *or* by reason of the *esse ideale* or mode in which it is present to, and apprehended by intellect, *or* on account of the *immateriality* of the presence it has in the intellect, and not otherwise, *that it is a universal.* As it really exists in any individual *datum* of sense, as it is apprehended through the percept or phantasm, it is individualized, singular, incommunicable; only as it is apprehended in the abstract by the intellect, and in that "immaterial" or "intelligible" condition seen by a reflex act of thought to be susceptible of indefinitely manifold realizations, is it "common to many things," or "formally universal".

Here, too, St. Thomas excels in the clearness with which he formulates the scholastic teaching of Moderate Realism. Of *humanity* or *human nature*, considered as an object of thought or conception, he says: "Human nature is *one* or *common* not *in reality* but only *under the consideration of the mind*" [1]

What we may call the content or connotation of the concept is real, is in extramental reality; but it is not real in the manner in which it is conceived, *i.e.* as a universal; for as a universal it

---

[1] " Unitas sive communitas humanae naturae non est secundum rem sed solum secundum considerationem."—*Summa Theol.*, i. Q. 39, a. 3.

cannot be extramental, it can only be a *thought*-object. "Universals considered formally as universals are only in the mind. But the natures themselves, which are thus universalized by the thought process, are extramentally real." [1]

The content or object of the concept is itself extramentally real—in the individual realities apprehended through sense. The universality which characterizes it as a thought-object is, however, no part or mode of its extramental reality, but is only a mode of its apprehension by intellect, a mental mode, a logical entity whose sole objectivity is that which it has for reflex thought. "The nature itself which is apprehended by intellect, which is abstracted and universalized, has its real being in the individual things [of sense]. But its actual presence to and apprehension by intellect, its abstractness and universality, are in the intellect. . . . The humanity which is apprehended as an object of thought by intellect is to be found really only in this or that individual man; but the apprehension of humanity without its individualizing conditions, its being subjected to abstraction and universalization,—all this belongs to humanity only inasmuch as it is perceived by intellect." [2]

On the one hand, then, as against Conceptualism, we attain, through conception, to an object which is real; on the other hand, however, as against Extreme Realism, this object is not real *as a universal*, as something formally "common to many". "Humanity is something *in the real order*, but in the real order it is not *a universal*, inasmuch as outside the mind (or, in other words, independently of thought) there is no such thing as *a humanity 'common to many'*; it is on becoming present to intellect, as a thought-object, that it receives, through the conception process, a mode or 'intention' whereby it is constituted a universal, or class-concept." [3]

---

[1] "Universalia secundum quod sunt universalia non sunt nisi in anima. Ipsae autem naturae, quibus accidit intentio universalitatis, sunt in rebus."—St. Thomas, *De Anima*, L. II., *l.c.*

[2] "Ipsa natura cui accidit intelligi, vel abstrahi, vel intentio universalitatis, non est nisi in singularibus. Sed hoc ipsum quod est intelligi vel abstrahi vel intentio universalitatis, est in intellectu. . . . Humanitas quae intelligitur non est nisi in hoc vel illo homine; sed quod humanitas apprehendatur sine individualibus conditionibus, quod est 'ipsum abstrahi,' ad quod sequitur intentio universalitatis, accidit humanitati secundum quod percipitur ab intellectu."—*Summa Theol.*, I., Q, 85, a. 2, ad 2.

[3] "Humanitas . . . est aliquid *in re*, non tamen ibi habet rationem *universalis* quum non sit extra animam aliqua humanitas *multis communis;* sed secundum quod

A clear apprehension of the fact that the abstract *thought-object* considered in the absolute, as a "fundamental" or "metaphysical" universal, is as such not yet judged to be "one-common-to-many" or "formally universal," or on the other hand to be "numerically manifold" in distinct individuals,—is absolutely essential to a right solution of the "universals" problem ; for it is the universal considered thus in the absolute that forms the rational connecting link between the "formal universal" of intellect and the "individuals" of sense, and thus solves the apparent antinomy which emerges from a comparison of intellectual cognition with sense cognition.

It is this apparent contradiction between the "universal" character of thought-objects and the "individual" character of sense-objects,—which makes it so difficult to determine which set of objects *are real* and which mode of cognition valid,—that has led to the formulation of so many different solutions of the problem,[1] and in modern philosophy especially to Kant's ambitious theory of phenomenalistic conceptualism. If the objects of sense are individual, manifold, and each individually incommunicable, and if the objects of thought are universal, if they are each one-in-many, and each communicable to many, how can the latter be identified with, and predicated (in judgment) of, the former ? Is not such an identification self-contradictory, and must we not rather opt for the validity of either mode of cognition only, at the expense of the other ?[2]

The answer is that we must uphold the validity of *both* modes and justify the judgment-process whereby we identify the universal with the individual in (affirmative) predication. And we can do so because—while it is one and the same real object which is manifold and individuated as it exists *in rerum natura* and as apprehended by sense, and which is one and universal as abstracted by intellect from the data of sense, and compared with these latter—this same object can be apprehended, and is apprehended by intellect, as to its real content, in an absolute condition in which it is neither judged to be universal on the one hand nor individual on the other.

accipitur in intellectu, adjungitur ei per operationem intellectus intentio secundum quam dicitur *species*."—I., Dist. 19, a. 5, ad 1.

[1] *Cf.* MERCIER, *op. cit.*, § 135, p. 346.

[2] *Cf.* MERCIER, *op. cit.*, § 133, p. 337 ; § 135, p. 346.

" There is," says St. Thomas, " a threefold way of considering any nature :
it may be envisaged in the mode of being which it has in individuals, as *e.g.*
the nature of a stone in the being which it has in this and that individual
stone ; again, it may be regarded in the mode of being which it has as an intelligible object, *e.g.* the nature of stone as conceived by the intellect. But
there is a third and absolute way of apprehending the nature, *viz.* without
taking into account either of the former modes of its being ; and considered
in this absolute condition the nature of a stone, or of any other thing, presents
to intellect merely whatever [notes or factors] are essential to such a nature." [1]

Now when we predicate the universal of the singular, in judgment, it is the absolute content of the universal concept and not
its universal mode, or, in other words, the metaphysical universal
and not the formal universal, that we so predicate. And we are
justified in doing so.

On the one hand, the content of the universal concept—*i.e.* the
fundamental or metaphysical universal, the universale *in se*—is
not *other* than its individual realizations in the manifold singular
subjects of which it is predicated. The absolute nature or object
signified by " man " is really in this, that, and the other individual
man, in John and James and Thomas, etc. It is really in them,

[1] " Triplex est consideratio alicujus naturae: una prout consideratur secundum
esse quod habet in singularibus, sicut natura lapidis in hoc lapide et in illo lapide
[how this apprehension can be *intellectual* as well as sensible, will be considered in
the following section, § 77] ; alia vero est consideratio alicujus naturae secundum
esse suum intelligibile, sicut natura lapidis consideratur, prout est in intellectu.
Tertio vero est consideratio naturae absoluta, prout abstrahit ab utroque esse, secundum quam considerationem consideratur natura lapidis vel cujuscumque alterius,
quantum ad ea tantum, quae per se competunt tali naturae."—ST. THOMAS, *Quod-
libeta,* Q. I., a. I. The universal considered in the first of those ways has been
called the " universale *in re*," *i.e.* as multiplied and individuated in actually existing
things *in rerum natura*. Considered in the second way, it has been called the " universale *in mente*," *i.e.* as a formally universalized object of human thought, as " one-
common-to-many ". Considered in the third way, it has been called the " universale
in se," *i.e.* the nature or object considered absolutely as to its real content, as to
what essentially constitutes it. The first has likewise been called the " universale
in essendo," *i.e.* in its actually existing reality as a manifold of individuals ; and the
second the " universale *in repraesentando*," *i.e.* as a universal *thought*-object representing to intellect the reality of those individuals. *Cf.* JEANNIÈRE, *op. cit.*, pp.
485-9. And since in the scholastic philosophy of Theism we must consider the
creation of things as guided, after the analogy of intelligent human production, by
ideal archetypes, *ideae exemplares*, in the Divine Mind, and these as *causae exemplares* of created things, such Divine patterns have been described by scholastics as
" universalia *in causando* ". Their consideration is connected with *Ontologism*.
Cf. supra, § 70; *infra*, § 80. Finally, the latter have been called " universalia *ante
rem,* vel *ante res*," *i.e.* in the Divine Mind, ontologically antecedent to created
things; while the real natures of the latter have been called " universalia *in re*, vel
in rebus "; and the formal universal as an object of thought in the human mind
(universale *in repraesentando*) has also been called the " universale *post rem*," *i.e.*
subsequent to, and abstracted by intellect from, actually existing things.

but, of course, with this difference in each, that it has in each *in_dividualizing characteristics* which are not included in it as it is when considered *in itself*, in its abstract condition as an object of thought, apart from the singulars of which it is predicated. In any individual man there are individualizing notes that are not in the abstract thought-object " man "; but there is nothing in the latter that is not in the former. The content of the abstract concept gives, therefore, an insight into the individual, which is *inadequate*, no doubt, but *faithful* as far as it goes. If it be a transcendental or generic concept of the individual it gives a comparatively shallow and superficial insight into the reality of the latter; and even if it be a *specific* concept, a concept of the *species infima* of the individual, it is still inadequate inasmuch as it abstracts from what makes up the individuality or *essentia atoma* of the individual.[1] But, so far as it goes, the content of the abstract concept, the metaphysical universal, reveals *what is really in* the individuals of sense. But the formally universal concept has precisely the same content as the abstract concept, *viz.* the thought-object considered *quoad rem*, fundamentally, absolutely, or in itself. The universal concept is, therefore, *objectively real.*

On the other hand, the *formal universality* of this abstract thought-object adds *nothing real* to its content, but only a logical relation, an *intentio logica* or *ens rationis ;* for what transforms the abstract thought-object or metaphysical universal into a formal universal is the relation of universality, or " communicability to many," or identity *quoad rem* with its manifold individual realizations,—a logical relation which the intellect superadds to it by a reflective act comparing it as it is in itself with its actual and possible concrete individual embodiments.[2] Therefore this act of reflective comparison whereby the thought-object is made formally universal does not in any way transform or metamorphose or falsify its *objective reality.* And finally we do not, in judgment, predicate this *formal universality*, this *intentio univer*

---

[1] *Cf.* § 77, *infra.*

[2] " Ratio speciei accidit humanae naturae secundum illud esse quod habet in intellectu. Ipsa enim natura habet esse in intellectu abstractum ab omnibus individuantibus, et habet rationem uniformem ad omnia individua quæ sunt extra animam, prout est essentialiter imago omnium et inducens in cognitionem omnium, in quantum sunt homines ; et *ex hoc quod talem relationem habet ad omnia individua,* intellectus adinvenit rationem speciei et attribuit sibi ; *unde intellectus est qui facit universalitatem in rebus.*"—ST. THOMAS, *De Ente et Essentia*, cap. iv.

18 *

salitatis, this mental or logical mode of the concept, of the individual, or attribute it to the individual ; it is only the content of the formal universal, *i.e.* only the fundamental or metaphysical universal, that we identify with the individual in judgment : and thus we avoid the antinomy or contradiction of asserting the same thing to be both singular and universal.   The difficulty might be put in this way : What is universal cannot genuinely or faithfully represent, or be truly predicated of, what is singular or particular ; therefore if it is the singular object of sense, the particular subject of the judgment, that is real, the universal object of the intellect, the universal predicate of the judgment, cannot be real ; or *vice versa ;* and in either case the validity of the judgment as a form of knowledge breaks down.   Or the same difficulty might be put in this alternative form : What is one cannot be identical with, or truly predicated of, what is manifold ; but the universal is one, and the individuals with which it is identified, and of which it is predicated, are manifold ; therefore, etc., as before.   The reply of course is that in judgments we do not attribute *the universality* of the universal to the individual, or its *abstractness* either, but only its absolute content.   We do not and cannot say " John is *humanity* " (in the abstract and universal) ; for the term " humanity " expresses human nature not as it is in John but as it is affected by the logical form or *intentio* of universality by and in the intellect.   But we can and do say " John is a *man* " or " John is *human* " ; for these terms " man " and " human " express human nature in itself, in the absolute, and this latter *is really in John* . not, however, as constituting his *whole* reality, inasmuch as he has also that which individuates this nature in him, and distinguishes it in him from all its other individual embodiments : but it is really in him, and it is therefore rightly attributed to him and identified with him.   The universal, therefore, *can,* by its absolute content, and apart from the mental mode of its abstractness and universality for intellect, faithfully (if inadequately) represent the particular ; what is one, *i.e.* one as a universal, one by the addition of a logical relation (of community or communicability or multiplicability) to an object which of itself prescinds alike from the unity of the universal and the multiplicity of the incommunicable individual—what is *thus* one *can* be identified with, and attributed to, the manifold of individuals, provided that it is the absolute object or content of the " one " or " universal " and not its " unity " or " universality " that we thus identify with, and attribute to, the individuals. The object of the universal concept, therefore, considered in itself, is *real ;* by a logical relation aris_ ing from the conception-process it is represented by thought as logically or conceptually one and self-identical in all its possible actualizations *in rerum natura ;* but if it does exist actually *in rerum natura* it exists there individuated and incommunicable, —and, of course, not as *really one* but as *really manifold* if there be a plurality of individuals in which the intellect truly finds it.

There are therefore " universal " *thought*-objects, but there are no " universal " realities.[1] Whatever is real, whatever actually exists or can exist is individual. When we think of "univer- sality" we are thinking of an object which is an *ens rationis*, a purely logical relation, which has no objectivity other than what it has in and for thought : our concept of " universality " is a *secunda intentio mentis*,[2] a reflex or logically universal concept. When, on the other hand, we think of " singularity," " individu- ality," " particularity," we are thinking of an object which is real : our concept is a *prima intentio mentis*, a direct universal concept, —like that of " whiteness," or " virtue," or " humanity," for in- stance,—because " particularity " is a real characteristic of real things : individuals are real.[3] Take any class of the individuals revealed through sense perception,—men, for instance. The *human nature* of each individual is a distinct reality, really dis- tinct and separate from the human nature of every other human individual. But these really and numerically distinct *human natures* are apprehended by intellect in the process of conception *without the features that differentiate them* in each ; and therefore that which constitutes each of the individuated natures appears first to intellect *as to what it is essentially* (the fundamental or metaphysical universal), and in the abstract as a definite concep- tual object, and then, by reflection on it in comparison with the individuals, as universal, or " one-common-to-all-of-them ".

Why are manifold individuals classified under a common or universal concept? Because they are really identical, or consti- tute one reality ? No ; for they are not really one ; but because they are *similar*. Why are they similar? What constitutes or

---

[1] " Quod est commune multis non est aliquid praeter multa, nisi *sola ratione*. · · ·" ST. THOMAS, *Contra Gentes*, i., 26.

[2] *Cf. Science of Logic*, i., § 19, pp. 31-2 ; *Ontology*, § 3, pp. 43-4.

[3] *Cf. infra*, § 77.

makes them similar? What is "similarity"? Is similarity partial *real* identity? No; similarity is a partial *conceptual* or *logical* identity : each individual of the manifold is so constituted that some factor of each, isolated by the abstractive power of the intellect from the other factors, appears to intellect as one definite self-identical object, and is apprehended as universal or as " one-common-to-all". The concept of "similarity," like that of " particularity," is a concept of something real : it has for its object a *real* relation grounded on the real natures of the individual things.[1]

It comes to the same thing to say that the formally universal concept has as its real foundation, and the ground of its objective reality, the fundamental or metaphysical universal which is apprehended as a definite thought-object in the manifold individuals, and abstracted from them, as to say, with Maher,[2] that "the real objective foundation for this universal concept" lies " in the perfectly similar natures of the members of the same class "

"The essence," he continues, "the constituent features, the nature, type, or ideal plan, of man, triangle, silver, is repeated and contained equally in each concrete sample of the class, however much these may accidentally differ. It is, of course, numerically different, and individualized by particular determinations in each instance. But considered in the abstract apart from these individual determinations it might equally well be realized in any member of the class. . . It is upon the perfect similarity of natures in all members of a class thus grasped in a universal concept that the objective validity of science rests."

In the foregoing exposition an important point to bear in mind is that the abstract thought-object, whereby the intellect apprehends the reality given in the sense *datum*, may reveal not the whole specific essence, the *species infima*, but only some wider and less determinate generic aspect, of the latter. When, therefore, it is said that the proper object of the human intellect is the *essence* of what is revealed in sense, the meaning is not by any means that whenever an individual sense *datum* is present in consciousness,—as when, for instance, we perceive an individual human being,—the intellect apprehends and understands forthwith the whole specific nature of this *datum*. In does not (72). It may apprehend in this *datum* only the widest possible aspect

---

[1] *Cf. infra*, § 81, C ; also *Ontology*, §§ 34-6, 81 (*b*), for analysis of the concepts of "identity," " distinction," " similarity," etc.

[2] *Psychology*, p. 249. *Cf.* JEANNIÈRE, *op. cit.*, pp. 491 *sqq.*

of its reality, the thought-object "being" or "something"; or, again, the less indeterminate aspect "substance"; or "corporeal"; or "living"; or "sentient"; or "rational". It is only by a prolonged process of synthesizing such abstract aspects of reality, —a process involving judgment, comparison, inference, induction,[1] —that we gradually build up our complex intellectual concepts of the specific essences or natures of the manifold data of sense experience.

77. GENERALIZATION. INTELLECTUAL APPREHENSION OF THE INDIVIDUAL.—From the conception of an object in the *abstract* the intellect passes to an apprehension of its *universality*. Here we must distinguish between what we may call the *possible* or *essential* universality of our thought-objects and their *actual* or *factual* universality,—between what a French psychologist has aptly described as their *universalité de droit*, and their *universalité de fait*.[2] The former sort of universality is essential to and inseparable from the abstract thought-object as apprehended by the intellect and compared, through a reflex act, with the individual sense *data* from which it was abstracted and elaborated.

---

[1] *Cf.* MAHER, *op. cit.*, pp. 294-303, and authors there referred to ;—MERCIER, *Psychologie*, p. 345 ; PEILLAUBE, *Theorie des Concepts*, pp. 302, 326, 332-5 ; COCONNIER, *L'Ame humaine*, p. 130.

[2] "Take for example the colour of an ivory ball. This colour is itself the colour of *this* individual ball, a mode indissolubly bound up with this ball and incapable of existing otherwise or elsewhere. But let this colour become the term of my intelligence, so that I have not merely the perception but the idea of it, at once and by this very fact, and without my knowing whether this quality is to be found elsewhere in nature, I apprehend it as applicable to an indefinite multitude of other ivory balls and possibly of other bodies. The same is true of every substance, mode and relation of whatever we understand. Whatsoever *datum* appears in our empirical consciousness acquires forthwith under the scrutiny of our rational consciousness a sort of *universality* which extends indefinitely. In every individual *datum* intellect apprehends an *essence*, and apprehends this essence as capable of indefinite realization or repetition through time and space. Thus, above the *universality of fact* ['*universalité de fait*'] there is a *universality of right* ['*universalité de droit*'] which has the peculiar feature of being essential to the thought-object, of being logical, absolute."—PIAT, *L'Intellect Actif*, p. 82—*apud* MAHER, *op. cit.*, p. 295, n. 4. *Cf.* also PEILLAUBE (*Revue de philos.*, Feb., 1911, p. 192) : "Generalization is the result of another operation of the intellect [consequent on abstraction]. Considering the [abstract] essence now no longer in itself but in relation to its actual existence the intellect apprehends it as realizable in an indefinite multitude of individual cases. *De jure* ['En droit'] the abstract essence is general; but to know if it is so *de facto* the intellect must consider not merely one unique object but a plurality of similar objects ; comparison of these will lead the intellect to assimilate or identify them in that which is common to them : a function which is possible inasmuch as the intellect has already abstracted the essence from its individualizing notes,"

Hence the scholastic maxim that "the proper object of the human intellect is the *universal*".[1] For whatsoever reality becomes an object of human *thought* becomes *eo ipso* thus potentially universal.

The apprehension of any such abstract concept or thought-object as potentially universal has been described as *formal* generalization. It does not need the consideration and comparison of a multiplicity of individuals in the domain of sense. Formally to universalize an abstract concept, to make it a class-concept with potential universality, "*universalité de droit*," we do not need " to see and compare several examples of the class " [2] One single instance is sufficient for the intellectual apprehension of its essence—more or less determinately—as a potential universal. Such apprehension " is not the outcome of a process of *comparison*, but of intellectual *intuition*".[3]

The *material* generalization of the concept, however, *i.e.* its apprehension as an *actual* universal, the discovery of its actual embodiment in a multiplicity of actually existing individuals, the determination of its *actual* extension, the proper adjustment of the content of the concept itself so that it may be truly representative of the individuals to which it is applied,—all this implies, of course, a prolonged process of observation, comparison, judgment, inference, induction, and verification.[4] It is only by observation of the actual data of sense perception, by interpretation of them and reasoning from them, that we can determine in each particular case whether the abstract thought-object elaborated from those sense data is an *actual* as well as a *possible* object ; whether it is materially or actually universal as well as formally or essentially universal ; whether, if actual, it is embodied only in one actually existing individual being, or equally in a plurality of numerically distinct individuals of the same species.

We have seen that the abstract thought-object as such has potential or essential universality. So much is guaranteed by its intrinsic possibility. The elementary conceptual factors which go to build up our complex concepts must of course themselves have been originally abstracted from *percepts* of *actually existing* physical things ; for imagination can only reproduce and remould or modify materials *originally given in perception*. But intellect

---

[1] " Differt sensus ab intellectu et ratione quia intellectus vel ratio est *universalium* quae sunt ubique et semper ; sensus autem est *singularium*."—St. Thomas, *De Sensu et Sensato*, l. 1.

[2] Maher, *op. cit.*, p. 295.   [3] *Ibid.*, p. 296.   [4] *Ibid.*, pp. 294-303.

can synthesize conceptual factors, abstracted from those imagina.
tion data, into complex thought-objects which as such are apprehended as *merely capable* of existence as individual realities,
but not as actually existing. Thus the intellect can form con.
cepts of *purely possible realities.* Each such reality it apprehends
not only as capable of actual existence, but—unless there be some
reason to the contrary in the nature of the thought-object itself—
as capable of existence in an indefinite manifold of individuals.

In the inadequate and analogical concepts which we form of purely
spiritual beings, there is, according to the teaching of St. Thomas and
Thomists,[1] a special reason against the possibility of the numerically multiple
mode of actual existence : the fact, namely, that spirits have in their constitution no element of that *materiality* which is the principle of numerical multiplication and individuation of abstract essences or thought-objects in the
conditions of their actual existence : each such purely spiritual object of
thought is necessarily, according to this theory, unique of its kind, so that the
distinction between a multiplicity of such beings is not properly numerical or
material, but rather specific and formal,—a distinction for thought and in the
thought-objects themselves.

But apart from this, which is a matter of opinion, there is one particular
thought-object which certainly includes in its very nature a reason for the
unicity of its mode of actual existence, namely, the concept of the absolutely
Unconditioned, Infinite, All-Perfect, Necessary Being. This particular
thought-object is such that we understand its essence to involve its actual
and unique existence ; so that even although each of the conceptual factors
which go to form this concept, together with their synthesis into one complex
whole, is potentially universal, we nevertheless realize that the Reality which
we imperfectly apprehend through this inadequate and analogical concept is
necessarily unique, and that the actual extension of our potentially universal
concept is necessarily limited to this one Self-Existent Reality, the Divine
Being.

- The process of *generalizing* the *abstract* concept or thought-
object, whether formally or materially, is an *intellectual* process,
involving reflection on that object ; apprehension of its embodi·
ment—or the embodiment of the separate conceptual factors of
which it is a synthesis—in the concrete individual sense data
from which those factors were abstracted ; conscious comparison
of the thought-object with these sense data present in perception or imagination ; and, in the case of *material* generalization,
a conscious identification of the thought-object with one or more
of what are interpreted as its actual individual realizations in
the physical domain of sense. Now these intellectual processes

[1] *Cf. Ontology*, § 32, pp. 128-30.

appear to imply not only that we are simultaneously conscious both of the objects of thought and of sense, both of the abstract and potentially universal thought-object and of the concrete and individual sense-object, but also that we have an *intellectual* apprehension of the latter object as concrete and singular : otherwise how could we *compare* the thought-object with the sense-object, and *apprehend a relation* (of identity) between them,— functions which are peculiar to *intellect ?* It would appear, then, that we have an *intellectual* apprehension of the *concrete and individual.* But how can this be, if the proper object of the human intellect is the *abstract and universal ?*

The problem has exercised all scholastics. And the proper solution seems to demand a distinction between our intellectual apprehension of the *essence (Quid* est?) and of the *existence (An* est ?) of the individual.

Of *the nature or essence* of any individual the intellect can never have an exhaustive or adequate concept. Since any individual *datum* of sense experience yields a theoretically indefinite multitude of abstract thought-objects,—transcendental, generic, specific, and individuating,—it follows that no matter how rich our complex intellectual concept of any individual reality may be in such conceptual factors, it can never *adequately* represent, or *exhaust* the intelligibility of, the concrete individual. What we call singular or individual concepts are those potentially or essentially universal concepts which include, beyond the abstract factors taken as constituting the specific essence or *species infima* of the individual, such a number of the individualizing conditions (each apprehended in the abstract) as will serve for practical purposes to mark off the actual individual in question from other possible or actual individuals of the same species. In so far as such " singular " concepts give an intellectual insight into the *individual nature,* the *essentia "atoma,"* of any existing individual in the physical domain of sense, they seem to be formed in the manner just indicated. But they never give an adequate insight into the *individuality* of the concrete sense individual,—for the simple reason that even such " singular " concepts are abstract and potentially universal. The consideration that the individual thing of sense is *material,* that matter is *the principle* of *numerical multiplication* and *individuation* of the specific nature or essence which is the object grasped by thought, and that this material factor is an " irrational element," an " ἄλογον "[1]—also goes to show why the individual as such cannot be adequately grasped by intellect.

How, in the next place, do we attain to an *intellectual* appre-hension or knowledge of the *actual existence* of any individual reality or *datum* of sense consciousness ? Such knowledge seems to be attained by applying the abstract predicate "exists"—by an implicit act of judgment—to the actual individual content of sense consciousness. The possibility of doing this has its root and explanation in the fact that intellect and sense are faculties of the same individual mind.[2]

It is through reflex thought, through intellectual reflection on all our cognitive processes, as they take place in our minds,— processes which, with their products and objects, are most in-timately present in their concrete reality to our thought,—that we apprehend intellectually both our own selves and the concrete data of our sense cognition as actually existing individuals. It is through external and internal sense perception that we be-come aware of our own existing selves, and of external existences as affecting us. It is from these conscious data that intellect derives the abstract ideas of "existence," "unity," and "multi-tude"; and it is by comparison of those data with one another, and reflection on their relations of similarity and dissimilarity, that it forms the abstract ideas of "individuality" and "univer-sality". Spontaneously, by an implicit judgment ("*I exist*") which accompanies the conception of the self as object, we apply the predicate "existence" to our own selves as objects of reflec-tion ; and by the same sort of implicit judgment we interpret the

---

[1] *Cf. Ontology*, § 32, p. 130.

[2] St. Thomas teaches that intellect apprehends the singular (*i.e.* the concrete singular, as distinct from the abstract thought-object "singularity") not directly, but by a sort of reflection on the mode and origin of its own act of abstract concep-tion, a process which leads it to the apprehension of the singular percepts or phan-tasma from which it derives its abstract concepts. The passage (*De Anima*, iii., 8 *b* ; *Cf.* MAHER, *op. cit.*, p. 94, n. 20) is obscure, but its meaning seems to be that intellect can apprehend objects as concrete and singular because it apprehends them as so given in perception and imagination : since they are so given, it abstracts the concept of "particularity" or "singularity" from their concrete presentation in sense consciousness, and then consciously applies this concept to them. The passage in the *De Anima* is as follows : "Non possemus cognoscere comparationem univer-salis ad particulare, nisi esset una potentia quae cognosceret utrumque. Intellectus igitur utrumque cognoscit sed alio et alio modo. Cognoscit enim naturam speciei, sive quod quid est, directe extendendo seipsum, ipsum autem singulare per quamdam reflexionem, inquantum redit super phantasmata, a quibus species intelligibiles abstrahuntur." *Cf.* MERCIER, *Psychologie*, II., § 172, pp. 38-9. *Cf.* similar passage from St. Thomas, *In* II. *Anal. Post.*, L. 20, quoted *infra*, § 78, p. 289, n. 3.

abstract thought-objects which we abstract from actual sense *percepts* as *actually existing*, as belonging to the *existential* domain of realities, and those which we abstract from *imagination images*, in the absence of percepts, as *really and intrinsically possible*, a belonging to the *ideal* order of possible essences.[1]

It is an undeniable fact that consciousness yields intuitions of existences, or existing realities. It is equally undeniable that the realities thus given in intuition as existing are each given as unitary, individual, concrete, and not as abstract or universal. Whether any such intuition—of the individual in the concrete— is to be ascribed to *intellect* rather than to *sense*, is perhaps a debatable question. There seems to be no sufficient ground for ascribing to intellect, as William of Occam seems to have ascribed to it, an intuitive knowledge even of external, material, individual things in their concrete existence. The contention that above and beyond our *sense* consciousness of our own living, feeling selves, our *intellect* is *directly aware* of its own *concrete, individual* processes of thought and volition, and of the individual self or mind, as revealed in them, is a much more plausible contention. But however that may be, this at least is certain, that the *abstract* concept of "existence," or "existing reality," which intellect abstracts from such data, is simultaneously an *abstract* concept of "unity," "singularity," "particularity," as opposed to the subsequently formed abstract concept of "universality," or of " the property of being one-common-to-many". That is to say, the *data* for the concept of "particularity," are *given*, and the content of the concept is objective, in the same sense as in the case of any other direct universal concept: so that there is no special ground for Kant's doctrine that " particularity" or "individuality" is an *a priori* form of thought.[2] And furthermore, the intellect sees such a self-evident relation between the notion of "actual existence" and the notion of "singularity," that it apprehends as axiomatic the judgment that "whatever actually exists, whatever is not merely possible but also actually existent, must exist *as an individual* (whether substance, accident, mode, etc.), and cannot exist *as a universal*".

Now it is by applying these abstract concepts of "existence" and "particularity" to certain data of consciousness, that intellect apprehends the "individual" or "singular" as existing in the

---

[1] *Cf.* MERCIER, *Criteriologie*, § 140, p. 383.

[2] *Cf. supra*, § 52; *Ontology*, § 29, p. 121.

concrete, and as distinct from the abstract and universal. It is thus that we have an intellectual apprehension of the self or *Ego* as a conscious, thinking, existing individual : whether or not we call such intellectual apprehension an "intuition" is of minor importance: at all events it is intuitive as opposed to *discursive* or *inferential;* and it is a direct intellectual apprehension of the individual in its actual, concrete existence, through concepts ab- stracted from data immediately given in consciousness. It is thus too that we have an intellectual apprehension of individuals other than the self, in their concrete existence, as constituting the whole physical universe of our direct conscious experience : according as they are given to us in actual sense perception we attain to an intellectual apprehension of them as actually existing, inas- much as intellect is rooted in the same individual mind as the sense faculties to which they are presented in their concrete in- dividuality. They are given in a stream or manifold of sense impressions. We interpret them as given in the form of really distinct and separate existing or subsisting individuals. These individual subsisting data we believe to be real,[1] and we interpret, as to their nature, by applying to them the abstract and universal concepts which we have garnered by intellectual abstraction from those same data.

We are thus face to face with the terms of the problem con- cerning the validity of intellectual knowledge or science. For all science is embodied in judgments whereby we affirm or deny an abstract thought-object, as predicate, of some subject. Now if this subject is itself abstract and universal, as, for example, in the judgment "Man is mortal," the question whether such a judgment gives us valid knowledge of reality will depend on the real significance not only of the abstract and universal predicate

---

[1] We have inquired elsewhere into the principles which formally *constitute,* and the principles which *reveal* to us, the numerical *multiplication* and *individuation* of our abstract thought-objects in the real world revealed by sense (*Ontology,* §§ 31-3) ; into what constitutes their subsistence as *supposita* or *persons* (*ibid.,* §§ 72-3) ; into the grounds for recognizing a major and adequate real distinction between actually existing individuals of the same species (*ibid.,* §§ 35, 37, 38) ; and into the nature of the distinction (virtual, not real) to be recognized between the various abstract thought-objects or "metaphysical grades of reality," which intellect apprehends in, and whereby it grasps the nature of, the individuals given in sense (*ibid.,* § 30 ; *cf.* JEANNIÈRE, *Criteriologia,* pp. 497 *sqq.*). For these topics, closely allied as they are with the present context, we must refer the reader to the sources indicated, and abstain from treating them here. We likewise assume here the thesis to be established later : that the data of sense consciousness which we interpret as revealing individuals of the real world do in fact put us into direct cognitive contact with reality.

"mortal," but also of the abstract and universal subject "man". For it is only on the assumption that "man" in turn can be similarly predicated of the *real* individuals, Socrates, Cicero, John, James, "*this* man," etc., and that *this predication gives us a valid insight into the nature of these real individuals,*—in other words, on the assumption that the *abstract and universal thought-object is somehow really in, and identical with, the real individuals* revealed through sense and included under the extension of the intellectual concept,—it is *only on this assumption* that the former judgment "Man is mortal," or any judgment whatsoever, can convey to us any *genuine knowledge of reality.* It is certainly about these individuals that the judgment purports to convey knowledge.

"Aristotle," writes Mercier,[1] "returns to this point again and again throughout the course of his *Categories*[2] and *Analytics.*[3] The *subject* in its primary acceptation is the *individual*, the *substantia prima*, πρώτη οὐσία. It is fundamental in the ontological order, for, while it does not inhere in any other mode of being, all other modes of being inhere in it. And in the *logical* order it is primary also, for while it can never be predicate, but always only subject, all thought-objects other than that of the individual are or can be predicates of the latter."

And he quotes the words in which a fifteenth-century schoolman, Cardinal Cajetan, emphasizes the importance of realizing that no science, no philosophical speculation, can be of any real value, as knowledge, unless it gives a genuine insight into the natures of the individual things of sense :—

"Just as the judgment of the practical intellect in the technical domain is imperfect, if it is inapplicable to details, *i.e.* to the individual, so, too, the speculative judgment must be imperfect unless it apply to the existing individual things of nature which are revealed through sense : for the purpose of philosophical speculation is surely not to have us talk in the air but to give us a knowledge of the realities which we apprehend as constituting the universe."[4]

The mediæval scholastics in stating and proving the doctrine of Moderate Realism assumed the validity of sense cognition, *i.e.* that the individual things and events revealed through the senses, and constituting the data of sense consciousness, are *real ;* and

---

[1] *Op. cit.*, § 132, p. 333.　　[2] *Cf. Categ.*, ii., iii.　　[3] *Cf. Anal. Priora*, i., xxvii.
[4] "　　　philosophia non quaeritur ut loquamur in aere, sed ut de rebus realibus quas universum integrare cernimus cognitionem habeamus."—CAJETAN, *In II. Post. Anal.*, c. 13—*apud* MERCIER, *l.c.*

they went on to state and prove that the abstract objects of thought—" the universals "—are really in these data. We shall prove later on that sense perception is valid. But there is no need to prove that the data of sense consciousness, the impressions of sense, taken at least as subjective facts of which we are aware, are real; no theory of knowledge can go behind them; these data are the necessary starting-point of all epistemology; no sceptic can question them, or ever has seriously questioned them (37). Mercier quotes [1] Sextus Empiricus,[2] Hume,[3] Mill,[4] and Kant,[5] as recognizing that there really are data of sense consciousness, that "*impressions really affect sense consciousness*". So invincible, in fact, is the feeling which is borne in upon us of conscious, cognitive contact with *reality* in our consciousness of the data of external and internal sense, that some of the very latest epistemological theories,—such as the Intuitionism of Bergson, certain forms of Pragmatism, and the German Philosophy of Immediate Experience,—claim that the only valid form of cognition lies in immediate intuition of the data of consciousness. This denial of all validity to *intellectual* apprehension is, of course, erroneous. The proof of Moderate Realism as expounded in the preceding sections of the present chapter, especially in § 76, will start from the assumption that the individual data revealed to us in the domain of sense consciousness are real, and will aim at showing that the abstract and universal objects of thought, the concepts which we use as predicates in judgment, are really embodied in, and constitute the reality of, those sense data : in other words, that our universal concepts *have objective reality*.[6]

78. PROOFS OF MODERATE REALISM.—Towards the end of § 73 a distinction was drawn between those simplest—transcendental and more remotely generic—concepts, which are comparatively unanalysable into simpler conceptual notes or factors, and the more complex specific concepts or class-notions which, resulting from syntheses of the former, are applied to the multitudinous classes of individual things and events which constitute the domain of sense experience. If the former have real objectivity in the

---

[1] *Op. cit.*, pp. 335-6.   [2] *Hypotyposes Pyrrhonienses*, c. x.
[3] *Treatise on Human Nature*, Book I., Part IV., Sect. 1 and 2.   *Cf. Ontology*, § 61, p. 215 n.
[4] *Exam. of Sir W. Hamilton's Philosophy*, chap. ix., pp. 157, 163.
[5] *Critique of Pure Reason*, pp. 15-17, quoted *supra*, §§ 51 and 74.
[6] *Cf.* MERCIER, *op. cit.*, § 131, p. 332.

data of sense, so, we may infer, have the latter: unless it be that the synthetic function whereby we conceive a complex thought-object, such as *human nature*, for instance, be not at all a conscious and objectively grounded synthesis of elementary conceptual factors,—in this case, "substance," "corporeal," "animate," "sentient," and "rational,"—but an instinctive synthesis of *a priori* thought forms or categories with a sense intuition. This contention of Kant will be disproved below (chap. xii., § 91). Here we confine ourselves to proving this main contention of Moderate Realism: that the elementary thought-objects which enter into all our specific and generic universal concepts, and which, as present to intellect, are abstract and universal, are *really in* the individual data apprehended by sense; that as to their content they are not fabrications of thought; and that, therefore, when they are predicated of individual sense data in judgment they give us valid knowledge about the natures of these sense data

The proof is really an appeal to introspection as bearing out the doctrine contained in the thesis and already expounded in §§ 75-7. It may be stated as follows[1]: Introspection reveals to us that in any individual datum of sense we apprehend not only its individuating notes, but also notes which correspond to our concepts of *substance*, or *accident*, or *agent*, or *body*, or *life*, or *quality*, or *space*, or *time*, etc.

"When that friend, Callias, instanced by Aristotle in his *Posterior Analytics*, approaches me, when I see him with my eyes, hear his voice, grasp his hand, etc., is it not evident that my universal concepts find their reality in the individual datum apprehended by sense? I understand most clearly that my friend Callias is a reality: that my concept of *being* is realized in him. I know, moreover, that a variety of circumstances affecting him may change, appear and disappear, while he remains nevertheless substantially and essentially the being that he is,—in other words, that he realizes in himself my concepts of *substance* and *accidents*. I know that he *acts*,—walks, talks, etc.,—in other words, that he realizes my concepts of *action, agent, cause*. And so on. All these thought-objects, *substance, accident, action*, etc., I apprehend as being intrinsically connected and bound up in him with certain individualizing traits which enable me to distinguish him from other individual men: so intimately bound up, indeed, that *spontaneously* I do not think of distinguishing or separating them: spontaneously I am rather likely to confound the object of my concept with that of my percept: so that I have to make an effort in order to convince myself by reflective analysis that there are taking place in me simultaneously *two* cognitive acts [intellectual concep-

[1] *Cf.* MERCIER, *op. cit.*, § 140, pp. 377-80; JEANNIÈRE, *op. cit.*, p. 221.

tion or thought, and sense perception], which have a common *material* object, but *formal* objects that are distinct and mutually irreducible." [1]

Hence, by reason of this unity of the material object of thought and sense, such common expressions as " I see a man," [2] when, as a matter of fact, what I *see* is only " something *coloured,*" —the quality of colour being the proper object only of vision,— whereas I *think* the *nature* or *substance,* " man,"—*substance* being *per se* an object of *thought,* an " objectum *intelligibile,*" and being an object of vision (or any other sense) not *per se,* but only *per accidens, i.e.* owing to the fact that the sensible quality, such as colour, affects the individual substance. [3] And when I realize, by introspection, that there is a twofold act of cognition, I simultaneously realize that they terminate in one and the same

---

[1] MERCIER, *l.c.,* pp. 377-8.   [2] *Cf.* JEANNIÈRE, *l.c.*

[3] St. Thomas, in a remarkable passage of his Commentary on Aristotle (*In II. Post. Anal.,* cap. xv.) asserts that *sense* has some sort of apprehension *even of the universal* (just as we have seen him claim for intellect some sort of indirect apprehension of the singular—*supra,* § 77). Here are his words : " Manifestum est quod singulare sentitur proprie et per se, sed tamen *sensus est quodammodo etiam ipsius universalis.* Cognoscit enim Calliam non solum in quantum est Callias, sed etiam in quantum est *hic homo,* et similiter Socratem in quantum est hic homo. Et exinde est quod tali acceptione sensus præ-existente, anima intellectiva potest considerare hominem in utroque. Si autem ita esset quod sensus apprehenderet solum id quod est particularitatis et nullo modo cum hoc apprehenderet *universalem naturam in particulari,* non esset possibile quod ex apprehensione sensus causaretur in nobis cognitio universalis " (*cf.* JEANNIÈRE, *op. cit.,* p. 491, n.). From the text reproduced in this passage of the commentary, Aristotle has been accused of teaching sensism, *i.e.* that sense can apprehend the universal, and that accordingly cognitive faculties of the sense order can account for our highest forms of knowledge. The perusal of an earlier passage, quoted by Mercier (*op. cit.,* p. 378, n. 2) from the context, would have shown how groundless is the charge. The meaning of the passage quoted above seems to be that sense apprehends the particular; that in the particular apprehended by sense, and through our sense apprehension of it, intellect apprehends the universal; that it can do so only because that which it grasps as universal is really and identically the particular (for that which individuates the specific nature grasped by intellect is not really but only virtually distinct from that nature: *cf. Ontology,* §§ 30, 31) ; that sense, on its side, apprehends not merely the individuating notes of the nature, but the *nature* which is individual (and which is apprehended by intellect in the abstract and as universal) ; that, therefore, sense may be said to apprehend the universal indirectly or *materialiter,* or *per accidens ;* that inasmuch as it is up to a certain point *similarly* affected by perception of *a plurality* of individuals of the same nature or class, and *is conscious* of this similarity, though it does not, of course, grasp its essence *as a relation of similarity* (in the abstract, as intellect does : *cf.* MAHER, *Psychology,* pp. 197-8, for sense apprehension of the *time*-relation in memory ; and what is said, *infra,* § 91, iii., regarding *individual* concrete relations as given to sense), sense can, therefore, also be said to apprehend *materialiter* the similarity of individuals, or, in other words, the *fundamental* universal (§ 76) : and, finally, that sense and intellect which thus apprehend the same reality under different aspects are *rooted in the same conscious mind or Ego.*

reality, that the object of thought is really in, and materially identical with, the object of sense. Consciousness, therefore, testifies "that intellect *finds* in the data of sense experience its proper object, *viz. the essences* of things : it *reads or deciphers in the core of the sense fact* ' *that which the thing is*,' to use an expression [' *quidditas*,' ' *quod quid est*'] of St. Thomas, who derives from this power of *reading into*,—' *intus legere*,'—the etymology of the word 'intellect'"[1]

This main contention of Moderate Realism, that the content of our universal concepts is really in the data of sense, and that therefore they have real objective validity (on the assumption, which will be established later, that the sense data themselves are objectively real)—is borne out by considering the dependence of our concepts on sense data, and seeking a satisfactory explanation of this dependence. The fact of this dependence is beyond dispute. For (*a*) diseases and abnormal conditions of the sense organs, the brain, or the nervous system, as instanced in delirium, insanity, etc., lead to disturbance and confusion of concepts ; (*b*) people totally deprived of the use of any particular sense, as in the case of those who are blind or deaf from infancy, are also destitute of the corresponding domain of concepts, *e.g.* of sounds or colours ; (*c*) we communicate to others *ideas* that are new to them by arousing in them *sense percepts* or *imagination images ;* (*d*) our intellectual activity is accompanied and conditioned by activity of the senses and imagination. But this dependence cannot be explained otherwise than by the recognition that it is one and the same reality which is apprehended in the concrete by sense perception, and in the abstract, apart from individualizing conditions, by the higher cognitive activity of conception or thought.[2]

The argument just set forth is given by Mercier as one of a number of what he calls "positive" proofs of the proposition that "the object of our universal concepts ('*formes intelligibles*') is contained materially in the sense percepts ('*formes sensibles*') of which it is predicated in the judgment".[3] The other argu-

[1] MERCIER, *l.c.*, p. 380.   [2] *Cf.* JEANNIÈRE, *op. cit.*, pp. 458-60.
[3] *Ibid.*, pp. 377-82. The proposition is there stated as major premiss of an argument of which the minor premiss is " But the object of the sense percepts ('*formes sensibles*') is real," and the conclusion, " Therefore the universal concepts ('*formes intelligibles*') express objective realities ". The minor is proved by vindicating the validity of sense perception. And the whole argument establishes the scholastic doctrine of Moderate Realism as a theory of knowledge in general, including both intellectual and sense cognition.

ments which he adduces in the context are, however, rather refutations of Kant's theory of conception, and therefore belong more properly to what he himself calls the "negative" method[1] of establishing Moderate Realism, *viz.* by showing that all the other alternative solutions of the "Universals" problem are untenable.   They will be given below when, in the course of our examination of those alternatives, we come to deal with Kant's theory (91).   The first of those defective solutions we purpose to examine is *Extreme Realism* in its various manifestations.

[1] *Op. cit.*, § 133, p. 337; § 135, p. 345.

CHAPTER X.

79. PLATO'S DOCTRINE ON UNIVERSALS.—The tenet common to all forms of extreme realism is this, that the objects apprehended by intellect in conception as universals exist also *as universals* outside the mind, or independently of thought. The Platonic form of this theory deserves attention both on its merits and because of its influence on all subsequent speculations. Plato's main concern, throughout the course of his dialogues[1] on universals, was to examine, and vindicate the validity of, scientific knowledge, and from an analysis of its characteristics of "necessity" and "universality" to discover the nature of its objects. The *objects* of thought Plato called "Ideas". For him conception is a process of *reminiscence* or *recollection*, of recalling to consciousness those objects, of which he conjectures the intellect or soul to have had a direct and immediate intuition in a previous state of its existence. This theory as to the *origin* of our knowledge may, perhaps, be one of those speculations which Plato intended to be taken allegorically or figuratively, rather than as a scientific exposition of literal fact.[2] Anyhow the main point of its significance is that the Ideas are in no sense products or constructions of our thought, but independent realities of which intellect has a direct and immediate intuition. The domain of these universal thought-objects is the *real* world *par excellence:* of it alone we can have certain and scientific knowledge (ἐπιστήμη), and that by means of intellect: hence he called this real domain—of stable, abiding, immutable self-identical universals, or objects of science — the "*intelligible. world,*" "τόπος νοητός," "mundus *intelligibilis*". Of what we call the "sense world," the whole domain of individual physical things and events, the transient, fluctuating, ever-changing data or phenomena revealed to our consciousness through sense per-

---

[1] *Cf.* especially *Phaedo*, xlix. *Cf. Ontology*, § 19, pp. 93-5.
[2] *Cf.* WEBB, *History of Philosophy* (Home University Library), pp. 36-7.

ception, we cannot have certain knowledge but only conjecture (δόξα); nor has it any substantive reality of its own, inde_pendently of the veritably real and intelligible world of uni_versals. But, then, do we not, in judgment, predicate these "intelligible" universals of those "sensible" singulars, and thus assert some sort of real community or identity as between the objects of both domains? Undeniably we do; and this is the crucial difficulty for Plato's—as, indeed, for every other—theory of knowledge. The language in which Plato attempts to solve it has met with widely different interpretations. And no wonder; for on the one hand he insists that the reality of the objects of intellect completely transcends, and is wholly separate and isolated from, the domain of the individual phenomena of sense: the universals are not *in*, but *above and beyond* the individuals (το ἐν παρα τα πολλα). Hence Aristotle, who may be presumed to have known the mind of his master, describes the Platonic universals as οὐσίαι χωρισταί, "entia separata," *i.e.* as wholly apart from the individual data of sense. Hence, too, Plato holds that of this real domain of intelligible objects, and of them alone, can we have scientific knowledge. Yet, on the other hand, he speaks of the individuals of sense as "participating," or "sharing" in the universals;[1] and it is in virtue of this "participation" that individual sense phenomena (*a*) have whatever sort of secondary or borrowed or reflected reality he accords to them, and (*b*) become, in predication or judgment, objects of an inferior sort of cognition which is not certain and scientific but only conjectural and unstable.

Now, whatever Plato means by this "participation" of the singular in the universal, he does not mean that the latter is really identical with, and apprehended by intellect in, the former for this theory of the *immanence* of the universal in the singular is precisely the theory of Moderate Realism which Aristotle opposed to the "transcendence" theory of his master: and what determined Plato to deny the real identity of the universal with the singular was precisely the apparent opposition and incompatibility which he apprehended between the "stable,"

---

[1] For interpretations of this "participation" and "transcendence," *cf.* TAYLOR, *Plato* (Constable's *Philosophies Ancient and Modern*), pp. 45 *sqq.*;—a very clear and interesting résumé of the Platonic philosophy by a brilliant present-day Platonist. The same author has contributed an equally clear and useful, if less sympathetic, brochure on *Aristotle* to Black's *People's Books.*

"immutable," "necessary" and "eternal" properties of the universal of thought, and the "transitory," "changeable," "contingent" and "temporal" properties of the individual of sense.

I. Now if the universal is in no real sense in the singular, but wholly apart, isolated, and transcendent in reference to the latter, the "participation" can mean really nothing more than a mere extrinsic denomination of the singular in terms of the universal, a denomination without any real ground, so that judgments in which we predicate the universal of the singular should be logically held to give us *no sort* of knowledge (*i.e.* interpretation, or insight into the nature) of the latter, *not even conjectural* knowledge; and the whole domain of sense experience, the whole world of physical nature, should be held to be wholly unknowable, and therefore to be, for aught we know, unreal.

Moreover, if the universal were a subsisting reality transcending the singulars, *all our singular judgments would be false.* It would be false, *e.g.*, to say "James is a man," if I mean by "man" a single, real, self-subsisting entity or nature above and beyond and apart from this qualitatively and quantitatively determined sense individual called James : for the judgment *identifies* what I mean by "man" with the individual subject "James"; and the most I could assert, on Plato's theory, would be that "James" somehow partially manifests, or reflects, or shares in, the transcendent reality which I mean by "man". But a theory of knowledge which is in such flagrant opposition to the common and spontaneous convictions of mankind, a theory which, purporting to explain to us how we come to know the world revealed to us through our senses, ends by asking us to believe that we do not know this world at all, that the objects of our knowledge are transcendent entities wholly other than anything which we perceive, and that finally all our singular judgments are false,—such a theory cannot be regarded as satisfactory.

II. Again, if each universal is, as such, extramentally real, then the "participation" of individuals in any universal which we predicate of them can only mean that they are partial manifestations of one and the same reality,—that John and James, for example, are partial manifestations of *one single reality, viz.* "universal humanity" or "human-nature-in-general"; that all individual "beautiful" things are beautiful because, and in so far as, they are identical with a single self-subsisting reality, *viz.*

"beauty-in-general".[1] But this is certainly not what we mean to assert in such judgments. On the contrary, reflection shows us that the *universality* of our universal predicates or thought-objects is not a mind-independent attribute of the reality of these objects, but a *logical relation*, an *intentio logica*, which is the product of the mind's mode of considering them : when I say of a man, a horse, and an oak, that they are "living" things, or endowed with "life," I do not fuse or confound or identify the three lives in one single real life ; on the contrary, I apprehend three numerically distinct real lives ; and because I intellectually apprehend each life in the abstract and apart from whatever really differentiates it from the others I apprehend it as a *conceptual unity*, and, as such, see it to be one-common-to-the-three, and to others indefinitely (76). The unity of the universal is logical, not real. "The objects which intellect considers separately or apart from individuating notes," says St. Thomas,[2] "need not have a separate real existence ; and hence universals should not be held to subsist as such apart from singulars, or the objects of mathematics [*e.g.* points, lines, surfaces, etc.] to subsist apart from the things of sense : for universals constitute the essences of the singulars, and mathematical objects the real terminations or limits of the corporeal things of sense."

III. *Plato's theory is based on a defective analysis of the conditions which render scientific knowledge possible, and leads to an erroneous interpretation of the objects of such knowledge.*

Plato rightly repudiated the teaching of Heraclitus that all reality consists in *change*, that there is no *stable* object within reach of human thought ; and the corollary drawn from this by Protagoras, that all knowledge is relative to the individual mind, that whatever appears to the individual is true for him, but that there is no absolute truth, no fixed standard for individual minds, that the individual "man is the measure of all things". He rightly accepted the undeniable fact that there is an *absolute* distinction between truth and error, a distinction valid for all minds ; and, furthermore, that there are judgments which, being necessarily, eternally, immutably, and universally true, are strictly scientific. But from the *stability* which science presupposes in its objects, as a condition of their intelligibility, he wrongly inferred that such objects can be in no true sense really *in*, or *identical with*, the ever-changing and transient individual phenomena which

[1] *Cf.* Phaedo, xlix. [2] *De substantiis separatis*, ii.

constitute the world of sense experience ; and that accordingly
they must be apart from, and give us no scientific knowledge of,
these latter.

Wrongly ; because he failed to distinguish between the mode
in which the objects of science *are present to intellect* and the
mode in which they *really exist ;* he failed to see that the stability,
necessity, eternity,universality, etc.,[1] which condition the relations
we establish between them in the necessary judgments of science,
are merely modes *of their intelligibility*, modes which affect their
presence to intellect, modes consequent on the abstract manner in
which intellect apprehends them ; that therefore those objects
may and do really exist without these modes *in the individual
data of sense ;* that when we predicate such thought-objects of
these data we do not attribute to these data the modes which
those objects have only in and for thought ; but that nevertheless
by predicating those objects, *as to their content*, of the data of
sense, we are attributing to these latter what is really in them,
and are therefore obtaining genuine if inadequate scientific knowledge about them.

The possibility of scientific knowledge is conditioned not by
the existence of universals *a parte rei*, as Plato thought, but by
the power which intellect possesses of abstracting and universalizing the natures which, independently of it, are concrete and individual.   Universality, as Cajetan remarks in his Commentary on
Aristotle, is not an *object* of science, but a *conditio sine qua non*
of science.[2]   The objects of science may have a mode of *real
being* other than the mode of their *being known*.   In order to be
known scientifically they must of course be *intelligible, i.e.* present
to intellect in a manner conformable with the nature of the intellect.   But this mode of their presence may be distinct from
that of their real existence ; and reflection on our processes of
thought and sense perception, processes of the same self-conscious
mind or soul, processes wherein we spontaneously recognize the

---

[1] *Cf. supra*, chap. vii., especially §§ 69, 70.

[2] " Propositio illa : scientia est universalium, quadruplici modo intelligi potest.
. . . Quartus sensus est : scientia est rerum quae habent universalitatem tanquam
conditionem, sine qua non sciuntur . . . quia scientiae *objectum* est res ipsa . . .
aliter scientiae reales non essent de rebus. Et quia res non potest intellectui objici
et sciendi actum terminare, nisi representatur absque conditionibus individualibus,
quod est representari universaliter et rem habere universalitatis conditionem, ideo
habentium universalitatem ut conditionem sine qua non, scientia est."—CAJETAN,
In I. Post. Anal., c. 9—*apud* MERCIER, *op. cit.*, p. 366, n. 2.

objects of thought and the objects of sense to be identical in reality,—reflection on these processes convinces us that things really exist and reveal themselves to sense in modes other than those which they assume on becoming objects of thought.[1]

Plato therefore erred in interpreting the objects of scientific knowledge, the "Ideas," as being in their reality essentially suprasensible, as transcending the domain of sense.[2] No doubt, as objects of knowledge, as conceived by intellect, they transcend the sensible mode of being, they are suprasensible or immaterial ; but they are not all or necessarily immaterial *positively;* they are for the most part immaterial *negatively,* by *abstraction* (71).[3] No doubt, too, they are conceived by us as *ideal exemplars* of the individual things of sense : but as such they have not a separate reality, a transcendent existence above and beyond, and superior to, that of the things of sense ; for our intellectual apprehension of them is not an intuition or reminiscence of a domain of immaterial realities, a τόπος νοητός, but is a process of intellectual abstraction and reflective universalization of the real natures of the things of sense.

No doubt, finally, there are positively eternal and immutable archetype ideas of the things of sense, existing antecedently both to these things themselves and to our knowledge of them, *viz.* in the Mind of Him who has created them ;[4] but, as we must now show against the error of Ontologism, it is not of these that we have or can have any intuition.

---

[1] *Cf.* ST. THOMAS, *In I. Metaph.,* l. 10 : " Patet autem diligenter intuenti rationes Platonis quod ex hoc in sua positione erravit, quia credidit quod modus rei in tellectae in suo esse est sicut modus intelligendi ipsam rem ; et ideo quia invenit intellectum nostrum . . . abstracta intelligere . . . abstractione intellectus posuit respondere abstractionem in essentiis rerum. . . . Hoc autem non est necessarium : nam in tellectus etsi intelligat res per hoc quod similis est eis quantum ad speciem intelligibilem per quam fit in actu, non tamen oportet quod modo illo sit species illa in intellectu, quo in re intellecta ; nam *omne quod est in aliquo est per modum ejus in quo est,* et ideo ex natura intellectus, *quae est alia a natura rei intellectae,* necessarium est quod *alius sit modus intelligendi quo intellectus intelligit, et quo res existit.*"

[2] It is remarkable that Kant, starting from the same assumption as Plato, *viz.* that we have scientific knowledge in necessary and universal judgments, drew the erroneous conclusion *contrary* to Plato's, *viz.* that the objects of knowledge are, as such, essentially *sensible,*—not sensible *realities* but sensible *phenomena* or *appearances,*—that we can have no knowledge of any realities, least of all of transcendent or suprasensible realities. *Cf.* TAYLOR, *op. cit.,* p. 52. The Moderate Realism of Aristotle and the scholastics avoids the errors of both extremes alike.

[3] *Cf. Ontology,* Introd., v. and vi.

[4] " Quod factum est in Ipso vita erat : whatever has been created was in Him life." That is, as St. Augustine explains (*In Joann.,* tr. i., 16 and 17), before things were created they were in the Divine Mind as to their plan or pattern, as the work of art is in the mind of the artist before it is executed ; and as such they were *life, i.e.* identical with the Living God. The present punctuation of the Vulgate, " . . . sine Ipso factum est nihil quod factum est. In Ipso vita erat . . ." is probably erroneous. St. Augustine read with a full stop after " nihil ". *Cf.* MERCIER, *op. cit.,* p. 369 n.

80. ONTOLOGISM.—The theory known as *Ontologism* explains both the origin and the nature or significance of universal concepts by the contention that the thought-objects which we apprehend through these concepts are Ideas in the Divine Mind. There appears to be no doubt that this was not Plato's meaning. For him the whole hierarchy of Ideas which constitute the τόπος νοητός is subordinate to the *Idea of the Good*. This supreme principle is for Plato the *Ens realissimum*, which gives order and intelligibility to the real universe.[1] He seems not to have considered God, any more than the soul, as an object of scientific knowledge; and whenever he speaks of God in connexion with the Ideas, as he does in the *Timaeus*, " the ' Ideas' are always referred to as objects existing independently of God and known by Him, never as owing their existence to His thought about them "[2]

The interpretation which identifies the Platonic Ideas with the Thoughts or Ideas of the Divine Mind can be traced to the Alexandrian Jewish philosopher, Philo Judaeus, who was a contemporary of Christ. It was partly espoused by Neo-Platonism, and adopted by St. Augustine towards the end of the fourth century. But neither St. Augustine in the fourth century, nor St. Bonaventure in the thirteenth, can be justly accused of Ontologism ; for they did not teach that intellectual conception is a direct intuition of these Divine Ideas by the human mind. They did indeed teach, in common with all Christian philosophers, that according to our mode of conceiving creation as the work of an Eternal, Divine Artificer, there are in the Divine Mind ideal plans, patterns, archetypes, *ideae exemplares*, of which all created essences are faint, far-off copies or reflections.[3] These Divine Ideas, identical with the Divine Being, are exemplar and efficient causes of created things ; and hence we may call them *universalia in representando et efficiendo*. But they are not the *formal* causes of created essences, intrinsic to, and identical with, the latter : they are not the *universalia in essendo*, the thought-objects which the human mind apprehends in conception. The error of Ontologism consists precisely in maintaining that the universal thought-objects of which we become aware are the Divine Ideas,

---

[1] *Cf.* WEBB, *op. cit.*, p. 45 ; TAYLOR, *op. cit.*, pp. 59-61. For the relation, in Plato's system, between *God* and the *Idea of the Good*, *cf.* DE WULF, *History of Medieval Philosophy*, § 24, pp. 20-1.

[2] TAYLOR, *ibid.*, p. 44.   [3] *Cf. Ontology*, § 19, p. 94.

and that through them we attain to an intellectual knowledge of the world of sense.

According to the French Cartesian, Malebranche (1638-1715), God is the " place of spirits " as " space is the place of bodies " He is intimately present to our intellects and in Him we *see all things* (*Vision en Dieu*). According to the Italian ontologist, Gioberti (1801-52), the primordial act of the human intellect is an intuition of *God creating existing things* (*Ens creans exist-entias*) : so that the Being that is first in the ontological or real order (God) is also first in the logical order, the order of our knowledge,—*Primum Ontologicum est Primum Logicum.* Thus, as Maher observes,[1] " Ontologism . . . inverts the true order of knowledge. We do not descend to a knowledge of the thing through the Divine Idea, but we ascend to the Divine Idea from the thing." Nor, finally, can the teaching of another Italian philosopher, Rosmini (1797-1855), be vindicated from the charge of ontologism, inasmuch as he virtually identifies the object of our concept of *Being-in-general*, which he holds to be innate, with the Being of God.[2]

The main reason which has induced ontologists thus to identify the " universals" apprehended in conception with the Divine Being, is to be found in the features of "necessity," " universality," " eternity," " immutability," " indivisibility," " incorruptibility," etc., which reflection undoubtedly reveals as characterizing the objects of our universal concepts. They argue that objects endowed with such attributes cannot possibly be apprehended in the concrete, contingent, individual data of sense ; that they must be really aspects of the Necessary, Eternal, and Immutable Being of God. But we have shown elsewhere [3] that this inference is based on an erroneous interpretation of the characteristics in question ; that, rightly interpreted, these can be quite satisfactorily accounted for by the *abstract* condition in which those thought-objects are apprehended by intellect in the data of sense.

Moreover, as a theory on the nature and validity of our universal concepts, the ontologist theory, which identifies them with

---

[1] *Op. cit.*, p. 260.   [2] TURNER, *cf. History of Philosophy*, pp. 631-2.
[3] *Cf. Ontology*, §§ 14-20, pp. 79-100. *Supra*, §§ 69, 70-72, 75. Among the standard works on Ontologism may be mentioned—ZIGLIARA, *Della Luce Intellettuale e del' Ontologismo; Propaedeutica ad Sacram Theologiam ; Summa Philosophica.* LEPIDI, *De Ontologismo.* SATOLLI, *In Summ. Theol. D. Thomae Aquinatis Prae-lectiones.* For criticism of ontologistic theory on the *origin* of our ideas, *cf.* MAHER, *op. cit.*, p. 259.

the Eternal Reality of the Necessary Being, is wholly inadmissible. For either our universal concepts would on this theory give us no valid insight into the nature of the things of sense, *any more than the Platonic Ideas ;* or else the objects of these concepts, *i.e.* the Divine Ideas, should be understood as formally constituting the reality of the things of sense,—*which would be Pantheism.* The question at issue in the whole "universals" problem is the question as to the nature and significance of the thought-objects which we apprehend in conception, and predicate of the individual data of sense in judgment, and of the consequent validity or knowledge-value of such judgments. And it is no answer to this question to confound or identify those thought-objects, those *universalia in essendo,* with the *Ideae Exemplares,* or *universalia in representando,* in the Divine Mind.

81. MEDIEVAL FORMS OF EXTREME REALISM.[1]—Aristotle had formulated at least in outline the doctrine of Moderate Realism on the nature and significance of universals. But the philosophers of the early Middle Ages had access only to a few of his logical treatises through the translations of Boëthius († 525); and to this writer's version of an elementary Greek commentary on the first of the Aristotelian treatises, the "Categories,"—a commentary called the *Isagoge* or *Introduction,*—by a neo-Platonic philosopher named Porphyry who flourished in the fourth century of the Christian era. In a single sentence of this unpretending brochure, which became a text-book in the medieval schools, Porphyry raises, and refuses to answer, the question of the significance of universals: "And now, (1) as to whether genera and species [*i.e.* universals] are real or are mere creations of the intellect, (2) and if they be real, whether they are corporeal or incorporeal, (3) whether they are apart from the data of sense or subsist in the data of sense, I shall not venture to say".[2] It was the first, and only the first of these questions, that was crudely debated in the schools down to the twelfth century. Boëthius himself abandoned the realist view—that universals are realities,—for the anti-realist view—that they are creations of our thought. In the ninth, tenth, and eleventh centuries we find on the one hand a succession of

[1] *Cf.* DE WULF, *History of Medieval Philosophy,* pp. 150-62; 178-98; 321-3; 336-7.

[2] " Mox de generibus et speciebus illud quidem sive subsistant sive in nudis intellectibus posita sint, sive subsistentia corporalia sint an incorporalia, et utrum separata a sensibilibus an in sensibilibus posita et circa haec subsistentia, dicere recusabo." *Cf.* DE WULF, *op. cit.,* p. 152; WEBB, *op. cit.,* pp. 114 *sqq.*

writers contending that each and every abstract specific or generic thought-object is as such a reality : they were called "*reales*" or "realists ". This theory led, as we shall see presently, to pantheism, and gradually fell into disrepute. Opposed to it we find on the other hand a line of writers adopting the purely negative view, that the objects of these universal notions are not things or realities, realized in the universal state in Nature, inasmuch as whatever actually exists in Nature must be individual, not universal.

The supposed implied inference that such objects were therefore *mere* creations of the mind ("*nuda intellecta*") has branded some of these writers—as, for instance, Abelard (1079-1142)—as *conceptualists ;* but they did not really draw the inference. The fact rather is that they were laboriously prosecuting the psychological analysis which terminated towards the middle of the twelfth century, by bringing to light the real relation between the abstract universal of thought and the concrete individual of sense, in the formula of Moderate Realism.[1] Similarly, the assertion ascribed to Roscelin (*circa* 1050-1100) that universals are mere *flatus vocis*[2] gained for such writers the title of "*nominales*" or "nominalists " ; though they were certainly not nominalists in the modern sense of denying the existence, in the mind, of genuinely universal representations as distinct from mere imagination images.[3]

A. *Empiric Realism.*—The early medieval form of extreme realism, which is sometimes called "*empiric* realism," and of which William of Champeaux[4] (1070-1120) may be taken as a typical exponent, differs from Platonic realism in this that it holds the universal to exist *formally as such*, not in a suprasensible domain, but *in the individual things of sense experience.* The generic universal is really one, unmultiplied, self-identical essence, shared by all its subordinate species ; and similarly the specific universal is numerically one reality shared by all its subordinate individuals :

---

[1] *Cf.* DE WULF, *op. cit.*, § 143, p. 157. For an instructive and interesting account of the various gropings towards a definite solution, in the " states," " aspects," " collection," and " indifference " theories of the early twelfth century, *cf. ibid.*, pp. 186-90.

[2] *Cf.* TURNER, *History of Philosophy*, pp. 269 *sqq. ;* MERCIER, *op. cit.*, § 134, p. 338.

[3] *Cf.* DE WULF, *op. cit.*, pp. 159-60.

[4] He modified his teaching repeatedly under pressure of the criticisms of his troublesome pupil, Abelard. *Cf.* DE WULF, *op. cit.*, pp. 179-80.

so that these latter differ from each other not really and substantially but only by the accidents whereby the common essence
is individuated in each.[1]

This theory has, over Platonism, the undoubted advantage of
safeguarding the validity of judgment and the possibility of a
genuine knowledge of the individual data of sense.   Nevertheless
it is wholly untenable.

I. In the first place, by destroying the distinct reality of the
individual, by denying a real distinction between individuals, it
is in too flagrant opposition to common sense.   Whether the
single " universal reality " apprehended *e.g.* through our concept
of " man," " humanity," " human nature," be held to be only
partially shared by each human individual, or to be " whole in all
and whole in each," [2] somewhat as the soul is " whole in the
whole body and whole in each and every part of the body," the
consequences are equally inadmissible.   For in the former alternative the validity of the singular judgment is sacrificed,—it
would not be true that " John is a man " but only that " John is
part of the single reality called man or humanity " ;—and in the
latter individuals are only phases or manifestations of the single
reality which is the specific universal.   Moreover, as will appear
presently, how any reality considered as having a real existence
independently of thought can likewise be conceived as universal,
as " one-common-to-many," is not easily intelligible.

II. In the second place, then, the theory we are examining
can be seen to lead logically to pantheism.   No doubt, most of
its medieval exponents merely contended that each and every
object of our specific and generic universal concepts is a distinct
reality, that these remain really distinct from each other in each
individual which participates in a number of them : that in the

---

[1] De Wulf, *op. cit.*, p. 179.

[2] *Cf.* Mercier, *op. cit.*, § 134, p. 343 : " Nearer to our own time, Ubaghs [*Le
problème ontologique des universaux*, 2 édit., Louvain, 1861] and Laforet [Louvain
professors] regarded *genera* and *species* as being in the individuals without losing
their universality there ".   And he quotes from the latter these sentences : " Realists
do not admit that the nature is multiplied with the individuals ; they see in all the
members of the human species the same nature, persisting as numerically one despite the multiplication of persons.   According to this view, which is also ours, we
have all the same human nature which neither changes nor is multiplied : a ' unity
in variety '. . . . If this view be well-founded the root difficulty of the mystery of
the Holy Trinity at once disappears . . ." (*Les dogmes catholiques*, 2e édit. i., pp.
148-50).   On which Mercier rightly remarks (*ibid.*, p. 373) that " it is futile and
dangerous . . . to attempt thus to explain mysteries philosophically : they are only
distorted by attempts to bring them down to the level of truths accessible to reason ".

individual man, for instance, there are as many distinct re.
alities as there are specific and generic concepts [1] under which
he can be classified. [2]   But then, they experienced the same
doubts and difficulties as had confronted Plato in regard to the
question whether each and every universal or class-notion of
ours,—even, for instance, our notion of " negation," of " nothing.
ness," of " deficiency," of " imperfection," etc.—has a reality, or,
as Plato would say, an " Idea," corresponding to it.   A greater
and more serious difficulty, however, is this.   If the reality of
each and every individual of a *species infima*—of human individ.
uals, for instance, as members of the *species infima* which is
" man,"—be the reality of that single specific thought-object it.
self, so that the individuals are not essentially and substantially
distinct realities, but are only parts or manifestations of the
single specific thought-object which is " man " : so too must the
reality of each and every *species* found under a higher *genus*,—of
" man " and " brute," for instance, under the *genus* "animal,"—
be the reality of this latter thought-object, which would thus be
not multiplied but numerically the same throughout all men and
brutes, whether partially or wholly manifested in each of these ;
and similarly animals and plants would be, each and all of them,
manifestations of the single reality which is "life"; living
things and inorganic bodies would be really the one self-identical
being which is "matter"; matter and spirit would be the one
real being which is "substance"; and finally, substance and
accidents would be manifestations of the one and sole reality
which is *Being.*   But this is monism or pantheism.   It is, as De
Wulf states, [3] "the logical and necessary outcome of extreme
realism, for if the attributes of *real* objects are modelled on the
attributes of *conceived* objects, the most abstract of all our concepts—that of 'being' in its widest sense—must have its cor-

---

[1] St. Thomas points out that if the universal *as such* had a distinct *real* existence, " sequeretur quod in Socrate et in Platone essent plura animalia, animal
scilicet ipsum commune, et homo communis, et ipse Plato ".   *Contra Gentes,* I.
c. 26.

   [2] In other words, that the " metaphysical grades of being " are in the individual
really distinct from one another.   *Cf. Ontology,* § 30, pp. 122-3.   Thus, then, these
writers draw the line of what is called " *real* distinction " (between the distinct realities which make up the admittedly *pluralistic* universe of our experience) *exclusively* according to what is one or manifold *conceptually,* or *for abstract thought,* and
equivalently deny that sense testimony or sense experience is in any way or to any
degree a criterion of *real* plurality within the domain of human experience.   This
view is criticized *op. cit.,* §§ 37, 38, especially pp. 147, 151-3.

   [3] *Op. cit.,* p. 154.

relative 'being' in the order of external Nature: and as all our concepts are determinations of this widest concept, so would all realities be mere determinations of this *one* real being".

The medieval realists, who were all supporters of the Christian philosophy of Theism, rightly shrank from this monistic conclusion. But many later philosophers have embraced it, and hence we may appropriately examine it on its merits here.

B. *Pantheistic Realism.*—The monistic variety of extreme realism, already attributed to Scotus Eriugena in the ninth century,[1] and expounded by Spinoza[2] (1632-1677) in the seventeenth, has gained a widespread acceptance in modern times owing to the influence of the monistic philosophy of Hegel[3] (1770-1831). It is a form of extreme realism inasmuch as it holds the universal as such to be real. But in the Platonic and Empiric forms of realism it is impossible to understand how the "Ideas" or the entities called "genera" and "species" can be endowed with universality, how they can be each a one-common-to-many, inasmuch as they are supposed to exist extramentally or independently of thought. How can anything which is supposed to exist extramentally be other than a numerically definite, incommunicable individual, which is the very antithesis of universal? The feature of universality, of being one-common-to-many, is intelligible only as a mental mode of a reality or object considered as a term of thought or conception, as present to or in some mind. The ontologists avoided the difficulty by regarding the universals as terms or objects of the Divine Thought in the Mind of the Deity. Now monistic realism appears to avoid it in another way: by boldly denying all distinction between the existence which reality has in and for the mind as an object of thought, and the existence which reality has in and for itself; by identifying the logical with the ontological, the thought-being or *esse ideale* of things, with their real being or *esse reale;* by proclaiming the duality of *subject* and *object* in knowledge to be always and necessarily a purely mental or logical distinction and never a real distinction, *i.e.* to be always the result of a presentation of reality *to itself,* or an

---

[1] DE WULF, *op. cit.*, pp. 168-72.

[2] "Mens (humana) et corpus unum idemque sunt individuum, quod jam sub cogitationis, jam sub extensionis attributo concipitur."—SPINOZA, *Ethica*, Pt. II., Prop. 21 (*apud* MAHER, *Psychology*, p. 261, n. 4).

[3] *Cf.* TURNER, *op. cit.*, pp. 561 *seq.*

opposition of reality *to itself.*[1] Thus reality, which is ever one
and the same, ever self-identical, is at once subject and object,
thought and thing, Mind and Nature, logical and ontological,
ideal and real. If we add to this that, all our concepts being
determinations of our widest concept of Being, all realities must
be likewise determinations of *One Sole* Reality, we have the
main outlines of monistic realism. This one sole reality, or
Absolute, is supposed to be evolving itself eternally, by an internal dialectic process of development, from absolute indeterminateness to its determinate manifestations in the categories,
genera, species, and individuals which constitute the domains of
Thought and Nature and Spirit. This is the sense in which the
Sole Reality is "universal," in which it is "one-common-to-
many": the evolution process, the process of constantly "becoming" or "determining itself," is *real* (and of course at the same
time, and identically, *ideal*); and the universality too is likewise
real (as well as ideal).

Now, in so far as this theory of the relation between thought
or knowledge and its objects is at all intelligible, what is the
most obvious criticism it calls for? It represents the familiar
logical thought-process whereby we "determine" or "narrow
down" our transcendental and generic concepts—of "being,"
"substance," "accident," etc.—to more and more determinate
specific concepts—of "man," "horse," "red," "triangle," "pat-
riotism," etc.—as being also and identically a process of *real*
evolution, becoming, or development of the Sole Existing Reality
into real manifestations or aspects thereof. The only criticism
we shall offer is this, that the theory is *self-contradictory.*

For, if the evolution of the Sole Reality, or Absolute, is *real*,
its manifestations must differ *really* from itself, at least in the
measure in which accidents differ from their substance: if the
manifestations do not differ really, at least to this extent, from
the evolving Absolute, the evolution of this latter cannot possibly
be claimed to be *real*. But if, in the real world, in Nature, there
is a *real* distinction between substance and accidents, then the
real world, or Nature, cannot consist of *one sole real being;* for
in the hypothesis of such a distinction, the concept or thought-
object which we designate "universal being" is the product of a

---

[1] Anything like an adequate presentation, much less a critical discussion, of
Hegelian monism, would be wholly beyond the scope of the present context. For
some brief remarks on the system, *cf. Ontology*, pp. 33, 46, 49-50, 67-8, 208.

process of *mental abstraction* the object of which is *considered as if it were unique* although it is in fact *multiplied* and really manifold in the substantial and accidental realities of Nature. But to admit that the "sole universal being" does not really exist as such, to concede that its universality is the result of a mental abstraction, would be to abandon the fundamental principle of monistic realism for the thesis of moderate realism according to which the universality of the thought-object or concept is a product of thought ("Ipsum intelligi vel abstrahi, ad quod *sequitur* intentio universalitatis"—St. Thomas). Hence the monistic realist cannot do so ; and accordingly, in maintaining simultaneously the *real* existence of the sole "universal being" and its *real* evolution, he is contradicting himself. He tries, no doubt, to escape the contradiction by contending that *the evolution of the Absolute, although real, is not positive, but purely negative or limitative.* But neither does this offer any real mode of escape ; for there are only these two alternatives : either the negation (or limitation) excludes from the Absolute something real, or it excludes nothing real. If it excludes nothing real, then all real diversity of beings is an illusion, the evolution itself is unreal, and we are outside the monistic hypothesis of a *real evolution.* If on the other hand the negation (or limitation) process does exclude from the Absolute something real, then we can understand the reality of the evolution, but also see as its inevitable consequence a real plurality of beings,— a pluralistic universe, which is the direct negation of monism.[1]

The fundamental error of monism is, of course, the assumption that the modes and relations under which abstract thought conceives reality are modes and relations of the conceived reality.

C. *The "Formalism" of the Scotists.*—A variety of realism known as "formalism" was propounded by John Duns Scotus (1266-1308) and gave the title of "formalists" to his disciples. In examining empiric realism we saw that the "metaphysical grades of being," *i.e.* the objects of the various universal concepts which we predicate of the individual, were regarded by these early realists as *really distinct* from one another in the individual. The earlier anti-realists contended on the other hand that the distinction between them—*e.g.* between the objects of our concepts of "substance," "corporeal," "living," "animal," "rational," "man," "individual," as predicated *e.g.* of John, and as actually in him,—is no more than a purely conceptual or logical distinction, without any foundation in the individual for their conceptual

---

[1] *Cf.* MERCIER, *op. cit.*, § 139, pp. 361-2, of which the text above is practically a paraphrase.

plurality. Moderate realists for the most part[1] have always maintained that the distinction is not indeed a real distinction, but neither is it purely logical ; it is a *virtual* distinction : that is to say, our concepts of the metaphysical grades of being in the individual are abstract concepts each of which in. adequately represents what is in reality one and the same being. For instance, "animality" and "rationality" are not two distinct realities com. posing the individual man, but two mentally distinct aspects of the single reality which is the individual man. And the ground for distinguishing them lies, no doubt, in the first place and subjectively, in the finiteness of our human mode of apprehending reality ;[2] but it also lies objectively in the nature of reality itself. What we might call the remote real ground of the distinction is the fact that there are various grades of perfection in the finite things of our experience,[3] and that the more perfect things include the perfections of the less : plants include the perfections of inorganic matter, and something else, namely, life ; animals all this and sensation ; man all this and also reason : so that the single reality of an individual man can be apprehended more or less adequately through the different concepts of "human "-" animal "-"living "-" corporeal" being. And what we might call the proximate real foundation of the distinction lies in the similarity and dissimilarity arising between things from the presence or absence of these perfections : thus, plants resemble inorganic things in that both are corporeal substances (*genus*), and differ from inorganic things in possessing life (*differentia*) ; man resembles the brute inasmuch as both have sentient or animal nature (*genus*) and differs from the brute in possessing reason (*differentia*).

Now although Scotists admit that the various metaphysical grades of being in the individual, the various abstract thought-objects which we pre- dicate of the individual, are not distinct *realities* in the individual, that the distinction between them is not real, nevertheless they contend that the distinction between them is not merely consequent on, and due to, our mode or process of conceiving or thinking the individual : it is more than a virtual distinction, which is a product of thought ; for the metaphysical grades,

---

[1] With a few exceptions : JEANNIÈRE (*op. cit.*, p. 449) refers to DE MARIA as maintaining that the distinction is real.

[2] "An understanding that could grasp through one single intuition all the reality of any being would have but one single concept for each being; so that the number and distinction of the concepts in such an understanding would correspond exactly with the number and distinction of the apprehended real beings in Nature. But the human understanding is not of that sort : abstraction, which is the law of our thought, must decompose the intelligible reality into a multiplicity of thought-objects ['*rationes objectivae*'] to enable us to reach an adequate comprehension of the reality ; for us this latter comprehension is possible only through a series of analyses followed by a total synthesis. We have therefore concepts which differ from one another in their respective contents, but which, nevertheless, derive these contents from the same integral reality. Consequently human science does not bear exclusively on the *extrinsic* relations of a concept to things, it has not for object purely *subjective* concepts, mere *signs* of the manifold individuals of Nature ; for first it represents to us *abstract objective aspects* of these individuals; and then it reveals these aspects synthesized into one and the same total object, and thus finally attains, laboriously but surely, to a faithful apprehension of reality."— MERCIER, *op. cit.*, § 137, pp. 358-9.

[3] *Cf. Ontology*, § 47, p. 173, § 36, pp. 140-2.

between which it exists in the individual, though they are indeed one and the same individual thing, are distinct *"formalities"* in the thing, and the distinction between them in the thing is *actually* there, grounded in and springing from *the nature of the thing*, altogether *independently of and prior to the exercise of our thought about the thing.* Hence the name of the distinction —*distinctio formalis actualis ex natura rei.* It is "formal" because the distinguished terms are not *realities* but *formalities;* but it is actually there in the nature of the thing, independently of thought: greater, therefore, than a virtual distinction, less than a real distinction.[1]

Thus, according to Scotism, any distinct metaphysical grade of being, "animality," for instance, or "rationality," has, in itself, as an object of thought in the real world, a unity of its own, a unity called "formal," which is *sui generis*, and which unites all its real, individual, manifestations in Nature into a "formal" unity ; and this unity is not a mere product of thought, any more than the "formal" distinction between any pair of such unities : both the unities and the distinctions are objectively actual independently of our thought. "Thus, the materiality apprehended by thought in all material things is one, not because it is made one by the abstracting and universalizing activity of thought, as most if not all other scholastic philosophers teach ; it is not merely *conceptually one* through our thought-activity, it is *formally one* apart from the latter ; and it thus knits into a 'formal' unity all material things. And so does 'life' all living things ; and 'animality' all animals ; and 'rationality' all men." [2]

Here we are obviously considering the "direct" or "metaphysical" universal, the *"universale in se,"* of which according to St. Thomas and Thomists we can predicate neither *unity* nor *plurality*.[3] No doubt it is one, self-identical object of thought, with a certain definite content, and has therefore through and for thought a "conceptual" unity which we may, if we wish, call formal : but this is a merely conceptual unity. No, replies Scotus : it has, corresponding to this "conceptual" unity in the *logical* order, a "formal" unity *in the ontological order.*[4]

I. Now this is what we must consider extreme or excessive realism, the "reifying" of the abstract thought-object as such. In the first place, therefore, we consider that to hold the unity of each "formality" or metaphysical grade of being, and its distinction from others, to be a unity and a distinction which are actually in reality independently of thought, involves inevitably the conclusion that such unities and such distinctions are real : and if so we are face to face with all the difficulty and unintelligibility of the abstract and universal existing *a parte re, in rerum natura.* It is, we think, unanswer-

---

[1] *Cf. Ontology*, § 39, pp. 153-7.   [2] *Ibid.*, p. 156.

[3] *Cf.* St. Thomas, *De Ente et Essentia*, chap. iv., quoted *supra*, § 76, with remarks thereon.

[4] "Licet enim [natura] nunquam sit sine aliquo istorum [*i.e.* individual 'manifoldness' or universal 'unity'], non tamen est de se aliquod istorum [*i.e.* and is itself neither an individual nor a universal], *ita etiam in rerum natura* secundum illam entitatem habet *verum 'esse' extra animam reale :* et secundum illam entitatem habet *unitatem sibi proportionabilem*, quae est indifferens ad singularitatem, ita quod *non repugnat illi unitati* de se, quod *cum quacumque unitate singularitatis* ponatur."—Scotus, *In L. Sententiarum*, 2, dist. iii., q. 7. *Cf.* De Wulf, *op. cit.*, p. 372.

ably argued against the Scotist position that between the virtual (logical) distinction and the real distinction there is no room for the Scotist distinc_ tion,[1] that this latter is intelligible only as a real distinction, whose terms, therefore, as such, must be realities. If the metaphysical grades of being are *actually distinct*, independently of thought, and not merely *distinguishable* by thought, how can the distinction be other than a real distinction?[2] The only distinct unity which any metaphysical grade of being has,—and the only unity which is compatible with its real multiplication, its *ontological* plurality or manifoldness in individuals,—is the unity which it gets in the *logical* order from the abstracting and universalizing functions of thought. To claim such distinct unity for it in the ontological order is to hold that the abstract and universal as such is real.

II. In the second place, if the unity of each metaphysical grade of being is a unity which is *actual*, independently of thought, then when we predicate any such grade of being of the individuals possessing it, and say they are " formally " one by possessing it,—*e.g.* when we predicate of all individual animals that they have " animal nature " and say they are formally one in pos- sessing it,—we can only mean that they are *actually* one (*i.e.* one animal nature), *independently of thought*. Now since individuality itself is a meta- physical grade of being, when we predicate of each and every individual being that it is " individual," and say of all of them that they are formally one in possessing this grade called individuality, are we not asserting that they are *actually* one individuality independently of thought? And the same can be applied to the predicate " being " : if all real beings, because they possess real being, are one " formally," and if this term, "*formally*," means also *actually* and *independently of thought*, then does it not follow that all indi- vidual beings are " one " ontologically? But all this points to pantheism.[3]

At the same time it must be admitted not only that pantheism has always been as strongly repudiated by Scotus and his followers as by other scholastics, but also that the inference to it has been always rejected by Scotists as invalid. And indeed if we interpret the " formal " distinction which they advocate, be- tween the metaphysical grades of being, as a *real* distinction, then pantheism could not possibly follow from the theory, inasmuch as pantheism is incom- patible with *real* distinctions. What would really follow from the theory would be rather that the lines of real distinction in things would be determined by abstract thought alone : all thought-objects between which conceptual analysis finds an adequate logical distinction would be regarded as distinct realities.[4]

Scotists, however, holding the formal distinction to be less than real, de- fend their theory from the charge of pantheism by recognizing a *real* distinc- tion *between the individuals* which share in the "*formal*" *unity* of any metaphysical grade of being, and by contending that the formal unity of any such grade of being is quite compatible with its " *real* " *plurality* and " *real* " *multiplication* in the numerically and really distinct individuals which are " formally " one by possessing or sharing in it : the formal unity of any meta-

---

[1] *Cf.* MERCIER, *op. cit.*, p. 374.   [2] *Cf. Ontology*, p. 155.
[3] *Cf.* MERCIER, *op. cit.*, p. 375 ; KLEUTGEN, P*hilos. der Vorzeit*, i., § 179.
[4] *Cf. supra*, p. 303, n. 2.

physical grade of being, although it is not a mere mental or *logical* but also an *ontological* and actual unity, and although it confers this unity on the individuals possessing such a grade of being, nevertheless does and cannot of itself fit this grade of being proximately for actual existence, and is therefore quite compatible with the ultimate determination of this grade of being by the individuating principles which are required to make it exist as a real manifold of individuals *in rerum natura*.[1]   But this reasoning ceases to be plausible the moment we ask ourselves how can unities or distinctions which are ontological and independent of thought be otherwise than real.

III. Our third and final difficulty against the theory is that the main argument on which it is based is inconclusive.   The argument is that the metaphysical grades of being in the individual are the respective grounds of mutually incompatible and contradictory predications about the individual ; therefore to avoid violation of the principle of contradiction it must be admitted that in the nature of the individual and independently of our thought these metaphysical grades must be actually distinct formalities.   For example, if the animality of Socrates were actually and formally identical with his rationality independently of our thought, then in asserting that " his rationality is the principle of his intellectual activities " we are asserting that " his animality (being formally and actually identical with his rationality) is the principle of his intellectual activities " : and it must at the same time be admitted as true that " his animality is *not* the principle of his intellectual activities " : in other words we violate the principle of contradiction.

The reply to this argument is twofold.   *Firstly*, if the argument were valid it should prove not only a formal but a real distinction between the respective grades of being in question : for if two such statements were mutually contradictory when made of what is actually the same " formality " *independently of thought*, so would they be contradictory when made of what is one and the same " reality " (independently of thought) : but Scotists admit that " animality " and " rationality " are the same *reality* in the individual independently of thought.   And as a matter of fact if the identity and unity be actually in the individual independently of thought, it is a real identity and unity ; and the distinction and multiplication of this reality into " formalities," can be only the product of thought.   In the *second* place the argument proves neither a real distinction nor a formal-actual distinction to exist between such grades of being in the individual independently of thought : it only proves that such grades of being are *distinguishable* for our imperfect and abstractive modes of thought, and are actually distinguished *by our thought*. The principle of contradiction is violated only by affirming and denying the same predicate of the same subject *under the same respect*, or, in other words, of *the same aspect* of the same reality.   It is not about realities as they are independently of our thought that we can make predications, contradictory or otherwise, but only of realities as they are apprehended through our imperfect and inadequately representative concepts of them.   The proposition " Socrates, as rational, is capable of intellectual activities " is a true proposition ;

---

[1] " Formal " unity, says Scotus, is " indifferens ad singularitatem, ita quod non repugnat illi unitati de se, quod cum quacunque unitate singularitatis ponatur."— *Cf. supra*, p. 308, n. 4.

so is the proposition "Socrates, as an animal, is *not* capable of intellectual activities ". Why are they not contradictories?—seeing that they affirm and deny the same predicate of that which, even on the admission of Scotists, is one and the same *reality*? Not because animality and rationality are actually distinct in the ontological order independently of thought,—for if they were they would be distinct realities (whatever name we give them : the title *formalities* does not alter the nature of the distinction), and Socrates would be an agglomeration of such distinct realities,[1]—but because they are logically or conceptually distinct mental aspects of one single reality, which, owing to the richness of its reality and the imperfection of our human mode of under-standing, is distinguishable by thought into such abstract and inadequate thought-objects.

[1] *Cf.* MERCIER, *op. cit.*, p. 376.

CHAPTER XI.

82. THE SO-CALLED MEDIEVAL NOMINALISM.—*Nominalism* is nowadays generally understood to designate the theory propounded by supporters of Sensism, Empiricism, and Positivism in regard to the significance of universals : the theory according to which the general or universal logical term (of language) has not even present in or to the mind a genuinely universal mental correlate or thought-object which would be intellectually apprehended as "one-common-to-many". If, however, we took *Nominalism* to include all theories opposed to any form of Realism, then obviously it would include Conceptualism which admits the presence of such genuinely universal objects in our thought but denies that these objects are in any sense extramentally real.

Now neither the earlier medieval " nominalists " represented by Roscelin (1050-1100), nor the later medieval " terminists " [1] represented by William of Occam († *c.* 1347), Gregory of Rimini († 1358) and Gabriel Biel (1425-95), denied the existence of genuinely universal concepts in the mind.[2]

The attitude of the former group was a purely negative attitude towards extreme realism.[3] That of the latter, which centred mainly on the distinction between the metaphysical grades of being in the individual, was more definitely conceptualist. Seeing that the objects of our generic, differenting and specific concepts,— *e.g.* of " animal," " rational " and " man,"—are embodied in *one* real individual,—*e.g.* Socrates,—and therefore cannot be distinct realities, these philosophers left it to be inferred that all such concepts of the individual have *intrinsically* the same content, the difference between them consisting solely in diversity of the

---

[1] *Cf.* DE WULF, *op. cit.*, pp. 418-32, 493.

[2] " Universale est intentio animae, nata praedicari de multis."—OCCAM, *In I. Sent., L. I.*, c. 15.

[3] *Cf. supra*, § 81, p. 301.

extrinsic relations of this concept or thought-object, and of the "word" or "verbal sign" which expresses it, to different indi_viduals. But if, as all scholastics held with Aristotle, the object of science is the universal, and if all the universal concepts which we have of any single individual are *intrinsically* one and the same thought-object, having a mere *extrinsic* connexion with the individuals of sense, we can understand how those "nominalists" or "terminists" could be plausibly charged with reducing all human science to a knowledge of mere words, mere *flatus vocis*— since the "word" would then express a thought-object not in_trinsic to the individual reality of sense.[1]

As a matter of fact, however, Occam and his followers meant by the "*terminus*" or "term," from which their theory gets its name, not the logical term, the spoken or written word, but the *mental* term or *intentio mentis*, the *thought*-object.[2] The distinction between these abstract and universal thought-objects apprehended by intellect in any individual, they held to be a *purely logical distinction*, without any foundation in the real, individual things for the various classes or collections of which these mental objects stood, and of which they were mere mental "signs" or representations. Thus, the abstract and universal object of intellectual conception is a mental sign which "stands for" or "denotes" a collection of individuals ; but its objective content, that which it implies, is nothing real, nothing in the real individuals for which it stands : it is exclusively a thought-product having a purely extrinsic, if natural, relation to those individuals.[3]

The error of this view lies mainly in its failure to recognize that the distinction between the abstract and universal grades of being which intellect apprehends in, and· predicates of, the individual, is more than a purely subjective and logical distinction. The distinction is not a merely subjective distinction between

---

[1] *Cf.* MERCIER, *op. cit.*, § 134, pp. 338-9.

[2] Occam "protested in advance against the absurd theory which would deny to the understanding the power of abstracting and thus identify sensation with intellectual thought. . . . In our understanding there are objects that are common, general, universal. The universal, therefore, is not a mere word (*vox, nomen*) devoid of thought-content, an empty sound (*flatus vocis*), a verbal label, but a conceived object (*intentio, terminus*), a mental substitute (*suppositio*) for a greater or less number of individual realities, according to the degree of its universality."—DE WULF, *op. cit.*, p. 423.

[3] "Illud quod praedicatur de pluribus differentibus specie, *non est aliqua res quae sit de esse illorum* de quibus praedicatur, sed est una intentio in anima naturaliter significans omnes illas res de quibus praedicatur."—OCCAM, *Expositio Aurea*, Praedicab. de Genere (*apud* DE WULF, *op. cit.*, p. 423, n. 4).

mental products whose sole relation to real individuals would be the extrinsic relation of standing as mental substitutes for these latter.[1] It is a logical distinction *with a foundation in the individual realities of sense*, a distinction between objects which for our thought are distinct as to their contents, but which, as to their contents, are really in the individuals of sense, and are mentally distinct, inadequate aspects of that which in the indi vidual is one reality.[2]

Occam's theory fails to assign any ground or justification for predicating the universal of the individual, or any reason why it is a "natural" sign of the latter. Nay, if the universal is "in no way extramental," [3] if it does not belong to the "substance or being" of individuals, if it is a mere "*intentio animae*," is not science, which is "of the universal," thereby rendered illusory, being thus divorced from reality? And, finally, does it not lead to the subjectivism in which the modern or Kantian form of conceptualism involves all speculative knowledge?

Although the germ of these consequences is indeed contained in Occam's "terminism," he himself would have disavowed and repudiated them. The real objectivity of science he seeks to uphold not merely by claiming a natural if extrinsic connexion of the universal with individual realities, but also by this other and quite distinct contention : that in addition to (intuitive) sense cognition, and abstract intellectual cognition (through universal concepts), the human mind has also an *intuitive intellectual cognition of the individual* (through "intuitive" concepts). This latter he holds, in common with Scotus and a few other medieval scholastics,[4] to be antecedent to, and necessarily presupposed by, abstract intellectual cognition. Although this contention is in itself very questionable, and seems to be based on a defective psychological analysis which mistakes the sense-percept for a concept, at all events it shows that Occam upheld the real objective validity of intellectual cognition. And it is certain that he

---

[1] " Nullum universale est extra animam existens realiter in substantiis individuis, *nec est de substantia vel esse eorum*."—Occam, *Expositio Aurea*, Praedicab. Proem., —*apud* De Wulf, *op. cit.*, p. 421.

[2] *Cf. supra*, § 81, p. 307, n. 2, passage quoted from Mercier, *op. cit.*, pp. 358-9, in explanation of this " virtual " distinction between the abstract objects apprehended by intellect in the individual reality.

[3] " *Nullo modo* est res extra animam quodcumque universale."—Occam, *Quodl.* V., Q. 12,—*apud* De Wulf, *op. cit.*, p. 421.

[4] *Cf. ibid.*, pp. 422, 426, 375, 292, 275. *Cf. supra*, § 77.

repudiated the Sensism which by confounding intellectual cogni_
tion with sense cognition has paved the way for modern Nomin_
alism.

83. MODERN NOMINALISM : GENERAL EXPOSITION AND
CRITICISM.—None of the theories we have been so far examining
endeavoured to reduce intellectual conception to a mode of sense
cognition, or denied the existence of the abstract and universal
concept as a mental object that is *sui generis* and wholly distinct
in character from any object present in sense cognition. The
last three centuries, however, have witnessed the rise and develop_
ment, both in England and on the Continent, of a philosophy
—Sensism or Empiricism—which attempts to explain all human
cognitive activities in terms of sense cognition. It is represented
mainly by Hobbes (1588-1679), Locke (1632-1704), Berkeley
(1685-1753), Hume (1711-76), John Stuart Mill (1806-73), Bain
(1818-1903), Spencer (1820-1903), Huxley (1825-95), and Sully in
England; by Herbart (1776-1841), Wundt, and the " Psychologist" school in Germany; by Condillac (1715-1780) and the
French materialists of the eighteenth century, and by Taine
(1828-93), Ribot and the " Positivist " school in France.

While differing more or less on the constructive side of their
theories of cognition, these philosophers all agree in denying to
the human mind any cognitive power of a higher order than that
of sense, or any apprehension *of a mental object that is properly
speaking universal in its capacity of representing reality.* They
speak, of course, of " intellect," " conception," " concepts,"
" thought," " abstraction," " generalization," etc., but these they
hold to differ not in kind, but only in degree, from organic sense
perception, imagination imagery, percepts, etc.,—explaining the
former rather as refinements or complex functions and products
of the latter. Neither do they deny the existence of some sort
or other of a *mental correlate,* some sort or other of a conscious,
cognitive process and *mental term,* corresponding to the common
name or general *logical term of language.* But inasmuch as they
deny to this mental term or object of awareness (19) all genuine
universality, maintaining that there is in the mind or present to
the mind no object which is " one-common-to-many," and thereby
confine universality to the verbal sign or name, they are properly
described as nominalists. Since, moreover, as we shall see in
dealing with sense perception, these philosophers generally hold
that knowledge does not and cannot extend beyond mental states,

phenomena, or appearances, or reach to the extramental, they must be set down as denying the real objective validity of knowledge.

Hume was among the first to teach that a universal idea[1] is only a singular idea associated with a general term, *i.e.* a term which has been habitually associated in our experience with other and similar singular ideas so that the mention of it easily revives these in our imagination.[2] We can *dissociate* any concrete sense impression into separate sense-elements by simple variation and successive concentration of our attention on the various parts of the complex whole. This is what they call "abstraction". Then by repetition of similar concrete experiences in consciousness we can fuse together again the similar separated elements, thus producing a sort of composite mental image which is made to signify or stand for the similar concrete experiences. This composite generic image[3] is what they call the "universal idea or concept," and its formation they describe as "universalization" or "generalization".[4] To this composite generic image, which of itself represents only the singular, concrete, actual content which it brings into consciousness,[5] we attach a common name or general term, associated by custom with the individual experiences fused together in the image, and thus make the image universal in its capacity of signifying or standing for such experiences—*universale in representando.* To the "habitual association" emphasized by Hume, Taine ascribes the existence of a *mental tendency* to attach a common name to the repeated similar perceptions;[6] and this he holds to be the sole mental correlate of the general logical term. Ribot finds the mental correlate of the "significative" or "meaning" function of general names in an *unconscious* mental concomitant of the verbal image in consciousness,—which unconscious element he describes as

---

[1] The word "idea" is used by all these writers in the widest possible sense to include any and every cognitive state of consciousness.

[2] *Cf.* HUME, *Treatise of Human Nature*, Bk. I., Part I., Sect. vii.

[3] *Cf.* SULLY, *The Human Mind*, p. 346,—*apud* MAHER, *op. cit.*, p. 277.

[4] *Cf.* MAHER, *op. cit.*, pp. 272-8; JEANNIÈRE, *op. cit.*, p. 454.

[5] *Cf.* MERCIER, *op. cit.*, § 124, p. 290.

[6] "When we explore what takes place whenever we extract a general idea from a number of perceptions, we find merely the formation, assertion, and preponderance of *a tendency which demands expression*, and, among other expressions, a *name*." —TAINE, *De L'Intelligence* (1870), t. i., p. 41. "An abstract and general idea is a name, nothing but a name, the name *understood* as *signifying* a series of similar facts, or a class of similar individuals."—*Ibid.*, t. ii., p. 259.

"stored potential knowledge,"[1] or "a hidden fund or capital of organized, latent knowledge ".[2]

If, then, as these few illustrative extracts would indicate, the "universal" is held to be merely a verbal sign attached to a mental correlate; if this latter is unconscious; or if, being conscious, it reveals merely a series of individual, concrete experiences, or at best a concrete, composite, individual mental product of their amalgamation,—it is clear that nominalists have suppressed the genuine epistemological problem of the real objective validity of *universal concepts* only by substituting for it the spurious psychological problem of accounting for the universal illusion whereby men have believed that in addition to concrete sense percepts and concrete sense images they possessed genuine universal concepts. It is to solve this problem that they have recourse to the theories of attaching the "common name" to "composite images," or "mental tendencies" springing from association, or "unconscious," "latent," "potential" sources of knowledge. But the psychological problem to which they set themselves is a spurious one; for the mental correlate of the "common name" is certainly not unconscious:[3] the *meaning* of the "common name," that which it implies, that in virtue of which it is applicable to an indefinite multitude of sense individuals, is something very definitely present in consciousness. Neither is it a mental tendency induced by association of individual perceptions with the name; nor is it a composite generic image, though this too may be and usually is present in consciousness. The mental correlate of the "common name" is none of these; it is a perfectly definite object, conceived in the abstract not by sense or imagination, but by thought, and apprehended by thought through a reflex act of comparison as indefinitely realizable in individual sense data, as "one-common-to-many" (77); in other words, it is a genuinely universal concept (73).

---

[1] "Savoir potentiel emmagasiné."—*Revue philos.*, nov. 1891, t. xxxii., p. 386. "Ce *substratum* inconscient, ce savoir potentiel, organisé."—*Ibid.*, p. 376. *Cf.* MERCIER, *op. cit.*, § 137, p. 357 n.

[2] "Im savoir organizé, latent, qui est le capital caché. . . ."—*L'Évolution des Idées générales*, p. 149.

[3] "Ribot's first mistake is to see in this ' potential ' mere sense elements, and his second is to make the universal concept consist in this ' potential '. . . . As a rule we know what we say, and our ideas are not potential but actual."—PEILLAUBE, *Theorie des concepts*, p. 112.

It is this object—apprehended by thought in the data of sense—that forms the content or connotation of the "common name," that is meant or implied by the name, and is the ground of the applicability of the name to all individuals in which the object is apprehended.

The fact that the presence of these abstract and universal concepts or thought-objects in consciousness is always accompanied by, and psychologically associated with, the simultaneous presence of concrete and individual sense-percepts or objects of imagination in consciousness,—combined with the superior vividness and force of sensation as compared with thought,—gives a certain amount of plausibility to the superficial psychological analysis whereby nominalists have sought to disprove the existence of the universal concept as a term of intellectual cognition or thought, as a mental object that is *sui generis* and irreducible to any product or complex of associated sense data. But a fuller and more searching psychological analysis of all our cognitive activities has shown so clearly and convincingly the opposite and mutually irreducible characters of the sense percept or imagination product on the one hand and the intellectual concept on the other; and the profound difference between what objects or data of consciousness *suggest* by *psychological association* and memory, and what they *logically mean* or *imply* for intellect,—that we deem it superfluous in the present context to reproduce the arguments furnished by such analysis.[1] As a general criticism of the nominalist position the following few considerations will suffice.

I. Introspection reveals the presence in consciousness of a mental correlate of the common name, a correlate of which the latter is the outward expression, and from which therefore the latter derives its function of standing for an indefinite multitude of individuals. This mental correlate introspection reveals to be not an individual sense datum, or a concrete portion isolated from each of a number of similar sense data, but to be a mental object apprehended *apart from all* the conditions of its actual existence in the similar sense data, but really in them and predicable of them : and it is because the common name *connotes* or *implies* this *abstract and universal mental object* that it can *denote*

---

[1] *Cf.* authorities referred to above, § 73, p. 256, n. 2; also MAHER, *op. cit.*, chap. xiv. ; JEANNIÈRE, *op. cit.*, pp. 456-8 ; MERCIER, *op. cit.*, § 124, pp. 289 90. *Cf. infra*, p. 320, n. 2.

or *stand for* an indefinite multitude of the similar sense data. Therefore universality is not merely or primarily in the name ; it is also and primarily in the *mental* term or object. And if some nominalists admit, as Sully seems to admit,[1] that the mind can attain to the conscious possession of an object which expresses what is indefinitely realizable in individuals, and therefore stands for those in which it is *de facto* realized,—by this admission such writers really abandon the nominalist position.

II. The main contention of nominalism is that the verbal term or name alone is universal ; and that the mental correlate, being itself sensuous and individual, derives the only universality we can ascribe to it from its uniform alliance with the name. But the *verbal* term or name can have, of and in itself, no *universal* significance unless its mental correlate be itself a universal *mental* term or object : since language derives its significance from thought, and not *vice versa*. If, therefore, the human mind had no power of apprehending any mental term or object other than a concrete, individual datum, or individual collection or fusion of such data ; if it had no power of apprehending an abstract and universal mental term or object,—then so far from the common name conferring universality on the former sort of mental term, the common name would be non-existent for us, it could have no meaning for us : in a word, we should be, like the lower animals, destitute of *language*, because like them we should be incapable of *thought* as distinct from sensation.[2]

Premising those general lines of criticism we may now profitably consider how it has come about that nominalists have so erroneously interpreted the facts of cognition as to confound intellect with sense, and the abstract and universal concept with a mental product of the sense order, asserted to be universal merely because of its inseparable psychological alliance with a common name. A brief glance at their way of understanding "abstraction" and "generalization" will supplement what we have already said (74-7) about these mental functions.

84. THE SENSIST AND POSITIVIST THEORY OF "ABSTRACTION" AND "GENERALIZATION".—There is no doubt that a series of partly similar sense perceptions,—*e.g.* of an individual poplar, pine, ash, beech, chestnut, sycamore, oak, elm,—leaves in the imagination a vague, blurred, fluctuating image of the successively recurring sense elements, *e.g.* of an "upright trunk

[1] *Cf.* MAHER, *op. cit.*, pp. 238, 276.   [2] *Cf. infra*, p. 323.

and spreading branches". But it is not this image that is universal: *it* cannot represent faithfully any member of the class, or be made to stand for any member of the class.[1] No one has brought out more clearly than Taine the differences between the image and the concept.[2] But, he continues, we attach to the former a *sign, i.e.* a *name,—e.g.* the name "tree" This sign indicates equally all the members of the class; it recalls them, and they recall it. Endowed with this double capacity of recalling individuals and being recalled by them, the name is what we call the *general idea*.[3] The isolated extract or residue which forms the composite image, to which the sign or name is attached, is, according to Taine, the result of *abstraction;* and the *generalization* of it, its transformation into a "general idea," is simply the attaching of a name or sign to it, whereby it stands for, and is recalled by, the individuals of the class. "Abstraction," then, for Taine, means

" the power of isolating the elements of facts and considering them apart. This, the most fruitful of all mental operations, proceeds by subtraction instead of addition ; instead of adding one experience to another it puts apart a portion of the former ; . . . it decomposes complex data into simple data. . . . It is this decomposition we seek when we inquire what is the nature of the object ; it is these components we seek when we endeavour to explore the inner being of a thing. We call them forces, laws, causes, essences ; . . . they are a portion, an extract, of the facts. . This operation . . . instead of going from one fact to another, goes from the same to the same, from the composite to its components. . . . It thus transcends observation and opens up a new task for the sciences, defining their limits, revealing their resources and indicating their aim." [4]

Now the procedure which Taine is here describing is not genuine abstraction at all, but a sense function which precedes and accompanies abstraction ; and apart from the latter it has not, and cannot have, the scientific value which he claims for it. What he is here describing is the process of *sense analogy* and

---

[1] *Cf.* MAHER, *op. cit.*, pp. 238, 276-8.

[2] *Cf. De L'Intelligence*, i., pp. 37-8 : " Between the vague, mobile image suggested by the name and the definite, fixed extract connoted by the name there is an abyss of difference. . . . It is impossible to imagine a polygon with ten thousand sides. . . . After five or six, twenty or thirty sides, the image fails and dissolves : but my conception of a myriagon is not an image of something vague, dissolving, falling to pieces, but of a perfectly complete and definite object. What I imagine I imagine very imperfectly ; what I conceive I conceive quite clearly : what I conceive, therefore, is not what I imagine."

[3] *Ibid.*, p. 26.

[4] *Le Positivisme Anglais*, pp. 114-18,—*apud* MERCIER, *op. cit.*, pp. 349-50.

the resulting sense experience,—endowments shared in large measure with man by the lower animals, whereas abstraction proper belongs to man alone. Animals have the power of as-sociating similar sense data, of attending to some portions of these to the exclusion of others, and so of "remembering" and "anticipating" sense experiences. And so has man in a higher degree. Man's practical life is largely guided by such memories and anticipations,—transitions from *one individual* sense datum to another *similar individual* datum. "Repeated sensations," Aristotle observed,[1] "leave impressions in the memory, and these engender experience (ἐμπειρια)." This experience, however, is of singulars; it goes from *similar* to *similar* individual; nor can it possibly bring into consciousness the universal. But there accompanies it a distinct mental activity of a totally different order, an activity ignored by Taine in common with all sensists, but which is none the less very real and operative : the activity by which we grasp mentally, in the singulars, but apart from individualizing conditions, something in them which appears to our mind one and identical,—the *abstract* nature or essence, which we *generalize* by apprehending it as *common* to all of them. This genuinely abstractive activity, as Aristotle continues in the same context, "separates from the particular instances *the one in relation with the many* (τὸ ἐν παρὰ τὰ πολλά), *i.e.* the universal. And the abstract, thus related to an indefinite multitude of individuals, is a principle of science and of art."

First, then, we have the passage by analogy from similar to similar individual, a sense process. Then we have the ab-stractive process proper, terminating in the apprehension of an *abstract* type, applicable *in its unity and identity* to an indefinite multitude of particulars,—the activity of a power distinct from, and superior to, that of sense. St. Thomas clearly distinguishes the two activities indicated by Aristotle, for in his commentary he continues :—

"The experience which apprehends something as common to the similar particular facts stored in memory involves comparison of the particulars,— which already involves a certain exercise of reason. Thus when we recollect that a certain herb has cured many people of fever we are said to gain the experience that *such an herb cures fever.* But reason does not stop in the

---

[1] *Anal. Post.*, II., c. 15. *Cf.* St. Thomas, *in loc.* Lect. XV.—"Ex sensu fit memoria. Ex memoria autem multoties facta circa eamdem rem in diversis tamen singularibus fit experimentum : quia experimentum nihil aliud videtur quam accipere aliquid ex multis in memoria retentis".

particulars : from the *many* experienced particulars it abstracts *a common element or object*, on which it fixes, and which it considers apart from the particulars whence it has been derived ; and this common object it sets up as a principle of science whether speculative or practical : as the physician does when he apprehends a *type or species* of herb as capable of curing a *type or species* of disease." [1]

This process of apprehending in each and all of the manifold similar data of sense consciousness the nature or essence which is in each and all of them, but of apprehending it apart from *all* the individualizing conditions of its actual existence in them, and hence of apprehending it as one and self-identical, and so of predicating it of each and all of them,—this is the real process of abstraction and generalization. It is wholly different from the process of concentrating attention successively on the various parts of a complex sense datum, dissolving this into its components,[2] associating individual sense data in memory, forming com-

[1] St. Thomas, *In Anal. Post.*, L. II., c. 15 ; *Cf. Science of Logic*, ii., § 208, pp. 33-4.

[2] Functions which have been improperly called *abstraction* (*cf.* Mercier, *op. cit.*, p. 352), and which would perhaps be more properly described as *extraction*. The following passage from a modern French scholastic contrasts very clearly the two procedures : " Between the abstraction of the senses and that of the intellect there is an abyss. The two procedures are irreducible. The sense 'abstract' is not really an abstract but a concrete. In the complexus *a, b, c, d, e, f*, which designate the qualities of a rose, you may fix your attention on *a*, but by doing so you merely isolate it from the other elements; it remains really individual. It is the colour of the rose, for example ; but it is still the concrete individual colour, after as well as before the act of attention. You can paint it or photograph it. But the abstract of the intellect cannot be depicted so ; for it is stripped of its concrete, individual, material features [it is abstract, *intelligible* colour : the essence or ' quidditas ' of colour]. So, too, you may trace on the blackboard an isosceles or a scalene triangle, but you cannot trace there the abstract triangle ; which is neither this isosceles, nor this scalene, nor any other particular triangle, but which nevertheless I clearly conceive and define as plane figure bounded by three intersecting straight lines, abstracting from the particular way in which they intersect.

" Again, the conceptual abstract is capable of being generalized, while the perceptual, sensible abstract is not. For this latter is essentially individual ; and between individual and universal there is an irreducible antinomy. What is individual cannot possibly be generalized without first having been freed by abstraction from all particular and concrete features. The generic image is not a universal : it is an average. A composite portrait of Cleopatra has been obtained by photography from a number of old coins. The beauty of the Egyptian queen was well-nigh indiscernible in any of the worn and rusty images, but the composite portrait revealed a pleasing figure, restoring in some sort the beauty of Cleopatra. The portrait was the optical mean or average of the medallion images. But an average has nothing universal about it. An average is a perfectly concrete particular quantity lying somewhere among certain other concrete particular quantities, to which it has certain concrete, particular relations : it is of the same order as these other quantities. So, too, the generic image, if it is a mean or average among similar images, must also partake

posite images of them, picturing in imagination this, that, or the other fancied combination of them. Such functions as these latter, exercised by animals in common with man, can never at_ tain to a *universal mental object*, but only to an individual sense datum, or an individual portion of it, or an individual synthesis of portions of such data, or a feeling of anticipation of the recur_ rence of some such individual datum. So far from their opening up avenues to progress in science they do not yield even the first essential mental requisite for rational knowledge, the *universal mental object*. Nor, in the absence of this sort of object, can the attachment of a common name to any mental correlate which re_ veals only an individual datum, make this correlate universal. For as a matter of fact were our minds only endowed with the power of apprehending individual data we should be incapable of using, or attaching any meaning to, the common names or terms of language.

Taine claims for the human mind only a "higher degree" of cognitive power than that possessed by the lower animals, and contends that this higher degree of it in man consists in his faculty of associating less obviously similar facts by *attaching to them a common name*. But it is not to any isolated sense element, or to any composite, average image resulting from composition of similar sense data, that we give the common name. The common name does not mean or imply a collection or fusion of *similar* data, but the conceptually *identical* nature apprehended by *thought* in all of them. But apart from this altogether, and no matter what may be the nature of the mental correlate of the common name, it is surely an inversion of plain facts to contend that the significance of the common name as a universal, its func- tion as a "sign," its power of denoting an indefinite multitude of individuals, is *communicated by* the name *to* the mental corre-

of the singular, the individual, the concrete, in a measure or degree which will be the mean or average of the degrees of singularity, individuality, and concreteness of the various other images. Hence neither *de facto* nor *de jure* does it embrace all the individuals of a series. The generic image of ' man ' reveals features which are not common to all people: all people are not of middle age or medium size. But young and old, great and small, male and female, are people ; and it is only the mental representation which embraces all of them that has any title to be called universal. Finally, the generic image is vague. The concept, on the contrary, is distinct. We cannot well imagine a myriagon, we can very well conceive it. . . . The conceptual abstract of intellect is therefore irreducible to the perceptual abstract of sense, and it reveals a chasm between man and beast."—PEILLAUBE, *Dict. de théol. cath.*, art. *Ame*, col. 1037 (*apud* JEANNIÈRE, *op. cit.*, pp. 462-3).

late. For as a matter of fact the name *derives* this power and function *from* the mental correlate, of which it is the verbal expression. Our cognitive processes, and their conscious, mental terms or objects, surely do not derive their intelligible meaning, their power of signifying reality, from the terms or names of language, but *vice versa*. But then, if no form of cognition attained to a *universal* mental term or object, a term or object which, as such, is " one-in-many," *implying* the "one" and *applying to* the " many,"—and nominalists contend that there is none such,—then, obviously, verbal terms or names could not derive their significance from their mental correlates ; and the only alternative left to nominalists is that of maintaining the incredible doctrine that language has its significance independently of cognition, and communicates this significance to cognition.

85. POSITIVISM AS A THEORY OF KNOWLEDGE.—The Sensist or Empiricist view of the human mind, by reducing all knowledge to *sense* experience, and by ignoring or misinterpreting the process of conception, the process of forming genuinely abstract and universal concepts, leads, as we have just seen, to nominalism. In an earlier chapter (chap. v.) we saw how this same attempt to account for all knowledge by association of the individual facts and events of sense experience involved a misinterpretation and an equivalent denial of the absolute necessity and universality of judgments and principles of the ideal order. According to this teaching, all judgments,—and therefore all knowledge, since it is in judgments that knowledge is embodied,— would consist of associations of past individual sense experiences in groups or classes according to their sensible similarities, and in feelings of anticipation of the future recurrence of such similar experiences.

Observing and classifying individual things and events in time and space ; noting their uniformities of co-existence and sequence ; and thus discovering the " laws " of phenomena,— "laws" in the sense of actually observed uniformities, but not at all in the sense of any intelligible real principles or causes of such uniformities,—these cognitive functions and their products would mark the highest efforts and the highest goal attainable by the human mind in the way of knowledge or science. The material alone, in its time-and-space manifestations, as related to sense and revealing itself in sense consciousness, as appearing to sense, as phenomenal, is the only object to which human knowledge can attain. It is only such judgments as refer to actual or possible sense experiences that can contain knowledge. They are true only in so far as they are verifiable by sense experience; their universality is limited by, and relative to, actual and possible sense experience; as universals, they are only empirical generalizations,[1] anticipations of future experiences, and, therefore, cannot be absolutely true but only more or less probable. The necessary character of such judgments is in no way absolute or ontological, but is only a psychological expression of the cumulative mental effect of some actually experienced uniformity. Causality is only sequence of time-and-space phenomena; and the "necessary" causality of Nature is only the actually experienced uniformity of its phenomena *plus* the mental anticipation of the continuation of such uniformity. Thus all genuine knowledge, all science and philosophy, are concerned only with *positive, i.e.* perceived or perceivable, things and events, and their time-and-space connexion and correlation within our positive sense experience. Hence the title *Positivism*, as descriptive of the constructive side of this general view of the scope of knowledge.[2]

Again, all the so-called knowledge hitherto believed to have been brought to light by *metaphysics*,—knowledge of the inner natures or essences of sense phenomena, knowledge of the "supra-sensible" and supposed "intelligible" aspects of these phenomena, knowledge of their first origin and final destiny, knowledge of a supposed suprasensible domain of being, knowledge of the soul and of God,—all this is chimerical and illusory. About the reality or unreality of such suprasensible objects of our conceptions, judgments and inferences, we *can know nothing*. For reason or intellect, of which these are the functions, being itself merely the mental faculty of elaborating, comparing, connecting, arranging, and systematizing sense data, cannot possibly transcend, or penetrate beyond, sense data, to furnish us with any genuine insight into what may lie within or behind or beyond such data. Hence the title *Agnosticism*, as descriptive of the negative side of the system.

Auguste Comte (1798-1857), who was the founder of this system in France,—as John Stuart Mill was its leading representative in England,—thought to support it by an appeal to history for a justification of his conception of the "three states".

---

[1] *Science of Logic*, ii., § 247.   [2] *Cf.* JEANNIÈRE, *op. cit.*, pp. 510-54.

According to his reading of history the human mind in its development has passed successively through three stages of evolution :—

"the *theological*, in which it explains natural phenomena by the interference of personal agents—supernatural beings : the *metaphysical*, in which it accounts for phenomena by metaphysical entities, occult causes, and scholastic abstractions—such as substances, forces, faculties and the like ; finally, the *positive* period, at last happily arrived, in which man abandons such futile investigations and confines himself to formulating the laws which connect phenomena ".[1]

This general theory of knowledge, superficial and one-sided as it is, suggests many obvious criticisms. The following will suffice :—

I. The fundamental principle of Positivism, put forward as if it were an axiom,—namely, that the sensible alone is knowable, that the suprasensible is unknowable,—is not an axiom but an inevident postulate, a gratuitous assumption which is neither demonstrated nor demonstrable, but is in fact false. That the individual's earliest knowledge is apprehension of concrete, material sense data, that the concrete data of external perception and introspection furnish the materials whence we derive all our knowledge,—must indeed be admitted (71). But that these can be apprehended by the mind only in their concrete, individualized condition ; that the mind cannot consciously apprehend as objects of knowledge, in and through these data, modes of being that are divested of the material, concrete, individualizing, time-and-space conditions which they have in and for sense perception and sense consciousness ; that it cannot infer from the reality of sense data the reality of positively suprasensible modes of being, —these contentions are neither demonstrated nor demonstrable. And introspection shows that they are false. As has been pointed out already (71, 72, 74, 75) the mind can apprehend,— and does apprehend when it answers the question, " *What is* this thing ?"—the essence or nature of reality, more or less adequately, and in an abstract condition in which it could not possibly be grasped by sense. And it is precisely because the mind can apprehend in this abstract condition the concrete data of sense that it can generalize, classify, compare, reason, and make progress in knowledge. The sensist theory of knowledge, on which positivists rely, misinterprets and misrepresents the mental

[1] MAHER, *op. cit.*, pp. 279-80 ; *cf. Science of Logic*, ii., §§ 224, 228.

process by which we really apprehend the abstract and uni_ versal thought-object in the concrete and individual data of sense (84).

If the principle of Positivism—that the sensible alone is know_ able—were *evident*, it would follow that *being* is evidently iden_ tical with *corporeal being*.   But this is not evident, for " corporeal " is an attribute not contained in the thought-object "being". " Being," therefore, is apprehensible by the mind apart from " corporeal " : it is knowable in itself, and has an intelligibility independent of "corporeal" being.   As objects of the mind's awareness the two objects are not identical.   Their real identity, therefore, cannot be asserted without proof.   Neither, of course, can it be asserted without proof that there are modes of real being which are not corporeal.   We do not and cannot see *a priori* the real possibility of an incorporeal or spiritual domain of real being ; but neither do we see *a priori* its evident impossibility ; nor, therefore, have positivists any right to assert *a priori* the impossibility of suprasensible or " metaphysical " knowledge. Such an assertion is mere gratuitous dogmatism.

In defending the possibility of a genuine metaphysical know- ledge against agnosticism, our method is to set out from the admitted facts of sense experience and introspection, and to show, on the basis of these facts, that *unless we admit the existence* of a suprasensible, immaterial, spiritual domain of reality, we not only find those facts inexplicable, but find ourselves involved in contradictions in any and every alternative attempt to explain them.   Hence, we argue, such a domain of being really exists. But if it exists it is possible ; and so the claims of metaphysics demand a hearing : to prejudge them as inadmissible is un- scientific, and positivism does prejudge them.

We admit that our knowledge of suprasensible, intelligible objects is of a different kind from our sense knowledge : supra- sensible objects cannot be seen, or heard, or smelled, or tasted, or touched, or pictured in imagination ; they can only be *thought* or *conceived*.   But apparently, because the *rational* cognitive faculty of the human mind, the intellect or understanding, does not apprehend its objects in the ways in which the corporeal, sense faculties apprehend their objects, positivists would have us believe that the former faculty and its objects are unreal and illusory.   We admit, too, that since reason or intellect apprehends its proper objects,—objects which are incorporeal or immaterial

only *negatively* or by abstraction (71): the essences or natures
of corporeal or material beings,—in and through the data of
sense, its concepts and judgments of positively and really incorporeal beings do not represent intuitively and immediately,
but only analogically and discursively, the real natures of those
incorporeal beings. But it is gratuitous to deny, with positivists,
that such imperfect knowledge is genuine as far as it goes (74).
We admit, finally, that whatever we claim to know about the
natures or essences even of corporeal things, whatever we know
about them as substances, agents, causes; about their faculties,
forces, energies; about their contingency, their origin, their purpose,—all this we know only by rational inference from their
visible behaviour in the phenomena of sense: on the principle
" *Operari sequitur esse* "; " *Qualis est operatio talis est natura* ".
But while positivists deny the validity of such inference and its
results, they themselves employ it in *classifying* phenomena and
bringing to light the *laws* of phenomena: for how can we classify
phenomena or formulate laws of their conduct without knowing
their *natures* or *kinds* ?

II. The kindred assertion of positivists, that the human mind
cannot know the *Absolute* but only the *relative*, is another piece
of dogmatism which derives any plausibility it has from its ambiguity.[1] It is meant of course to convey that we can attain to no
knowledge of God, who is the Absolute in the full and proper
sense; or of any suprasensible factors of sense phenomena, fac
tors not apprehensible by, or related to, sense cognition. That
whatever is *knowable* must be *referable* to the mind, and that
whatever is *known* must stand *in actual relation* to the mind, it
would be self-contradictory to deny. This, however, merely involves that the suprasensible cannot be known *by sense*. If we
understand by the relative and the absolute the sensible and the
suprasensible respectively, then we can know the absolute if we
have a faculty of knowledge, *viz.* intellect or reason, into relation
with which the suprasensible can be brought. And as a matter
of fact it is by intellect or reason that we know the sensible as
relative. We cannot know phenomena to be phenomena unless
we know them to be phenomena or appearances *of something, i.e.*
of some substance or substances; we cannot know them as effects
unless we know them to be effects *of something, i.e.* of some cause

[1] *Cf.* MAHER, *op. cit.*, pp. 158-9, 280. For division of *being* into *absolute* and
relative, cf. Ontology, § 5, pp. 47-9.

or causes.   And, in general, as Maher observes,[1] " Reason knows the absolute by the very fact that it cognizes the relative *to be relative*.   Knowledge of the relative, *as such*, involves as its necessary consequence, knowledge of the absolute " ;—and not only knowledge of the *existence* of an absolute, but by reasoning from effect to cause, from operation to essence, some degree of genuine knowledge of the *nature* of the absolute.

III.   Comte's conception of the three stages in the mental development of the race is a subjective and fanciful misreading of history, prompted by the needs of his own theory.[2]   Certain epochs have been characterized by a *predominant* interest in the problems of religion, or in metaphysical problems, or in the special problems of the positive sciences of observation and experiment, respectively.   But the contention that these three preoccupations have been *distinct*, *successive*, and *mutually exclusive*, is not only a discredited travesty of history : it is no less a palpably prejudiced account of the interests, the efforts, and the aspirations of the human mind confronted with the problems of experience.   To deny that men have at all times, and by their very nature must have, interested themselves in the three great domains of inquiry, the religious, the philosophical, and the scientific, is no less futile than to assert that in this latest and so-called " positive " epoch they will eschew religion and philosophy, to devote themselves to classifying facts and cataloguing the " laws " or observed " uniformities " of facts.

[1] *Op. cit.*, p. 280.   [2] *Cf.* Mercier, *op. cit.*, § 129, pp. 323-6.

CHAPTER XII.

VALIDITY OF CONCEPTS: CONCEPTUALISM; KANT'S DOCTRINE.

86. GENERAL VIEW OF CONCEPTUALISM.—We have now to examine the theory which admits that the human intellect can form genuinely universal concepts, and can by means of each such concept apprehend as a mental or conceptual unity an indefinite multitude of similar individual data of sense ; but denies that there is in these latter any real ground for the concept, anything really represented or apprehended through the concept; and therefore concludes that the universal concept gives us no genuine or valid insight into the nature or reality of the data of sense.

Occam and certain other scholastics of the fourteenth and fifteenth centuries [1] propounded this doctrine under the title of *Terminism*. We have already examined this form of conceptualism (82), and seen that it imperils the real objectivity of human knowledge,—a defect which is inherent in every form of conceptualism. Since it is by attributing universal predicates, in our judgments, to singular or individual subjects, that we attain to whatever intellectual or scientific knowledge we have of these subjects, if the universal predicate reveals nothing that is really in the singular subject we cannot escape the consequence that intellectual knowledge is an illusion. [2]

Certain very recent writers of the anti-intellectualist or *Pragmatist* school [3] boldly accept, and proclaim the accuracy of, this sceptical conclusion. It is not by intellect, they say, but only by the immediate and direct intuitions of sense experience

---

[1] *Cf.* JEANNIÈRE, *op. cit.*, p. 477.

[2] The conclusion from moderate realism, which recognizes that the universal is really in the singular, is, of course, that intellectual knowledge of the latter, though never exhaustive or comprehensive, is or can be genuine and accurate as far as it goes.

[3] *Cf.* BERGSON, *Introduction à la métaphysique, Rev. de Mét. Mor.*, 1903, pp. 7-25 (*apud* JEANNIÈRE, *op. cit.*, pp. 478, 493) ; *L'Évolution créatrice*, c. iv., pp. 203-6, 217, 2:0, 370, etc.; JAMES, *A Pluralistic Universe*, Lect. V.-VIII.; *cf. La théorie des concepts chez M. Bergson et W. James* in the *Rev. de Phil.*, Decr., 1910.

that we attain to genuine knowledge of reality. The real, as presented in sense intuition, is a dynamic, ever-flowing, ever-evolv_ ing continuum ; whereas the intellectual concept presents us with something wholly heterogeneous and antithetic to this, *viz.* an object that is static, fixed, isolated. Hence the intellectual con_ cept cannot be said to reveal reality. Intellect itself is an evolved faculty, evolved to meet the practical need of defining, control_ ling and directing the current of intuitional sense experience ; and this it does by means of those intellectual products called concepts.

Bergson and his disciples thus exaggerate the truth that in_ tellect cannot give us an *exhaustive view* of the concrete, indi_ vidual reality, into the error that it can give us *no insight* into the latter. Had he distinguished, or rather appreciated the dis_ tinction recognized by scholastics for centuries, between the *mental mode* of the universal concept, *viz.* its *abstractness* and *universality*, and its *objective content* (76), he would have seen how the universal can, without contradiction, be predicated of the singular, and can validly reveal to us the reality of the singular.

The most prevalent and ambitious form of conceptualism in modern times is, however, that which Kant has embodied in his philosophy. In the preceding chapter (85) we connected positiv_ ism with nominalism and with the sensist theory on the neces_ sity and universality of ideal judgments (chap. v.). We must now similarly take up, in direct connexion with the Kantian theory which based the necessity and universality of such judg_ ments on *a priori* mental forms (chaps. vi., vii.), the Kantian theory in regard to the validity of concepts.

87. CONCEPTUALISM OF KANT'S DOCTRINE.—Kant's solu_ tion of the question whether our universal concepts are repre_ sentative of, and validly applicable to the concrete data furnished to us in and through sense perception, is generally described as a form of *conceptualism*, inasmuch as it vindicates, against empiricism and nominalism, the mental existence of genuinely universal con_ cepts, but fails to find for these latter in the domain of sense consciousness any ground for their existence in the understanding, or any real correlate to which he can prove them to be validly applicable. If, however, his doctrine is conceptualism, it is a peculiar form of conceptualism. It is not conceptualistic in in- tention ; for Kant labours hard to prove that the universal con- cepts which lie at the basis of all knowledge, *viz.* the categories

of the understanding, *are* validly applicable to the intuitions of sense. But in effect his doctrine is conceptualism ; because his account of the mode of formation of the *empirical* concept, as a synthesis of a sense intuition with a pure *a priori* category of the understanding, makes it impossible for this latter to yield a genuine insight into the nature of *what is given* in the sense intuition. This will appear from the following simple consideration.

According to Kant it is because we unify the manifold which is given in sense intuition, by synthesizing it with the pure categories of the understanding, that we can apprehend *in the products* of such synthesis, *i.e.* in *phenomena*, relations that are " objective," "necessary" and "universal," and thus constitute scientific knowledge. We therefore apprehend such relations and connexions in the data of sense intuition only *because we have superinduced on these* the pure *a priori* forms of the understanding.[1] Hence the empirical concepts so formed, and the judgments in which we utilize them as predicates, can give us no knowledge of the character of the manifold data in the domain of sense consciousness, but only of a product subjectively derived from these by permeating them with the pure categories of the understanding.[2]

We must now see whether the universal concepts which we use in our judgments, and whereby we interpret what is given in sense perception, are syntheses of *a priori* forms of the understanding with a manifold given in sense intuition, and whether therefore they reveal, not any characteristic of the manifold, but merely the nature of the synthesized product.

88. IF ALL CONCEPTS INVOLVE A PRIORI SYNTHESES, WHAT MOVES OR DETERMINES THE MIND TO FORM SUCH SYNTHESES?—Kant allows that in relating two concepts in a judgment we determine the particular form of the judgment by *analysis* of the concepts ; and also that in bringing individual perceptions under a concept—*e.g.* " This body is divisible,"—we find the concept ("divisible") *in* the perception ("this body") by *analysis* of the latter.[3] But his main contention is that we form *all* such universal concepts—*e.g.* the concept of "divisible," which we use in the judgment just illustrated, and the concept of " body " which we use in the singular judgment whereby we

---

[1] *Cf.* PRICHARD, *op. cit.*, p. 165.   [2] *Ibid.*, pp. 212-13.
[3] *Cf. ibid.*, p. 166, n. 3.

interpret an individual datum of sense perception, "This is a body"—by an *a priori* synthesis whereby we think whatever manifold we designate " divisible" as an *attribute*, and whatever manifold we designate "a body" as a *substance*. And so for all other universal concepts. Hence *all* our universal concepts— *even those of lesser universality, specific and generic concepts*, which can be subsumed under the *ultimate* and *widest* concepts or " categories"—involve, and are originated by, the function of synthesizing *a priori* a *pure* form or concept of the understanding with a manifold given in sense intuition.[1]

By performing this synthesis the understanding establishes " objective" connexions and relations that are necessary and universal among the data thus conceptually synthesized. It is not that the understanding *discovers* these relations or any ground of them in the manifold of sense; it *puts* them *into* the latter. Then the problem for Kant is, *What guides or determines the understanding in establishing the specific relations which it does establish in its conceptual syntheses of sense data ?*

We must also note here that Kant's view of the concept as a synthesis of a manifold apparently excludes from the purview of his treatment those concepts which philosophers have traditionally described as " simple," or unanalysable into constituent notes or elements, and confines his attention mainly, if not exclusively, to complex concepts.[2]

It would, however, be perhaps more accurate to say that for Kant even concepts that are simple in the sense of being unanalysable into more elementary concepts,—*e.g.* redness, equality, etc.,—are *all* complex in the sense that they are each a synthesis or unification (under a category) either of an empirical manifold or of a *pure a priori* manifold such as he supposes to be

---

[1] *Cf. Critique*, p. 64 : " Before we can proceed to an analysis of our representations, these must first be given, and, as far as their contents are concerned, no concepts can arise analytically. Knowledge is first produced by a synthesis of what is manifold (whether given empirically or *a priori*)." The whole section referred to (pp. 63-9) is of the first importance. *Cf.* Prichard, *op. cit.*, pp. 161 *sqq.*; Mercier, *op. cit.*, § 140, pp. 380-1. The reference to " *a priori* " in the last sentence quoted finds its meaning in Kant's view that *space* and *time* are *pure a priori perceptions*. As we shall see later, they are abstract concepts of the understanding.

[2] Criticizing Kant's *Postulates of Empirical Thought* in connexion with the categories of Modality (*cf. Critique*, pp. 178-91), Prichard writes : " In this context, as in most others, Kant in speaking of a conception is thinking, to use Locke's phraseology, not of a ' simple ' conception, such as that of equality or of redness, but of a ' complex ' conception, such as that of a centaur, or of a triangle in the sense of a three-sided three-angled figure. It is the apprehension of a ' complex ' of elements " (*op. cit.*, p. 310).

given in the pure *a priori perceptions* of space and time.[1] Thus, presumably, the concepts of " redness " and " equality " would be empirical concepts, but they would presuppose and involve the synthesis of the pure concepts of " inherence " (or " attribute ") and " plurality " (?), respectively, with the manifold supposed to be given in the pure *a priori* perception of " space " (or " time ").[2] Now, abstracting for the present from the possibility of a *pure a priori* perception of a spatial or temporal manifold,[3] it is an undoubted fact that every definite concept is a representation which brings before the mind something as a (conceptual, abstract) *unity;* and when this unity involves a manifold (of constituent notes or elements), as it does in the case of complex concepts, it is very important to discover what it is, according to Kant's theory, that *guides and determines the mind to form such complex representations.*[4]

Again, as we have seen already (49), the mere conceivability of a certain complex of notes or elements as a self-consistent whole or unity is, according to Kant, no index to the *real* or *objective possibility* of such a complex :[5] to be objectively possible the complex must be known to " express *a priori* the relations *of perceptions*[6] in every kind of experience " : in other words, it must be known not to be *suprasensible* or *transcendent.*[7] This, of course, is a mere assertion of the arbitrary principle involved in Kant's theory of knowledge, " that everything knowable must conform to the conditions involved in its being an object of possible experience,"[8] and must therefore be presentable in *sense* intuition. Rejecting this arbitrary limitation, scholastic philosophers hold that any complex of manifold notes or elements seen by the mind to constitute a self-consistent unity is *eo ipso* really and objectively possible.[9] Not that the complex in question is possible *because* it is conceivable, but that it is conceivable because it is possible ; conceivability being the

---

[1] *Cf. Critique*, p. 179: " A concept is to be considered as empty, and as referring to no object, if the synthesis which it contains does not belong to experience, whether as borrowed from it (in which case it is called an empirical concept), or as a synthesis on which as a condition *a priori*, all experience (in its form) depends, in which case it is a pure concept, but yet belonging to experience, because its object can only be found in it ".

[2] *Cf. supra*, § 49.   [3] *Cf. infra*, chap. xxi.

[4] *Cf.* MERCIER, *op. cit.*, § 140, p. 381.

[5] *Cf. Critique*, p. 179 : " It is no doubt a necessary logical condition, that . . . a concept must contain nothing contradictory, but this is by no means sufficient to establish the objective reality of a concept, that is, the possibility of such an object, as is conceived by a concept ".

[6] *Ibid.*, p. 180,—italics ours.

[7] *Ibid.*, p. 178 n. *Cf.* PRICHARD, *op. cit.*, p. 212, n. 3.

[8] *Ibid.*, p. 309.   [9] MERCIER, *op. cit.*, § 131, pp. 330-2.

a posteriori test and index of possibility.[1] Thus, whatever
scholastic philosophers may think that this objective and real
possibility ultimately involves,[2] they do not make the human
mind the measure of the possibility of things; whereas Kant
makes the human mind the measure not only of the *possibility*,
but of the *actual existence*, and even of the absolutely *necessary*
existence of the *objects* of its knowledge, or of *things in so far as*
they are knowable. This startling conclusion is a necessary con.
sequence of his doctrine that the categories of modality (possibility or impossibility, *existence* or *non-existence*, necessity or
contingency) "express only a relation [of the object of know-
ledge] to our faculty of knowledge"[3]

Thus, then, according to Kant, in order to know that a concept is "objectively possible," or, in other words, that its complex content is a really possible object, we must either (1) have
sense experience of the actuality of such an object, or (2) know
it to fulfil the *a priori* conditions of experience, *i.e.* to be representable in an *a priori* space-and-time sense intuition and apprehensible under the pure *a priori* categories of the understanding.
And it is to be noted that even the concepts whose possibility is
known in the former way can be thus known to be possible only
because they too have already conformed to the conditions in
the second alternative. This is important; because while Kant
seems to *allow* that in forming empirical concepts the synthesis
is guided and motived by "experience," he *really denies* to *what*
is given in "experience" any determining influence in the formation of the concept, inasmuch as the "experience" must, on his
theory, be already determined to be what it is by the *a priori*
application of the pure categories of the understanding to the
unknown and unknowable data of sense intuition. Hence in
all cases of intellectual conception what makes the conceived synthesis or complex a possible object, what differentiates it from
merely subjective, "arbitrary,"[4] "fictitious"[5] combinations, or
tricks of thought, or "mere cobwebs of our brain,"[6] what gives
it its "knowledge" value, is *not* the extramental *datum*, or the
concrete content or manifold in sense perception, *but* the in-

---

[1] *Cf. Ontology*, § 16, p. 86.   [2] *Ibid.*, §§ 18, 19, pp. 89-100; *supra*, § 70.
[3] *Critique*, p. 178. The position escapes absurdity only by being based on the
fundamental error that all "objects of knowledge" are mental appearances.
[4] *Cf. ibid.*, p. 181.   [5] "*Gedichtete*," *ibid.*
[6] *Ibid.*, p. 180.

stinctive, unconsciously operative, determining influence of the *a priori* categories of the understanding.[1]

89. KANT'S VINDICATION OF UNIVERSAL CONCEPTS AS A PRIORI SYNTHESES OF THE CATEGORIES WITH THE MANIFOLD OF SENSE INTUITIONS.—We may now state Kant's main contentions in regard to the nature of conception and the rôle of concepts in knowledge: All knowledge implies and depends on concepts; and the function whereby we form concepts is a function whereby we combine an *a priori* form or category of the understanding with a manifold of sense intuition. This manifold consists in itself of mere isolated units.[2] The imagination, as *productive*, first synthesizes these in an image, and, as *reproductive*, can recall them as thus unified.[3] But in order to be thus capable of synthesis and reproduction they must have themselves a certain *affinity*[4] whereby they are synthesized not arbitrarily but in a fixed, orderly way, according to a rule.

This affinity, however, has not its ground in the manifold of sense but in "the principle of the unity of apperception . . . according to [which] all phenomena, without exception, must so enter into the mind or be apprehended as to agree with the unity of apperception".[5]

---

[1] *Cf.* PRICHARD, *op. cit.*, p. 311; MERCIER, *op. cit.*, § 140, pp. 380-1.

[2] " We cannot represent anything as connected in the object, without having previously connected it ourselves."—*Critique*, p. 744. *Cf.* PRICHARD, *op. cit.*, p. 170.

[3] The faculty here described by Kant as the *imagination* must be merely the *intellect* or *understanding* working spontaneously or unreflectively. *Cf.* PRICHARD, *op. cit.*, pp. 167-9, 175-7.

[4] *Cf. Critique*, p. 100.

[5] *Ibid.*, p. 100. That is, the " affinity " (of the sense-manifold), which is an *a priori* condition for the function of empirically producing definite mental images (as unities) by associating the isolated sense elements, and reproducing these images, implies " that the act by which the data of sense enter into the mind or are apprehended, *i.e.* the act by which the imagination *apprehends and combines* the data of sense into a sensuous image, must *make* the elements such that they have affinity, and therefore such that they can subsequently be recognized as parts of a necessarily related whole."—PRICHARD, *op. cit.*, p. 225. The author points out (*ibid.*, n. 1) that on this interpretation " Kant's argument formally involves a circle. For . . . he argues that the synthesis of perceptions involves reproduction according to rules, and then, . . . that this reproduction presupposes a synthesis of perceptions." The main point is, however, that according to Kant all affinity or connectedness of phenomena or objects of knowledge comes *from the mind's activity*. And he means by this affinity *the Uniformity of Nature*: " If cinnabar were sometimes red and sometimes black, sometimes light and sometimes heavy, if a ' man could be changed now into this, now into another animal shape, if on the longest day the fields were sometimes covered with fruit, sometimes with ice and snow, the faculty of my empirical imagination would never be in a position when representing

All unity, therefore, all connectedness, of the contents of any empirical concept, is due not to what is given in sense intuitions, but is *superinduced on this by the unifying function of the understanding.* This systematic connectedness of the manifold of sense can be effected only by the categories of the understanding, and *on the assumption that the functions of the categories presuppose a "transcendental apperception," or "a priori unity of self-consciousness".*[1]

red colour, to think of heavy cinnabar. . . ."—*Critique*, pp. 83-4. For the resulting phenomenism, *cf. ibid.*, pp. 102-5, 94, 765; PRICHARD, *op. cit.*, pp. 211-13.

[1] " No knowledge [Erkenntnisse] can take place in us, no conjunction or unity of one kind of knowledge with another, without that unity of consciousness which precedes all data of intuition, and without reference to which no representation of objects is possible. This pure, original, unchangeable consciousness I shall call *transcendental apperception.* . . . The numerical unity of that apperception therefore forms the *a priori* condition of all concepts, as does the manifoldness of space and time of the intuitions of sense."—*Critique*, p. 88. *Cf.* PRICHARD, *op. cit.*, pp. 187-9.

Of course what is really presupposed by all knowledge, and especially involved in memory, is a real, permanent, abiding, self-identical, knowing subject or mind. But that *consciousness* of such a self is a transcendental or *a priori* condition of knowledge, or that such consciousness is *possible*, as " a condition which precedes all experience, and in fact renders it possible " (*ibid.*, p. 88), Kant nowhere proves. He merely assumes the necessity of such a consciousness (*cf.* PRICHARD, *op. cit.*, p. 198), and contrasts it with "the *internal sense*, or the empirical apperception" which is " empirical only, and always transient," and which, being merely a " stream of internal phenomena," can yield "no fixed or permanent self ". This presupposition of a " fixed or permanent self " or of a " transcendental unity of apperception" Kant holds to be necessarily implied by the possibility of knowledge as a synthesis of a manifold through the categories of the understanding. Without this " transcendental ground of the unity of our consciousness . . . it would be impossible to add to our intuitions the thought of an object, for the object is no more than that something of which the concept predicates such a necessity of synthesis " (*ibid.; cf.* PRICHARD, *op. cit.*, p. 187). Thus the objectivity of the concept is simply the realization that as a synthesis it implies this transcendental ground; and this "transcendental ground " this " fixed or permanent self " cannot itself be an object of knowledge : it is the *noumenal Ego*, and therefore itself an unknowable *x*.

Here Kant attributes the unity and objectivity of the concept, as a synthesized product, ultimately to the unknowable influence of the *noumenal Ego*. Earlier in the same context he appears to have attributed it to the equally unknowable influence of the thing in itself, or the *noumenal non-Ego*: " We find that our conception of the relation of all knowledge to its object contains something of necessity, the object being looked upon as that which prevents our cognitions [Erkenntnisse] from being determined at haphazard, and causes them to be determined *a priori* in a certain way, because, as they are all to refer to an object, they must necessarily, with regard to that object, agree with each other, that is to say, possess that unity which constitutes the concept of an object " (*ibid.*, pp. 86-7; *cf.* PRICHARD, *op. cit.*, p. 178. By the influence of the "object" Kant here means the influence of the transcendental reality, or thing in itself; *cf.* his recognition of an " affinity " in the manifold of sense, *supra*, p. 214, n. 2). But he concludes that " since we have only to do with the manifold of our representations, and the *x*, which corresponds to them (the object), since it is to be something distinct from all our representations, is for

The recognition of a manifold of sense as thus obtaining the necessary and systematic unity *of a certain kind*[1] bestowed on it by conception, is *eo ipso* the recognition of it as a representation that is not merely subjective and arbitrary, but as one that is *objective*, or "related to an object". This object is, of course, the noumenal or transcendental *x*: the something which, though unknowable, Kant holds we must think of as the noumenal *Ego* or "transcendental unity of apperception". Through relation to this *a priori* condition of knowledge the manifold of sense intuition is recognized as necessarily and systematically unified by the combining function of the categories as modes of this transcendental unifying function of the mind's self-consciousness.

Thus Kant argues *both* from the possibility of conception or knowledge as *objective*,—or representative of mental objects or phenomena as systematic, orderly, mental products, synthesized according to rules or laws or principles,—*and* from the possibility of a necessary, transcendental self-consciousness in the apprehension of such products[2] (which self-consciousness he does not prove, and which really implies that the transcendental *Ego* is a *Necessary Being*, an *Ens Necessarium*), to the conclusion that both knowledge and self-consciousness imply that all our concepts are mental syntheses of *a priori* forms of the understanding with the data of sense intuition, and reveal to us the mental products of these syntheses as objects of knowledge.

Before criticizing this doctrine it will be convenient to state and criticize his completion of it as contained in his theory of the "schematism of the categories".

90. KANT'S ACCOUNT OF THE TRANSITION FROM INDIVIDUAL TO UNIVERSAL IN COGNITION.—The categories of the understanding are, after all, a very small number of abstract

us nothing, the unity which the object necessitates can be nothing else than the formal unity of consciousness in the synthesis of the manifold of representations" (*ibid.*, p. 87; PRICHARD, *op. cit.*, p. 182).

It is no wonder that Kant thus wavers between attributing the unity of the concept to the *noumenal Ego* or to the *noumenal non-Ego*, for since both are an unknowable *x* he has no right to distinguish between them. "Up to this point," says PRICHARD (*op. cit.*, pp. 182-3), "it is the thing in itself which produces unity in our representations. Henceforward it is we who produce the unity by our activity in combining the manifold. The discrepancy cannot be explained away, and its existence can only be accounted for by the exigencies of Kant's position. When he is asking ' What is meant by the object (beyond the mind) corresponding to our representations?' he is thinking of the unity of the representations as due to the object. But when he is asking ' How does the manifold of sense become unified?' his view that all synthesis is due to the mind compels him to hold that the unity is due to us."

[1] And not merely a systematic unity in general. *Cf.* PRICHARD, *op. cit.*, p. 185.
[2] *Cf. supra*, p. 214, n. 2.

conceptions which do not in themselves seem applicable to the concrete data of sense intuition. The former are static, change_less, and timeless. How can the transient, changing, temporal manifold of sense intuition be subsumed under them? It is the old question of the relation of the concept to the percept, of the universal to the singular; of the transition from sense to intellect (72, 75-77). And Kant effects the transition by a doctrine no less artificial than that of his metaphysical deduction of the categories from the forms of judgment: the doctrine of "the schematism of the pure concepts of the understanding".

- We saw above that Kant ascribes to the faculty which he calls *productive imagination* (and which must be interpreted to mean the understanding or intellect working unreflectively) the transcendental function of effecting an "*a priori* synthesis founded upon rules," and of thereby introducing "affinity" into phenomena.[1] He now calls in the aid of the imagination to produce a sort of mediating concepts, called *schemata* (52), between the pure forms of the understanding and the intuitions of sense, and thus to render possible the subsumption of the latter under the former: for even the images resulting from the *a priori* synthesis of the productive imagination are concrete, sensuous, and heterogeneous as compared with the pure concepts, or forms of the understanding.[2] Prichard[3] thus summarizes Kant's statement and solution of the problem:—

"Whenever we subsume an individual object of a certain kind, *e.g.* a plate, under a conception, *e.g.* a circle, the object and the conception must be homogeneous, that is to say, the individual must possess the characteristic which constitutes the conception, or, in other words, must be an instance of it. Pure conceptions, however, and empirical perceptions, *i.e.* objects of empirical perceptions, are quite heterogeneous. We do not, for instance, perceive cases of cause and effect. Hence the problem arises, 'How is it possible to subsume objects of empirical perception under pure conceptions?' The possibility of this subsumption presupposes a *tertium quid*, which is homogeneous both with the object of empirical perception and with the conception, and so makes the subsumption mediately possible. This *tertium quid* must be, on the one side intellectual and, on the other side, sensuous. It is to be found in a 'transcendental determination of time,' *i.e.* a conception involving

[1] " Only by this transcendental function of the imagination does even the affinity of phenomena, and with it their association and, through this, lastly their reproduction according to laws, and consequently experience itself become possible, because without it no conceptions of objects would ever come together into one experience." —PRICHARD, *op. cit.*, p. 223 ; *Critique*, p. 101.

[2] *Cf. Critique*, pp. 112 *sqq.*   [3] *Op. cit.*, p. 248 ; *cf. Critique, l.c.*

time and involved in experience.   For in the first place this is on the one side
intellectual and on the other side sensuous, and in the second place it is so far
homogeneous with the category which constitutes its unity that it is universal
and rests on an *a priori* rule, and so far homogeneous with the phenomenon
that all phenomena are in time.   Such transcendental determinations of time
are the schemata of the pure conceptions of the understanding." [1]

Now the schema of any category, according to Kant, is not
the image synthesized by the imagination, though it " is in itself a mere product of the imagination ".   It is rather the

" representation of a general procedure of the imagination to supply its image
to a conception [or category].   The fact is that it is not images of objects,
but schemata, that lie at the foundation of our pure sensuous conceptions.
No image could ever be adequate to our conception of a triangle in general.
For it would not attain the generality of the conception which makes it valid
for all triangles, whether right-angled, acute-angled, etc., but would always be
limited to one part only of this sphere.   The schema of the triangle can exist
nowhere else than in thought, and signifies a rule of the synthesis of the imagination in regard to pure figures in space.   An object of experience or an
image of it always falls short of the empirical conception to a far greater
degree than does the schema ; the empirical conception always relates immediately to the schema of the imagination as a rule for the determination of
our perception in conformity with a certain general conception.   The conception of ' dog ' signifies a rule according to which my imagination can draw
the general outline of the figure of a four-footed animal, without being limited
to any particular single form which experience presents to me, or indeed
to any possible image which I can represent to myself *in concreto*.   This
schematism of the understanding in regard to phenomena is an art hidden in
the depths of the human soul, whose true modes of action we are not likely
ever to discover from Nature and unveil.   Thus much only can we say : the
image is a product of the empirical faculty of the productive imagination,
while the *schema* of sensuous conceptions (such as of figures in space) is a
product and, as it were, a monogram of the pure *a priori* imagination, through
which, and according to which, images first become possible, though the
images must be connected with the conception only by means of the schema
which they express, and are in themselves not fully adequate to it.   On the
other hand the schema of a pure conception of the understanding is something which cannot be brought to an image [' was in gar kein Bild gebracht
werden kann ' : ' which can never be made into an image '—MÜLLER, p. 116] ;
on the contrary it is only the pure synthesis in accordance with a rule of unity
which the category expresses, and it is a transcendental product of the imagination which discerns the determination of the inner sense in general
according to conditions of its form (time) with reference to all representations,

---

[1] *Op. cit.*, p. 248.   The author rightly notes that Kant's argument here is inconclusive inasmuch as " transcendental determinations of time," although homogeneous with the categories in the sense of being universal and *a priori* are not
homogeneous with the categories in the way required, *viz.* in the sense of being
instances or species capable of subsumption under the latter.

so far as these are to be connected *a priori* in one conception according to the unity of apperception." [1]

We have quoted this passage *in extenso* not only to help the reader to catch the general drift of Kant's meaning, but also to call attention to the curious analogy which one cannot help observing between Kant's attempt to effect the transition from percept to concept, from concrete and singular to abstract and universal, and the scholastic treatment of the same problem. For the unconscious function of the scholastic *intellectus agens*, using the *phantasma* of the imagination to generate the *species intelligibilis impressa* in the *intellectus possibilis*, and so mediate the full conception of the *verbum mentale* or universal concept (75), we have here the transcendental function of the imagination producing a *schema* (partly sensuous and temporal, partly intellectual and timeless, or abstract and universal) whereby the *image* is brought to, and mediately subsumed under, a pure conception or category of the understanding. Moreover, just as medieval scholastics felt the obscurity of the process and differed as to the precise nature and relations of the respective functions of the *intellectus agens* and the imagination ; and just as modern scholastics are content to explain the co-operation of the abstractive faculty of the intellect and the concrete image-producing faculty of the internal sense by the simple consideration that both are faculties rooted in one and the same individual mind or soul,[2] without claiming to throw any further light on the process whereby intellect and sense co-operate in knowledge,—so Kant likewise confesses that the process whereby the intellect con ceives in the abstract what the senses perceive in the concrete, is "an art hidden in the depths of the human soul, whose true modes of action we are not likely ever to discover".

But if Kant means by the *schema* of a category or conception "the thought of the rule of procedure on our part by which we combine the manifold in accordance with the conception, and so bring the manifold under the conception," [3]—and this is certainly the meaning his language conveys,—then *the schema is useless for the purpose for which Kant required it.* For if the *schema* is merely a conception of the mind's mode of procedure it cannot represent or relate to the concrete sense intuition, nor can it

---

[1] PRICHARD, *op. cit.*, pp. 249-50, quoting the *Critique*, pp. 115-16.
[2] *Cf.* MAHER, *op. cit.* (4th edit.), pp. 308-9, 311 ; *supra*, §§ 75, 77.
[3] PRICHARD, *op. cit.* p. 252.

mediate the process of subsuming this under the category: it cannot be what for Kant's purpose it ought to be, *viz.* something in the nature of a "more concrete conception [than the category] involving the thought of time and relating to objects".[1]

Moreover, in his whole treatment of the subsumption of the individual objects of sense under universal conceptions or categories, no less than in the passage quoted above, he treats as a *mental image* what really is, and what on his own theory ought to be, an *individual object*. Owing to his fundamental error—which will be examined later—of identifying *objects in nature* with *mental appearances*, he confounds in the present context the mental image of an individual with the individual itself. What he set out to explain was the possibility of subsuming under a category or universal concept individual instances or objects, whereas he represents the *schema* as the rule of procedure whereby the imagination presents an *image* to the category.[2]

Finally, if we examine the respective *schemata* which he professes to discover for the categories—*number* as the *schema* of *quantity*, *intensity or degree of sensation* as the *schema* of *reality*, *permanence* as the *schema* of *substance*, *succession* as the *schema* of *causality*, *co-existence* as the *schema* of *reciprocity*, etc.—we shall find that the temporal element or time determination, which enters into the *schemata* as explained by Kant, refers only to *our process of apprehension*, and not (as it should, in order to serve the purpose of subsumption) to *the things or objects apprehended*.[3]

Let us now revert to the general doctrine set forth in the preceding section, and see how Kant's account of universal concepts as *a priori* syntheses of the categories with the manifold given in sense intuition fails to explain the facts of knowledge. We shall first endeavour to show that even on Kant's own assumption—that conception is an *a priori* synthesis of a sense-manifold with a category—his theory fails to account for the facts of knowledge ; and secondly that conception is not such a synthesis.

---

[1] PRICHARD, *op. cit.*, p. 255.   [2] *Ibid.*, p. 251.

[3] " The main confusion . . . is, of course, between temporal relations which concern the process of apprehension and temporal relations which concern the realities apprehended.   Kant is continually referring to the former as if they were the latter.   The cause of this confusion lies in Kant's reduction of physical realities to representations."—*Ibid.*, p. 259.   This cause of confusion will be examined below (93).

91. GENERAL CRITICISM OF KANT'S THEORY OF UNIVERSAL CONCEPTS.—A. THE THEORY FAILS TO ACCOUNT FOR THE FACTS.—I. *If conception consisted in combining or unifying systemati_cally a sense-manifold, and if this manifold were in itself wholly unsystematic and chaotic, then we should expect not a plurality of categories or ways of combining it into concepts, but one general activity of mental synthesis.*[1]

" Thus,"—to take the example given by Prichard,[2]—" suppose the mani_fold given to the mind to be combined consisted of musical notes, we could think of the mind's power of combination as exercised in combining the notes by way of succession *provided that* this be regarded as the only mode of combination.   But if the mind were thought also capable of combining notes by way of simultaneity, we should at once be confronted by the insoluble prob_lem of determining why the one mode of combination [or category] was exercised in any given case rather than the other.   If, several kinds of syn_thesis [or categories] being allowed, this difficulty be avoided by the supposi_tion that, not being incompatible, they are all exercised together, we have the alternative task of explaining how the same manifold can be combined in each of these ways [or why it is not *always* combined *de facto* in *every* way, *i.e.* by the simultaneous exercise of *all* the categories : which reflection on our cognitive processes reveals never to be the case].   As a matter of fact, Kant thinks of manifolds of different kinds as combined or related in differ_ent ways ; thus events are related causally and quantities quantitatively.   But since, on Kant's view the manifold as given is unrelated and all combination comes from the mind, the mind should not be held capable of combining manifolds of different kinds differently.   Otherwise the manifold would in its own nature imply the need of a particular kind of synthesis [or, in other words, would have ' affinities '] and would therefore not be unrelated."

Since what is given in the manifold of sense intuition is, ac-cording to Kant, a chaotic manifold of isolated sense impressions,

---

[1] As a matter of fact the mental process of *knowing, i.e.* of interpreting, apper-ceiving, recognizing (8), is fundamentally one and the same, whether it be conceiv-ing, judging, or reasoning.   It is essentially a mental apprehension and assertion of something, some datum, as real.   Reasoning not only involves judgment, but is it-self judging: it is apprehending relations of dependence in the reality given to thought, and thus asserting reality to be such or such (*cf. Science of Logic*, i., §§ 79-80, pp. 160-2 ; § 148, pp. 296-7).   Judging, in turn, is using concepts to interpret the real, and thereby implicitly asserting that the content or object of the concept is real ; while conceiving is itself intellectually apprehending, and implicitly asserting to be real, what is given in and through sense perception.   Reality as *known intel-lectually*, as object of *intellect*, has the features of *abstractness* and *universality :* the only features which reflection shows to belong not to the content, but to the mode, of thought.   And that there are different kinds of concepts, judgments and in-ferences is due of course to the *complexity* and *variety* of the *given reality* determin-ing those differences in our cognitions.

[2] *Op. cit.*, p. 214.

in themselves unknowable, he has really no right to assume
" different kinds of manifolds ".

This line of criticism is so destructive of Kant's theory that
we will add an alternative statement of it by a scholastic writer :—[1]

> " Suppose the conception of the object of the understanding were a result
> of the natural [synthetic *a priori*] functioning of the mind in presence of the
> passive impressions of the sensibility, should not the same impressions [and
> *impressions* are *always* the *same :* a chaotic manifold of unknowable isolated
> units] necessarily determine the same functioning, the exercise of one and the
> same category? And on this hypothesis how are we to explain that *one and
> the same matter* [or *datum*] originates *different* concepts, sometimes, *e.g.* that
> of substance, sometimes that of cause or action, etc. ? "

If, therefore, conception were a function of systematically
combining *a priori* into definite unities a chaotic manifold given
in sense intuition, it is inexplicable why there should be a
plurality of categories, or why, granted such a plurality, any one
rather than any other should be called into operation in any
given case of conception.

II. In the second place, even if such plurality of the categories were explained, and such selective employment of them
accounted for, it would still be true that *each category is in itself
utterly inadequate to account for the numerous distinct modes of its
application ;* or, in other words, *there would need to be as many
categories in the understanding as there are universal concepts, specific
and generic, which the understanding can form*, and not merely the
dozen or so which Kant maintains to be exhaustive and to ac
count adequately for *all* our conceptions.

When Kant is explaining how knowledge and self-conscious
ness alike imply the synthesizing of a manifold by *a priori* forms
or principles of synthesis his illustrations clearly show that each
such synthesis

> " requires a *particular* principle which constitutes the individual manifold
> a whole of a *particular kind* [*e.g.* 'a triangle' or 'a sum of five units ']. But
> if this be the case, it is clear that the categories, which are merely *concep-
> tions of an object in general*, and are consequently quite general, cannot
> possibly be sufficient for the purpose. And since the manifold in itself in-
> cludes no synthesis and therefore no principle of synthesis, Kant fails to
> give any account of the source of the particular principles of synthesis
> required for particular acts of knowledge." [2]

---

[1] Mercier, *op. cit.*, § 140, pp. 383-4, 3*me. arg.*
[2] Prichard, *op. cit.*, p. 207 (italics ours). *Cf. ibid.*, p. 177, n. 2; *supra*, § 89.

For instance, he illustrates the process (of combining a sense manifold through a category), whereby the sense-manifold acquires " objectivity " *in general,* or " relation to an object " *in general,* or " systematic unity and connectedness " *in general,* by the example of

" a synthesis on a *particular* principle which constitutes the phenomenal object an *object of a particular kind.* The synthesis which enables us to recognize three lines as an object [a triangle][1] is not a synthesis based on general principles constituted by the categories, but a synthesis based on the *particular* principle that *the three lines must be so put together as to form an enclosed space.*" [2]

If the categories " can only contribute a general kind of unity, and not the special kind of unity belonging to an individual object," [3] or class of objects, then it is clear that the categories cannot account for the conception of all the numerous specific and generic " unities" which are the objects of our universal concepts :—

" Suppose it to be conceded that in the apprehension of definite shapes we combine the manifold in accordance with the conception of figure, and, for the purpose of the argument, that figure can be treated as equivalent to the category of quantity.[4] It is plain that we apprehend different shapes, *e.g.* lines [5] and triangles,[6] of which, if we take into account differences of relative length of sides, there is an infinite variety, and houses,[7] which may also have an infinite variety of shape. But there is nothing in the mind's capacity of relating the manifold by way of figure to determine it to combine a given manifold into a figure of one kind rather than into a figure of any other kind ; for to combine the manifold into a particular shape, there is needed not merely the thought of a figure in general, but the thought of a definite figure. No cue can be furnished by the manifold itself, for any such cue would involve the conception of a definite figure, and would therefore imply

---

[1] In this example (*Critique*, p. 87 : " Thus we conceive a triangle as an object, if we are conscious of the combination of three straight lines, according to a rule, which renders such an intuition possible at all times "), the process " plainly requires a synthesis of a very definite kind " (PRICHARD, *op. cit.*, p. 217, n. 1), and not merely a synthesis according to the general category of *quantity.*

[2] *Ibid.*, p. 185. According to Kant, to know a sense-manifold as having systematic unity in general is to know it as an object, or as objective ; and it is made objective by the application of a category. In order, therefore, to apprehend a sense-manifold as objective, *i.e.* in order to exercise the function of a category, we should not need to know the *particular kind of systematic unity* which the manifold is to have. Yet, from his examples, it is clear that we must know the latter as a means to knowing the former. *Cf. op. cit., ibid.*

[3] *Ibid.*, n. 1.

[4] It is *de facto*, a more concrete conception than the category, and therefore more favourable to Kant's contention.

[5] *Critique*, p. 749.   [6] *Ibid.*, p. 87.   [7] *Ibid.*, p. 764.

that the particular synthesis was implicit in the manifold itself, in which case it would not be true that all synthesis comes from the mind." [1]

Thus, then, the categories can give at most only the widest and most generic sort of so-called " objectivity," or "systematic unity," to the manifolds of sense intuition ; they cannot originate our specific and generic universal concepts.

Nor does Kant prevent this breakdown of his theory by ascribing the principles of the less universal syntheses to the productive imagination, for with Kant this faculty must mean the understanding itself working unreflectively; and anyhow he fails to account for the intermediate principles of synthesis which he locates in it. We have seen how in explaining the synthetic *a priori* function of these faculties he felt forced to admit an " affinity " in the elements of the sense-manifold. But the exigencies of his theory prevented him from ascribing this " affinity " to any " real " or " extra-subjective " or "extramental " factor : "since the manifold is originated by the thing in itself, it seems *prima facie* impossible to prove that the elements of the manifold must have affinity [of themselves, or derived from their real source, *viz.* things in themselves], and so be capable of being related according to the categories ".[2] Accordingly, he tried " to carry out to the full his doctrine that *all* unity or connectedness comes from the mind's activity," by

"maintaining that the imagination, acting *pro*ductively on the data of sense and thereby combining them into an image, gives the data a connectedness which the understanding can subsequently recognize. But to maintain this is, of course, only to throw the problem one stage further back. If reproduction, in order to enter into knowledge, implies a manifold which has such connexion that it is capable of being reproduced according to rules, so the production of sense-elements into a coherent image in turn implies sense-elements capable of being so combined. The act of combination cannot confer upon them or introduce into them a unity which they do not already possess. The fact is that this step exhibits the final breakdown of his view that all unity or connectedness or relatedness is conferred upon the data of sense by the activity of the mind." [3]

We see then that if *all* our universal concepts be, as Kant claims, *a priori* syntheses of forms of the understanding (or the " productive imagination ") with sense-manifolds, the mind should be furnished with a separate and distinct synthesizing principle or form for every specific or generic class-notion which it can conceive.

[1] PRICHARD, *op. cit.*, p. 216.   [2] *Ibid.*, pp. 219-20 ; *supra*, p. 214, n. 2.
[3] *Ibid.*, p. 226.

III. *Whether the* a priori *categories of the understanding, whether the* a priori *schematizing and image-producing functions of the "productive imagination" be one, or few, or indefinitely numerous, the sort of synthesis ascribed to them by Kant is incapable of originating the universal concepts which* de facto *enter into our knowledge.*

To synthesize or combine the elements of a manifold is to *relate* them somehow to one another as *terms* (and, in Kant's meaning, also to recognize them as systematically inter-related, as forming a conceived "objective" unity). But in order that the elements be capable of entering into relation with one another they must, as terms, (1) be adapted to the *general nature* of the relationship to be effected; and (2) to the *special kind* of relation to be effected within that general order of relationship. For example, (1) "if two terms are to be related as more or less loud they must be sounds";[1] if "as right and left" they "must be bodies in space"; if "as parent and child" they must be "human beings," etc. And similarly, (2) "if one sound is to be related to another by way of the octave, that other must be its octave"; "if we are to combine or relate a manifold into a triangle, and therefore into a triangle of a particular size and shape, the elements of the manifold must be lines, and lines of a particular size"; "if . . into a house, and therefore into a house of a certain shape and size, the manifold must consist of bodies of a suitable shape and size," etc. Hence "the manifold must be adapted to fit the categories not only . . . in the sense that it must be of the right kind, but also in the sense that its individual elements must have that orderly character which enables them to be related according to the categories". But in Kant's theory the manifold to be related consists solely of a chaotic stream of sensations, or isolated space-and-time perceptions.[2] The question therefore returns, Whence have these isolated data of sense the characteristics of affinity which fit them, as terms, for the relations which the mind is supposed to establish between them by synthesizing them into systematic objective unities or concepts?

For Kant the chaotic manifolds of sense data are originated by the extramental reality, which, though according to his own theory unknowable, he always thinks of in the plural, as *things*

---

[1] *Cf.* Prichard, *op. cit.*, pp. 218-19; 226-9.   [2] *Ibid.*, p. 218.

(in themselves), or *individuals*.[1] His first distinction between sensibility and understanding was "that between the passive faculty by which an individual is given and the active faculty by which we bring the individual under, or recognize it as an instance of a universal".[2] Then he came to regard the "given individuals" as *terms*, and the function of the mind (the understanding and the productive imagination) as that of *relating* those terms. Thus he confounds the two quite distinct processes of bringing individuals under a universal and establishing between the given manifold of terms relations which transform these manifolds into definite, systematic unities or objective concepts,—describing both as if they were one and the same process of *a priori* synthesis, and thus ascribing all unity or connectedness to the activity of the mind. But it is plain that before an individual can be brought under a universal it must first be apprehended as an individual. The process by which we recognize an individual plane figure as an instance of the universal "triangle" cannot be the same as the process by which we recognize the given sense manifold (of perception or imagination) as a consciously apprehended individual sense datum. According to Kant the latter process is one by which we so relate among themselves and unify the isolated elements of the given manifold that we apprehend the *products* as an "individual-space-bounded-by-straight-lines". But it is impossible for Kant to hold, consistently with his general theory, that the isolated elements of the manifold are given *as terms*, and that the mind contributes the unifying *relations*. For in the first place, if the elements are given *as terms* they are given as *having mutual affinities* whereby they are *of their own nature* mutually referable by the mind apprehending them : but Kant denies that the elements of the manifold have in themselves, or derive from things in themselves, any affinity whatsoever: indeed he holds that the manifold given in sense does not and cannot enter into consciousness at all *as it is*, but only *as unified* by the activity of mental *a priori* forms. And in the second place, if the manifold of sense be given as a manifold of *terms*, *i.e.* of elements which have mutual affinities, which of their nature demand and necessitate certain relations,—and it is thus that the manifold of

---

[1] And implicitly identifies with bodies in space (56-59),—PRICHARD, *op. cit.*, pp. 67 n. ; 77 n., 257 n.·; 265.

[2] *Op. cit.*, p. 228.

sense is *de ʔacto* given,—then the *ground* of such relations, and the *motive* for the mind's formally establishing or apprehending them, are *given with* the sense-manifold, and are apprehended *in* it by the mind: and so Kant's main thesis falls to the ground, *viz.*, that the mind, in inter-relating the manifold of sense con_ sciousness, in interpreting the given by means of concepts and judgments, in "knowing" the given as an orderly system of objects of scientific knowledge, is not *guided by evidence* furnished to it in and with the data of sense; but through an *instinctive, subjective process* of synthesizing unknowable data with *a priori* mental factors creates for itself a system of mental products which *are* the phenomenal world, or physical Nature.[1]

That not only a manifold of individual *terms* (and not a chaotic stream of isolated sense impressions), but a manifold of individual *relations*, is given in sense consciousness, introspection itself clearly testifies.[2]　To illustrate this in the case of the (perceptive or imaginative) apprehension of an individual sense datum Prichard takes "Kant's favourite instance . . . the apprehension of a straight line"[3]

> This, according to Kant, "presupposes that there is given to us a manifold, which—whether he admits it or not—must really be parts of the line, and that we combine this manifold on a principle involved in the natuie of straightness.

[1] As a matter of fact since Kant holds that the *real*, whether *Ego* or *non-Ego*, is *unknowable*, and since he represents the categories as *transcendental* functions, or functions of the *noumenal Ego*, he is inconsistent in maintaining that reflection on our processes of cognition can discover the grounds of the laws and relations which make the objects of knowledge a *system* or *cosmos*, in the categories, or in these with the "transcendental unity of apperception,"—for this position implies that we can after all discover something as to the character of the *noumenal* or *real Ego*. *Cf. supra*, §§ 59, 89, p. 336, n. 5 ; p. 337, n. 1.

[2] We here appeal to consciousness as testifying that the grounds of our conceptions and judgments are given with the data of sense-consciousness, and are apprehended by intellect therein.　Kant would probably object that nothing can come into consciousness except already synthesized products ; that the reason why the products are such as they are cannot be found in consciousness but must lie beyond consciousness, in the *transcendental Ego*. (Query : Why there, rather than in the *transcendental non-Ego ?*) ; and that therefore it is impossible to argue from the facts of consciousness against his theory (*cf. supra*, p. 215, n. 1).　We join issue with this position in pointing out that Kant's theory, by denying that the grounds of conception and judgment can be discovered in the facts of consciousness, thereby contradicts facts of consciousness; for while his main contention—that these grounds are transcendental—is practically an agnostic confession that they are ultimately undiscoverable, our contention is that they are discoverable in the data of consciousness and knowledge, that they are discovered there in the process of cognition, and that they guide the mind in this process.

[3] *Op. cit.*, p. 226.

Now suppose that the manifold given is the parts AB, BC, CD, DE, of the straight line AE. It is clearly only possible to recognize AB and BC as contiguous parts of a straight line, if we immediately apprehend that AB and BC form one line of which these parts are identical in direction. Otherwise we might just as well join AB and BC at a right angle, and in fact at any angle ; we need not even make AB and BC contiguous.[1] Similarly the relation of BC to CD and of CD to DE must be just as immediately apprehended as the parts themselves. . . . Relations then, or in Kant's language, particular syntheses, must be said to be given in the sense in which the elements to be combined can be said to be given." [2]

Hence the apprehension of a sense-manifold as an individual unity is not to be confounded, as Kant confounds it, with the apprehension of this individual unity as an instance of a universal

" For, on the one hand, a relation between terms is as much an individual as either of the terms. That a body A is to the right of a body B is as much an individual fact as either A or B. And if terms, as being individuals, belong to perception and are given, in the sense that they are in immediate relation to us, relations, as being individuals, equally belong to perception and are given. On the other hand, individual terms just as much as individual relations, imply corresponding universals. An individual body implies ' bodiness ' just as much as the fact that a body A is to the right of a body B implies the relationship of ' being to the right of something '. And if, as is the case, thinking or conceiving, in distinction from perceiving, is that activity by which we recognize an individual, given in perception, as one of a kind, conceiving is involved as much in the apprehension of a term as in the apprehension of a relation. The apprehension of ' this red body ' as much involves the recognition of an individual as an instance of a kind, *i.e.* as much involves an act of the understanding, as does the apprehension of the fact that it is brighter than some other body." [3]

That the systematic unity and connectedness of the concept is not due to any instinctive synthesizing operation of the transcendental and unknowable *Ego* on a chaotic sense-manifold originating in the mind from an equally unknowable *non-Ego,* but that it has its ground in the apprehended sense-manifold itself,—this is a doctrine of such capital importance, as against Kant's theory, that we will now further illustrate the real nature of the synthesis involved in conception, by Mercier's statement [4] of the line of argument we have been so far developing :—

---

[1] " In order to meet a possible objection, it may be pointed out that if AB and BC be given in isolation, the contiguity implied in referring to them as AB and BC will not be known."

[2] *Ibid.*, pp. 227-8.   [3] *Ibid.*, pp. 228-9.

[4] MERCIER, *op. cit.*, § 140, pp. 380-3.

Any *specific essence* [he writes] is composed of notes [or elements, or factors] each of which is contained in the data of sense, and the formation of its concept is constantly guided by these. The formation of a [concept of a] specific essence [or "kind" of thing] is conditioned by a series of judg. ments all of which refer to one and the same subject [or datum] of sense ex. perience, the notes successively abstracted therefrom by the mind. According to Kant . . . the *first*[1] combination of the notes that constitute a conceived object would be an exclusively subjective function of the mind devoid of any guarantee that such combination corresponded with things [or reality], so that our concepts would perforce be destitute of real objectivity. Now this account *misrepresents the process* of conception. No doubt the conception of an intelligible object [or "kind" of thing] is a work *of synthesis*. The human mind at first apprehends only fragmentarily, so to speak, what a given thing is : such is the law of its finite nature. The adjustment of several fragmentary notes into a whole is therefore the inevitable consequence of our abstractive mode of apprehending the intelligible aspects of reality, and is accordingly the *sine qua non* condition of our knowing an essence [or kind of thing]. But the union of any two elements of an intelligible object presupposes their *comparison*, and hence a judgment. But comparison implies intuition of the terms compared, and judgment the intuition of their compatibility or incompatibility. And since the total synthesis of any conceived object is only the sum of the partial syntheses of its elements, it is the product of comparisons and judgments. But what is it that determines the mind to operate these partial syntheses and to gather them into a total synthesis? A subjective law of the mind? On the contrary, it is *the real unity of the sense datum* perceived by the external senses or reproduced by memory. The mind is conscious of representing to itself, by the aid of a plurality of abstract notes, a thing which in its concrete reality is one ; and it is moreover aware that it must unify these [successively apprehended] notes into one single [whole or] essence in order to gain for itself a faithful representation of the reality. It is therefore undoubtedly the intuition of the unity of the objective reality that guides the mind in the formation of concepts.

To illustrate this let us suppose that in presence of a person whom I actually see I form the concept of " a being subsistent-corporeal-living-sentient-rational ". Before uniting the two notes *being* and *subsistent* I have apprehended that what is *subsistent* is a *being ;* before uniting with *subsistent being* the note of *corporeity* I have apprehended that a *body* is a *substance* and a *being ;* and so, likewise, the notes of *life, sentiency* and *rationality* have revealed themselves as compatible with those of corporeity, subsistence and being, before I combine the former with the latter. In a word, whenever I unite any two notes [or factors] to form synthetically an intelligible essence I am conscious of comparing them firstly and then by an act of *judgment* attributing the one as predicate to the other as subject ; and I am conscious, moreover, that such a union, so far from being a fusion [or synthesis] of which I could see merely the result and in nowise apprehend the determining reason, is formally an act of *cognition*. Now the partial syntheses terminate

---

[1] Or earliest, or fundamental : *cf. supra*, § 88, p. 333, n. 1, where it was noted that *synthesis* must precede *analysis*, that *all* concepts are *synthetic-a-priori.*

in an act of total synthesis whereby I conceive the intelligible essence. And what determines the mind to effect this total synthesis? The sense reality, apprehended by [sense] experience. The individual person whom I saw with my eyes drew upon himself the active attention of my mind and furnished to it the material for abstractive acts whereby I successively conceived abstract being, abstract substantiality, abstract corporeity, and so on. But while I was successively abstracting those various notes [or aspects] I was well aware that, in the person I saw, these notes did not exist mutually isolated from one another; on the contrary I was aware of them as united in one single reality, and of myself as unable nevertheless to grasp them mentally by one single effort of thought. *The irresistible tendency which naturally impels me to conform my concept with the thing in Nature* [the given reality] *made me combine again the notes which analysis had separated. Clearly, therefore, it is the sense reality that furnishes the notes* [or factors] *of conceived essences* [or objects]*; and it is on a* [ground or] *substrate in sense that the* [synthesis or] *unification of those elements into a conceived essence is based.*

Sometimes this sense substrate is an *image:* then the intellect grasps the notes of the essence [or objective concept] in *imagined representations*, and the concept is of the *ideal order.* Sometimes the sense substrate is given in *perception :* the intellect apprehends the identity of the notes of the essence in a *datum* of actual sense experience, and then the concept is said to be of the *real*, or more strictly, of the *existential order* (10). But imagination can only *re*present elements given in perception. So that in ultimate analysis we must always find the notes or factors of our concepts in some previous or original percepts, *before* synthesizing them [into a conceived object]. Consequently Kant's presentation of the process of conception as an *a priori* synthesis, to account for the formation of objective concepts, is in conflict with the testimony of consciousness.

92. B. CONCEPTION IS NOT AN A PRIORI SYNTHESIS WHEREBY OUR MENTAL REPRESENTATIONS ARE MADE "OBJECTIVE" AND THUS BECOME COGNITIONS.—I. *Conception is not a Synthesis which Constructs the Objects of Knowledge.*—In the preceding argument we have seen in what sense conception [1] is really a "synthesis," *viz.*, in the sense that it is a conscious comparison of abstract aspects of reality, aspects isolated by previous analysis, a recognition of their real identity, and a consequent mental synthesis of them into a definite, specific object of thought. This is not a process of *mental fabrication*, as it were, of an object ; it is a process of *discovering* an object, of recognizing the given sense-manifold as an object. Now Kant meant something wholly different from this by describing cognition as a process of synthesis. Having in mind the synthesis "of spatial elements into a spatial whole," or, in other words, "the

---

[1] Including judgment and inference (*cf. supra*, 91), and therefore as meaning cognition or knowledge in general.

construction or *making* of spatial objects in the literal sense," Kant really represents the synthesis in which knowledge consists as "that of making or constructing parts of the physical world, and in fact the physical world itself, out of elements given in perception ".[1] Knowledge, for him, is really a process of manu. facture, a process by which the mind creates the physical universe. That this is really Kant's view will appear firstly from his own express statements, and secondly from the fact that it is only such a synthesis that can fit in with his theory of the categories.

His statements are unmistakable : " It is we, therefore, who carry into the phenomena which we call nature, order and regularity, nay, we should never find them in nature, if we ourselves, or the nature of our mind, had not originally placed them there ". . . .[2] " The understanding therefore is not only a power of making rules by a comparison of phenomena, it is itself the lawgiver of nature." . [3] " However exaggerated therefore and absurd it may sound, that the understanding is the source of the laws of nature, and of its formal unity, such a statement is nevertheless correct and in accordance with experience." [4]

[1] PRICHARD, *op. cit.*, pp. 233-4. The author rightly notes that Kant uses " mathematical illustrations of the synthesis " because they are " the most plausible for his theory. While we can be said to construct geometrical figures, and while the construction of geometrical figures can easily be mistaken for the apprehension of them, we cannot with any plausibility be said to construct the physical world."

[2] *Critique*, p. 1c2. [3] *Ibid.*, p. 103.

[4] *Ibid.*, p. 104. This Kantian view, that physical nature, as known through the mathematical and physical sciences, is but a system of mental conceptions whose function is purely *regulative* and confined to the mental products of our thinking processes, but in nowise *representative* of extramental reality, is very prevalent among those of our present-day scientists who carry their speculations into the philosophical domain. *Cf.* MACH's theory of science as a *Denkoeconomie*, POINCARÉ's *Science et hypothèse*, etc. Stated baldly, the view that the mind creates physical nature appears absurd and incredible. The absurdity is partly concealed, and the view rendered superficially plausible, by Kant's other and underlying contention that the " physical world" thus created is a world of *mental representations only*. " It sounds no doubt very strange and absurd that nature should have to conform to our subjective ground of apperception, nay, be dependent on it, with respect to her laws. But if we consider that what we call nature is nothing but a whole [' Inbegriff '] of phenomena, not a thing by itself, we shall no longer be surprised that we only see her through the fundamental faculty of all our knowledge, namely, the transcendental apperception, and in that unity without which it could not be called . . . nature" (*Critique*, p. 94). " It is no more surprising that the laws of phenomena in nature must agree with the understanding and its form a *priori*, that is, with its power of *connecting* the manifold in general, than that the phenomena themselves must agree with the form of sensuous intuition a *priori*. For laws exist as little in phenomena themselves, but relatively only, with respect to the subject to which, so far as it has understanding, the phenomena belong, as phenomena exist by themselves, but relatively only, with respect to the same being in so far as it has senses. Things by themselves would necessarily possess

Secondly, it is only if conception or cognition be a process which *literally constructs its objects*, that the categories can even lay claim to validity :—

If knowing is really making, the principles of synthesis must apply to the reality known, because it is by these very principles that reality is made. Moreover . . . we are able to understand why Kant should think (1) that in the process of knowledge the mind *introduces* order into the manifold, (2) that the mind is limited in its activity of synthesis by having to conform to certain principles of construction which constitute the nature of the under-standing, and (3) that the manifold of phenomena must possess affinity. If, for example, we build a house, it can be said (1) that we introduce into the materials a plan or principle of arrangement which they do not possess in themselves, (2) that the particular plan is limited by, and must conform to, the laws of spatial relation and to the general presuppositions of physics, such as the uniformity of nature, and (3) that only such materials are capable of the particular combination as possess a nature suitable to it. . . . We can understand why Kant should lay such stress upon the " recognition " of the synthesis, and upon the self-consciousness involved in knowledge. For if the synthesis of the manifold is really the making of an object, it results merely in the existence of the object ; knowledge of it is yet to be effected. . . This recognition, which Kant only considers an element in knowledge, is really the knowledge itself. Again, since the reality to be known is a whole of parts which we construct on a principle, we know that it is such a whole, and therefore "that the manifold is related to one object," because, and only because, we know that we have combined the elements on a principle. Self-consciousness, therefore, *must* be inseparable from consciousness of an object.[1]

For Kant, therefore, conception or cognition is an *a priori* synthesis whereby the mind literally makes or constructs its objects. This being so, we may briefly express the one insuperable and sufficient refutation of the theory in the words of the author we have been quoting :—

The fundamental objection to this account of knowledge seems so obvious as to be hardly worth stating ; it is of course that knowing and making are not the same. The very nature of knowing presupposes that the thing known is already made, or to speak more accurately, already exists. In other words knowing is essentially the discovery of what already is.[2]

their conformity with the law, independent also of any understanding by which they are known. But phenomena are only representations of things, unknown as to what they may be by themselves. As mere representations they are subject to no law of connection, except that which is prescribed by the connecting faculty " (*ibid.*, p. 765). The error of this contention, that we cannot know things in themselves, will be exposed in our treatment of sense perception.

[1] PRICHARD, *op. cit.*, pp. 234-5.

[2] [*I.e.* is already *actual* if known as actual, or already *possible* if known as possible.]

Even if the reality known happens to be something which we make, *e.g.* a house, the knowing it is distinct from the making it, and, so far from being identical with the making, presupposes that the reality in question is already made. Music and poetry are, no doubt, realities which are in some sense "made" or "composed," but the apprehension of them is distinct from and presupposes the process by which they are composed. . . .[1]

It is simply *impossible* to think that any reality depends upon our know-ledge of it, or upon any knowledge of it. If there is to be knowledge there must first *be* something to be known. In other words knowledge is essenti-ally discovery, or the finding of what already is. If a reality could only be or come to be in virtue of some activity or process on the part of the mind, that activity or process would not be "knowing," but "making" or "creating," and to make and to know must in the end be admitted to be mutually exclusive. [2]

The fact seems to be that the thought of synthesis in no way helps to elucidate the nature of knowing, and that the mistake in principle which underlies Kant's view lies in the implicit supposition that it is possible to eluci-date the nature of knowledge by means of something other than itself. Knowledge is *sui generis* and therefore a "theory" of it is impossible. Knowledge is simply knowledge, and any attempt to state it in terms of something else must end in describing something which is not knowledge.[3]

II. *Conception is not a Process whereby our Sense Representa tions are rendered "Objective," or "Related to an Object".*—Ac-cording to Kant, the sense-manifold, which is in itself a mere mental representation, a mere modification of the mind through sense impressions (1) is combined into a unity by the operation of a category, (2) is recognized as being thus combined according to a principle, and (3) by being thus recognized is apprehended as "objective," or as an "object," *i.e.* as being not a mere arbi-trary play of thought but as having a certain necessity and uni-versality. But clearly, the only "objectivity" or "relatedness to an object," which the manifold can derive from (1) the com-bining activity, is the relatedness of the separate elements of the

---

[1] PRICHARD, *op. cit.*, pp. 235-6.
[2] *Op. cit.*, p. 118. The author suggests three reasons why Kant thus resolved "knowing" into "making": (1) the idea that "knowing" can he "explained" by resolving it into something else, combined with the fact that in knowing we are *active* and therefore "*do*" or "*make*" something; (2) the fact that "Kant never relaxed his hold upon the thing in itself," regarding it as "the fundamental reality . . . though . . . inaccessible to *our* faculties," and therefore did not consider it unreasonable that the mind should "make" the sort of secondary reality or "ob-ject" which is a mere mental phenomenon or appearance; and (3) the fact "that Kant failed to distinguish knowing from that formation of mental imagery which accompanies knowing," and that he further confounded these mental images with the individual things of physical nature (*op. cit.*, pp. 238-41).
[3] P. 245. *Cf. supra*, § 6, p. 25 n.

23 •

manifold to this same manifold as a mental whole; and thus we reach no object distinct from the sense-manifold itself. And (2) the *recognition* of the manifold as combined into a unity, though it gives this manifold as a mental product a relation *to us* as thus recognizing it, certainly does not give this manifold any objectivity other than that which it already possessed as a mere object of awareness (19, 20).[1]

A little consideration of this whole question of the objectivity of our mental representations will reveal the futility of all attempts to find an object for them once the erroneous assumption is accepted that our sense perceptions are perceptions of our mental states, and not of realities as objects. It will show that Kant's attempt is rendered barely plausible only by his constantly juggling with the term " representation " [" Vorstellung "], taking it now as "the function of apprehending something," now as the " something apprehended," according as the context of his argument requires.

First, then, when Kant asks, How do our representations acquire relation to an object? he is really asking a meaningless question ; for the question implies that it is possible to think of a representation as not having an object. But it is impossible to do so, for a representation, or apprehension, or idea, or cognition, —call it what you will,—is essentially a representation, apprehension, etc., *of an object, i.e.* of *something*, which something is the *object* of the said representation, etc.

"If there is no object which the apprehension is 'of,' there is no apprehension. It is therefore wholly meaningless to speak of a process by which an apprehension *becomes* the apprehension of an object. If when we reflected we were not aware of an object, *i.e.* a reality apprehended, we could not be aware of our apprehension ; for our apprehension is the apprehension of it, and is itself apprehended in relation to, though in distinction from, it. It is therefore impossible to suppose a condition of mind in which, knowing what 'apprehension' means, we proceed to ask 'what is meant by an object of it?' and 'How does an apprehension become related to an object?' for both questions involve the thought of a mere representation, *i.e.* of an apprehension which as yet is not the apprehension of anything."[2]

---

[1] *Cf.* PRICHARD, *op. cit.*, pp. 236-8.

[2] *Ibid.*, pp. 230-1 ; *cf. ibid.*, p. 180. *Cf.* MERCIER, *op. cit.*, § 131, p. 330: " Every cognition is ' objective,' it has inevitably an ' object,' *aliquid menti objectum*. A representation which would not represent anything, and would be purely ' subjective,' is pure nonsense. Even an *ens rationis*, a logical entity, has its objectivity."

But Kant commenced with the assumption that in sense per-ception we become aware, not of the reality or thing in itself which is assumed to produce impressions on our sensibility, but of the conscious state aroused through these impressions. He thus

"interposes a *tertium quid* between the reality . . . and the percipient, in the shape of an 'appearance'. This *tertium quid* gives him something which can plausibly be regarded as at once a perception and something perceived. For, though from the point of view of the thing in itself an appearance is an ap-pearance or perception of it, yet, regarded from the point of view of what it is in itself, an appearance is a reality perceived of the kind called mental."[1]

But since (1) he considers that such appearances do not reveal things in themselves as perceived objects, and since (2) as per-ceptions they are themselves psychic facts or events, or realities of the mental order, he proceeds to regard them on the one hand as "mere" representations (or mere "determinations of the knowing subject") and asks "How do they get objects?" and to regard these self-same mental facts or states on the other hand as "related to an object," or as "objects" (which phrases he uses as synonymous, though obviously they are not synonymous), when he sees the representations to have that systematic unity and connectedness which actually (in his theory) makes of them the physical universe, or the world of material objects in time and space.[2]

But this identification of any cognitive process or state with that of which it is a cognition is as utterly unwarranted in prin-ciple as it is inadmissible in the results which Kant reaches by persisting in it throughout his whole theory. He first drops the thing in itself as an object of perception; then he regards the latter as a mental appearance or a mental fact apprehended by the mind, a fact which he considers a "mere" apprehension or re-presentation (without any object); then he finds a new object for this "mere" representation by erecting *itself* into an object, *viz.* into a physical thing or event or "phenomenon" in time and space: which latter feat he achieves by merely discovering that it

[1] *Op. cit.,* p. 137.
[2] Those of the conscious states that have not such systematic connectedness he regards as mere subjective plays of fancy, mere arbitrary fictions; but even these have the distinct twofold character of (1) being mental facts, and (2) mental facts of a *special* kind, *viz. representative of* "something," which "something" is an "object," *aliquid menti objectum seu menti praesens.*

(the representation) has the systematic order, connectedness, unity, etc., which characterizes the physical universe.

Such a plan of getting objects for cognitive acts is plainly illegitimate. It confounds two distinct aspects of the same mental act, the subjective or psychic or mental, and the objective or representative. We are entitled, for example, to call an act of perception a mere mental fact (and we can reflect upon it as such and make *it* an *object of reflection,* and study all its mental, subjective relations to the percipient mind) ; but we are not entitled to take advantage of its special character as *representative* for the purpose of calling *it* the *object of perception,* or, in other words, for the purpose of confounding *it* with *its own object,* merely because we detect in the latter (the "something" of which it is a perception, apprehension, representation, etc.) a certain systematic unity and connectedness.[1]

Moreover, if this confusion of the "representation" with the "thing represented" conceals more or less the absurdity of an "objectless apprehension," it has the serious defect of rendering insoluble the problem of knowledge even as Kant himself conceives it, *i.e.* the problem of explaining how it is that we form concepts and judgments which give us valid knowledge about the physical universe of time and space :—

For if a representation be taken to be an appearance or a sensation, the main problem becomes that of explaining how it is that, beginning with the apprehension of mere appearances or sensations, we come to apprehend an object, in the sense of an object in nature, which, as such, is not a sensation but a part of the physical world. But if the immediate object of apprehension were in this way confined to appearances, which are, to use Kant's phrase, determinations of our mind, our apprehension would be limited to these appearances, and any apprehension of an object in nature would be impossible. In fact it is just the view that the immediate object of apprehension consists in a determination of the mind which forms the basis of the solipsist position. Kant's own solution involves an absurdity at least as great as that involved in the thought of a mere representation, in the proper sense of representation. For the solution is that appearances or sensations become related to an object, in the sense of an object in nature, by being combined on certain principles. Yet it is plainly impossible to combine appearances or sensations into an object in nature. If a triangle, or a house, or a "freezing of water"[2] is the result of any process of combination, the elements combined must be respectively lines, and bricks, and physical events ; these are objects in the sense in which the whole produced by the combination is an object, and are certainly not appearances or sensations. Kant conceals the difficulty from himself by the use

---

[1] *Cf. op. cit.,* pp. 231-2, 180-1.   [2] *Critique,* p. 764.

of language to which he is not entitled. For while his instances of objects are always of the kind indicated, he persists in calling the manifold combined "representations," *i.e.* presented mental modifications. This procedure is of course facilitated for him by his view that nature is a phenomenon or ap. pearance, but the difficulty which it presents to the reader culminates when he speaks of the very same representations as having both a subjective and an objective relation, *i.e.* as being both modifications of the mind and parts of nature.[1]

There are several passages of the *Critique* in which Kant openly adopts this latter gratuitous and unwarranted procedure.[2] Among these there is one in particular where, on account of the importance of the issues at stake, the fallacy of the procedure needs to be exposed. It is the rather lengthy passage [3] in which he endeavours to vindicate, against Hume, the "objectivity" of the Principle of Causality.

93. THE CONCEPT OF CAUSAL OR NECESSARY SUCCESSION OF EVENTS IN PHYSICAL NATURE IS, FOR INSTANCE, NOT MADE OBJECTIVE BY THE APPLICATION OF AN "A PRIORI" MENTAL RULE TO MERE MENTAL REPRESENTATIONS.—We have already noted [4] that Kant understood by "cause" the "necessitating *phenomenal* antecedent" of an event, or what is nowadays described as a "physical" cause; that the necessity he was thinking of was the *contingent* or *conditional* necessity of the laws of physical nature, the necessity which produces the *order* or *uniformity* of physical nature; and that he wrongly conceived this necessity as *absolute*, like mathematical and metaphysical necessity. In the same context (65) arguing from what is involved in the concepts of "contingent being," "change," "happening" or "beginning to exist," we vindicated the analytical character of the Principle of Causality rightly understood.[5]

[1] PRICHARD, *op. cit.*, pp. 232-3.

[2] A notable example is the passage (*Critique*, p. 752) in which he distinguishes the *judgment*-relation, or *objectively valid* relation, of two representations ("bodies" and "heavy") from the *association*-relation or subjectively valid relation between *the very same representations*. Upon which Prichard rightly remarks (*op. cit.*, p. 209, n. 3) : "There is plainly involved a transition from representation, in the sense of the apprehension of something, to representation, in the sense of something apprehended. It is objects which are objectively related ; it is our apprehensions of objects which are associated. . . . Current psychology seems to share Kant's mistake in its doctrine of association of ideas, by treating the elements associated, which are really apprehensions of objects, as if they were objects apprehended."

[3] *Critique*, pp. 155 *sqq.*; pp. 774-5. [4] *Cf.* § 64, p. 224, n. 3 ; § 66.

[5] It is interesting to note that while Kant *ostensibly* rejects this kind of proof "from conceptions" and what is implied in them, as "dogmatical," and *professes* himself to establish such principles as that of causality by arguing "transcenden-

Abstracting now from Kant's misinterpretation of the *nature* of the *physical* necessity by which events in the physical world are connected as cause and effect, we will here examine his attempt to vindicate "objectivity" for this necessity, as he conceived it, against the subjectivism of Hume.

Hume had reduced causality to a subjective feeling of expectation. He had

" denied that we are justified in asserting any causal connexion, *i.e.* any necessity of succession in the various events which we perceive, but even this denial presupposed that we do apprehend particular *sequences in the world of nature* [*e.g.* the positions of ' a boat going down a stream '], and therefore that we succeed in distinguishing between a sequence of events in nature [*i.e.* a sequence that is ' necessary' at least in the sense of 'regular,' ' uniform,' 'irreversible'] and a *mere* [' reversible'] *sequence of perceptions* such as is also to be found when we apprehend a coexistence of bodies, in space [*e.g.* 'the parts of a house']." [1]

Holding, as he did, "that in all cases of perception *what we are directly aware of is a succession of perceptions*," [2] Hume was of course utterly unable to explain how it is that we can, and do *de 'facto*, make such a distinction. Kant recognized the fact that we do make the distinction, and, *while accepting Hume's assumption*—that what we are directly aware of is always *a mere sequence of perceptions or representations*,—he attempted the impossible task of showing that the distinction is compatible with the assumption, and of explaining how, on the assumption, we come to make the distinction. Recognizing the fact that we make the distinction, he contends that the reason we can make it is because, and only because, by virtue of an *a priori* rule of the understanding (the pure category of cause and effect) we can think two representations (which, apart from this category, are only successive representations in the imagination, successive " internal determinations of our mind " [3]) as *phenomena* or *objects*, by " rendering necessary the connexion of [these] representations in a certain way, and subjecting them to a rule ". [4]

The possibility, therefore, of apprehending certain of our

---

tally," *i.e.* from the *possibility* of perceiving, conceiving, etc., to what is implied *a priori* therein, his arguments are *as a matter of fact* from conceptions. For instance, he seeks to establish the objectivity of the concepts of " substance " and " cause " by what is involved in the *nature* of *change* as such. *Cf.* PRICHARD, *op. cit.*, pp. 269, 274-5, 300-1.

[1] *Ibid.*, p. 277,—italics ours.   [2] *Ibid.*,—italics ours.
[3] *Critique*, p. 161.   [4] *Ibid.*

representation-sequences as "objective," or as necessarily deter‑
mined in an irreversible order, involves the function of a trans‑
cendental, *a priori* rule of the understanding, which rule is the
Principle of Causality, or the Law of Necessary Connexion of
Events as Cause and Effect.

Let us see what all that means. Kant's starting-point is
that "the manifold of phenomena is always produced in the
mind successively. . The representations of the parts follow
upon one another."[1] But since he assumes the fundamental
error of phenomenist idealism, common to himself and Hume
(*cf.* p. 186, n. 3)—that "how things may be by themselves (with‑
out reference to the representations by which they affect us)[2] is
completely beyond the sphere of our knowledge,"[3]—and since,
therefore, "we have always to deal with our representations
only,"[4] he is once more confronted with the problem of finding
an "object" for these representations. Whether I indulge in a
reverie, or gaze successively on the parts of a house, or watch a
boat gliding down a river, I have in all cases alike a sequence of
representations. And this sequence of mental facts is, according
to Kant's fundamental assumption, all that I am ever directly
aware of. How then is it that in the third case alone, not
merely have the *representations* a temporal sequence, as in the
other two cases, but have a temporal sequence which is "neces‑
sary," "determined by a rule," "irreversible"? Because, Kant
answers, in this case they have become the special kind of "ob‑
jects" which we call "events" by being connected "causally"
by virtue of the transcendental, *a priori* function of the category
of causality. Which reply prompts us to ask, Does a sequence
of representations, then, *become its own object* by the fact that
the mind *a priori* and transcendentally endows it with a certain
kind of connectedness? And now Kant's answer is a confession
that this is so: "Since therefore phenomena [mental appearances]
are not things by themselves, and are yet the only thing that
can be given us to know, I am asked to say what kind of con‑
nexion in time belongs to the manifold of the phenomena itself
[*i.e.* co-existence, as in the parts of a house, or sequence as in the

---

[1] *Critique*, p. 155.
[2] Or, indeed, he might say, "even with reference to these latter," since he
holds that the "representation" does *not* "represent" or in any way reveal the
"things" to us.
[3] *Ibid.*   [4] *Ibid.*

boat going down the stream], when the *representation* of it is *always* successive. . . . Here, that which is contained in our successive apprehension [*i.e.* the temporal succession or flow of mental states] is considered as representation, and the given phenomenon, *though it is nothing but the whole of those representations*, [is considered] as *their object*, with which my concept . is to accord."[1]   Kant had assumed gratuitously that things in themselves are unknowable, that they cannot be the objects of our representations, that the objects of these latter must be themselves mental, must be themselves representations or ideas ; but since it is the things and events of physical nature, bodies in space and events in time, that are really the objects of which we are aware, the objects of our representations, his theory leaves him no option but to assert these physical objects to be mental, to be in fact identical with the representations themselves[2]— unified and connected according to *a priori* transcendental principles of the understanding.   But this assertion that "the object of representations consists in the representations themselves related in a certain necessary way"[3] only shows the futility of starting with representations that are *mere* (*i.e.* objectless) representations, and trying to restore an object to them. It is "open to two fatal objections":—

"In the first place, a complex [or whole] of representations is just not an object in the proper sense, *i.e.* a reality [or 'something' whether 'physical' or 'mental'] apprehended. It essentially falls on the subject side of the distinction between an apprehension and the reality apprehended. The *complexity* of a complex of representations in no way divests it of the character it has as a complex of *representations*. In the second place, on this view the same terms have to enter at once into two incompatible relations. Representations have to be related successively as our representations or apprehensions—as in fact they are related—and, at the same time, successively or otherwise, as the case may be, as parts of the object apprehended, *viz.* a reality in nature. In other words the same terms have to enter into both a subjective and an objective relation, *i.e.* both a relation concerning us, the knowing subjects, and a relation concerning the object which we know. 'A phenomenon in opposition to the representations of apprehension can only be represented as the object of the same, distinct therefrom, if it stands under

---

[1] *Critique*, p. 156,—italics ours. *Cf.* PRICHARD, *op. cit.*, pp. 280-1.

[2] But we never thus "confuse an apprehension with its object, nor do we take the temporal relations which belong to the one for the temporal relations which belong to the other, for these relations involve different terms which are never confused, *viz.* apprehensions and the objects apprehended".—PRICHARD, *op. cit.*, p. 280.

[3] *Ibid.*, p. 281.

a rule which distinguishes it from *every other* apprehension, and renders necessary a mode of conjunction of the manifold.'[1]   A representation, however, cannot be so related by a rule to another representation, for the rule meant relates to realities in nature, and however much Kant may try to maintain the contrary, two representations, not being realities in nature, cannot be so related.   Kant is in fact only driven to treat rules of nature as relating to representations, because there is nothing else to which he can regard them as relating.   The result is that he is unable to justify the very distinction, the implications of which it is his aim to discover, and he is unable to do so for the very reason which would have rendered Hume unable to justify it.   Like Hume he is committed to a philosophical vocabulary which makes it meaning-less to speak of relations of objects at all in distinction from relations of apprehensions.   It has been said that for Kant the road to objectivity lay through necessity.[2]   But whatever Kant may have thought, in point of fact there is no road to objectivity, and, in particular, no road through necessity. No necessity in the relation between two representations can render the relation objective, *i.e.* a relation between objects.   No doubt the successive acts in which we come to apprehend the world are necessarily related ; we certainly do not suppose their order to be fortuitous.   Nevertheless, these relations are not in consequence a relation of realities apprehended."[3]

It is unnecessary now to examine in detail the long, laboured passage[4] in which Kant seeks to show that although we can be aware only of representations, and that in these we always observe a temporal sequence, yet we can discover that *their objects*, though in some cases [*e.g.* the parts of a house] necessarily coexistent, are in other cases necessarily successive [*e.g.* the positions of a boat going down a stream], and that we can do so because in the latter class of cases the objects are rendered necessarily successive by the fact that the corresponding repre-sentations are synthesized under an objective (?) rule of necessary sequence—the law of causality.   For since, with him, " objects of apprehension " are really and identically " apprehensions of objects," he makes out to be a causal law which gives necessity to a sequence of objects or events in nature what is really a subjective rule which gives a necessary or irreversible sequence to our representations themselves.[5]

He starts with the fact that we observe the sequence of our apprehensions to be in some cases irreversible ; but " any attempt to argue from the irreversibility of our perceptions to the ex-istence of a sequence in the object must involve a ὕστερον

---

[1] *Critique*, p. 156,—italics not in original.   [2] Caird, i., p. 557.
[3] Prichard, *ibid.*, pp. 281-2.
[4] *Critique*, pp. 156-64.   *Cf.* Prichard, *op. cit.*, pp. 283-301.
[5] *Ibid.*, p. 284.

πρότερον," for we cannot know them to be irreversible unless "we already know that what we have been perceiving is an event,"[1] *i.e.* unless we already know the objects of these perceptions to be subject to the law of causality; but we cannot know this from the mere sequence of perceptions "at a stage where we are not aware of any relation in the physical world at all".[2]

As a matter of fact Kant identifies, and must identify, the two irreversibilities (just as he had to identify objects with representations) for the simple reason that "he has only one set of terms to be related as irreversible, *viz.* the elements of the manifold, which have to be, from one point of view, elements of an object, and, from another, representations or apprehensions of it".[3]

Hence we can see the necessarily futile character of Kant's vindication of "objectivity" for the law of physical causality in nature :—

He is anxious to show that in apprehending AB as a real or *objective* succession we presuppose that they are elements in a causal law of succession. Yet in support of his contention he points only to the quite different fact that where we apprehend a succession AB, we think of the *perception* of A and the *perception* of B as elements of a necessary, but *subjective* succession.[4]

And, moreover, when we do think of two *perceptions*, A and B, as necessarily successive, it should follow, on Kant's theory, that, the succession being *eo ipso* "objective," the necessity should consist in the fact that A is the cause of B. But no; the causal rule, being general, only determines that in the state preceding B (the state of which A is a part or item) there must be a "correlate, *though a still undetermined correlate*,"[5] which necessitates B. He has to adopt this position (1) in order to avoid the alternative inference "that all observed sequences are causal, *i.e.* that in them the [temporal] antecedent and consequent are

---

[1] PRICHARD, *op. cit.*, pp. 288-9; *cf.* p. 299: "The view that in our apprehension of the world we advance from the apprehension of a succession of perceptions to the apprehension of objects perceived, involves a ὕστερον πρότερον. As Kant himself in effect urges in the *Refutation of Idealism* [*Critique*, pp. 778-81], self-consciousness in the sense of consciousness of the successive process in which we apprehend the world, is plainly only attained by reflecting upon our apprehension of the world. We first apprehend the world and only by subsequent reflection become aware of our activity in apprehending it." *Cf. supra*, § 61, p. 214, n. 1.

[2] *Ibid.*, p. 276. [3] *Ibid.*, p. 291. [4] *Ibid.*

[5] *Critique*, p. 162,—*apud* PRICHARD, p. 292.

always cause and effect, which is palpably contrary to fact ".[1] and (2) because the causal law " is quite general, and only as. serts that something must precede an event upon which it follows always and necessarily ".[2]   But if the law is thus quite general, and if therefore, as Kant himself elsewhere admits,[3] "experience is needed to determine the cause of B," then it is admitted "that the apprehension of objective [and ' causal'] successions is *prior to* and *presupposed by* any process which appeals to the principle of causality.[4]   . In other words, the process by which, on Kant's view, A and B become, and become known to be, events [*i.e.* causally connected] presupposes that they already are, and are known to be, events." [5]

The fact is, of course, that our representations have objects, that these objects are things and events, and orderly sequences of events, in physical nature ; that the ground of this order, uniformity, physical necessity of sequence, physical causality, lies not in any *a priori* mental rule, productive of such characteristics, but in the things and events themselves, in the *apprehended realities.* When, therefore, Kant gratuitously denies that *realities* are the objects of our apprehensions, when he makes out the objects of our apprehensions or representations to be these apprehensions or representations themselves *as endowed with necessary relations and connexions,* it really matters very little whether he locates the grounds and principles of such necessity in the "unknowable" things-in-themselves (the "transcendental object or *non-Ego*") or in the equally "unknowable" reality of the "transcendental subject or *Ego*" which is the seat of the *a priori* categories and their functions.   In either case, knowledge is confined to the conscious states of the individual mind, and solipsism is the unavoidable conclusion.[6]

The general conclusion, therefore, to be derived from the discussion is that the "conceptualism" of Kant is indefensible and erroneous, that the concept is not applicable merely to a fictitious object constructed by the understanding operating *a*

---

[1] PRICHARD, *ibid.   Cf. Science of Logic,* vol. ii., § 219, p. 76, for the same difficulty in Mill's account of causality.
[2] *Ibid.*   [3] *Critique,* pp. 765-6.
[4] PRICHARD, pp. 293-4.   *Cf. supra,* § 91, ii., for this failure of the categories to accomplish their supposed function.
[5] *Ibid.,* p. 295.
[6] *Cf.* PRICHARD, *op. cit.,* p. 123, for the observation that "the real contrary to realism is *subjective* idealism ".

priori on "unknowable" sense data, but that it is really applicable to, and really grounded in, the data of sense perception.

94. RETROSPECT; PSYCHOLOGICAL GROUNDS OF CONCEPTUALISM.—The chapters in which we examined the objective validity of necessary judgments find their natural development in those we have just devoted to the objective validity of conception and concepts. Thus, what is called Sensism, Empiricism, Positivism (chap. v.) in regard to judgment, appears as, Nominalism in regard to conception (chap. xi.). This general interpretation of intellectual cognition leads inevitably to subjectivism or scepticism and is nowadays largely and justly discredited. Again we may naturally connect all forms of Extreme Realism in regard to concepts (chap. x.) with the errors of Platonism and Ontologism (chap. viii., § 70) in regard to the ultimate implications of the necessary character of judgments of the ideal order. These theories are exaggerations of the true interpretation of concepts and necessary judgments—the scholastic theory of Moderate Realism (chap. ix.) and Intuitive Objective Evidence (chap. viii.). They, too, imperil the validity of *intellectual* knowledge by divorcing it from the domain of *sense*. Finally, we have the theories which accord to intellectual knowledge, expressed through concepts (chap. xii.) and necessary judgments (chaps. vi., vii.), an ideal validity within the domain of the mind itself, but which either formally or equivalently deny to such knowledge all claim to give us any genuine insight into extramental reality.

This theory, which we may describe in general terms as conceptualism (87), has not only been much more ably defended, especially by Kant and his followers, but is also perhaps in itself more plausible, than any of the other erroneous theories. For while it is really futile to deny that the intellect apprehends mental objects which are genuinely universal, it is not at all evident at first sight that these objects are in any true sense real. Nay, when we contrast these intellectually apprehended "universals" with the "individuals" of sense perception we are naturally impressed by the overwhelming sense of reality borne in upon us by the concrete, intuitively perceived individuals of sense, as compared with the abstract universals of thought. And the same feeling of what we may perhaps call the comparative unreality, or questionable reality, of the universal as compared with the individual, is conveyed by contrasting the abstract, necessary and universal judgments of science with the singular judgments of experience. As Prichard aptly observes,[1] "there is an inveterate tendency to think of universals, and therefore the connexions between them, as being not objective realities[2] but mere ideas. In other words, we tend to adopt the conceptualist attitude, which regards individuals as the only reality, and universals as mental fictions." And, noting that "Kant may be fairly supposed to have been unconsciously under the influence of this tendency," he proceeds to give this other psychological excuse for conceptualism : "In the second place we apprehend a universal connexion by the operation of thinking. Thinking is essentially an activity; and since activity in the ordinary sense in which we oppose action to knowledge originates something, we tend to think of the activity of thinking as also originating something, *viz.* that which is our object when we think.[3] Hence since we think of what is real as independent of us, and therefore as something which we can discover but in no sense make, we tend to think of the object of thought as only an idea. On the other hand, what is ordinarily called perception, though it involves the activity of thinking, also involves an element in respect of which we are passive. This is the fact pointed to by Kant's phrase 'objects are *given* in perception'. In virtue of this passive element we are inclined to think that in perception we simply stand before the reality in a passive attitude. The reality perceived is thought to be, so to say, there, existing independently of us. . . ." And so, the reality of the universal of thought is as it were eclipsed by the more vivid reality of the individual of sense. Moreover, this first impression, .militating as it does against belief in the reality of the universal, will be strengthened by the consideration that while perception seems to give us a *direct* and *intuitive* insight into that which we regard as extramentally real, intellectual thought, being *discursive, elaborated,* and *mediated* through sense, seems almost *too remote* from the extramental reality to secure for us a genuine cog-

---

[1] *Op. cit.,* pp. 21-2.

[2] " *I.e.* as not having a place in the reality which, as we think, exists independently of the mind."

[3] As a matter of fact thinking does originate something, *viz.* the *mental modes* of its objects, their *abstractness* and *universality*. But it is only such *entia rationis* that thinking does or can originate. It does not and cannot originate the objects themselves as to their *real content.* Kant's mistake of thinking that it can do so even partially has been already exposed : *cf.* § 92.

nitive contact with this latter (*cf.* 74). In our general exposition
and criticism of Kant's theory of knowledge we saw (55) how he
misstated the general problem of the validity of knowledge by
confining it to necessary and universal judgments, and the con
cepts involved therein,—apparently under the impression that
the real validity of perception and empirical judgments is self-evi
dent and raises no problem.

Such, then, is the general prepossession or prejudice of
spontaneous thought in favour of conceptualism. But a closer
reflection on all the facts of knowledge inevitably dissipates this
prejudice and substitutes for it the conviction that the "universal" of thought is, and must be, in some true sense real,—
in the sense, namely, of Moderate Realism. Carrying out this
process of reflection (chaps. ix., xii.), we realize what an illusion
it is to think that while reality lies within the scope of sense it
escapes the grasp of intellect. If we pronounce that the object
of sense is extramentally real notwithstanding the fact that in
order to be *perceived* it must be *related to sense*, we have no right
to deny that the object of intellect is real because of the fact that
in order to be *conceived* it must be *related to intellect*. In the
following passage [1] Prichard not only emphasizes the point that
the reality of an object, whether of thought or of sense, is not
sacrificed or compromised, so to speak, by its having to be related to mind in the process of cognition ; he also vindicates the
reality of the object of thought on the precise lines of the
moderate realism of the scholastics :—

Perceiving and thinking alike presuppose that the reality is immediately
object of the mind, and that the act of apprehension in no way affects or
enters into the nature of what we apprehend about reality. If, for instance,
I assert on the strength of perception that this table is round, I imply that I
see the table, and that the shape which I judge it to have is not affected by
the fact that I am perceiving it ; for I mean that the table really is round.
If some one then convinces me that I have made a mistake owing to an effect
of foreshortening, and that the table is really oval, I amend my assertion, not
by saying that the table is round but only to my apprehension, but by saying
that it looks round. Thereby I cease to predicate roundness of the table
altogether ; for I mean that while it still looks round it is not really so. The
case of universal judgments is similar. The statement that the straight line
is the shortest distance between its extremities means that it really is so.
The fact is presupposed to have been in no way altered by our having apprehended it. Moreover, reality is here just as much implied to be directly object

[1] *Op. cit.*, pp. 20-1.

of the mind as it is in the case of the singular judgment. Making the judgment consists . . . in *seeing* the connexion between the direction between two points and the shortest distance between them. The connexion of real characteristics is implied to be directly object of thought.[1] Thus both perceiving and thinking presuppose that the reality to which they relate is directly object of the mind, and that the character of it which we apprehend in the resulting judgment is not affected or altered by the fact that we have had to perceive or conceive the reality.

The foregoing passage is at this stage of our inquiry extremely suggestive. No sooner does it assert, as a presupposition of all cognition, "that reality is immediately object of the mind, and that the act of apprehension *in no way affects or enters into the nature of* what we apprehend about reality," than it points to a fact which apparently contradicts, or at all events raises a difficulty against, the assertion,—the fact, namely, that things may *look* otherwise than they *are*. For we may ask, How can we know them to be otherwise than they look? It is easy to understand that we can know what or how things look. But how can we know anything further about them? Particularly, if they really *are* otherwise than they *look*, how can we possibly know this "otherwise"?

Hence arises the whole question of the real validity of sense perception, the relation of mind to the extramental, the nature and significance of the processes and objects of sense cognition, the right interpretation of these as purporting to reveal a real material universe, the justification of our spontaneous conviction that we know not only the real existence of such a universe, but something also about its nature. These inquiries will be our next immediate concern.

[1] "In saying that a universal judgment is an immediate apprehension of fact, it is, of course, not meant that it can be actualized by itself, or, so to say, *in vacuo.* Its actualization obviously presupposes the presentation of individuals in perception or imagination. Perception or imagination thus forms the necessary occasion of a universal judgment, and in that sense mediates it. Moreover, the universal judgment implies an act of abstraction by which we specially attend to those universal characters of the individuals perceived or imagined, which enter into the judgment. But, though our apprehension of a universal connexion thus implies a process, and is therefore mediated, yet the connexion, when we apprehend it, is immediately our object. There is nothing between it and us."—*l.c.*, p. 21, n. 1.

END OF VOLUME ONE.

INDEX TO VOLUME I.[1]

[1] The numbers refer to the pages. For references to the main topics of the volume, which are not included in the Index, the reader will please consult the Table of Contents.

24 *

PRINTED IN GREAT BRITAIN BY THE UNIVERSITY PRESS, ABERDEEN

Made in the USA
Columbia, SC
22 August 2021

44153594R00215